DUTCH REFORMED EDUCATION

Dutch Reformed Education
Immigrant Legacies in North America

Edited by Donald A. Luidens
    Donald J. Bruggink
    Herman J. De Vries Jr.

© 2020 Van Raalte Press
All rights reserved

Van Raalte Press is a division of Hope College Publishing

A. C. Van Raalte Institute
Theil Research Center
9 East 10th Street
PO Box 9000
Holland, MI 49422-9000

vanraalte@hope.edu
www.hope.edu/vri

Printed in the United States of America
978-1-7320854-4-2

Library of Congress Control Number: 2020945842

Editor-in-Chief: Jacob E. Nyenhuis
Project Editor: JoHannah Smith
Page Layout: Russell Gasero, Archivist Emeritus, Reformed Church in America
Cover Design: Marena De Leau

Papers from the Twenty-Second Biennial Conference of the Association for the Advancement of Dutch American Studies, held 14-15 June 2019, at Calvin Universtiy, Grand Rapids, Michigan.

*This volume on Dutch Reformed Education
is dedicated to
Dr. Jacob E. Nyenhuis:
Consummate Dutch American Educator,
Graduate of a Christian Day School and Calvin College,
and Long-Time Dean and Provost of Hope College.*

Contents

Acknowledgments   xi

Introduction
Tending the Legacies   xiii
    Donald A. Luidens

I. Institutional Legacies

1. Present from the Beginning: Reformed Dutch Day Schools in North America, 1638-2019   3
    Henk Aay
2. Meester Mulder and Orange City's Un-American Christian School   39
    Earl Wm. Kennedy
3. Wisconsin Memorial Academy   65
    Mary Risseeuw
4. Christian Education in the Calumet Region: A Pictorial Memoir   83
    Ken Bult
5. Cultivating a Community, Expanding a Church: Religion and Immigrant Education on the Frontier   91
    Andrew Klumpp
6. "The joyous, jolly Academy days": Northwestern Classical Academy, Iowa, 1882-1928   103
    Douglas Firth Anderson
7. From Dutch Reformed to Nondenominational: Transitions at Timothy Christian Schools of Chicagoland since the 1970s   127
    Robert P. Swierenga
8. Creating the Third Way in Canada: The Ontario Alliance of Christian Schools, 1952-2018   145
    Adrian Guldemond
9. School as the Vessel of Hope: The Experience of Faith and Dutch Immigrant Culture in Ontario Christian Schools   165
    Phil Teeuwsen

10. Calvin Seminary and University as the Full-Size Kampen 183
    George Harinck

II. Race- and Gender-Based Legacies
11. Members Only: The Founding of Erasmus Hall
    Academy, 1786-1813 201
    Stephen Staggs
12. The Integration of Grosse Pointe Christian Day School 217
    Douglas J. Vrieland
13. Educating the North American Indian: Dutch Christian
    Reformed Contributions and Their Legacy 237
    Pieter Hovens
14. Writing about Education: Gendered Visions in Dutch
    American Letters and Memoirs from the Turn of the
    Twentieth Century 255
    Suzanne M. Sinke
15. Women in Higher Education: The Case of Five Reformed
    Institutions 273
    Rhonda Pennings
16. The Development of Diversity at Western Theological
    Seminary 289
    Donald J. Bruggink

III. Other Legacies
17. Dutch Immigrants and Education: Where Winning
    Meant Losing 305
    Robert Schoone-Jongen
18. Farming across the Line: An Historical Reflection on
    the Hollander Fires 323
    Keith Fynaardt
19. Publication as Pedagogy: How Dutch Reformed Churches
    Used Reading to Inspire Congregants 331
    Justin R. Vos
20. Fifty Years of Dutch Studies at the University of Michigan 347
    Ton Broos
21. Betsy DeVos's Dutch Heritage, Media Reporting, and
    the Misuse of Dutch American History 355
    Michael J. Douma

22. All but the Saloon: Nineteenth-Century Dutch Immigrants, the Wilderness, and the Idea of Progress 373
    Jan J. Boersema and Anthonia Boersema-Bremmer
23. Teaching the Past: History Education among Dutch Americans 389
    David Zwart

Contributors 401
AADAS Conferences 1977 to 2019 409
Index 413

Acknowledgments

This volume has its origin in the Twenty-Second Biennial Conference of the Association for the Advancement of Dutch American Studies (AADAS), held in June 2019 on the campus of Calvin University (née College) in Grand Rapids, Michigan. This event marked the fortieth anniversary of AADAS as a promoter of outstanding Dutch American scholarship.[1]

It is both a fitting marker and an encouraging omen that the 2019 conference featured one of the largest number of presentations ever, a fact that is mirrored in the twenty-three contributions in this volume. Nearly all of the AADAS presenters submitted their work for this volume, and we thank them for that.

As a board member and recent president of AADAS, I can affirm that the cooperation of the Van Raalte Press (VRP) with AADAS has been a spectacularly fruitful effort. It has resulted in a unique series of volumes that does scholarly justice to the compelling and varied stories of Dutch immigrants to North America. AADAS is indebted to

1   A complete list of the AADAS conference topics and resulting publications is provided at the end of this volume.

the VRP and its editor-in-chief, Jacob E. Nyenhuis, for their continued commitment to publishing the finest efforts of scholars on Dutch American topics.

The present volume is the product of a team effort. Donald A. Luidens, Donald J. Bruggink, and I all contributed in many and various ways to the project. Thanks go to Russ Gasero for the volume's layout. Henk Aay graciously contributed the cover map. The unsung hero of a scholarly volume is often its copy editor. As a result, our special thanks go to JoHannah Smith for her outstanding work as project editor.

Herman De Vries
Past President AADAS

Introduction: Tending the Legacies

Donald A. Luidens

Sola scriptura, decreed the Reformers, and thereby launched a literacy frenzy. The newly christened "priesthood of all believers" necessitated that even the lowly layman know how to read and reflect on Holy Writ. Buoyed by the mushrooming bourgeoisie that boasted exceptional resources and unprecedented discretionary time, and fueled by geopolitical and mercantile demands, literacy—steeped in approved Christian dogma—became a widespread expectation throughout seventeenth- and eighteenth-century Europe.

These high expectations for Christian education crossed the Atlantic with succeeding waves of Dutch Reformed immigrants and set the stage for a remarkable flourishing of academic institutions, from the earliest grades through postgraduate training. During the colonial era, while broad-scale literacy was the impetus for establishing primary and secondary schools for young folk—principally males—the demand for an educated clergy and a well-trained professional class prompted the founding of postsecondary schools. Reformed congregations and individuals were at the forefront of both initiatives—literacy training for the layman and theological training for the clergy. The resulting institutions were augmented in their educational tasks by a nascent publishing industry that produced a broad range of Christian literature and commentaries.

Most of the essays in this volume provide snapshots of the ongoing drive for a self-consciously *Christian* education that was embedded in the Dutch Reformed immigrant movement. These essays are happily complemented by chapters that reflect on the broader implications of the Dutch immigrant experience in other spheres of the educational enterprise. The multidisciplinary approaches that appear here make this volume particularly engaging. Along with a preponderance of historians, a scattering of cultural anthropologists, language and literature scholars, theologians, and even a photographer will make their appearance in the following pages. The rich variety of lenses that they bring to bear enlivens our imaginations and extends our understanding of the Dutch immigrant experience.

Initial forays into the business of Reformed Christian education—such as Erasmus Hall Academy, begun in 1786 in the Flatbush section of Brooklyn—were harbingers of the vibrant array of local schools, academies, and colleges that blossomed across the country. As late as the 1950s, the impetus was alive and well among Reformed folk intent on preserving their religious traditions, resulting in the founding of Dordt College in Iowa and Trinity College in Chicago.

Along the way, these scholastic establishments were beset by a number of cultural crosscurrents. Almost all were buffeted by competition from public schools that provided comparable scholarly fare but without the religious framework. Whether in nineteenth-century Iowa or in twentieth-century New Jersey, Illinois, Michigan, or Ontario, these tussles were painful, poignant, and variously resolved, sometimes to the favor of the Christian schools, sometimes not.

To confound matters, public schools came free, whereas Christian education demanded a direct, personal price. Early on, the Reformed Church in America branch of the Dutch diaspora made its peace with this divide, committing itself to public education within an assumed (Protestant) Christian context; teachers and administrators, after all, would be Christian, and prayers would open the day. Later immigrants, who largely affiliated with the Christian Reformed Church, took the opposite view and insisted on specifically Christian schools. Consequently, they had to seek creative ways to pay for education so that it would not be prohibitive to parents. Along with denominational support (especially for church-related colleges), many congregations assumed the responsibility to cover at least part of the cost incurred by member-parents.

Establishing educational institutions was always a costly challenge, but maintaining them was equally so. The passage of time and the change in demographics both played deleterious roles as Dutch immigrant waves receded during the twentieth century and as second- and third-generation Dutch Americans and Dutch Canadians felt less connected with their religio-ethnic pasts. The solution for many Reformed schools was to seek a broader constituency, often reaching into non-Dutch and non-Reformed circles. The resulting "ecumenicity" sometimes flew in the face of conventional Calvinism, further eroding the unique heritage that had been at the core of the institutions' founding. A generic, highly personalized, evangelical piety often replaced the more stoic and formulated Dutch Reformed Calvinism. In many places, what it took to be a "Christian" school generated considerable debate and angst as the twentieth century yielded to the twenty-first.

Twentieth century "culture wars" also left their indelible marks on schools in the Reformed fold. The place of women—especially in postsecondary domains—was a source of tension through the last decades of the nineteenth and well into the twentieth century. In the early years, since women were not expected to be professionals—much less, clergy—there was little reason for them to enroll in institutions of higher learning, the argument went. And yet, women persisted in their desire for parity with men. The most recent battleground of the gender struggle has been in the seminaries, where the place of women in the pulpit has been fought in theory and in practice. Crucially, the struggle for institution maintenance has joined in this debate. How could colleges and seminaries stay fiscally afloat if the student body was limited to men? Why should women's tuition and contribution be denied? The result has been to generate programs (initially teaching and nursing degrees in colleges, Christian education degrees in seminaries) that have opened the door for women to wedge into academe. But the status of women in Dutch Reformed academic circles remains a complicated one, sometimes painful and sometimes encouraging.

The Dutch immigrant community has faced the realities of ethnic dilution with considerable trepidation and ambivalence. "If you're not Dutch, you're not much," moved from the realm of jocular banter among self-satisfied immigrant insiders to a more strident indictment of Dutch insularity. Many Dutch immigrant communities, reinforced in their isolation by Dutch language usage in churches and schools, set themselves apart from their "American" compatriots. The issue of ethnic isolation became even more of an issue as historic "Dutch" neighborhoods yielded to African American newcomers. This confrontation often came to a head in school board meetings, as competing visions of Reformed theology tugged back and forth. Should African Americans be admitted into "Dutch Reformed" schools? Did they have to be members of Christian Reformed or Reformed Church congregations in order to qualify for admittance? What responsibility did congregations have to their neighbors in an ethnically changing world?

The impact of the Christian education movement was felt far beyond the local communities. Educational initiatives followed Dutch folk into the mission field around the globe. Indeed, the training of missionaries was seen as a pivotal rationale (along with the training of clergy) for the founding of several Reformed colleges. Illustrative of the fruit of those labors is an extensive mission endeavor undertaken by the Christian Reformed Church to Native Americans in New Mexico and Arizona. Although often guided by perspectives with a decidedly racist edge, these efforts of benevolent outreach were widely supported in local congregations and opened the doors of education to many Native Americans who might otherwise not have been served.

In sum, the impetus for Christian education within the Dutch Reformed immigrant community has produced a remarkable legacy of stories and memories. Many of them are vivid and hopeful; yet some are riven with agony and anger. All are valuable records, as these brief introductory notes will illustrate.

The structure of this volume is to reflect on these rich legacies. At almost every turn, when Dutch immigrants hit the New World, they established schools right on the heels of establishing their churches. Indeed, worship and scholarship often occurred in the same building, under the same pastor-educator. Thus, the first legacy of the Dutch Reformed immigrant experience is the wide array of primary and secondary schools—"day schools"—that they founded in their determination to fashion new homes in a foreign land. Animated accounts of a sample of these schools are told in part 1. A second set of legacies is more problematic. As generations passed, the initial Dutch Reformed, immigrant enclaves ran up against a diversifying world. Issues of race and gender in particular created challenges for the schools and their minders. These struggles, too, are seminal heirlooms of the Christian educational enterprise and appear in part 2. Finally, the impact of Christian education as practiced by the Dutch Reformed community has had implications for communities and institutions far beyond the borders of Dutch immigrant enclaves. Whether in the worlds of linguistics, local or national politics, or the teaching of Dutch, these legacies are central to the Dutch Reformed immigrant experience and appear in part 3.

Part I: institutional legacies

These rich stories begin with a broad-stroke mapping of the Dutch Reformed American and Canadian experience by geographer and retired Calvin University professor, Henk Aay (ch. 1). Aay charts and maps the founding of Reformed immigrant schools from colonial times into the twenty-first century. As succeeding waves of immigrants landed on New World shores, their settlements rippled across the continent and were marked by the schools they left in their wake. Decade by decade, as communities attained a critical mass, churches and parents insisted that their children be educated in Reformed Christian schools. Many initially conducted their classes in Dutch, but that vestige of the past frequently became the first target in the march toward Americanization, as students, teachers, and parents began to insist that instruction be in English. For the earliest settlers—the colonial era Dutch and their descendants—the transition to English often came with the transition from church-run schools and to public education. When this happened, Reformed day schools were unable to compete for students, and many shut their doors. Later generations of immigrants and their descendants, especially those who formed the Christian Reformed Church, resisted this pattern and have continued to found and operate schools well into the twenty-first century. Aay's charting of these stages is a significant table setter for the subsequent articles.

The struggle between church-sponsored education and public education was at the core of civic debates in late nineteenth-century Orange City, Iowa, as it was in many other communities. Earl Wm. Kennedy, emeritus professor of religion at Orange City's Northwestern College, describes the heated controversy that rippled through that community around 1900 (ch. 2). The imbroglio absorbed the community's leading lights in lively repartee in the local newspaper—a "thriller," with new episodes in the form of impassioned epistles from one side and then the other appearing in each week's edition. Among the issues that riveted readers was whether Christian schools were—or should be—the sole carriers of Christian values; readers were reminded that even the public school day began with prayer and Bible reading and that classes were conducted by good Protestant educators. In a time of intense patriotism, the public school proponents suggested that Christian day schools were inherently un-American. But the supporters of these schools, largely recent immigrants and predominantly members of the Christian Reformed Church, maintained that the schools reflected the educational views of Abraham Kuyper and their memory of Christian schools back in the Netherlands. The "un-democratic" nature of Christian schools was also debated, with the clear implication that the cost of a Christian education appealed primarily to the elite of the community and was, by implication, therefore un-American.

The founding in the late nineteenth century of the Wisconsin Memorial Academy was a response to the lack of Christian secondary education in the remote villages of eastern Wisconsin. Genealogist and independent historian Mary Risseeuw explains that, in the face of the high cost of a religious education, a coalition of supporters from across the Midwest helped to found the academy (ch. 3). Of particular note is the central role played by the Reformed Church in this process, a rare instance of RCA support for private rather than public schooling. True to form, the academy was instrumental in educating a disproportionate number of clergy and missionaries—including a significant number of women who became educational and medical professionals.

Photographer and culture observer Ken Bult has contributed a pictorial essay (ch. 4). Bult portrays the establishment of the Christian education system in the Calumet, Illinois, region. His picturesque renderings of the times and settings of Christian schools in this boggy borderland conjoining Illinois and Indiana remind us of the hope and challenge that confronted all immigrant communities struggling to find a footing on the frontier in the late nineteenth century.

Northwestern College in Orange City, Iowa, began life as another "academy" in a Reformed Church community. Andrew Klumpp, editor of the *Annals of Iowa*, recounts that it was seen from the outset as an instrument "extending [Orange City's] influence throughout the region and even the globe" (ch. 5). The founding of Northwestern Classical Academy was an expression of the Dutch immigrants' grand worldview, one that reached far beyond their local environs. With such ambitious intentions in mind, it is not surprising that the émigrés poured considerable resources—including their offspring—into making the academy a vital and growing institution. Drawing its students from congregations as far flung as Minnesota and the Dakotas, the academy lived up to its founders' intentions of having a region-wide impact. By sending its most promising graduates on to colleges elsewhere, the academy extended its influence far beyond the region. By the second decade of the twentieth century, it was possible to say that the academy had lived up to all founding expectations.

Douglas Firth Anderson, himself a professor at Northwestern College, embellishes the story of Northwestern Classical Academy by focusing on its students and alumni (ch. 6). Their individual and collective successes were a vital testimony to the effectiveness of the academy's teaching and mentoring. B. D. Dykstra (Class of 1892), Hendrina Hospers (Class of 1897), and James Muilenburg (Class of 1914) were all distinguished graduates of the academy, making marks far beyond the Dutch enclave in northwestern Iowa. Anderson reflects on the importance of the ever-evolving curriculum as a significant factor in the remarkable effectiveness of the academy. Moreover, he found that campus life was lively and enriching, happily augmenting the classroom experience. As his title suggests, the resulting exuberance left (at least) one alumnus recalling, nostalgically, "the joyous, jolly Academy days" of his youth.

How to maintain a Christian identity in the face of demographic change has been a recurring struggle within the Dutch Reformed academic enterprise. As historian Robert P. Swierenga found in his study of the Timothy Christian Schools in Chicagoland, this challenge has led succeeding boards of trustees to broaden the scope of Christian identity far beyond the initial bounds of orthodox Calvinism (ch. 7). As financial and demographic exigencies pressed on them, Timothy Schools found that a "nondenominational" articulation of Christianity became increasingly necessary to fill their desks. As a result, Timothy Schools continue to flourish, even though their connections with their Dutch immigrant past and their Reformed theological foundations have become muddled. Among the gestures that have marked this passage have been changes in official mission statements as well as in the compositions of the board of trustees and faculty.

The status of Christian schools in relation to state-run, public schools has also been a challenging issue in Canada. Canadian educational administrator Adrian Guldemond maintains that the resolution of this dilemma has been a unique one north of the United States border (ch. 8). The provincial organizations representing the

Reformed Christian Schools in Canada have been able to articulate a "Third Way," which provides for both limited autonomy in curricular matters and substantial state funding that together maintain the distinctive character of Christian schools. By building coalitions with other religious communities, the Ontario Alliance of Christian Schools was able to persuade civic authorities to legislate measures that benefitted both private and parochial schools throughout the province.

Drawing on his doctoral research, Redeemer University College professor Phil Teeuwsen found that Christian schools in Ontario served as critical mediating agents in their communities' transitions from immigrant to Canadian status (ch. 9). On the one hand, the obvious roles of distilling and maintaining "Reformed" and "Dutch" immigrant traditions were clearly manifested in the stories and identities of Christian schools. On the other hand, the secondary role of shaping Canadians out of Dutch immigrant students was also widely accepted. More unexpectedly, Teeuwsen found that for many of their parents, the transition to full citizenship often involved claiming the local Christian school as "our" school. With this adoption of a known entity as their own place to start, the transformation from foreigner to Canadian began.

Postsecondary education became a critical issue soon after Dutch immigrants had established their frontier communities. Dutch historian George Harinck suggests that, in characteristic fashion, the Dutch Seceders in Grand Rapids looked back to the Netherlands for inspiration about how to develop a postsecondary, truly Reformed, model of higher education (ch. 10). He argues that they found their ideal model in the founding principles of the Theologische School in Kampen, the Netherlands. Since almost all of the early rectors and docents who undertook the theological education of young Dutch (Christian Reformed) immigrants in the United States were graduates of Kampen, they naturally mimicked the curriculum and training practices with which they had become familiar. As precursors to what became Calvin College[1] and Calvin Seminary, these early educators drew on a model that had been touted as an ideal for Kampen itself. Indeed, Harinck suggests that the happy marriage between Calvin College and Calvin Seminary was the embodiment of a vision that was never fully realized in Kampen. In a parallel narrative, Harinck posits a similar pattern for Christian higher education developing in South Africa as

---

1   Calvin College was renamed Calvin University in 2019.

Seceder immigrants sought to respond to educational expectations there.

Part II: race- and gender-based legacies

Invariably, as Dutch Reformed, immigrant, educational institutions matured, they confronted challenges from their American social and cultural contexts. As the articles in part 2 demonstrate, these confrontations often revolved around issues of race and gender. "Dutchness" often implied a racial (and cultural) separatism. As a result, the immigrants' encounter with racial and ethnic differences was often a direct challenge to their ethnic particularity. On a similar note, Dutch Reformed patriarchy found the growing expectations of women to be very problematic. Not surprisingly, one arena in which the resulting confrontations took place was the academic one.

Stephen Staggs, a Calvin University historian, maintains that the challenge of race was built into the very founding of one of the earliest academic institutions established by Dutch immigrants to the New World (ch. 11). Staggs reveals that the founders of Erasmus Hall Academy in Brooklyn, New York, were unequivocally committed to educating white males. Imbued with the prevailing understanding that nonwhites were incapable of feats of learning, the very notion of including blacks never crossed their minds. Indeed, as they lived out their professional lives, many graduates of Erasmus did what they could to keep black Americans from attaining their full potential. In that way, the legacy of their early education was to confirm the racist structures of eighteenth- and nineteenth-century societies. As the demographics of Brooklyn evolved, however, Erasmus Hall went from having a largely segregated, white student body to a highly diverse one and then back to a largely segregated one. Paradoxically, the last, most recent, stage is one in which the student body is almost exclusively black.

In the mid-twentieth century, the issue of race came to a dramatic head in Christian schools throughout the United States. Douglas Vrieland, retired Navy chaplain and former student in the Grosse Pointe Christian Day School, brings a front row perspective to the issue of race as it unfolded in Detroit (ch. 12). A letter from a local African American congregation requesting their children be admitted to the Grosse Pointe Christian School could not have been more timely, since it came one month before the city's July 1967 riots. As Vrieland recounts, in the aftermath of the rebellion, the school board grappled with questions of what it meant to be a "Christian" day school and the implications of their conviction that all covenant children be given a Christian School education. With a concerted effort to get to the answer "yes" to the parent's request, the school society, board, and teachers (along with a courageous pastor in the background) all pulled together to respond warmly and graciously to these profound questions, teaching the students valuable lessons about race in the process.

Also problematic has been the educational outreach by the Christian Reformed Church to Native Americans. Dutch anthropologist Pieter Hovens has examined the history of the denomination's work among Navajos and Zunis in the American southwest (ch. 13). Many communions established schools on reservations, but the CRC efforts seem to have been met with singular ambivalence. On the one hand, CRC schools delivered substantive curricular material that students and their parents greatly appreciated; on the other hand, the rigid Calvinism of the educator-missionaries found stiff resistance from students and parents. It is noteworthy that, in the early twenty-first century, the CRC mission community came to realize this unfortunate legacy and sought, through official policy and practice, to change course.

Historian Suzanne Sinke has found that gender played a significant role in framing immigrants' understanding of education when they arrived in America (ch. 14). Drawing on a cache of letters written by Dutch immigrants, she found that the prevalence in America of female teachers in the lower grade levels was a surprise to the newcomers. In the Netherlands, even primary school education was in the hands of men—often clergymen. The immigrants adapted to this existing pattern quite quickly, however, and before long, most of their primary and secondary Christian schools were staffed by female educators. For many immigrants, this shift in their expectations about appropriate roles for women teachers became a harbinger of other changes to their assumptions about gender-specific involvements.

Although women were quickly accepted into the ranks of primary and secondary school educators, the place of females in Dutch Reformed institutions of higher learning has been a more mixed story. At times, females have been severely limited, and at other times, heroically championed. College administrator Rhonda Pennings recounts that circuitous journey as it has applied to women in Reformed and Christian Reformed colleges (and, more recently, universities) (ch. 15). The inclusion of female students was a significant milestone for the older colleges. Indeed, this seemed to be a significant "wedge" decision, for with the matriculation of women students came the demand for women administrators (especially deans of women) and women faculty. Not surprisingly, the early courses for women were designed to promote "traditional" roles, such as teachers or nurses. Tellingly, parity between females and males was woven into the fabric of the most recent Reformed-related colleges as they built on the legacy of the past.

Parity prevailed at the college level by the middle of the twentieth century, but Reformed Church historian Donald Bruggink points out that the inclusion of women in Western Theological Seminary (WTS) was much longer in coming (ch. 16). Founded to provide Dutch Reformed, immigrant churches with regionally trained clergy, WTS was from the outset focused on male education. Christian education became the vehicle by which women were drawn into WTS. The burgeoning demand in the 1950s and 1960s for church-based Christian education resulted in a significant demand for trained professionals. Women teachers were found throughout academe, so it was easy to argue that women should be trained to become "Christian" educators, as well. The first female professor at WTS arrived in 1962; she was a key architect of the Christian Education curriculum and set the stage for other female faculty to follow. Surprisingly, however, of the twelve MCE degree graduates in the 1960s, only two were women. Beginning with the Christian education programs, demand for female access to other degree programs—including the master of divinity degree—were logical consequences. Logical or not, the resistance that women encountered—and sometimes continue to encounter—was painful for all concerned.

Part III: other legacies

In Dutch Reformed immigrant enclaves—especially in sections of the Midwest—the establishment of "Christian" schools implied the establishment of Calvinist Reformed schools. In early twentieth-century New Jersey, however, the title of "Christian" was also claimed by Lutherans, Catholics, and others. Robert Schoone-Jongen, in his keynote address to the 2019 Association for the Advancement of Dutch American Studies (AADAS) conference, reflected on the experience of the Dutch community in the polyglot city of Paterson, New Jersey (ch. 17). The raucous, multiethnic neighborhood that housed the Dutch Reformed immigrant school (in this case portentously named "Amity Street Christian School") was an unseemly place, and recruiting students was an unending, arduous task. Newcomers to the community, especially those who arrived in the later Dutch immigrant waves, found themselves quickly being absorbed, willy-nilly, into this most American of American contexts. Retaining their Dutchness was a virtual impossibility, and their unique, Calvinist theological heritage was also soon in jeopardy. Internal debates among the various Reformed congregations further compounded the challenge of maintaining the Christian school's viability. The final challenge to the Dutch Reformed school was the development of a wide-ranging public school system that provided a solid education for free. While "winning" their new American identity, the Christian schools of Paterson "lost" their distinctive Dutch Reformed heritage.

The uniqueness of Dutch identity was also under assault in rural Iowa. Northwestern College English professor Keith Fynaardt reports on the "Hollander fires" that greeted Dutch immigrant farmers moving into Prairie Township, Iowa, at the turn of the twentieth century (ch. 18). The "jingoist nativist element" in that section of central Iowa, near Pella, was especially virulent during and after the First World War. Dutch newcomers, often successful farmers in other sections of Iowa and therefore able to buy new tracts of Prairie Township outright, were conflated with German sympathizers. An unholy alliance between local businessmen and disgruntled "nativists" resulted in a number of cases of arson. Fynaardt suggests that, even a century later, there continue to be strains in the relationship between the "American" and "Dutch" heirs of those earlier confrontations.

Graduate student Justin Vos reminds us that "education does not begin or end with schooling." Rather, in chapter 19, he emphasizes the formative role that such denominational publications as the *Banner* have played in engaging and guiding the Dutch Reformed community. Whether it was to digest and report on currents in politics, science, and popular culture, or to reaffirm the importance of the special burden of being truly Reformed in a religiously heterogeneous society, church publications were instrumental community builders. In addition, publication houses—such as Eerdmans and Zondervan—have been central to the mission of informing and affirming the unique identity of the immigrant—and postimmigrant—members of their Reformed readership. What the members of the Dutch Reformed community read, mattered.

One of the key distinctives of many early immigrant schools was the use of Dutch in the classroom. Within a few generations of their founding, however, most of the schools had abandoned that language and moved on to English. Ton Broos reminds us that by the late twentieth century, Dutch was so rare that it had to be resuscitated as a "foreign" language, even among formerly Dutch-speaking constituencies (ch. 20). He reviews the fifty years that Dutch has been part of the University of Michigan's curriculum and provides dynamic reasons why it should be maintained into the future. In addition to its value as the language of a vivid and sumptuous literature, Broos feels that understanding Dutch serves to enhance our understanding of own national history (the Dutch were the first to acknowledge the independence of the American colonies) and the unique culture that has enveloped Dutch immigrants from colonial times until the present. In addition, John Adams sent his (somewhat unruly) young sons to a Dutch tutor, believing that a Dutchman would be their best possible mentor.

Perhaps a better understanding of the Dutch language would serve to modulate the stereotypical (mis)understanding of Dutch Americans in the minds of American media mavens. Michael Douma argues that real ignorance of Dutch American history has manifested itself in a very unfair portrayal of Secretary of Education Betsy De Vos (ch. 21). Characterizing the media's mentality as fixated on the phrase, "If you ain't Dutch, you ain't much," Douma maintains that De Vos has been unfairly described as stuck in an ethnic myopia common to all Dutch immigrants and their offspring. Rather, he contends, a true understanding of Dutch American history would show that descendants of Dutch immigrants are much more variegated than assumed—even within the politics of West Michigan. After all, he points out, Holland, Michigan, De Vos's hometown, has a Democratic majority that belies the narrow-minded image of the stereotype.

How they understood their own experience in the New World mattered a great deal to Dutch immigrants. As Jan J. Boersema and Anthonia Boersema-Bremmer recount in chapter 22, the notion of "progress" permeated their interpretation of the transformation they were undergoing. Whether it was a matter of "clearing" the wilderness for the construction of "civilization," the eradication of "wild" animals and the domesticating of beneficial ones, or the invention and adoption of implements of new technology, the immigrants absorbed it all with great enthusiasm. Moreover, the embrace of "progress" was often seen as an inevitable part of their Christian experience, emblematic of their unilinear march toward a more Edenic society that reflected true Christian virtues and values.

If the media has it all wrong, what *should* the children of Dutch immigrants be taught about their past? That question drives the essay by David Zwart (ch. 23). Zwart has found that the teaching of Dutch American immigrant history has evolved in close parallel with the transitions in the teaching of history beyond the confines of Reformed educational circles. When the approach *au currant* among professional historians was to emphasize the memorization of facts and events, that mode was taught in Christian schools. When the prevailing pedagogy emphasized analyzing and critiquing social structural fault lines and the need for social change, that, too, was reflected in how Dutch American history was taught. In this way, Zwart suggests, Dutch Americans may have found themselves "more 'American' than they would like to admit."

That may be a fitting epitaph for this volume. Dutch Reformed immigrants to the New World worked assiduously to retain their unique theological and cultural heritage and transmit it to succeeding generations, and in the long run, the schools they created to carry out that mission were strongly supported. But the Americanizing forces that they confronted were overwhelming. Distinctive Dutch Reformed traditions have had to contend with demographic and cultural waves far beyond the control of the Dutch immigrants and their children and grandchildren.

And yet, and yet, the schools remain. Legacies of wholehearted and faithful forebears, these enduring establishments—battered and yet unbowed—serve as living talismans of the unique treasure that Dutch Reformed immigrants shared with North America.

Part I

Institutional Legacies

CHAPTER 1

Present from the Beginning: Reformed Dutch Day Schools in North America, 1638-2019

Henk Aay

Introduction

The field of Dutch American studies has been siloed into two congenial scholarly camps: those who research and write about the colonial Dutch and their continuing legacy in New York and New Jersey (the "old" Dutch) and those who do much the same work for Dutch immigration to the Midwest and beyond, which began in the mid-1800s and continued throughout much of the twentieth century (the "new" Dutch). This partition has resulted in a neglect of attention to connections, comparisons, and continuities between these two principal historical periods and regions.[1] Episodes in Dutch American

---

[1] In 2015 the New Netherland Research Center (NNRC), located in Albany, New York, tasked with scholarship about the colonial Dutch and their continuing legacy, and the Association for the Advancement of Dutch American Studies (AADAS), focused on the Midwestern Dutch, held a joint conference for the first time. One of their goals was to bring scholars from both sides together for professional and personal dialogue. The conference theme, The Dutch in America across the Centuries: Connections and Comparisons, was chosen to encourage researchers to consider the connections, continuities, and comparisons between these two periods

history of "old" and "new" Dutch working together—cooperating, sheltering, financing, advising, disagreeing—or not—and of continuities in Reformed Dutch religion and education are examples of such joint and lasting enterprises. This essay surveys the history of Reformed Dutch day schools as one such continuity.[2] From one perspective, the Reformed Dutch day school in Breuckelen (now Brooklyn), New York, in 1661, and the one in Drenthe, Michigan, in 2019, could not be more dissimilar, from the school buildings to the subjects, curriculum, classrooms, teaching, and just about anything else one would care to consider. From another perspective, there are compelling continuities—

---

and areas. Yet most presenters stayed within their silos; very few wrote papers that tackled such issues. We ended up *sharing* our different pasts rather than connecting or comparing them; the editors expressed that sentiment in the title of the book that resulted from the conference and regarded sharing our pasts as a first step to connecting them. Most of the papers presented at this particular conference are found in Henk Aay, Janny Venema, and Dennis Voskuil, eds., *Sharing Pasts. Dutch Americans through Four Centuries* (Holland, MI: Van Raalte Press, 2017).

[2] Throughout this essay, I will use either the somewhat unusual name "Reformed Dutch day schools" or "Reformed Dutch American/Canadian day schools," even though individual schools hardly ever take a name that includes the word "Reformed." Most other Christian day schools in North America do include denominational names (e.g., Baptist, Lutheran, Catholic). The reason why "Reformed" is not used in school names in North America is that, except for those who are members of the various Reformed denominations, very few people understand what it refers to and means; for many, the word is associated with penal institutions where offenders undergo reformation. This has led Reformed Dutch American and Canadian day schools to commonly use the generic name "Christian" together with a geographic designation, for example, Listowel [Ontario] Christian School. This naming convention brings to mind a broadly ecumenical and nonparochial community institution to those unfamiliar with these schools and interested in Christian education for their children. That is a positive perception and a worthwhile goal, but it does obscure what they have been for more than a century: denominationally Reformed and ethnically Dutch American/Canadian. Their governance, umbrella organizations, administrators, teaching staff, and students have continued to be largely made up of Dutch Americans and Canadians who are members of Reformed denominations, principally, the Christian Reformed Church.

The other reason for my use of the word "Reformed" in reference to these schools is that, unlike the denominational markers for some other kinds of Christian schools, that word, from the late nineteenth century on, came to refer to a comprehensive Christian worldview no longer restricted to theology, faith, and the church but decisive for every arena in society, including education. Another naming variant for this denominational/worldview combination is "Calvinist." Some have labelled these schools Calvinist Christian schools. For a succinct introduction to a Reformed (neo-Calvinist) worldview, see Albert Wolters, *Creation Regained: Biblical Basics for a Reformational Worldview* (Grand Rapids, MI: Eerdmans, 1985). Both the denominational and worldview definitions of "Reformed" or "Calvinist" are, to varying degrees and in different times and places, relevant for these Christian schools.

Dutch ancestry, unifying Reformed confessions, the transmission of Reformed Dutch educational institutions, philosophy, and practices. I will give an account of this history in five periods.

Period 1 (1638-64): parochial/public schools in New Netherland

The schools of New Netherland were replicas of the village schools in the home country. Such schools were present throughout the republic; the Netherlands had achieved high accessibility to elementary education during the seventeenth century, although not all parents took advantage of its availability.[3] In nearly every settlement with a church, there was a coeducational elementary (Nederduitse) school. Only cities offered education at and beyond this level in what were called Latin schools, as well as in various private academies, some for particular subjects and training. These elementary schools throughout the country were both public and parochial at the same time. Civil magistrates and ecclesiastical authorities (ministers, church consistories) together governed and administered the schools.[4] They were public schools in that they were usually the only school in the village or town and its surroundings, open to all children without regard to their religious affiliation or their parents' ability to pay tuition.[5] They were parochial schools in that both the teacher and the curriculum explicitly communicated the teachings, practices, and theology of the Reformed Church. The balance between such joint civil/ecclesiastical governance varied in time and place. In matters of religion—what was taught as part of religious education, the orthodoxy of the teacher, local supervision—the Reformed Church held sway; in matters of civil authority—financial support, the school building, the powers of appointment, licensing, and admission—the magistrates were in control. Of course, the civil authorities themselves were also Calvinists. The Reformation had earlier replaced the Roman Catholic

---

[3] For the history of schools during the Dutch Republic (1581-1795) see P. Th. F. M. Boekholt and E. P. Booy, "Het Onderwijs voor 1795," in *Geschiedenis van de School in Nederland* (Assen/Maastricht: Van Gorcum, 1987), 1-85; William Heard Kilpatrick, *The Dutch Schools of New Netherland and Colonial New York* (Washington: Government Printing Office, 1912), 19-38; D. Langedijk, "Het Schoolwezen tijdens de Republiek," in *Kort Overzicht van de Geschiedenis van het Christelijk Onderwijs* (Groningen: Wolters, 1947): 5-8.
[4] Kilpatrick, *Dutch Schools*, 19-25.
[5] Not many children from indigent families, however, were able to take advantage of this edict of the Synod of Dordt. Boekholt and Booy, *Geschiedenis van de School in Nederland*, 42-45.

governing authorities at all levels with Protestant adherents who introduced and enforced Calvinistic regulations respecting church and school. Teachers were required to be members of the Reformed state church and, following the mandates of the Synod of Dordt (1618-19), to sign the so-called Three Forms of Unity: the Belgic Confession, the Heidelberg Catechism, and the Canons of Dordt.[6] Those who would not, were dismissed.[7]

These schools in the Netherlands and in New Netherland were parochial in other important ways as well. Invariably, the teacher of the school also held a paid position in the church; because of his education, he commonly served as cantor (*voorzanger*, in Dutch), lay reader (*voorlezer*), and sometimes as sexton (*koster*).[8] The cantor would start and lead congregational singing or sing verses solo; as lay reader, the teacher would read to the congregation from the Bible, the confessions, or liturgical forms. The sexton was the property manager of the church and tasked with a variety of services, such as readying the church for Sunday worship. The school (often in the teacher's home) was in close proximity to the church, a reflection of this dual affiliation.

The common, three-part curriculum of religion, reading, and writing taught in these elementary schools also underlined the parochial character of the schools; a large block of in-school learning was devoted to Bible studies, prayer, singing of the Psalms, and studying the Ten Commandments, the Reformed creeds, and the Heidelberg Catechism.[9] Religious texts would serve as the subject for practice reading and writing. Students might well learn the Bible reading and psalms to be sung at the upcoming Sunday church service.[10] They could be asked to recite Bible passages and parts of the Heidelberg Catechism in front of the congregation. In these ways, the school served the role of what would much later become the church's Sunday school. The dominant

---

[6] Ibid., 19. This four-hundred-year-old requirement will be very familiar to today's educators in many Reformed Christian day schools, colleges, and universities in North America.

[7] The phasing in of the Reformation throughout the Republic, also in regard to Calvinist schooling, took time and generated opposition among the public who clung to their traditional Catholic religious beliefs and practices. Many teachers were Catholics and could not be easily replaced. Catholics ran their own clandestine schools for more well-to-do parents; these were often tolerated by the local authorities and population. Ibid., 17-21.

[8] Ibid., 67-71.

[9] Ibid., 33-41.

[10] Kilpatrick, *Dutch Schools*, 200.

Present from the Beginning 7

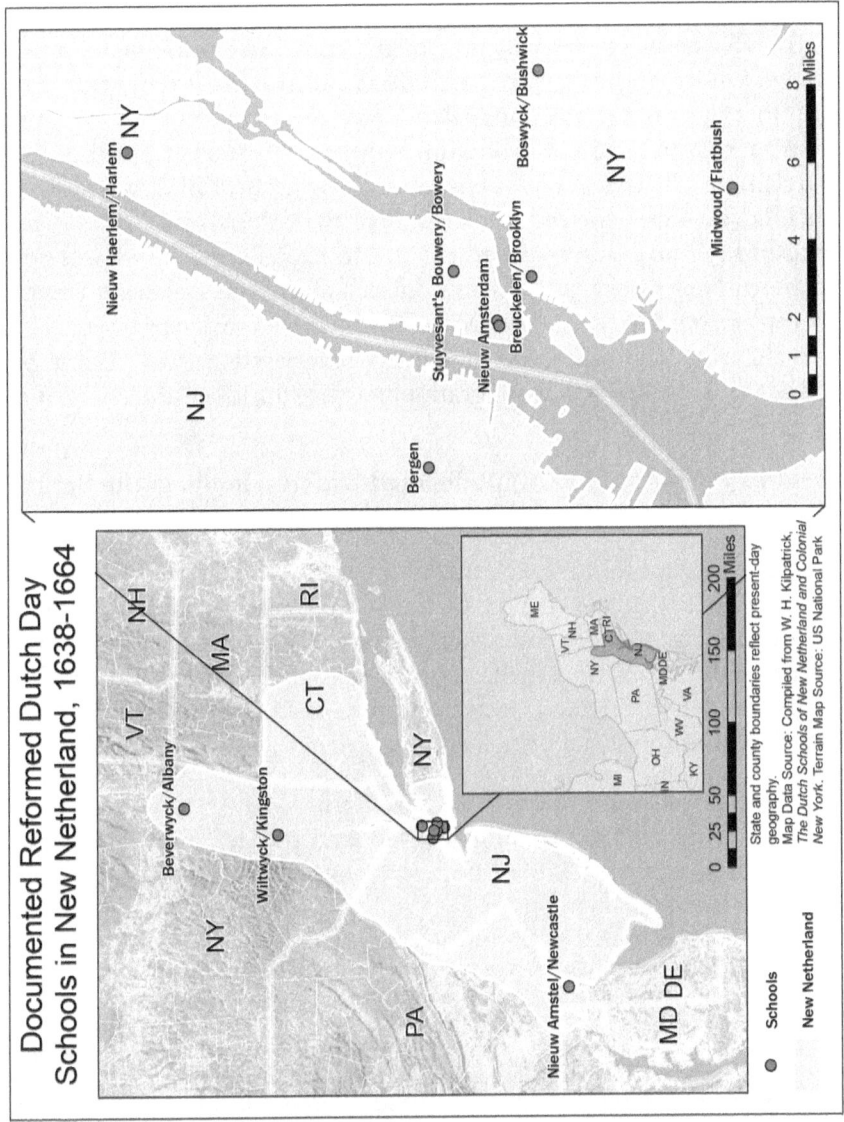

Fig. 1

Reformed quality of these elementary schools was fixed by the Dutch Calvinistic establishment, especially the national synods, during and after the successful revolt against Spain (1568-1648).[11]

There were ten documented Reformed public elementary schools and one Latin school in New Netherland from 1638 to the

[11] Ibid., 19-20.

surrender of the colony to England in 1664 (fig. 1).[12] They were found in the chartered Dutch villages, towns, and other settlements along the Lower Bay and valley of the Hudson River: Breuckelen, Midwoud, and Boswijck on western Long Island, now the borough of Brooklyn in New York City; Nieuw Amsterdam, Stuyvesant's Bouwerij, and Nieuw Haerlem on the island of Manhattan; Wiltwijck and Beverwijck along the Hudson River, the economic spine of the colony; and in two other areas of emerging Dutch settlement and control, Bergen, in what is now northern New Jersey, and Nieuw Amstel, along the Delaware River.[13] Nieuw Amsterdam on Lower Manhattan, the largest settlement, also had a Latin School for the higher and moneyed classes, offering a classical education with Latin grammar and texts, logic, and rhetoric as its curriculum.[14]

Period 2 (1664 to ca. 1776): Reformed Dutch schools in the British colonies

Most schools in New Netherland were founded during the 1650s and 1660s, late in the history of the colony, when Dutch settlement began to increase more rapidly. The first—in Nieuw Amsterdam—was established in 1638 and the last—in Bergen and Boswijck—just before the surrender to England. Most persisted as Dutch Reformed public schools throughout the British colonial period.

In Flatbush, however, there were no private schools, one school must do all the teaching and meet all the demands. Hence the presence [since 1758] of both languages in the curriculum of the

---

[12] Ibid., 119-41. Kilpatrick reviews the archival records related to schools (financing, tuition, school building, duties of the teacher, etc.) for each of the chartered villages with a school. See also, Janny Venema, *Beverwijck. A Dutch Village on the American Frontier, 1652-1664* (Albany: State University of New York Press, 2003), 148-54.

[13] The maps in this essay were produced as part of the Dutch American Mapping Project; its goal is to publish an atlas of Dutch American history and culture, 1609-2019. Several students from Calvin University (Christina Bohnet, Megumu Jansen, and Matt Raybaud) and Hope College (Isabelle Rembert) worked on the section of this project devoted to Dutch Americans/Canadians and education. They digitized the records and created databases from the yearly directories of Christian Schools International (CSI), formerly the National Union of Christian Schools (NUCS), the principal association for Reformed Dutch American/Canadian day schools. They did the same with the yearly records of several other Dutch American/Canadian Reformed denominations that operate their own Christian Schools. Maps were made from these databases and from published works (such as Kilpatrick's, *The Dutch Schools of New Netherland and Colonial New York*) that included the locations of these schools.

[14] Kilpatrick, *Dutch Schools*, 95-109.

school. The town meeting even followed much later in the use of English, its last record in Dutch being of date April 4, 1775, the first in English a year later . . . [Church] services in English were not introduced until 1792 and even then were confined to the afternoon service. Not until 1805 was English the exclusive language of the church service. For still many years, Dutch was used in the privacy of many of the old families.[15]

Ninety-four years after the British takeover, the Flatbush, Long Island, school in 1758 finally had a teacher who could teach in English as well as Dutch. There are records for another six schools established after the English takeover: four in the Hudson and Mohawk Valleys and two in villages that today are part of the Borough of Brooklyn, New York (fig. 2). These records show that they were exactly the same kind of schools as during the New Netherland period and that all the schools in the Dutch villages kept these characteristics (including Dutch as the language of instruction) until the time of the American Revolution.[16] As historian W. H. Kilpatrick calculates:

> It appears more or less certain that Albany, Bergen, Bushwyck, Brooklyn, Flatlands, Kingston, New Utrecht, Schenectady, and probably many other villages more or less exclusively Dutch in stock and language kept up schools similar to the schools already studied [New Haerlem and Flatbush]. It is quite possible that whenever was found a village predominantly Dutch in language and of sufficient size to maintain a church (but not necessarily a pastor), there—had we the data—one would find almost invariably a school, public in some sense, controlled more or less by the consistory and taught by the *voorlezer* of the Dutch church.[17]

Fig. 3 maps the 102 Dutch Reformed churches, then known as the Reformed Protestant Dutch Church (RPDC) for 1770. Rather than the seventeen documented Dutch Reformed schools, Kilpatrick's calculation would have resulted in five times that number in the Dutch villages in Long Island, Manhattan, northern New Jersey, and the Hudson and Mohawk Valleys during the century after the British takeover.

Here a Dutch way of life was continued without interference; the chartered villages and their surroundings were centered on a Dutch

---

[15] Ibid., 199.
[16] Ibid., 201-15.
[17] Ibid., 201.

10 DUTCH REFORMED EDUCATION

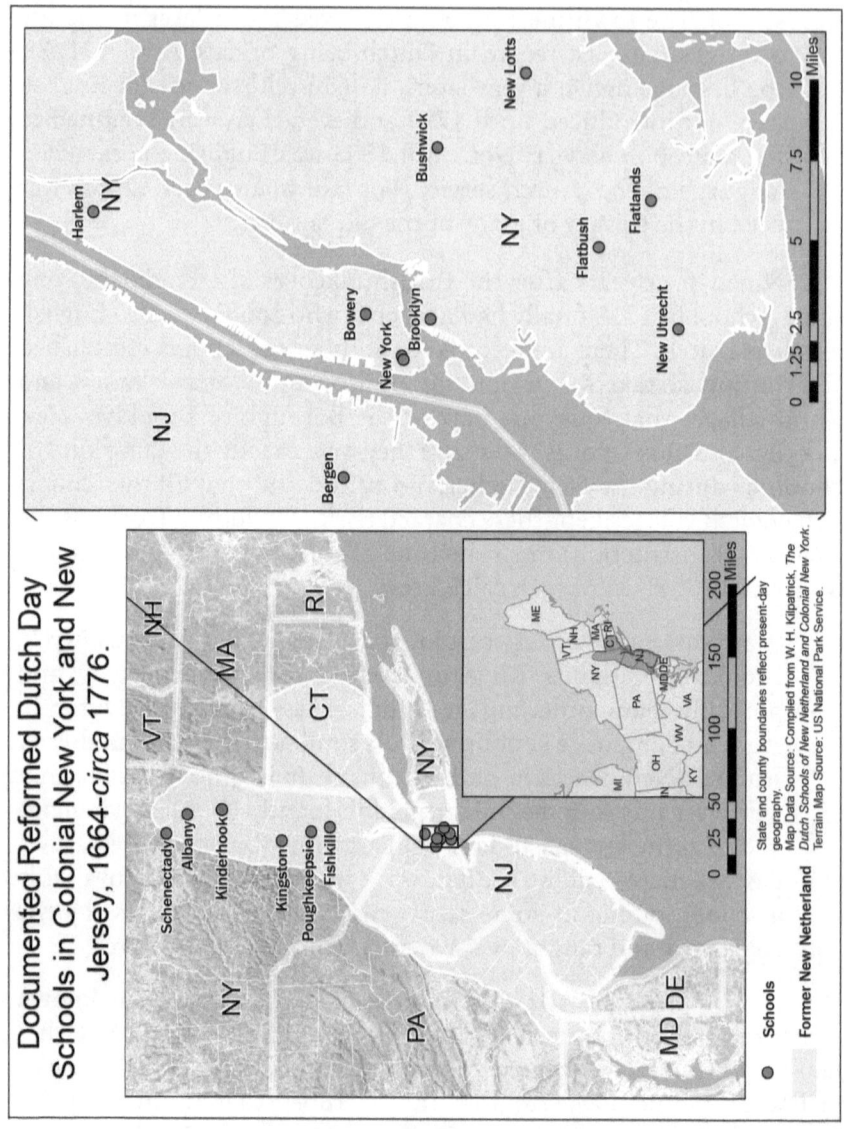

Fig. 2

Reformed church and preserved a Dutch way of life that included a parochial school governed and financed by both church and village council. The Dutch local governmental offices continued with their new English names, such as "constable" and "overseers." Officeholders were now elected by the people at a public town meeting, called for

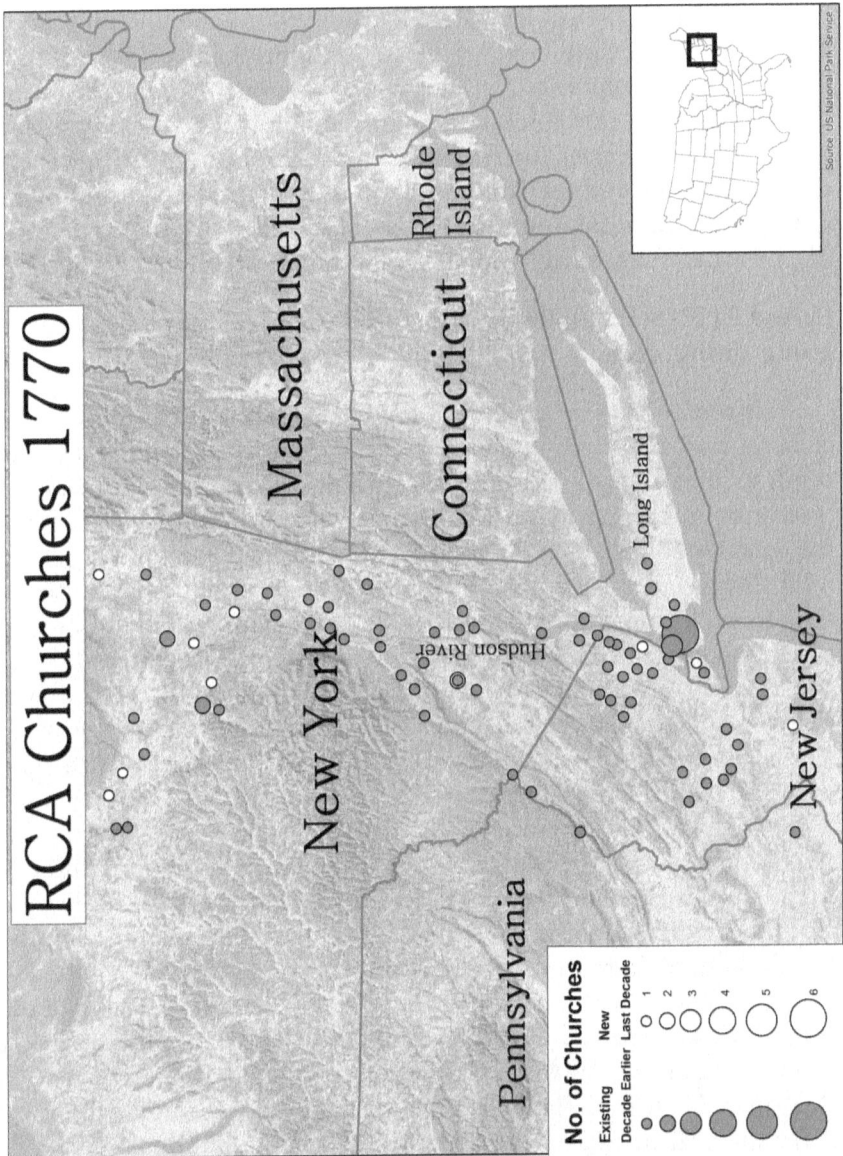

Fig. 3. Dutch Reformed Churches (RPDC) in 1770

all householders. The council sold public land and levied taxes; it had considerably more authority than in New Netherland in what we would now call church matters: setting the ministers' salaries and selecting school masters, as well as the church wardens. The church, however, as in New Netherland, was not separate from the civil authorities.

Dutch was the spoken language and that of church and school. The close relationship between these two continued: students would learn to read and write in Dutch and become familiar with the Reformed creeds, catechism, and psalms so that they could understand and participate in the church service. As the Dutch population grew by natural increase, and with the arrival of other Reformed believers, such as the Huguenots, new farmlands were occupied, villages founded and chartered, and Reformed churches and schools established.[18]

Period 3 (1776-1870): Reformed Dutch American day schools— going, going, gone

It took a very long time (as long a century) for this hegemonic cultural tradition with respect to schooling in the Dutch villages to begin to break down. During the last half of the eighteenth century (the years leading up to the War of Independence and early decades of the new republic), these Reformed Dutch elementary public schools were slowly superseded, place by place, by either nonparochial public schools or, in some towns and cities, by truly parochial schools. I have not found published research on this transition, but what is clear is that the era of the Reformed Dutch public/parochial school—a replica of the elementary school in the Netherlands that had persisted for more than a hundred and forty years in New York and New Jersey—came to an end in post-Revolutionary America.

With the growing power of local democratic governance during this transitional period, the traditional clerical control in the community— led by the minister and the consistory—became increasingly challenged and sidelined.[19] School affairs slowly fell into the hands of the common people and their representatives on the town and village councils. People affiliated with other churches began to settle in these Dutch communities, especially on the frontiers of Upstate New York; they could not be expected to send their children to—or pay for—the local Reformed day school, the only elementary education program in town. After the United States was founded, schools were also increasingly

---

[18] Kilpatrick, *Dutch Schools*, 201-15. Surprisingly, more than a century after Kilpatrick published this highly original work, very little new published research has been added to our knowledge of these schools, even though a steady stream of Dutch documents has been transcribed and translated. It would require a comparative examination of the records of these chartered villages and of their Dutch Reformed churches. There is a PhD out there for a graduate student in Dutch American history or in the history of American education.

[19] Ibid., 215

regarded as one important avenue to build a sense of nationhood and citizenship that would transcend ethnic, class, and religious differences and instill democratic values and civic virtues. A parochial, largely ethnic school ran counter to such goals. Once a local village council was entirely responsible for schooling (finances and governance), the Dutch Reformed school closed or became a public school, albeit, still very much Protestant but without much explicit religious instruction. The distinguishing close ties (staffing, Dutch Reformed schoolmasters, Reformed religious education) between school and church were cut. Dutch rural villages could not support both public and parochial schools. In larger centers, such as New York and Albany, there was room for both public and private schools. Here, the Reformed Dutch school could transition into a truly parochial school funded entirely by the church and its parents and, in that way, continue its longstanding educational practices.[20]

The perceived advantages of public or common schools—for example, free for everyone—led to political campaigns in many states for such schools during the first half of the nineteenth century.[21] New York State was a very early adopter (1812) of the common school system for the entire state; this made it impossible for parochial schools to receive public moneys; any remaining Reformed Dutch parochial/public schools had to either close or become entirely private schools. From the very beginning, New York State was a stronghold of these common schools.

The decision of the state of New York to establish a common school system statewide in 1812 led to a decisive and surprising reversal of what had been the RPDC's staunch and continuous mandate to form and maintain Reformed day schools. As part of the Classis of Amsterdam of the church in the Netherlands from 1621, as its own classis of the Reformed Church in the Netherlands from 1754, and as a national synod for an entirely separate and independent denomination beginning in 1793, the Reformed community had steadfastly sustained this mandate.

Indeed, in 1809, three years before New York State adopted the common school system, the General Synod of the RPDC adopted the most extensive and final set of resolutions on the necessity of Reformed

---

[20] Ibid., 147-59.
[21] Carl Kaestle, *Pillars of the Republic: Common Schools and American Society, 1780-1860* (NY: Hill and Wang, 1983).

Christian schooling.[22] It began with republishing the decree in six resolutions (with words such as "shall" and "must") as set forth by the Synod of Dordt related to schools, teachers, the poor and education, religious education, and school supervision. It then applied these to the current RPDC, with four resolutions of its own (with words such as "recommend" and "duty") on the division of each congregation into school districts; the appointment of consistory members as school trustees in each district; the recruitment and examination of suitable schoolmasters by the trustees; the supervision by the trustees of the schoolmaster, especially on the teaching of Reformed doctrines; and the supervision of the schools and the schoolmaster by the pastor of the congregation as school trustee, *primus inter pares*.

Three years later, in 1812, New York State adopted the common school system, and from then on, the RPDC as a body no longer regarded Christian day schools as imperative or essential. It is instructive that the synod's sweeping attention to Reformed Christian schools in 1809 is entirely silent about financial matters. This suggests that the committee that produced the report did not regard these schools as private, parochial institutions; it fully expected that the customary and historic pattern of the government paying for local schooling would continue and that the Reformed day schools would continue to carve out a place in a public educational system as they had in the past. Public moneys, tuition from parents, and contributions from the Reformed Church would together pay for education.

The New York State legislation for the common school system, however, directed that all public moneys go to the common schools, and that meant the end of public funding for Reformed Christian day schools. In the transition from the 1809 synodical resolutions on Reformed day schools to the next synodical action on this topic, Tanjore writes: "In 1812 the Common School System was adopted in New York State, after which, the suggestions of the Synod of 1809 could not generally be carried out. There is no reference to parochial schools in the Revised Constitutions of 1833 and 1874."[23] Indeed, there are hardly any further entries under parochial schools in subsequent digests of synodical legislation. In hindsight, it is startling how orthodox the 1809 synodical action was, given the precarious state of the Reformed day schools at the time. But this is clearly the turning point in the RPDC's

---

[22] Ibid., 478-79.
[23] Ibid., 479.

transition from parochial Christian education as a requirement to that of an option for its members.

In sum, after the American Revolutionary War, with the growing power of local government and the erosion of clerical authority, the expanding denominational diversity in Dutch American communities, and the increasing appeal (also among RPDC congregants) of common (public) schools as builders of the new nation and of common civic virtues—all of these societal changes being external to the denomination—Reformed parochial/public day schools began to weaken and become crowded out, replaced, and eliminated. The implementation by legislation of the common school system completed this process.

At the same time, and in response to these dramatic changes, the laity and leadership of the RPDC began to revisit its generally accepted position on schooling. In the process, the responsibility of parents and the church in the religious education of their children was reemphasized. As a result, the public schools, still overwhelmingly Protestant in staffing and cultural outlook, were lobbied to include prayer, Bible reading, the importance of religion in civic life, and opportunities for different local clergy to provide religious education for their students during designated school hours.

There were those who fought a rearguard action to revive Reformed day schools on the ground that public schools were secular institutions that could not prepare students for their life as Christians. Samuel Schieffelin, a wealthy New York pharmaceutical manufacturer, made sizeable donations to the church's board of education to establish a parochial school fund to establish and support such schools and to publish Christian textbooks.[24] During the last half of the nineteenth century, Schieffelin's fund helped support as many as sixteen schools, mainly among the Midwest's new Dutch and German immigrant churches. Synod went along with these initiatives but regarded them as inexpedient and urged its churches to focus instead on instruction of their youth in Sunday school programs. By the early twentieth century, the number of schools helped by this fund had steadily declined, and this program came to an end, and with it, the parochial schools of what had become the Reformed Church in America (RCA).[25] By 1957 there

---

[24] Corwin, *A Digest of Constitutional and Synodical Legislation*, 479-83.
[25] The RPDC was renamed the Reformed Church in America in 1867, thereby affirming its American home rather than its Dutch roots.

was only one such school—a high school operated by the Reformed Church of German Valley, Illinois.[26]

Period 4 (1870s-1920): re-emergence of Reformed Christian Day Schools

Immigration from the Netherlands to America amounted to just a trickle during the British colonial period and the first seventy years of the new republic. But after 1846, a second wave of Dutch immigration began in earnest. Between 1840 and 1940, more than two hundred thousand Dutch immigrants arrived, settling primarily in the Midwest.[27] They came from a country in the middle of a protracted, century-long, religio-political struggle about education that was not resolved until 1920 when public, Protestant, Catholic, and Jewish schools were granted equal, financial public support.[28]

During the eighteenth century, the Reformed Church of the Netherlands came increasingly under the influence of the Enlightenment; reason and deism had gained the upper hand, rather than, as before, the revelation of the Scriptures and the Reformed creeds and confessions based on them.[29] For example, teachers could talk about Jesus Christ only as an embodiment of virtues for students to follow rather than as the Son of God who died for humankind. Reason explained everything, rather than revelation through faith. Hand in hand with rationalism was the principle of tolerance. So as not to offend Protestant, Jewish, or Catholic students, teachers could speak to their class only about an

---

[26] "The Relationship of Public and Parochial School Education: A Statement of the Board of Education, Reformed Church in America" (NY: Board of Education, RCA, 1957), 20. This report was sent to all the churches for study. This is the last comprehensive report by the RCA on Christian schooling. It reiterates the positions held since the early 19th century: Christian schools are not essential but an option; they can easily become sectarian; and RCA members should strive to keep religion in the public schools.

[27] Hans Krabbendam, *Freedom on the Horizon: Dutch Immigration to America, 1840-1940* (Grand Rapids, MI: Eerdmans, 2009), app. 1, 361-62.

[28] For histories of the struggle for Christian education in the Netherlands consult: D. Langedijk, *Kort Overzicht van de Geschiedenis van het Christelijk Onderwijs* (Groningen: J. B. Wolters, 1947); D. Langedijk, *De Geschiedenis van het Protestants-Christelijk Onderwijs* (Delft: Van Keulen, 1953); Boekholt and Booy, "De Schoolstrijd," and "Naar een Gedifferentieerd Onderwijssyseem, 1860-1920," in *Geschiedenis van de School in Nederland*, 132-228; Donald Oppewal, *The Roots of the Calvinistic Day School Movement* (Grand Rapids: Calvin College Monograph Series, 1963), 8-15. Oppewal's monograph suffers from not consulting the extensive Dutch literature on the topic.

[29] Boekholt and Booy, "Naar een Nieuwe Tijd," in *Geschiedenis van de School in Nederland*, 80-85.

all-knowing supreme being and religious virtues. The public school had become an institution for students belonging to all creeds.[30]

Beginning with their secession from the state Reformed Church in 1834, political and church leaders of more orthodox Protestant Christian communities resisted this state monopoly on education and the increasingly non-Christian character of Dutch public schools. They persistently advocated for the right to establish and operate their own schools, something that was finally granted in principle in the revised Dutch Constitution of 1848. It took another nine years for a new national education law to be enacted in 1857. It fully funded public schools, made them neutral with respect to religion, and allowed for the establishment of special religious schools (Protestant, Jewish, Catholic) but without any funding or subsidies from the state. For the rest of the century and until 1920, the political fight was about increasing the financial support for these special religious schools; these efforts met with modest incremental successes. The *holy grail*—full financial equality with public schools for special religious schools—was finally granted, first in the revision of the constitution in 1917 and then in legislation in 1920.[31]

After 1857 orthodox Reformed as well as Catholic and Jewish communities in the Netherlands began to establish their own—then largely unsubsidized—schools. In 1880, when Dutch immigrant congregations in the American Midwest were just beginning to found their own Reformed day schools, some 25 percent of students in the Netherlands attended religious schools, then partially subsidized; by 1920, just before the organization of the Reformed day schools in the United States into the National Union of Christian Schools (NUCS), 45 percent of students in the Netherlands attended fully funded religious schools.[32]

Nineteenth-century Dutch Protestant immigrants to the United States were very much aware of the battle for Christian education in the Netherlands; many families had lived through its changing fortunes. It is little wonder that in the 1870s, once they had established a firm foothold in their new communities, they began to duplicate the Reformed Dutch day schools. Unlike the protracted struggle in

---

[30] Langedijk, *Kort Overzicht van de Geschiedenis*, 5-8; Langedijk, *De Geschiedenis van het Protestants-Christelijk Onderwijs*, 1-6.
[31] Langedijk, *Kort Overzicht van de Geschiedenis*, 42-49; Langedijk, *De Geschiedenis van het Protestants-Christelijk Onderwijs*, 325-37; Boekholt and Booy, *Geschiedenis van de School in Nederland*, 218-23.
[32] Boekholt and Booy, *Geschiedenis van de School in Nederland*, 221.

the Netherlands to even establish such schools, there were no legal impediments in the New World, although there was plenty of resistance within some Dutch immigrant communities.[33]

One condition that worked against the establishment of such schools on the frontier was that the RPDC did not regard Reformed day schools as essential, and therefore, as a denomination, it did not actively work to encourage and establish them. Instead, its members were expected to send their children to the public schools once a school district was established. On the frontier, state control in education was limited at first, and local school boards and public school teachers could more easily implement the wishes of parents when it came to Bible reading, prayer, and religious education.

The immigrant churches joined the RPDC in 1850 which, until 1857, was the only Dutch Reformed denomination on the frontier. Thereafter, it was joined by the Christian Reformed Church (CRC). Although Christian education did not factor into the secession of 1857 that created the CRC, many of its members then and in the future were seceders from the Dutch state church (from the secessions of both 1834 and 1886). Within this body of adherents, there had developed a strong commitment to and experience with Christian schools as a reaction to what they regarded as secular public education in the Netherlands and the United States. Once the CRC was established, it began to act on these convictions. In 1870 the CRC General Assembly called upon every congregation—where feasible—to establish a Christian school.[34] With remarkable vigor, this new Reformed denomination became the champion of Reformed day schools.

The new Dutch immigrant communities began establishing schools during the late nineteenth century at a notable pace.[35] The

---

[33] Gerhardus Bos writes about the combative opposition to Christian schools among Dutch immigrants in the working-class neighborhoods of Paterson, NJ. Gerhardus Bos, "Schools of the East," *Yearbook of the Free Christian Schools in America, 1923-24* (Chicago: Materson-Selig, 1924), 125.

[34] Janet Sjaarda Sheeres, ed. *Minutes of the Christian Reformed Church* (Grand Rapids, MI: Eerdmans, 2013), 297, Art. 36, General assembly, 15 and 16 June 1870. The article reads: "Primary education is discussed again and the entire Assembly is unilaterally convinced that the school is the place for cultivation of and support for the Church, and that, therefore, it must be the obligation of each congregation to see to it that they acquire free schools and if this is not possible, to provide as much as possible for Dutch and Reformed instruction. The Assembly recommends this most emphatically to each church council and congregation."

[35] In 1924 NUCS asked a number of individuals closely involved with Reformed Dutch Christian day schools and its pioneers in the early years in different parts of the country to submit articles to its yearbook. These are valuable first-person

yearbooks of the CRC from 1881 to 1900 list forty-five different schools: twenty-six regular day schools and nineteen supplementary schools. Locally, they were often called Holland Christian Schools or just Holland Schools.[36] The supplementary schools taught the Dutch language and the Reformed creeds, confessions, and catechism during the summer (commonly known as vacation schools) and on weekends and evenings during the school year, just as the 1870 CRC General Assembly had recommended. Such extra schooling was feasible for Dutch immigrant communities that were too small, without sufficient resources, or without available instructors to organize a full-fledged day school. As immigrant communities grew, their supplementary schools became day schools, and new supplementary ones emerged in newly established centers.

Fig. 4 maps these forty-five different Reformed Dutch schools. Overall, the regular day schools are where one would expect to find them: in West Michigan, Chicago, south central and northwestern Iowa, and northern New Jersey. The supplementary schools are also found there, but they are also present on the margins of the Dutch settlement zone: Cincinnati, Ohio; Lafayette, Indiana; and New Holland and Ridott, Illinois. Here the Dutch communities were either too small or unable to support a Christian day school. What the map does not show because of its scale—though the yearbooks do—is that the two principal Dutch colonies—Holland, Michigan (and many of its surrounding villages), and Pella, Iowa, had no Reformed day schools in this 1882-1900 period. Unlike the mixed ethnicities of larger cities, these pioneer areas in Ottawa and Allegan Counties in Michigan and Marion County in Iowa consisted nearly entirely of immigrant Dutch populations. Here the district public schools had only Dutch children, Dutch teachers, and Dutch parents; their public schools apparently were a mirror of their populations in language and religion.

Until the turn of the century, the Reformed Dutch day schools were parochial schools, extensions of the church and governed ultimately by its consistory and minister. Beginning in 1882, school

---

accounts. H. Jacobsma and Henry Kuiper, "Schools of the Middle-West," *Yearbook of the Free Christian Schools in America, 1923-24* (Chicago: Materson-Selig, 1924), 101-22; R. Postma, "The Christian School Movement in Michigan," *Yearbook of the Christian Schools of America, 1925-1926* (Chicago: Onze Toekomst, 1926), 81-102; Gerhardus Bos, "Schools of the East," 123-32; C. Aue, "Schools of the West," *Yearbook Free Christian Schools, 1923-1924*, 133-47.

[36] For any given year, these statistics are incomplete; some churches neglected to submit their school information.

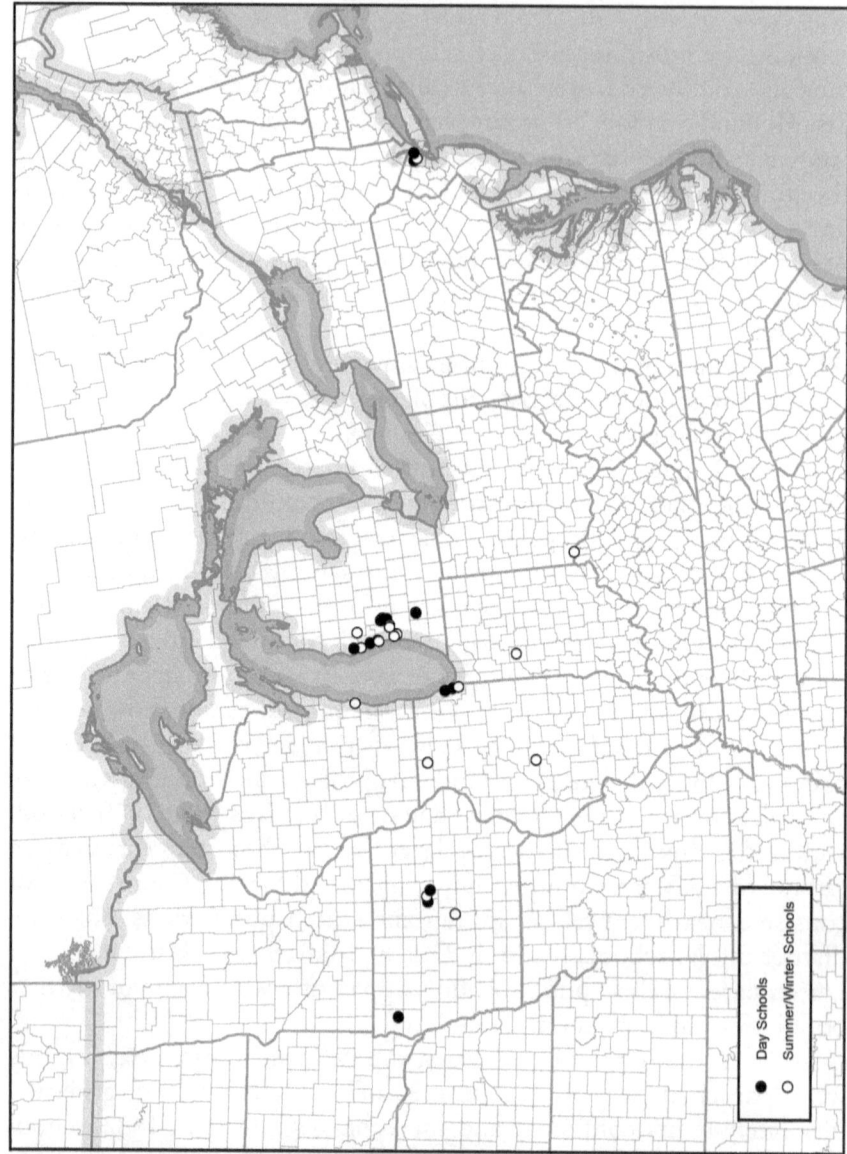

Fig. 4. Parochial Reformed Dutch Day Schools, 1881-1900
(*yearbooks of the CRC*)

statistics were reported annually in the yearbook of the CRC. The schools were oriented to the church rather than the nation, tasked with cultivating its future congregants rather than educating future citizens. Teachers were hired by the church and often hailed from the Netherlands. Especially the smaller schools were regularly housed in the church itself. The language of instruction was mainly in Dutch; later, in some of the larger cities, such as Grand Rapids and Chicago, there was instruction in Dutch and English. Because the church services and catechism instruction were in Dutch, it was considered important that the children could read, sing in, and understand Dutch, much like the children in the Dutch Reformed communities of the seventeenth and eighteenth centuries in New Netherland and the English colonies.

In the first decade of the twentieth century, the language of instruction in the schools began to change to English. The use of Dutch was considered an obstacle to Americanization and disadvantaged students when they transferred to public schools. As long as church services were held in Dutch, however, some Dutch language instruction remained. For most of the Reformed day schools founded during the late nineteenth century, there were from ten to twenty-five years of Dutch instruction. H. Jacobsma stresses how different the early Reformed Dutch day schools were from those at the time he wrote (1924): "The older schools passed through three periods: namely, first, Holland; second, Holland-English; third, English-Holland; and are now going into the fourth, English."[37] Although there clearly were many fewer years of Dutch instruction during this period when compared to the century of Dutch language usage during the New Netherland and British colonial periods, this does not minimize how culturally "closed" the Dutch American community was during the nineteenth century.

With continuous new immigration from the Netherlands, another form of school governance and organization began to take hold in the Reformed Dutch day schools in the United States at the turn of the century. The belief that schools should be free not only from the state but also from the church and that schools should have their own nature and independence had taken hold among neo-Calvinist Protestants in the Netherlands and changed the governance of Christian schools there. This conviction came over with the immigrants and began to change the Reformed Dutch schools in North America as well. Besides, adopting the doctrine of freedom for schools, principals, and other professional educators, revealed that consistories and ministers were not well qualified to govern schools, often gave them a low priority, and resisted Americanization.[38] These new perceptions led to the development of parental schools. Parents and other school supporters became members of an educational society for a particular school and

[37] Jacobsma and Kuiper, "Schools of the Middle-West," 103.
[38] Postma, "Christian School Movement in Michigan," 91-94.

elected a board from its members to govern the school. One can find the first reference to educational societies in the 1901 CRC yearbook.[39] During the changeover period, the school statistics in the yearbooks distinguished between church- and society-governed schools. Some ten years later, all the schools were run by societies, and the statistics were expanded to also include the number of society members and the name of the board president. The size of the society provided a measure of how close the community was to establishing a school.

From their very beginning in 1638, the Reformed Dutch day schools, as noted, had been parochial schools; that era had now come to an end, but it must be made clear that nearly every education society member was also a member of a local CRC. The schools, although not parochial in a strict sense, were very much denominational. By 1920 the CRC yearbook no longer included Christian day school statistics. NUCS—founded in 1920 to pursue the schools' common objectives for teacher training, textbooks, curriculum, supervision and standards, and relations with local and state governments, among others—took over and began reporting school statistics in its first yearbook in 1922.[40] Now named Christian Schools International (CSI), the organization continues to pursue these objectives.

Fig. 5 maps all the places (96) in North America that in 1915 had either operating schools/summer schools run by school societies or school societies that planned to open such schools in the near future. Twelve were summer schools. There were fifty-three day schools with societies and seventeen stand-alone societies; unfortunately for our records, another twenty-six places that had a Reformed educational presence failed to report any particulars to the yearbook.[41]

The distribution of these schools and educational societies followed the existing and expanding settlement pattern of Dutch immigrants. The schools thickened in the more densely occupied Dutch settlement zones of West Michigan (and farther north), Chicago,

---

[39] *Jaarboekje ten dienste der Christelijk Gereformeerde Kerk in Noord Amerika voor het Jaar 1901* (Grand Rapids, MI: J. B. Hulst), 103.

[40] NUCS, *A Survey of our Free Christian Schools* (Chicago: Matherson-Selig, 1922).

[41] *Jaarboekje ten dienste der Christelijk Gereformeerde Kerk in Amerika voor het Jaar 1915* (Grand Rapids, MI: Eerdmans), 128-31. Without historical research on each of the places with a Reformed Dutch educational presence that did not supply information to the 1915 yearbook, it is not possible to determine whether an educational society or a school was present. B. J. Bennink's yearbook of 1917-18 lists 66 schools, all but one with societies. B. J. Bennink, *Year-Book, Schools for Christian Instruction, 1917-1918* (Grand Rapids, MI: n.p.)

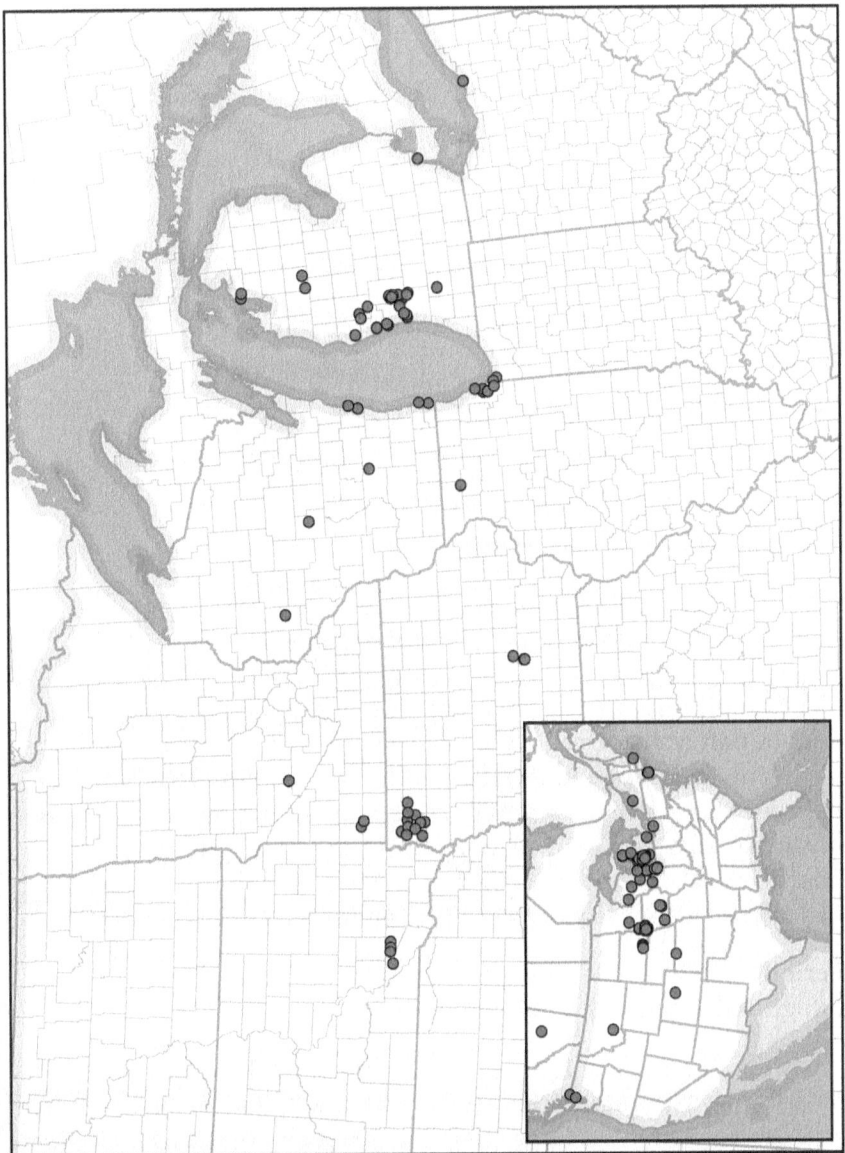

Fig. 5. Reformed Dutch American day/summer schools and stand-alone educational societies in 1915 (*Yearbook of the CRC, 1915*)

and Paterson, New Jersey; a new cluster of schools and societies arose in the corner zone where Iowa, Minnesota, and South Dakota come together. And outliers, such as Whitinsville, Massachusetts; Luctor, Kansas; Denver, Colorado; Manhattan, Missouri; Lynden, Washington;

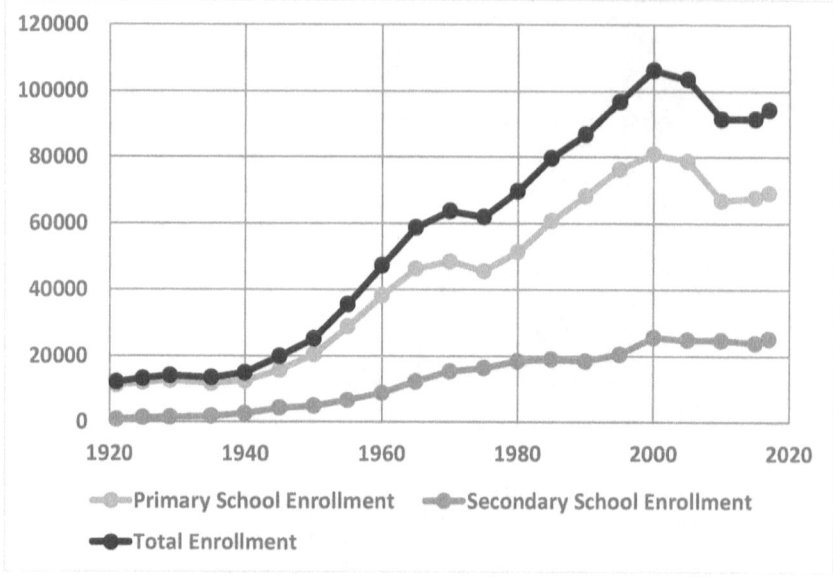

Fig. 6. Enrollment in NUCS schools, 1922-2018
(*NUCS/CSI yearbooks and directories*)

and Edmonton, Alberta, began to give a continent-wide cast to the distribution of Reformed Dutch day schools and educational societies.

This fourth period reversed the decline and near disappearance of Reformed Christian day schools in North America. A new denomination of immigrants schooled in the Netherlands brought the prevailing Dutch model of Reformed Christian education to the United States and by the end of the period had readied it for Americanization.

Period 5 (1920-2000): growth and educational development in an integrated system of schools

The distinguishing traits and history of the Reformed Dutch day schools in the twentieth century have been well documented, debated, and interpreted in a large and diverse body of literature.[42] There

---

[42] An excellent selection of this literature until 1977 is found in Harro W. Van Brummelen, *Telling the Next Generation. Educational Development in North American Calvinist Christian Schools* (Lanham, MD: University Press of America, 1986). Van Brummelen's study is the most comprehensive account of the history of Reformed Dutch day schools in North America. See also: Harro W. Van Brummelen, "Molding God's Children: The History of Curriculum in Christian Schools rooted in Dutch Calvinism" (PhD diss., University of British Columbia, 1984), 419-51; George Stob, "The Christian Reformed Church and her Schools" (ThD dissertation, Princeton

Present from the Beginning 25

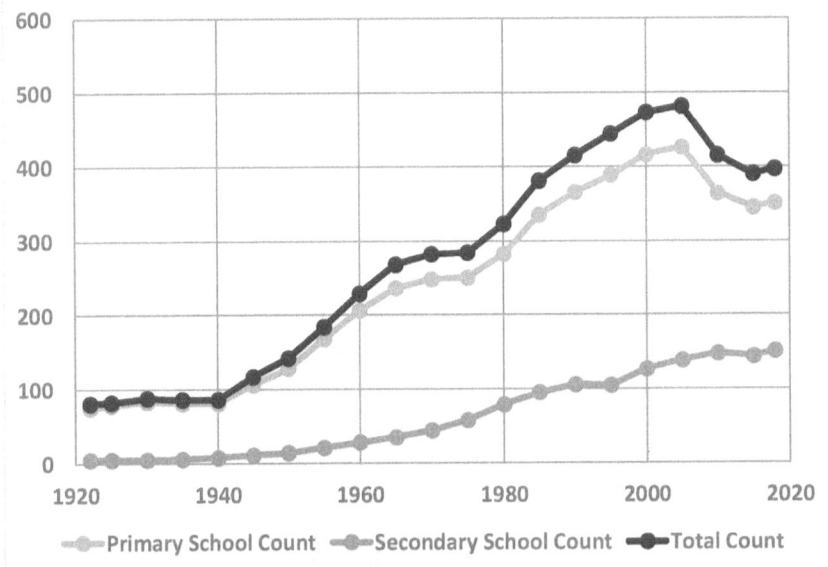

Fig. 7. Number of NUCS/CSI schools, 1922-2018
(*NUCS/CSI yearbooks and directories*)

is no need here to cover that ground except to outline the principal features that stand out in this fifth period in the continuing history of Reformed Dutch day schools in North America. I will touch on four distinguishing features of this most recent period: growth and geographic expansion, the private nature of the schools, educational development, and denominationalism.

The first of these traits was the overall sustained geographic expansion and remarkable numerical growth in enrollment and number of schools (elementary and high schools) that marked this period. Fig. 6 graphs the primary, secondary, and total enrollment from 1922 to 2018.[43] Total enrollment increased from around 12,000 to 104,000 students, with elementary school enrollment around six times that of high schools in 2000. Growth was sustained throughout the entire period, with the exception of the early 1970s, which marked the end of both the baby boom and high immigration, both of which which had benefitted school enrollment. The rate of growth in elementary

---

Theological Seminary, 1955).

[43] Calvin University and Hope College students scanned the summary tables in NUCS/CSI yearbooks and directories into Excel to produce these and many other maps and graphs.

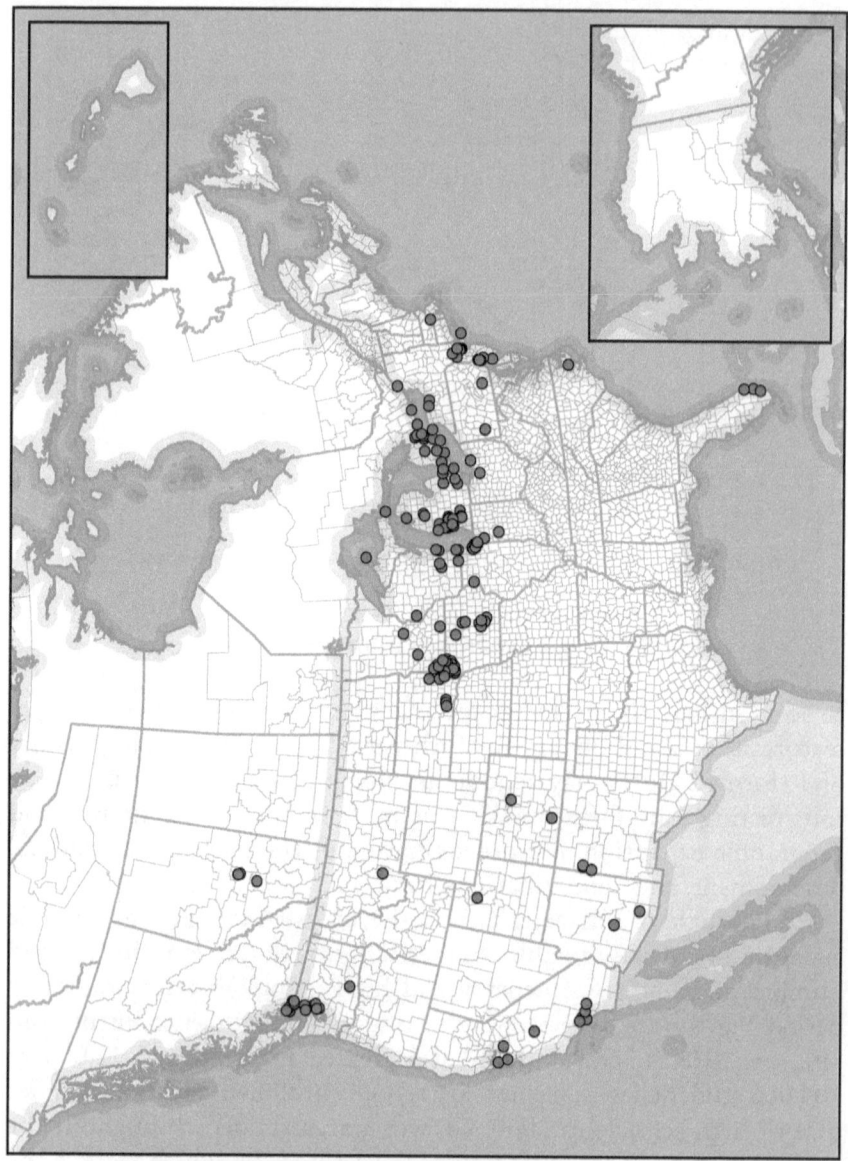

Fig. 8. Schools in NUCs, 1960 (*NUCS directory, 1960-61*)

school enrollment was consistently higher than that of high schools, a reflection of the lack of availability of high schools in outlying areas and their higher minimum enrollment requirements. The total number of schools also climbed steadily from fewer than a 100 (fig. 7) to more

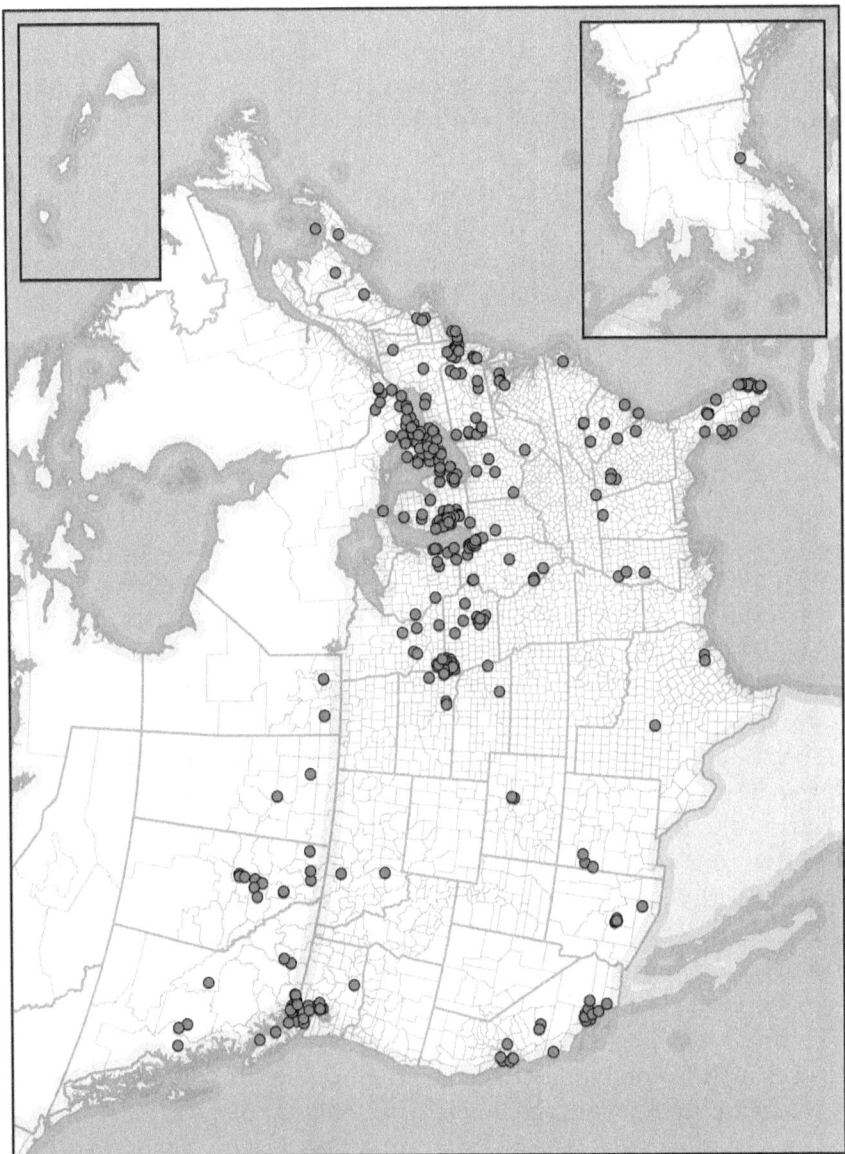

Fig. 9. Schools in the National Union of Christian Schools, 1990
(*NUCS directory, 1990-91*)

than 475; especially the high schools grew from just a handful in 1922 to more than 125.[44] The arrival of post-World War II Dutch Reformed

---

[44] In the face of more junior high and middle schools and the increasing diversity of grade ranges in individual schools in recent years in general, we stayed with

immigrants and their settlement in new areas (southwestern Ontario and California, for example), the postwar baby boom, and the mandate of the CRC for Christian education, all figured into steady increases in both enrollment and number of schools.

A comparison of the 1915 geographic distribution (fig. 5) of Reformed Dutch American and Canadian day schools (and societies) with that of 1960 (fig. 8), shows there was significant additional densification of schools in the established core areas of the Midwest. Both the Northeast and the West Coast of the United States now showed clusters of schools oriented to major conurbations. Entirely new was the appearance of a thick constellation of schools (both urban and rural) in southwestern Ontario, the result of high, post-WWII, Dutch immigration into the province. Elsewhere, there was a smattering of additional schools in the southwest and the initial appearance of schools in Florida. The additional schools in new areas were associated with the relocation of Dutch Americans and the arrival of Dutch immigrants. The school societies and enrollments were closely connected geographically to Christian Reformed congregations.

Thirty years later, in 1990, further notable regional changes in the distribution of Reformed Dutch American and Canadian day schools had become apparent (fig. 9). In Canada, the Prairies—especially Alberta—and the Maritimes had gotten on the map. In the United States, two new regional bands had appeared, one with mainly relocated urban Dutch Americans south of the established settlement core, from eastern Pennsylvania to southern Illinois. The other band of new schools grew largely without Dutch Americans, from North Carolina to western Mississippi. This second band broke new ground; here schools of other Christian communities committed to Christian education had joined NUCS. Elsewhere, in the already-established zones of Dutch American (Florida and along the West Coast) and Canadian (Ontario, Alberta, and British Colombia) settlements, the number of schools continued to increase; in the West, the cluster of schools in northwest Washington state and southwest British Columbia is noteworthy. The more dense, core area of Reformed Dutch American and Canadian day schools,

---

elementary/primary schools (pre-K to 8) and secondary/high schools (9-12, or 9-13 for some years in Ontario). The classification of any school in NUCS yearbooks and directories was made on the basis of its grade range belonging more to one than the other type. The reporting of school systems with multiple schools or campuses with more than one school also presented challenges to counting and classifying schools.

from northwestern Iowa to eastern Ontario, was by 1990 surrounded by a continent-wide, lower-density distribution of schools.

A second defining trait of the Reformed Dutch American and Canadian day schools in this period of its history is their status as privately funded schools. In spite of compelling arguments made for confessional pluralism in public education and follow-on equal funding by local and state/provincial governments, the schools in the United States were and have remained fully private, funded entirely by parents, church communities, and philanthropists. In this way, these schools are very different from their sister schools in the Netherlands, which had achieved equal public funding by 1920. The Canadian western provinces have, by contrast, indeed provided increased funding for independent schools, including NUCS/CSI schools.[45] There were those who called for either a path to financial equalization with public schools or, more modestly, tax credits and subsidies for particular public educational services. The strict separation of church and state in the United States, the presence of other denominational systems of religious schools (such as Lutheran, Baptist, and Roman Catholic), and concerns about possible governmental interference that might come with public funding, however, all kept Reformed Dutch American (and most Dutch Canadian) day schools private. This trait would have a significant impact on their place in the larger national educational enterprise compared with the Dutch public/religious schools from which they came. They, along with all other religious and independent schools, would not become part of the publicly funded school system with equal opportunities for all Christian parents to enroll their children. This limited these schools' overall Christian education impact on society.[46]

A third and multifaceted defining trait of this period in the history of Reformed day schools was the drive for professionalization and educational development. It proceeded along a number of fronts: organizational (by geography and function), curricular, teaching, teacher education, and publications. This drive largely paralleled similar developments in other school systems in the twentieth century.

---

[45] Adrian Guldemond, *Inspired by Vision . . . Constrained by Tradition. Conflict, Decline and Revival in Christian Schools in Ontario* (Ancaster, ON: Monarch Educare Solutions, 2014), 110-13.

[46] For works that examine the position of equal funding and financial aid for NUCS/CSI schools, see John A. Vander Ark, *22 Landmark Years, Christian Schools International, 1943-65* (Grand Rapids, MI: Baker Book House, 1983), 119-39; Gordon Spykman et al., *Society, State and Schools. A Case for Structural and Confessional Pluralism* (Grand Rapids, MI: Eerdmans, 1981).

What had been a loose assemblage of schools without much contact and concerted effort steadily developed into a more integrated and professional system with local, regional, and national organizations and leadership. When schools transitioned from parochial to parental governance in the first decades of the twentieth century, Dutch American communities established societies for Christian education that fostered leadership, sponsored speakers and other promotional activities, and, together with the schools themselves, served as an informal educational network for Reformed Dutch communities. In 1917 and 1918, for the first national directory of Reformed Dutch day schools, Christian educational pioneer B. J. Bennink compiled profiles of every school and their society, as well as data on board members, tuition, enrollment, teachers, grade range, and so forth. This directory preceded the establishment of NUCS in 1920 and was superior to the rather unreliable summary tables in the yearbooks of the CRC.[47] In 1922 NUCS/CSI began publishing its own directories and until recently had continued to do so. The directories and NUCS itself also helped establish the perception that this was a system of schools found throughout North America with common aims and practices, part of the Reformed Dutch world. When a Dutch American or Canadian family moved into a community, they looked not only for a Reformed church but also a Reformed day school.

Before the founding of NUCS in 1920, regions and urban centers with a concentration of Christian schools had already established organizations for teachers, principals, and board members to meet, present, discuss, and cooperate on common issues. For example, the Society for Christian Instruction, based on Reformed principles, was established in 1892 by a group of Michigan schools; later it became the Michigan Christian School Alliance.[48] Similarly, New Jersey, South Dakota, Iowa, and Chicago early on had principals' clubs, alliances of Christian schools, and teachers' associations.[49] Soon after its founding, NUCS began organizing annual national conventions of delegates and other educational professionals; it set policy for the organization, developed an *esprit de corps*, facilitated networking, and made it possible for those with similar educational responsibilities to engage around particular topics and issues at a national and international level. The keynote addresses, given by church and educational leaders in the

---

[47] Bennink, *Year-Book, 1917-1918.*
[48] Postma, "Christian School Movement in Michigan," 90.
[49] NUCS, *A Survey*, 83-84.

Dutch Reformed community, cut across a broad swath of foundational educational issues. These were regularly published either in NUCS yearbooks or in separate NUCS convention papers for the benefit of the entire educational community.

As schools opened in other regions of North America, professional organizations soon followed. The 1970-71 NUCS directory, for example, lists fourteen teachers' and fourteen principals'/administrators' associations, ranging from California to Florida and from the Canadian Prairies to Pella, Iowa.[50] The Christian Educators' Association (CEA) began as a Michigan organization in 1924 and today still organizes conferences throughout the Midwest. NUCS/CSI itself also divided North America into administrative districts, each with its own board. In sum, a highly differentiated organizational structure was put into place that, when all was said and done, also helped teachers, principals, and board members deliver more effective Reformed Christian education to a growing number of students.

Educational development on other fronts was also required. Teacher education for Reformed Christian schools was clearly a high priority. Reformed Christian colleges launched teacher education programs, and their graduates staffed NUCS/CSI schools, as well as other Christian and public schools. Scholars at Christian colleges and other educational leaders worked to develop and articulate a Reformed philosophy of and *raison d'etre* for Christian education that gave it coherence and meaning.[51] NUCS/CSI, together with sister organizations, helped schools attain accreditation and teachers receive certification and continuing education. News and issues related to Christian education became regular rubrics in CRC magazines, such as *De Wachter* and the *Banner*. For Christian school parents and school supporters, there was *Christian Home and School* (from 1922) and for educators, the *Christian Educators' Journal* (from 1961). These publications shared news about NUCS/CSI schools and their educational issues with parents and educators and published professional articles, literature reviews, and curriculum evaluations.

Although there was consensus throughout this fifth period of Reformed Dutch day schools on the importance of the Reformed

[50] NUCS, *Directory 1970-1971* (Grand Rapids, MI: n.p., 1971), 200-202.
[51] See, for example, John L. De Beer and Cornelius Jaarsma, *Toward a Philosophy of Christian Education* (Grand Rapids: NUCS, 1953); Henry N. Beversluis, *Christian Philosophy of Education* (Grand Rapids: NUCS, 1971); Van Brummelen, *Telling the Next Generation*; Nicholas Wolterstorff, *Educating for Responsible Action* (Grand Rapids, MI: Eerdmans and CSI, 1980).

confessions and theology for education, there continued to be divergent and contested interpretations of the nature and purpose of Reformed Christian education. Earlier Dutch American immigrant communities often followed a more pietistic and theological path in Christian education with an emphasis on Bible study, devotions, and spiritual formation; these practices often went together with cultural abstinence and isolation. Later Protestant Dutch immigrants were raised in and more often followed a neo-Calvinist orientation, one of cultural engagement. When applied to education, this approach meant delivering the Christian perspective in all subjects throughout the curriculum; such education prepared students to be Christians engaged in society. The Reformed day schools in Canada, in general, embodied more of this engaged orientation. The shifting middle ground between these two stances—pietism versus engagement—supplied much of the internal debate in Reformed day school discussions.

If the lifeblood of a Christian school is the Christian teaching of a Christian curriculum, then the NUCS/CSI staff and related writers prepared a spate of Christian curriculum units and textbooks over the years for every subject, along with appropriate teaching methods. These were piloted, published, and adopted by many schools both within and outside of the organization.[52] This was new and pioneering work for Christian educators. Twentieth-century day schools required teaching a growing list of subjects, something that Reformed Dutch American and Canadian day schools had not done before. Instruction in science, history, literature, languages, government, and geography with a Christian curriculum was uncharted territory. After three centuries, the lines between the church and school education in the Reformed world had to be redrawn, leaving schools with less responsibility and time for ecclesiastical matters and more for teaching about the wider world. The subjects of Bible and religion were still there, but they were less closely tied to the church; much more curricular space and time was devoted to learning about the fullness of God's world and humanity's place in it.

One last defining trait of the Reformed Dutch American and Canadian day school system was the impact of denominationalism.

---

[52] Van Brummelen, in *Telling the Next Generation*, 305-8, includes a list of NUCS/CSI curriculum materials; Van Brummelen, in "Molding God's Children," 423-33, lists curriculum articles published by NUCS/CSI writers and curriculum units developed for NUCS/CSI schools. See also, Harro Van Brummelen, *Steppingstones to Curriculum. A Biblical Path* (Seattle: Alta Vista College Press, 1994), and G. Steensma and H. Van Brummelen, *Shaping School Curriculum: A Biblical View* (Terre Haute, IN: Signal, 1977).

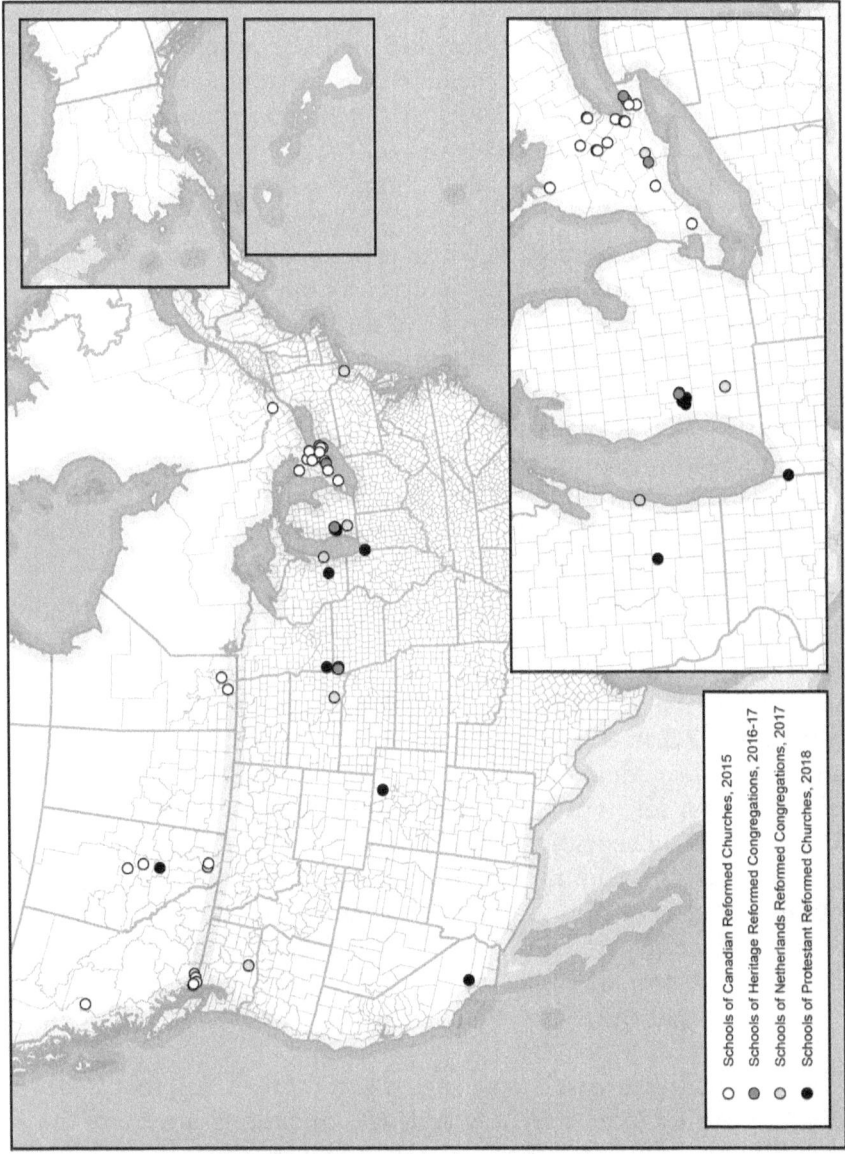

Fig. 10. Reformed Day Schools of the Smaller Dutch Reformed Denominations, 2015-18 (*yearbooks of the Dutch Reformed denominations identified on the map*)

From the beginning, NUCS planned to be a big, inclusive tent for students from all the different Dutch Reformed denominations. Because the CRC was the largest such denomination with strong support for Christian education, students from the CRC dominated the enrollment throughout the period. In 1937 the split in enrollment among Dutch Reformed churches in NUCS schools was 85 percent CRC, 7 percent Protestant Reformed Church (PRC), and 5 percent RCA. Thirty-three years later, in 1970, this split was still over 77 percent CRC, 4 percent RCA and less than 1 percent PRC.[53] Similarly, the teacher corps and the leadership of NUCS and of local schools were overwhelmingly CRC. NUCS and local schools worked with all Dutch Reformed churches and families to recruit students; they booked a lot more success with the CRC. In spite of the demographic weight of the CRC on enrollment, NUCS/CSI, its member schools, and other educational organizations were able to develop their own educational domain independent of the CRC.

Especially after World War II, denominationalism began to leave other marks on Reformed Dutch day schools. Several smaller, more theologically conservative denominations began to establish their own school societies and schools: among these were the PRCs, the Netherlands Reformed Congregations, the Canadian Reformed Churches, the Heritage Reformed Congregations, and United Reformed Churches. This had a significant impact on NUCS-related school enrollments. For example, as the PRC established its own schools, PRC enrollment in NUCS schools fell sharply. The United Reformed Church—seceded from the CRC in 1996—kept its associations with existing schools and established some new ones. Fig. 10 maps the recent distribution of schools for four of these smaller Dutch Reformed denominations. Most notable, of course, are the Canadian Reformed schools clustered in southwestern Ontario and scattered in the western provinces. Altogether, the distribution of these schools is coterminous with the outlines of Dutch American and Canadian settlement geography. In the larger Dutch American and Canadian population centers, there were enough adherents of these smaller denominations to establish congregations and schools.

Although these schools are not parochial in governance, their connections to local churches and denominations are quite close. Information about the schools is commonly found in the yearbooks of the denominations. Students are mainly, although not exclusively, drawn from the congregations of these individual denominations; teaching staff and boards are even more closely affiliated with the denomination and specific congregations. The desire to maintain

---

[53] NUCS, "1970 NUCS Decade Survey," *1970-1971 Directory*. (Grand Rapids, MI: NUCS, 1971), 243-66.

their Reformed theological emphases and lifestyles is the main reason for operating their own schools and system-wide educational organizations. The Protestant Reformed Schools (15 in 2007) have their own Federation of Protestant Reformed School Societies, and its Protestant Reformed Teachers' Institute holds annual conventions and publishes its own magazine, *Perspectives in Covenant Education*. Similarly, the schools (more than 20 in 2000) of the Canadian Reformed Churches have their own League of Canadian Reformed School Societies, the Canadian Reformed Teachers Association, and the Covenant Canadian Reformed Teachers College.

This fifth period in the history of Reformed Dutch American and Canadian schools is the most heady and groundbreaking. On the one hand, it mirrors the developments that were taking place in all elementary and secondary school systems in North America—professionalization, curriculum and textbook writing, teacher education, and networking by way of professional meetings and conferences. On the other hand, the period demonstrated that an immigrant and postimmigrant Reformed Christian educational system could grow, expand, professionalize, thrive, and transform itself in and for North America. It could go head-to-head with any other system of schools to give students skills and knowledge for their place in society and the world. It could shape students' spiritual formation and life by means of a Christian lens on the world through Christian teaching of Christian curricula in all subjects.

The twenty-first century: the making of a new chapter? More Protestant and less Reformed, less ethnic and more diverse

During the first two decades of this century, total enrollment at CSI dropped by more than ten thousand students, from 104,539 in 2000-2001 to 93,969 in 2017-18.[54] This decline was and continues to be fueled by a variety of interlocking factors. Demography is one: the membership of the CRC—the principal enrollment source for CSI schools—has fallen from 316,000 in 1992 to 228,000 in 2018, a 28 percent drop. The decline in birth rates is a large part of this falling membership and declining CRC enrollment in the schools: 6,192 children were baptized in 1988, 2,834 in 2018.[55]

---

[54] CSI directories, 2000-2001 and 2017-18.
[55] Neil Carlson, "Church Decline? Blame the Baby Bust," in *Charting Church Leadership*, blog, 12 Oct. 2015, patheos.com. The data shown in the blog has been updated several times, most recently for 2018.

A number of additional factors are relevant to account for the decline in the enrollment in CSI schools. The real cost of a quality Christian education has continued to increase and take a larger share of a family's budget. Reformed Christian schooling from pre-K to college has become unaffordable for a large percentage of families; they now have to make decisions about which level of Christian education is optimal for their children. The homeschooling movement has become an alternative for Christian parents, also in the context of these rising costs. In the United States, many parents who have chosen CSI schools because of their dissatisfaction with the quality and security of the public schools have moved over to selective charter schools with good reputations and attractive programs. More theologically conservative Reformed parents —often with large families—have enrolled their children in the schools of the smaller correspondingly conservative Dutch Reformed denominations. And operating at a deeper cultural level is the inevitable de-ethnicization—the hollowing out and erasure of Reformed Dutch American/Canadian identity, meaning, commitments, and comportment through intermarriage, assimilation, and neglect.

All together these factors have led to a decline in the percentage of students in CSI schools from the CRC. In eastern Canada (Ontario and the Maritime provinces), for example, the percentage of CRC members supporting Christian schools declined steadily from 1960 to 2010, reaching 47 percent in 2000 and 30 percent in 2010. At the Reformed day schools in eastern Canada, the percentage of students from other than Reformed churches has steadily increased in the schools since the 1980s, reaching 48 percent in 2010.[56] The exact numbers will be different in other CSI regions and schools, but these two trends—declining CRC and increasing non-Reformed enrollment—are setting the stage for a new chapter. Were it not for these new students, smaller Reformed day schools could not remain viable.

To further promote mainline Protestant enrollment in Christian education, consideration needs to be given to broadening the confessional basis for teachers, parents, and educational organizations beyond the Three Forms of Unity to include other ecumenical creeds. The well-honed and widely respected Christian philosophy of education and Christian curricula developed in the Reformed day school movement can also rest on such creeds and be accepted by non-Reformed parents. Other mainline denominational school systems (Lutheran schools, for example) may well be invited and pulled into

---

[56] Guldemond, *Inspired by Vision*, 105-6, table C-3.

such a mainline Protestant Christian school coalition. Although the more narrow denominationalism of the conservative Reformed schools will remain part of the Christian school scene, CSI can take the lead in charting a path to a less denominational and more ecumenical system of Christian schools. Reformed day schools as such may disappear; their contributions to Christian education, however, will endure through their tried-and-true practices and materials, parents, educational leaders, and teachers.

CHAPTER 2

Meester Mulder and Orange City's Un-American Christian School

Earl Wm. Kennedy

On Monday, September 5, 1904, Orange City's two elementary schools opened their doors—the already-established public school with 364 pupils and the newborn Christian one with 125.[1] The latter became the first (Reformed) Christian school west of the Mississippi River to survive infancy and endure to the present. Because of the unexpectedly large number of pupils who appeared that day at the Christian school, it immediately hired a second female teacher to assist the principal. The town also quickly decided to lay a sidewalk for the school.[2] The original plan had been to use a vacant two-room building of the public school, but given the large number of pupils, the consistory room of the Christian Reformed Church had to be brought into service as well. The school board also then decided to enlarge the school building by adding a second story to it, so that the two rooms became four by

---

[1] *De Volksvriend* (hereafter *VV*), 8 Sept. 1904. The present article is heavily dependent on this weekly newspaper, since it is virtually the only available source with detailed, first-hand information on this topic.
[2] *VV*, 8 Sept. 1904.

Orange City's First Christian School, 1904

the next summer.³ The Society for Christian Instruction, meeting on Saturday evening, September 24, 1904, celebrated the school's initial success, with the treasurer reporting $3,933.50 in pledges. The tuition was set at $.60 per month for one child, $1.00 for two children, and, if one family had additional children, the cost would be proportionately reduced. The school by that point had grown to about 150 pupils.⁴

The first principal of Orange City's School for Christian Instruction (its official name in the early years), not yet twenty-three years of age, was Benjamin Henry (baptized Berend Hendrik) Masselink. He was born in Overisel, Michigan, to immigrant parents, members of the Overisel Christian Reformed Church (CRC), who had come from the County of Bentheim on the Dutch-German border. A 1901 graduate of the preparatory school of Hope College of the Reformed Church in America (RCA),⁵ Masselink headed the Orange City school for only a year, departing in 1905 to continue his studies at the University of Michigan (DDS, 1908), followed by a long career in

---

3   VV, 15 Sept. 1904. The fall 1905 school opening was delayed slightly by the construction. VV, 15 June, 10 and 31 Aug., and 7 Sept. 1905; "Orange City Christian School: A Brief History," at http://www.orangecitychristian.net/editoruploads/files/BriefHistory7_23.pdf.
4   VV, 29 Sept. 1904; girls were in the majority in the early years of the school.
5   Catalogue of the Officers and Students of Hope College, Holland, Michigan, 1903-1904 (Holland, MI: Holland City News Presses), 104.

dentistry. He did not, however, break all ties with Sioux County, since he soon (1908) wedded one of its daughters, a 1904 graduate of the RCA's Northwestern Classical Academy.[6]

Masselink was succeeded in the fall of 1905 by a locally well known, seasoned teacher, Meester (schoolmaster) Yge Mulder (1859-1930), who had to be coaxed to return to Orange City,[7] where he had once led the "prehistory" of the town's "School for Christian Instruction." He would head the Orange City Christian School for only three years before resigning.[8] But we now need to go back to the beginning to see how the story of Orange City's elementary schools unfolded.

Orange City's elementary schools in the 1870s and 1880s

Orange City was founded in 1870 in Sioux County in northwest Iowa—a region with rich soil—as a daughter of Pella, Iowa, where cheap land had become increasingly scarce. The new colony was a quarter century further removed than Pella and Holland (Michigan) from the religious fervor of the Afscheiding (Secession) of 1834. A further dissimilarity was that its leader was not a minister but a layman—Pella's mayor, the entrepreneurial Henry Hospers. But within a year, Orange City had both a big RCA congregation and a feeble CRC congregation, with the veteran Rev. Seine Bolks, a protégé of Holland's Rev. A. C. van

---

[6] In 1908 Masselink (1881-1973), having received his DDS degree from the University of Michigan, was married in Orange City to the daughter of an Orange City pioneer; the best man was Bernard Braskamp, who later became chaplain of the US House of Representatives. The young couple went to the United Kingdom for the groom's further study, after which, he taught dentistry briefly in South Africa and then returned to spend the rest of his long career as a Grand Rapids, Michigan, dentist. While still a novice in the field, he published an article with the hopeful title, "The Advent of Painless Dentistry" (1910). Thomas Masselink, "The Masselink and Kleine Masselink Family Genealogy from 804 to 2019," at http://masselinkgenealogy.weebly.com/b.html; *VV*, 11 May and 15 June 1905; 25 June, 13 Aug., and 3 Sept. 1908; www.findagrave.com; www.ancestry.com (1900, 1910, and 1920 federal census; IA, Marriage Records, 1880-1940).

[7] Mulder had been trained as a teacher, and Masselink had probably not. After Mulder declined the school's initial call, it offered the position to another man, who also refused, so Mulder was called again, at a higher salary, which he accepted. He arrived in Orange City in early October, after school had commenced, with ninety pupils; the public school had 302. The Sioux Center Christian school, begun 1905, had twice as many CRC as RCA students; no statistics on this comparison are available for Orange City, but they would probably be similar. *VV*, 6 and 20 July, 3, 10, 17, and 31 Aug., and 14 Sept. 1905.

[8] After his resignation from the Orange City school, he seems to have continued teaching part time and combined that with other occupations; he was never again principal. For more on his later activities, see note 38 below.

Raalte, soon to come as pastor of the First Reformed Church.

The children in the new colony—of whom there were not a few, since most of the settlers had young families—needed schooling, so by mid-1875, the county had seventeen schoolhouses with instruction in English, commonly provided by young, single American women (generally in short supply).[9] Around this time, an argument about the area's schools erupted in the local weekly papers (*De Volksvriend* and the the *Sioux County Herald*)—in English and Dutch—between two medical doctors: an American-born county supervisor of schools and a fascinating Dutch immigrant. Neither man belonged to either of the two Orange City Dutch churches.

The immigrant, Dr. Adolph Frederik Henri de Lespinasse (l'Espinasse), Delft-born but of French-Swedish extraction on his father's side, was a university-educated, cultured physician, with many publications and a long medical practice behind him in the Netherlands. He came to the United States in 1870, sojourned briefly in Chicago, and turned up in Orange City in 1874, where he had hoped to employ his considerable abilities not only to cure the body but also to uplift his fellow immigrants.[10] In a series of ten articles appearing in *De Volksvriend* between November 1874 and February 1875, De Lespinasse expressed, somewhat condescendingly, his low opinion of the American (and local) public school system, criticizing the poor quality of instruction (and instructors), as well as any teaching of religion through Bible reading and prayer; he thought that the schools should be "neutral" (i.e., secular), as in the Netherlands. Also, he was opposed to church schools, especially Roman Catholic ones, maintaining that the general education of children should be entirely free from the church, only inculcating virtues like justice, truth, and humanity.[11]

---

[9] *VV*, 18 June 1875.
[10] De Lespinasse worked as a physician and also as a druggist, whose store sold not only drugs to heal the body but also wines, liquors, cigars, and candies; *VV*, 8 and 22 June 1876. For more on this fascinating outsider and his career, see Nella Kennedy, "Dr. A. F. H. De Lespinasse, the Man from Helmus," in *A Century of Midwestern Dutch American Manners and Mores—and More*, at https://dutchamericans.files.wordpress.com/2017/03/1995_03_kennedy.pdf ; Hans Heesen, "A.F.H. de Lespinasse (1819-1881), een Nederlandse schrijver in een Amerikaanse roman," at https://www.academia.edu/11779224/A.F.H._de_Lespinasse_1819-1881_een_Nederlandse_schrijver_in_een_Amerikaanse_roman.
[11] *VV*, 5, 12, 19, and 26 Nov., and 10, 17, and 24 Dec. 1874; 7 and 30 Jan., and 13 and 25 Feb. 1875. De Lespinasse opposed using the public school to "force religion" on children; *VV*, 20 Jan. 1876. Around this same time, Roman Catholics were also trying to remove (Protestant) Bible reading and prayer from the public schools in the East, while at the same time setting up their own parochial schools; and

De Lespinasse's younger American adversary was Dr. Edward O. Plumbe, a native Iowan and monolingual anglophone, who replied more briefly in the *Sioux County Herald*. Plumbe noted that American law required that public grade schools be "unsectarian," with no "sect" favored above another; although only a tiny fraction of the school year was for released time for religious instruction, it was a critical component of the overall educational enterprise.[12] In sum, De Lespinasse argued for primary education, with no religious instruction (only morality was to be taught), while Plumbe defended the American (Iowan) status quo, namely, nonsectarian Bible reading and prayer in the public schools.[13]

In any event, the primary schools of Orange City and Sioux County were, from all appearances, quite safely in the hands of Protestant (if not Reformed) Christians in the 1870s and 1880s. Nevertheless, the idea of an alternative to the American public school began to gain traction in the Dutch American world by around 1890, including in Sioux County. This was especially true in the CRC, which got a boost in the 1880s, just when Dutch immigration was peaking, from an influx of seceders suspicious of the RCA because of its recent decision to tolerate

---

Abraham Kuyper was promoting his idea that Christian schools should be "free" from the spheres of both the church (only superficially, De Lespinasse might concur with this) and the state, in a sphere unique to themselves (note the Free University, 1880). For further context on "nonsectarian" public schools, the views associated with Horace Mann of Massachusetts and J. R. Thorbecke of the Netherlands should be consulted.

[12] *Sioux County Herald*, 18 Feb. 1875. Plumbe, like De Lespinasse, opposed the "religious fanaticism" of the Roman Catholics and their schools.

[13] A curious sidelight to this whole debate is that De Lespinasse established a secular, medical minicollege in Orange City (1875-77), with himself as the sole instructor and with the full public support of Hospers and Bolks, even though the latter had come to Orange City as a pastor in 1872 on condition that a Christian academy be set up (by the RCA), which soon occurred, in 1882, after De Lespinasse was dead. The fact that De Lespinasse was a fervent Freemason (theologically deistic and legalistic), opposed to traditional Christianity, must have given Bolks and Hospers pause, but the sources give no hint of this; local pragmatic boosterism seems to have prevailed. De Lespinasse, probably the only university graduate in the colony, was a sophisticated big fish in an unsophisticated small pond. His presence in Orange City was evidently viewed, at least by some, as a distinct asset for the young colony, especially as it faced local American nativist opposition, the Panic of 1873, and the grasshopper plague of the mid-1870s. The energetic, "heretical" doctor organized a short-lived modernistic "Dutch Free Reformed Church" in Orange City; *VV*, 4 May 1876. Presumably unknown to the town leaders, however, were the facts that De Lespinasse, the outspoken moralist, was apparently a bigamist, as well as a wife and child deserter. Kennedy, "De Lespinasse," 3-6; Jacob Van der Zee, *The Hollanders of Iowa* (Iowa City: State Historical Society of Iowa, 1912), 280-81, 415-16.

Freemasons.[14] The Sioux County CRC congregations in Orange City and Sioux Center began to flourish then. Abraham Kuyper's vision for separate, independent, Christian day schools, "free" from both the state and the church, was eventually mandated by the CRC Synod toward the end of the nineteenth century. Moreover, it was familiar to, if not accepted by, many of the newcomers (as well as some of the earlier immigrants).[15]

Unsurprisingly, Kuyper's views did not find especially fertile soil in the more Americanized RCA, including in Orange City. This disapproval reflected the attitude expressed by the denomination's 1892 General Synod that "the Common School is vitally essential to the fusing of the heterogeneous elements of our population into one nation." The Synod strongly opposed any public money going to Roman Catholic parochial schools, the Catholic hierarchy being hostile to "our non-sectarian Common School system."[16]

Forerunner Meester Mulder's Christian school efforts 1889-1898

The first public hint of possible interest in Christian day schools in the Orange City area may have come in the summer of 1883[17] in

---

[14] Robert P. Swierenga and Elton J. Bruins, *Family Quarrels in the Dutch Reformed Church in the Nineteenth Century* (Grand Rapids, MI: Eerdmans, 1999), 130-33.

[15] Janet Sheeres, ed., *Minutes of the Christian Reformed Church* (Grand Rapids, MI: Eerdmans, 2013), 297, 328-29, 343-45, 446; Robert P. Swierenga, *Holland Michigan: From Dutch Colony to Dynamic City* (Holland, MI: Van Raalte Press; Grand Rapids, MI: Eerdmans, 2014), 539-40. Robert P. Swierenga, *Dutch Chicago: A History of the Hollanders in the Windy City* (Grand Rapids, MI: Eerdmans, 2002), 356. Dutch Reformed Christian day schools in larger American urban centers led the way, following the example of their Reformed coreligionists in the Netherlands; in both places, "secularism" was generally more apparent than in the smaller rural communities in the United States; the Bible was banned from the public schools in Chicago in 1907.

[16] *Acts and Proceedings of the General Synod of the ... Reformed Church in America, ... June 1892* (NY: Board of Publication of the RCA, 1892), 661-62; Swierenga, *Dutch Chicago*, 355, 357-61. For the RCA's earlier temporary, tepid, partial support of parochial schools, by implementing the 1854 plan of Samuel B. Schieffelin, as well as A. C. van Raalte's largely futile efforts to promote this in the colony in Holland, Michigan, see Earl Wm. Kennedy, "Van Raalte and Parochial Schools," in *The Enduring Legacy of Albertus C. Van Raalte as Leader and Liaison*, ed. Jacob E. Nyenhuis and George Harinck (Holland, MI: Van Raalte Press; Grand Rapids, MI: Eerdmans, 2014), 171-95; Earl Wm. Kennedy, *A Commentary on the Minutes of the Classis of Holland 1848-1876* (Holland, MI: Van Raalte Press, 2018), 428-29.

[17] In 1875 the first pastor of Orange City's CRC had reported to the June meeting of the denomination's General Synod that his congregation was "too small to be able to establish a Dutch [Christian church] school"; Sheeres, *Minutes of the Christian Reformed Church*, 344.

Meester Yge Mulder in later years
(*courtesy Pamela Mulder Nelson*)

connection with the brief visit there of Yge Yges [Jr.] Mulder (1859-1930).

Having crossed the Atlantic to see his immigrant father and siblings, who were living just south of Orange City, Yge took time to visit Kasper Tietema (1836-1898), editor of that town's weekly newspaper, *De Volksvriend*. Tietema, evidently hoping that Mulder might settle there as a teacher,[18] noted that young Yge was an instructor at the Groen van Prinsterer School (opened 1878) in Doetinchem, Gelderland, an interdenominational Reformed teacher training institution, rated highly by the editor.[19]

---

[18] *VV*, 19 July and 2 Aug. 1883. Yge was the son of a Seceder Reformed deacon of Sint-Annaparochie, Het Bildt, Friesland, who had emigrated as a widower with all of his other children in April 1881, settling on a farm in Le Mars, Iowa, seven miles south of Orange City; J. Wesseling, *De Afscheiding van 1834 in Friesland*... (Groningen: Uitgeverij De Vuurbaak bv, 1981), 2:310, 312, 314-15; *WieWasWie*.

[19] Rev. John van Dijk (1830-1909), the school's founder, served both Seceder Reformed and Hervormd congregations during his ministerial career. Mulder delivered Van Dijk's greetings to his friend Tietema, which was presumably why Mulder went to the editor's office in Orange City; incidentally, all three men were Frisians. Van Dijk was a proponent of both Groen van Prinsterer's and (by extension) Kuyper's views on independent Christian schools. *VV*, 2 Aug. 1883; Joh. de Haas, *Gedenkt uw voorgangers*, 2nd ed. (Haarlem: Uitgeverij Vijlbrief, 1984), 2:81-83. Upon his return to teaching in Doetinchem, Mulder published a report on Orange City and its schools; *VV*, 20 Dec. 1883; he soon married and began a family.

Later that same summer (1883), Tietema welcomed the opening of the Northwestern Classical Academy in Orange City (the future Northwestern College) at the start of its first year of operation (there was no local public high school at the time). He endorsed the academy's avowedly Christian stance, contrasting it with the public primary schools that by law had to be religiously neutral, their religious character in this respect being wholly dependent on the individual teacher. Tietema expressed his happiness that hundreds of Christian schools had been set up by societies in the Netherlands in the half century since the Afscheiding.[20]

Six years later, in 1889, a new *De Volksvriend* editor, Antonie Jacob Betten Jr., welcomed the return of Yge Mulder Jr., who this time had come to stay.[21] Five weeks after announcing Mulder's arrival, the paper reported talk of setting up a local "Dutch" (Hollandsche) primary school, although details were not yet known. A month later, in early October, Mulder revealed the details in *De Volksvriend* under the caption "Hollandsch Christelijk *Onderwijs*" (Dutch Christian instruction). On behalf of the "school committee," he said that teaching in the Dutch Christian School would begin on Tuesday, October 8, in the consistory room of the Dutch Christian Reformed Church. The opening address, to which all were invited, would be delivered on the evening before by Rev. Seine Bolks, the retired minister of Orange City's First Reformed Church (which he had served from 1872 to 1878), who was also the first chairman of the board of Northwestern Classical Academy.[22]

Given Bolks' long association with Van Raalte and thus with the Christian education cause in Michigan (which had had mixed results),[23] his support of Christian primary schools in Iowa (albeit in a predominantly Christian Reformed context) was surely more genuine than his endorsement of De Lespinasse's educational dream in the 1870s. In any case, the involvement of Bolks, a representative of the RCA, showed that the Orange City Christian school promoters, although largely from the CRC, aimed from the beginning (and consistently, if not always successfully, in the future) to be inclusive; they were not

---

[20] Tietema was also thankful for orthodox men like Van Dijk and Kuyper, still within the Hervormde Kerk (the Dutch public church, from which the Seceders seceded beginning 1834). *VV*, 13 Sept. and 18 Oct. 1883.
[21] Mulder, accompanied by his ailing wife and toddler son, was then lodging temporarily with his father. *VV*, 29 Aug. 1889.
[22] *VV*, 5 Sept. and 3 Oct. 1889.
[23] Kennedy, "Van Raalte and Parochial Schools."

interested in having a CRC parochial school. The new "Dutch" school began with twenty-eight pupils, rising to forty-one the following week. In addition, a "Dutch evening school" (presumably for adults) was announced by Mulder, to start in early November 1889.[24] After this flurry of news about Mulder's educational efforts, *De Volksvriend* dropped the subject in the coming months.

Interestingly, in the same issue of *De Volksvriend* that Mulder announced the opening of his primary school, Dr. Henry Peter Oggel (1844-1926), an instructor at the Northwestern Classical Academy and future editor of *De Volksvriend* (1891-1926), issued an appeal for parents to send their children to the academy, because from forty to fifty ("Christian") teachers were needed in the Sioux County public schools to keep them from falling into the hands of either Roman Catholics or unbelievers.[25] As we shall see, Oggel's approach would be typical of the majority RCA attitude toward primary education, in contrast to the majority CRC vision of separate Christian schools.

Some fifteen months later, in January 1891, Mulder's Christian school, then still housed in the CRC consistory room, announced that it would continue on a broader scale; the annual meeting of its supporters had decided to enlarge the four-man school committee by adding five new members, including some from the RCA. The school by this time had ninety households backing it "with interest, money, or children," with the goal of educating their offspring in their mother tongue (Dutch)—and many also with the aim of raising their children under God's Word. Nevertheless, the school acknowledged here that, sooner or later, its pupils would have to go on to a public school, where, admittedly, the education was good and conducted in English, with likeable teachers. Still, whereas public school teachers were not free to use the Bible as the basis (*grondslag*) of their teaching, even though they were allowed to read it in the classroom, Christian school teachers, in a Christian school, could speak out freely as Christians and teach Christian truths to children.

---

[24] *VV*, 3, 10, 17, and 31 Oct. 1889. This prehistory of the Orange City Christian School (opened 1904) has apparently never been told, even though Yge Mulder was involved in both.

[25] *VV*, 3 Oct. 1889. Hendrik Pieter (later Henry Peter) Oggel, a loyal RCA layman and the youngest brother of Van Raalte's son-in-law, was an 1855 immigrant and a graduate of the Holland Academy and Hope College. He had practiced medicine and edited a newspaper in Pella before coming to teach at Northwestern Classical Academy. Earl Wm. Kennedy, "Prairie Premillennialism: Dutch Calvinist Chiliasm in Iowa 1847-1900, or the Long Shadow of Hendrik Pieter Scholte," *Reformed Review* 46, no. 2 (winter 1992): 160, 163-64, 166.

Therefore, Orange City's Dutch school was to be supplemented and expanded, to become an English-Dutch school—even an "American Christian school." Its orientation was not ecclesiastical (*kerkelijk*); it was not an extension of any denomination—CRC or RCA—but rather operated under a committee made up of members of both denominations, teaching the children the standard subjects, together with the Bible and biblical truths, in relation to God and Jesus Christ. It would be "hard to overcome prejudices," but the children were worth it. The public school provided twenty-six hours of instruction a week in secular subjects but only two hours of Bible and catechism; a little time once a week was inadequate for instruction in Christian things. It was well and good that some parents instruct their children daily at home in these matters, but what about their neighbor? *All* children should have a Christian education. The committee's report ended with an appeal for money to buy land and to erect a school building.[26]

The advertised makeover of the school, however, failed to invigorate it. It limped through the 1891-92 school year, with Meester Mulder apparently moonlighting by trying, against the odds, to breathe life into the local, factionally divided YMCA (composed of both RCA and CRC youth), which had been ailing as well.[27]

In any event, Mulder changed direction in the fall of 1892. Having closed his three-year-old Christian school,[28] he moved to Le Mars to attend "a business college," the Le Mars Normal School, the later Westmar College (recently defunct); it was located south of Orange City and near where his deceased father had once lived.[29] At the end of the 1892-93 school year, having done well in his examinations at the normal school, which prepared teachers for the public schools, Mulder took a position during the 1893-94 academic year as instructor in a country (public?) school, under "Mr. Jasper," its "director," two miles from Le Mars. Yge's work there began in August 1893, the same month his long-ailing wife died.[30] It was thus a very hard time for him, losing

---

[26] *VV*, 22 and 29 Jan., 5 Feb. 1891. The committee's report seems to be here setting forth, in brief compass, a kind of "Kuyperian" view of the integration of faith and learning.

[27] *VV*, 5 Feb. 24 Sept., 1 Oct., and 31 Dec. 1891.

[28] The persistent strong support by the RCA of the American "nonsectarian" public school, primarily in opposition to Roman Catholic parochial schools, certainly provided little encouragement for efforts such as Mulder's; note the paper adopted at the General Synod in June 1892; *Acts and Proceedings* (1892), 661-62. Of course, the CRC, Mulder's denomination, supported Christian schools.

[29] *Sioux County Herald*, 7 Sept. 1892; *VV*, 8 Sept. 1892.

[30] *VV*, 3 and 24 Aug. 1893; 15 March 1894. "Mr. Jasper" was evidently Jacobus Jans

a spouse and with work scarce during the financial crisis of the Panic of 1893.

Then after a two-year absence, the widower Mulder made a fresh start by returning to Orange City, where he was remarried in September 1894 by its CRC pastor to a widow, the sister of two of Mulder's brothers' wives. The same month, the newlyweds became American citizens.[31]

Yge Mulder remained in Orange City for the next four years (1894-98), making use of his training as a teacher as best he could, while also trying to make a living, which was not easy in the wake of the 1893 financial downturn. For four summers, from 1894 to 1897, he taught a five-week (in July and August) "Dutch" summer school in the Christian Reformed consistory room, a venue certainly familiar to him. He advertised in *De Volksvriend* that he was mainly teaching children to read and write the Dutch language, "which we can all speak" but not read and write. He was also available to teach a little arithmetic, if it was desired. He was able to use the textbooks (gratis) from the former Dutch school. The cost for the five weeks was a dollar per child. Unfortunately, Mulder had some competition during the first summer (1894) from a Dutch-born Northwestern Classical Academy student (and future RCA minister), who also gave Dutch lessons (for six weeks).[32]

Jasper (1840-1896), who, like Yge Mulder, was an immigrant from Friesland and who became a well-to-do farmer four miles southwest of Orange City. He and his wife had emigrated in 1871, joined Orange City's First Reformed Church the next year, and were in trouble with its consistory in 1890 and 1891 for quarreling with their neighbors (fellow church members) as well as for several years' absence from worship; the couple refused to submit to consistorial discipline and wanted to secede to the CRC, which request was denied; Consistory Minutes, First Reformed Church, Orange City, IA, 4 Aug., 1 Sept., 27 Oct., 24 Nov., 29 Dec. 1890; 31 Aug. and 21 Sept. 1891. They seceded anyway, and Jacobus Jans Jasper died suddenly of a heart ailment in 1896; his funeral was conducted from Orange City's Christian Reformed Church. Ancestry.com (First Reformed Church, Orange City, IA, Indexes and Membership list; Netherlands emigration records; 1880 federal census); "A Pioneer's Sudden Death," in the *Sioux County Herald*, 9 Dec. 1896, at http://iagenweb.org/boards/sioux/obituaries/index.cgi?read=341651.

[31] At that time, wives were automatically naturalized on the basis of their husbands' American citizenship. "Researching Akke de Jong Hoekstra," in "The Shoe Box Under the Bed," at https://roordawrite.wordpress.com/2015/01/05/researching-akke-de-jong-hoekstra-ancestor-152; *VV*, 13 and 29 Sept. 1894; ancestry.com (IA, Marriage Records, 1880-1940).

[32] The young man was Henry P. Schuurman (1865-1933). *VV*, 7 and 28 June, 12 and 19 July 1894; 11 July 1895; 2 July 1896; 24 June 1897. Mulder's "Dutch" summer schools may well have been part of the CRC's early efforts to facilitate Christian schools in any way possible; Sheeres, *Minutes of the Christian Reformed Church*, 297, 343, 345.

In addition to this summer work, Mulder opened a "Dutch reading library" in a local store that same fall (1894). H. P. Oggel, now editor of *De Volksvriend*, gladly recommended this as a place where one could get "unobjectionable reading" (*degelijke lectuur*).[33] Mulder even appears to have become a teacher in the Orange City public school, for at least part of his four years in the town.[34] Extracurricular activities for him, in 1895 at least, included serving as vice president of the newly organized Christian Reformed Missionary Society in Orange City, substituting once for H. P. Oggel as editor of *De Volksvriend* during the latter's absence, and giving the keynote address on American history at the annual "Christian" (i.e., Christian Reformed) observance of the Fourth of July, celebrated as a missions festival in a grove near town.[35]

Nevertheless, Mulder may well have jumped at the opportunity in 1898 to become the full-time principal and teacher of English at the well-established Christian school in Roseland, near Chicago. He received the call in April and soon vacated his house (and sold his household goods) across from the Orange City CRC.[36] He would remain at Roseland for six years, serve at the Kalamazoo Christian school for only a single year, and then return (apparently reluctant to leave Kalamazoo so soon) to Orange City to be the second principal at the recently (re)founded Christian school. Remaining there for only three years (1905-8), Mulder retired, seeming abruptly, from full-time teaching, not yet fifty years old.[37] Perhaps burnout and ill health were contributing, if not decisive, factors. The last two decades of his life were spent, still in the Orange City area, in various part-time activities, including some country-school teaching.[38]

---

[33] *VV*, 4 Oct. 1894.

[34] *VV*, 17 Dec. 1896. He is here included in a list of public school teachers; other lists were not found.

[35] *VV*, 21 March, 9 May, 27 June, and 11 July 1895.

[36] *VV*, 28 April and 15 Sept. 1898.

[37] *VV*, 28 April, 15 Sept. 1898; 17 March 1904; 20 July, 3, 17, and 31 Aug., 14 Sept., 12, 19, and 26 Oct. 1905; and 25 June 1908.

[38] Mulder, to quote his obituary, was "engaged in Christian school work for more than 40 years. For 15 years he was treasurer of the [CRC] classis, Orange City, was vice president of the Pioneer [retirement] Home association [in Orange City], and agent for many Holland [that is, Dutch] papers." "Pioneer School Master Passes," in *The Alton Democrat*, Alton, IA, 28 Nov. 1930, https://www.findagrave.com/memorial/33439121/yge-yges-mulder. His post-1908 teaching, presumably part time, is noted occasionally, for instance, in Holland Township in the 1910 census, and in Nassau Township, near Orange City (he had taught a student graduating from a rural school; *VV*, 11 June 1914). He appears in a Nassau Township teachers list in 1913 and in attendance at the Sioux County Teachers' Institute in 1915; *Alton*

As for the fate of Mulder's summer Dutch Christian school in Orange City, it was continued in 1898 and for a few years thereafter by young men (mostly Christian Reformed), such as William Stuart (1898), J. F. van den Berg (1899), H. J. L. Fortuin (1901), and J. Voogd (1903), initially in the CRC consistory room but soon in Orange City's public "ward school."[39] When Fortuin appealed to the Christian Reformed consistory in April 1901 for permission to conduct a Christian summer school, it suggested that he approach the pastor of the First Reformed Church to cooperate in this endeavor; no record of this request, however, appears in the Reformed congregation's consistory minutes.[40] These summer Christian schools, with classes of around thirty or forty pupils, were modest forerunners of the Orange City Christian School that would begin in 1904.

The context of the 1903-4 Orange City Christian School debates

The same week in April 1898 that Yge Mulder's impending departure from Orange City was announced, the three-month Spanish-American War began. Editor H. P. Oggel of *De Volksvriend* incarnated the fervent patriotism that swept the community and nation at that time,[41]

Democrat, 25 Oct. 1913 and 9 Oct. 1915; http://www.iowaoldpress.com/IA/Sioux/1913/OCT.html and http://www.iagenweb.org/sioux/Schools/1915_Institute.htm. He was a census enumerator in 1919 and listed in the 1920 census as without employment. He also seems to have farmed on the side. *VV*, 25 June 1908, 25 March 1909, 11 June 1914, 4 Sept. 1919; ancestry.com (1910, 1920, and 1930 federal census). Incidentally, just after Mulder retired as principal, it was reported that "Mr. Eertmans" (William B. Eerdmans, soon to found the eponymous publishing company) of Grand Rapids was lodging with "Mr. Y. Mulder"; *VV*, 24 Dec. 1908.

[39] *VV*, 23 and 30 June 1898; 8 June and 6 July 1899; 23 May, 20 June, and 4 July 1901; 23 and 30 July and 27 Aug. 1903. Stuart would become a CRC minister. Fortuin was a son of the well-known, ardent Kuyperian immigrant Rev. Foppe Fortuin, who was briefly pastor of the Free Grace Reformed Church of Middleburg, near Orange City (1901-3), but who quickly returned to the CRC. The younger Fortuin had already been a successful teacher in Roseland and Chicago. The summer school of Voogd in 1903 closed prematurely due to lack of students.

[40] Fortuin's father had just arrived from a Christian Reformed congregation to serve as the pastor of the Middleburg Reformed Church, so this may have seemed like a propitious moment to request interdenominational support, especially since Nicolaus Martin Steffens, the pastor of the First Reformed Church of Orange City (1899-1901), was, like the elder Fortuin, a devotee of the thought of Abraham Kuyper, who, incidentally, had visited Orange City in 1898, when the RCA and CRC pastors there and in nearby Sioux Center appeared together in an unusual display of ecumenicity. Consistory Minutes, First Christian Reformed Church, Orange City, IA, 27 March 1901; *VV*, 3 and 10 Nov. 1898; 19 Jan. 1899.

[41] Partly due to the influx of large numbers of non-WASP immigrants, this was the decade that saw the appearance of the Pledge of Allegiance and the Flag Salute to foster American unity and patriotism ("social glue").

Editor Dr. Henry Peter Oggel
(*www.findagrave.com*)

reinforced among the immigrants by memories of the sixteenth-century Dutch war for independence from Spain. An additional unifying force locally was the Boer War in South Africa (1899-1902), which revived the immigrants' latent anti-English bias, stemming from the seventeenth-century Anglo-Dutch wars (lost by the Dutch), not to mention the American Revolutionary War. Oggel's faithfully Republican weekly reflected the outlook of the majority of the Sioux County Dutch voters, although its rival, the Democratic weekly, *De Vrije Hollander*, actually outdid it in enthusiasm for the cause of the Boers.[42]

Religiously, though, Oggel tried to maintain the appearance of neutrality vis-à-vis the RCA and the CRC, although he was predictably partisan when it came to Roman Catholicism, Mormonism, and the

[42] The Dutch immigrants were especially impassioned about the plight of the South African Boers, so that the Republican president McKinley's failure to support the Boers embarrassed Oggel as he competed in supporting the underdog Boers with the passionate Martin D. van Oosterhout, editor of *De Vrije Hollander*, a Boer proponent par excellence. At the same time, Van Oosterhout was embroiled in a long, bitter dispute about South Africa with a Republican elder in his congregation—and eventually found guilty of slander by the consistory; Consistory Minutes, First Reformed Church, Orange City, 31 March 1904. Van der Zee, *The Hollanders of Iowa*, 349-62, 423-25. Incidentally, Jacob Van der Zee, a Northwestern Classical Academy graduate and University of Iowa student who became a Rhodes Scholar at Oxford University beginning in 1905, was excoriated in an editorial by Van Oosterhout for accepting the award funded by "the low-lived" Cecil John Rhodes, the oppressor of the Boers; 18 March 1905, *De Vrije Hollander*, quoted in translation in *The Hollanders of Iowa*, 424-25.

like. Nevertheless, he did not always conceal his RCA sympathies, given his early, close association with it in Michigan as an eyewitness of the 1857 CRC secession, as well as his long involvement with it throughout his adult life.[43] Accordingly, Oggel endorsed any effort to reunite the two denominations and, beginning in 1896, published the interdenominational *De Heidenwereld* (The heathen world), a missionary monthly initially coedited by the Orange City RCA and CRC pastors.[44] Not surprisingly, therefore, he doubted the need for a Christian elementary school in Orange City, sensing (correctly) that it would reinforce the division between the CRC and the RCA when they ought to unite to proclaim the gospel to the world.[45] As shall be seen, Oggel was essentially content with the American public school system, at least as it existed in the Dutch enclave in Sioux County, Iowa.

Whereas Orange City public opinion was largely coalescing with respect to the faraway Spanish-American and Boer Wars, the storm clouds of division were gradually gathering around the Christian school question, which had already been (or soon would be) debated among the Dutch Reformed immigrants elsewhere in the United States, as had earlier occurred in the Netherlands.[46]

A few harbingers, chosen somewhat at random, of the impending arguments on this matter in *De Volksvriend* may be noted. For instance, several RCA and CRC pastors were reported as leading religious exercises in the local public schools beginning around 1900, which, Oggel observed, showed the link between church and school in a "Christian

---

[43] See note 25 above.
[44] This publication, later called *Missionary Monthly*, finally ceased publication in 2003.
[45] The RCA and CRC at this time supported two rival Orange City Fourth of July celebrations (the CRC had a more edifying, "Christian" emphasis on the Fourth, whereas the RCA had a more fun and games "National" one; both were "patriotic"); there were eventually also two separate annual (in August) mission festivals in Sioux County (that of the RCA stressed foreign missions, while the CRC focused more on domestic missions); the latter had begun as part of the CRC Fourth of July celebration. *VV*, 27 June, 4 and 11 July 1895; 25 June and 9 July 1896; 24 June and 8 July 1897; 30 June and 7 July 1898; 15 and 22 June, 13 July, 17, 24, and 31 Aug. 1899 (Rev. N. M. Steffens of the RCA, who tried to bridge the gap between the two denominations, spoke at *both* Fourth of July celebrations in 1899!); 28 June, 5 July, 23 Aug., 6 and 13 Sept. 1900; 20 and 27 Aug. 1903.
[46] Note also the Schieffelin Plan for parochial schools adopted by the Reformed Church's General Synod in 1854, as well as the brief attempt at its implementation in several of the Dutch immigrant congregations in the Midwest, including those of Van Raalte in Holland, MI, and Oggel's older brother in Pella, IA. Kennedy, "Van Raalte and Parochial Schools," in Nyenhuis and Harinck, *Enduring Legacy*, 171-95; Kennedy, *A Commentary*, 428-29, 487-89, 680-82, 793, 833-34, 846, 851, 864, 913, 1313.

society like ours."⁴⁷ Also, in December 1900, Oggel penned an editorial affirming Christians' responsibility toward the public school, this "unique American institution," which was "a gift of God," so as "lovers of the Fatherland" and as believers, they should pray for the schools and make sure that they were ruled by moral and religious influences—and that the Bible had a place in them.⁴⁸

Three months later, Oggel approved the defeat at the ballot box of a proposal to have "uniformity of textbooks" in Sioux County (Orange City was the county seat). This initiative would have taken away "our local Reformed Hollanders' Christian freedom to have textbooks which suit our children," not so-called "neutral" but in reality "unbelieving, naturalistic, and evolutionistic" textbooks. He felt that, under the guise of neutrality, public schools in the Netherlands had become godless. The Iowa State Code stated that the Bible should not be excluded from any public school; only "sectarian" teaching was barred. The law did not forbid parents from sending their children to Northwestern Classical Academy to become Christian teachers, nor did it forbid teachers to be Christians or textbooks (selected by locally elected school boards) to respect "the one true religion." Oggel thus concluded that the local schools were not "godless."⁴⁹

In February 1902, a flurry of writers, including Oggel, expressed a variety of opinions in *De Volksvriend* on whether Christian schools were good for the United States in general and for Orange City in particular.⁵⁰ A year later, a society for Christian education on a Reformed basis was formed in nearby Sioux Center, with both CRC and RCA members and with the local CRC minister, Rev. Jan Smitter, as president. At the society's invitation, Rev. Martin Broekstra, an RCA minister from Michigan (of whom, more later), and Rev. Klaas Kuiper, a Christian Reformed minister from Illinois, soon came to energize Hollanders "in the West" for the cause of Christian education.⁵¹

Sioux Center having led the way, Orange City soon followed, with the organization of a society for Christian education in late summer

---

47 One of these was Rev. Jerry P. Winter of Orange City's American Reformed Church (of whom more later); *VV*, 7 June 1900; 18 Dec. 1902; 18 Jan. 1903; 25 Dec. 1905.
48 At the same time, Chicago had just banned Scripture reading to avoid "sectarianism," which action concerned the Orange City folk. *VV*, 6 Dec. 1900; 21 July 1892; Swierenga, *Dutch Chicago*, 353-54, 359-60.
49 *VV*, 7 March 1901.
50 *VV*, 6, 20, and 27 Feb. 1902.
51 *VV*, 19 and 26 Feb., 12 March, 2 April, and 2 July 1903. Both Smitter and Broekstra were young men.

Rev. Idzerd van Dellen and wife
(*courtesy Heritage Hall, Calvin University*)

1903, spearheaded by the new pastor of the local Christian Reformed Church, the energetic, young Rev. Idzerd van Dellen (1871-1965). Van Dellen was a product of the theological school of Kampen, where his favorite teacher was Herman Bavinck, whose views on Christian education, similar to those of Kuyper, he adopted. He had thus organized a Christian school (as well as a tuberculosis sanitarium) in Maxwell, New Mexico, where he had been pastor before he went to Orange City. It was in the latter place, however, that Van Dellen led in setting up the first permanent Reformed Christian school west of the Mississippi; Sioux Center's Christian school would only open a year later.[52]

Taking advantage of the current flurry of publicity regarding Christian education, Northwestern Classical Academy published an ad in *De Volksvriend* that same summer (August 1903): "Want Christian schools and education? Now then, here is a Christian school—a school with the Bible." The academy assured the public that the faculty had been selected with two factors in mind: competence and an authentic Christian spirit born from "faith in God and a love for Christ's church."

[52] Idzerd van Dellen, *In God's Crucible: An Autobiography* (Grand Rapids, MI: Baker Book House, 1950), 39-43, 64, 85-86; *VV*, 14 Sept. 1905.

Moreover, the faculty had to be communicant members of a Reformed congregation.[53]

The Winter-Van Dellen debate

The same month (October 1903) that both the First Reformed and Christian Reformed churches in Orange City installed electric lighting, Oggel began an open forum in *De Volksvriend* that would sometimes generate more heat than light about the impending Christian grade school. The man to lead in objecting to the new institution was, quite appropriately, the *American*-born (second generation) Rev. Jerry P. Winter (1869-1963), pastor of the English-language, *American* Reformed Church of Orange City, a member of the town's *public* school board, and also Oggel's own pastor. Winter contributed a letter that Oggel, in publishing it, recommended for his readers "to ponder"; the piece appears to have been the mild-mannered Oggel's way of surreptitiously promulgating his own position.[54]

In "A Parochial School for Orange City?" Winter recounted that he had made a few remarks at the end of his previous Sunday morning sermon about setting up a parochial elementary school. He held that the American public school is "the nursery of Democracy and Patriotism," but "our church-school people" would take away one of the chief God-given means of assimilating diverse groups of immigrants.[55] Winter claimed that there was no need locally to discard textbooks teaching

[53] *VV*, 20 Aug. 1903. Over the years, Northwestern would educate many CRC students in addition to RCA ones (often future ministers); also, some RCA youth would attend the slowly growing Orange City public high school. Interestingly, there was a proposal, eventually rejected by the CRC Classis Iowa, for a "Union Northwestern Classical Academy." The plan was to have a board of trustees composed of eight RCA members and six CRC members (with half of the teachers RCA and half CRC), to obviate the CRC starting a "parent-controlled" second academy in Sioux County in Hull (which eventually occurred) or elsewhere. Van der Zee, *The Hollanders of Iowa*, 270, 414; *VV*, 18 May, 22 June, 3 and 10 Aug., 23 Nov. 1911; 21 March, 25 April, 2 and 16 May, 20 June, 12 Sept. 1912. This story is worth telling at another time.

[54] Jerry P. (originally Jurrien Pieter) Winter, a graduate of Hope College and Western Theological Seminary (where his uncle, Rev. Egbert Winter, taught 1895-1904), was ordained in 1894; the American Reformed Church, where he served from 1899 to 1909, was his third charge. *VV*, 15 Oct. 1903; Kennedy, "Prairie Premillenialism," *Reformed Review* 46, no. 2 (winter 1992): 163. According to Van Dellen many years later, Winter's congregation harbored non-Calvinists (Arminians, whose views were rejected by the Canons of Dort) and Freemasons (anathema to the CRC and many in the Midwestern RCA); Van Dellen, *In God's Crucible*, 63-64.

[55] The public school was viewed by many Americans as the ideal means for assimilating the masses of non-Protestant immigrants from southern and eastern Europe who were pouring into the United States, seemingly threatening "WASP" America.

Rev. Jerry P. Winter in later years
(courtesy Fairfield Reformed
Church, Illinois)

evolution, since the city's public school principal had challenged anyone to show where that was taught in any of the school's books. "Our friends want a positive Christian influence. Good. We have it in our Orange City schools," since the principal (who belonged to the American Reformed Church) and all the teachers are professing Christians; most teachers have grown up in Orange City's Christian homes; and all are active in local churches. Moreover the Bible is read in school, biblical history is taught, and daily prayer occurs. "What more do you want?"[56]

The following week, Van Dellen, the first president of the local Christian school society, who had already contributed two articles on the present subject to *De Wachter* (CRC weekly), responded with a letter, "The Ideal is neither Parochial nor Public," the usual Kuyperian position. In the article, Van Dellen avers that Winter errs in thinking that the Christian school is a parochial school, attached to a church. Rather, the Christian school society met deliberately in the city hall, not in a church, and its first speaker was the RCA's Rev. Marinus Broekstra.[57] The

---

[56] J. P. Winter, "Eene Parochiale School voor Orange City?" in *VV*, 15 Oct. 1903.
[57] Coincidentally, Marinus E. Broekstra (1872-1940) was with Van Dellen at the theological school in Kampen. Russell L. Gasero, *Historical Directory of the Reformed Church in America* (Grand Rapids, MI: Eerdmans, 2001), 49; Van Dellen, *In God's Crucible*, 43. Since Broekstra had been invited by the Sioux Center Christian school society to speak for it, the Orange City Christian Reformed church requested that he come to Orange City as well; Consistory Minutes, First Christian Reformed Church, 20 May and 22 June 1903; *VV*, 25 June and 2 and 9 July 1903. Orange City's First Reformed Church consistory minutes contain nothing about Broekstra.

society's constitution stated that it was not "ecclesiastical" (*kerkelijk*). At its last general meeting, five of the nine board members chosen on the first ballot were RCA, despite the fact that a huge majority of the voters were CRC. If the society does not get RCA support, "they cannot be forced to join it." In any case, "the public school is a failure" and will be more and more so: witness the Netherlands, where the state school has been "the nursery of unbelief and socialism." A state school must be neutral (especially that of the United States with such a diverse citizenry) and can never be Christian; "neutrality and Christianity are incompatible"; evolution is being taught to teachers at institutions of higher learning. Not only does the school form the people, but the people form the school, and as the public becomes less Christian, so does the school. The new immigrants, as well as native-born Americans, could also thwart the schools in their efforts to teach democracy and patriotism.[58]

Winter's second article noted that public schools maintain the equality of citizens, rich and poor, promote democracy, and do not separate social classes. The last named is one of the parochial school's dangers, that is, lack of sympathy for others, exclusivism, Pharisaism; "I'm a little better than you." These dangers grow when parochial schools are in the hands of those who oppose free institutions, like the Roman Catholics, with their "Old World doctrine of papal authority, which is against the spirit of our national life." It is much harder for pupils to become intelligent American citizens if they go to parochial schools. In a third article, Winter argued that the American public school has contributed to our material progress, as have factories.[59]

Van Dellen, taking his turn in a second article, answered the closing question of Winter's first article ("What more do you want?") by explaining that his people do not want a vague Americanism in their schools, made up in big cities of a mix of diverse elements (Jews, Russians, Italians, and others), but rather, a common mind, which begins with the fear of the Lord that brings wisdom; the Spirit of the Lord gives liberty, and that will make good citizens. About textbooks, Van Dellen claims that it is never said in the society's meetings that evolution was taught in Orange City public schools, so why is the principal so

---

[58] I. van Dellen, "Geen parochiale en geen publieke school het ideal," *VV*, 22 Oct. 1903.
[59] J. P. Winter, "De Publieke School en de Landverhuizing," *VV*, 22 Oct. 1903. Unfortunately, this second Winter article appears on the same page as Van Dellen's first one, so it has no response to the latter. Winter's third article also ignores Van Dellen's piece; J. P. Winter, "De Publieke School en Productie," *VV*, 29 Oct. 1903.

defensive about it? But even if evolution is not taught there, children should avoid neutral schools and instead be educated according to God's Word. Nevertheless, public schools need to be made as good as possible for the general public. It is fine that Orange City schools have Christian teachers, but Winter fails to see that the issue is not primarily about the persons of the teachers but about the character of the school. By law, the public school must be neutral; this is insufficient, even if begun with Bible reading and prayer and conducted by truly Christian teachers. What is needed is positive Christian instruction, particularly education steeped in Reformed principles. But this is not education as a sort of Reformed catechism class. Rather, children should be educated for a full, rich life for church, state, and society, so that they can operate as Christian citizens in every terrain of life. Thus, all subjects must be taught in relationship to God. For instance, when children learn history, they must learn not only that America is great but also that God's hand is in history and that all nations and peoples (including America and Americans), compared to him, are as a drop in the bucket.

In a hurried postscript to this article, Van Dellen answered Winter's second article, which he had not known would appear simultaneously with the former's first article. Van Dellen held, among other things, that Christian schools promulgate a true equality in Christ, whereas public schools offer a false equality, like that of the French Revolution; that Christian schools cannot be equated with Catholic parochial schools regarding our true fatherland; that Christian schools do not want a caste school, where some (such as Americans) are better than others, as is done in public schools; God made of one blood all peoples; we want a school for both rich and poor. Besides, the solution for the immigration problem is not to send our children to schools with "Italians, Poles, unbelievers, and the half-civilized, who endanger our children" (consecrated to the Lord); the fear of the Lord is above love of fatherland; we as patriotic citizens seek the good of the United States but not at the cost of our children. Finally, we believe that, although the state has a stake in education, the public schools are insufficient for our covenant offspring. We do not, however, want them to disappear until a better solution is found; moreover, we think that setting up special (*bijzondere*) schools will lead to finding a solution. In this search, the rights of the family (parents) are over those of the state, which has secondary rights. In all of this, Van Dellen sounds very Kuyperian.[60]

---

[60] I. van Dellen, "*Wat we willen op schoolgebied*," *VV*, 29 Oct. 1903.

Winter's fourth article, "The Public School and Christianity," asked Van Dellen why he is still living in the United States and paying taxes to support the public school under a government which is "neutral" and thus un-Christian and against Reformed principles? Actually, however, the Constitution was given by many with Christian character and the Christian religion has been recognized as part of American common law. As for the future, is God dead? Is Van Dellen a prophet? Why must public opinion influence the school negatively when it is our duty to make public opinion Christian? Also, if we are to have Christian instruction, not just Christian influence, will that schoolwork not suffer if the teacher has to add a sort of little sermon (*preekje*) along with the lesson? Our teachers are busy enough, and making minisermons is not easy. Also, if the "Christian" school is to be on "Reformed principles," does not that exclude many American Christians? So we end up with parochial schools. Finally, although Christian education at school does no harm, the proper places for that are the home and church. Do not give the honor of the family to a Christian school.[61]

Van Dellen responded to Winter in a third article, "On the Family and the School." With regard to Winter's question on how Van Dellen, as a Reformed Christian, can remain in the United States and pay taxes, he simply points to Romans 13 and Matthew 22:21 (about the Christian's duties to the pagan Roman government). Winter says that the Unites States is not hostile to Christianity, and that Christianity is part of our common law. But not much of genuine Christianity (which claims to be the one true religion) is left in the state, since the American Constitution can support only a least-common-denominator religion (like at the 1893 World's Parliament of Religions in Chicago), which ipso facto makes the state un-Christian. In such a situation, what does freedom to read the Bible mean? Moreover, Winter fails to distinguish properly between state and school, because the state and the school are in separate spheres.[62] In fact, the school has no separate sphere but belongs to that of the family; children are not in the first instance members of the state (which is a socialist idea) but of the family (so it is erroneous to say that the state can corrupt the school). The state must be neutral between the various Christian denominations (but ruling according to God's Word), but the family may never be neutral in baptizing their children and educating them in the Reformed faith. We must support the public school, however, because children must be

---

[61] J. P. Winter, "*De Publieke School en het Christendom,*" *VV*, 12 Nov. 1903.

[62] Kuyper's doctrine of sphere sovereignty is clearly in evidence at this point in Van Dellen's argument.

taught, and as long as the family does not grasp its right and calling, the state must step in as guardian and educate these children, and since Van Dellen is a member of the state, he shares the responsibility to see that the state exercises its duty as well as possible. Thus, he cannot, as a citizen, desert the public school, but even more, as a Christian, he may not let the family remain a ward of the state. And so his aim is that the family be mature (*mondig*) and set up its own schools. Winter concludes by saying, do not give the honor of the family to a Christian school, but instead, Van Dellen retorted, it is the state that now robs the family of its honor. More next week.[63]

Van Dellen's promised sequel, "The School Question," concluded his part of the debate. He had said earlier, against Winter's optimism, that the public school would become increasingly un-Christian because of the influence of the unbelieving immigrants and native-born Americans and also because of the signs of the times here and in Europe that foretell a falling away.[64] Winter wrongly assumes that we support schools that educate the few and let the masses grow up in ignorance, but in fact, we want all children to get an education. The ideal is a school, under the oversight (*toezicht*) of the state but as an extension of the family. Winter keeps saying we are for parochial schools. NO! Parochial schools (such as the Catholic schools) need to exist if people want them, but they are under the church. Instead, we want a school that is based on the Three Forms of Unity (Reformed principles). But, Winter will say, there goes the precious (*kostelijke*) equality of American citizens—in separate schools. The United States, however, already has great diversity, which will not be diminished if all children are put in public schools. Better that we are like a forest with all different varieties of trees. Not the state school but Christian freedom must make and keep us one people. Let us make Christian soil in the United States. Finally, Winter's tired argument about Christian teachers adding minisermons to the lessons, long used against Christian schools in the Netherlands, is countered by the analogy of a cook blending ingredients: Christianity is to be integrated with, not tacked onto, the subject matter in school.[65]

[63] I. van Dellen, "*Het Huisgezin en de School*," *VV*, 26 Nov. 1903.
[64] This sounds like premillennial "pessimism."
[65] I van Dellen, "*De School - Questie*," *VV*, 3 Dec. 1903. Nearly a half century later, the relatively moderate Van Dellen, in his autobiography, acknowledged—regarding the Orange City Christian school discussions—that "there was an element of truth in the arguments of the opposition," such as, that "most of the teachers, especially in the country school, were members of the Church," and some began instruction with prayer and Bible reading; also, love for Christian education was indeed an import from the Netherlands, "but that does not make the school unpatriotic." Van Dellen, *In God's Crucible*, 86.

This ended the main debate—between Winter and Van Dellen—about the Christian school in *De Volksvriend*, although the discussion droned on for another half year, with input from both sides.[66] Oggel terminated it and declared his own position openly for the first time. He averred that he would never speak against Christian education but that the public school does a fine job of giving good morals to children from diverse backgrounds and all classes. It teaches them to be good citizens in a new land, to honor our flag, to obey our laws, and to love their new Fatherland. Sioux County can expect even more from the public school. Is it important for America and worth our support? "I, for one, say that it is of incalculable worth for our land."[67]

Concluding observations

Why was a countercultural, divisive, "un-American," Orange City Christian school[68] "here to stay" in 1904 but not in 1889, when Mulder first opened one? Briefly, the key elements appear to have been the critical mass of recent CRC immigrants imbued with Kuyper's views on education, the leadership of the energetic new CRC pastor Van Dellen, the example of Christian schools elsewhere obeying the CRC synodical mandates, the growing secularization of urban American public schools, and the end of the economic downturn that began in 1893.[69]

---

[66] Many of the talking points were reiterated and refined and a few new ones added. Oggel aimed to give each side opportunity to speak. There is little evidence that minds were changed; rather, battle lines seem to have hardened. People from Orange City and elsewhere weighed in, including Seine Bolks' son-in-law, RCA pastor Rev. James de Pree of Sioux Center (pro public school) and the young Orange City school principal (Orris W. Herr) but not the (possibly ailing) pastor of First Reformed Church, Rev. Evert W. Stapelkamp, who remained silent. One of his elders, Garrit de Jong, however, was a vocal proponent of the public school and a sharp antagonist of maverick newspaper editor Martin D. van Oosterhout, a member of his congregation; interestingly, this church gave money ($34) to Christian schools in the Netherlands in 1904 but not to the one in Orange City; Consistory Minutes, First Reformed Church, Orange City, 30 March 1904. The lengthy school debate was also carried on in Van Oosterhout's rival Orange City Dutch weekly, *De Vrije Hollander*; although he was a member of the RCA, Van Oosterhout was more sympathetic than Oggel to the Christian school; Van Dellen, *In God's Crucible*, 85-86. Unfortunately, no copies of *De Vrije Hollander* are known to exist; a bit of its content is available mainly from references to it in *De Volksvriend*.

[67] *VV*, 30 June 1904.

[68] The opponents of the Christian school repeatedly implied that it was unpatriotic and un-American; Van Dellen, *In God's Crucible*, 85; Van Dellen denied the charges, but his Americanism was nevertheless relatively muted.

[69] For a relatively impartial, general, contemporary overview of the Christian and public school situation in Orange City and Iowa in general around the turn of the twentieth century, see Van der Zee, *The Hollanders of Iowa*, 266-75, 413-15. His one

Curiously, both the deist Freemason De Lespinasse and the orthodox Calvinist Van Dellen had somewhat similar assessments of the public school in the United States—the former believing that, happily, it *should* be secular and the latter believing that, sadly, it *would* be secular. The Plumbes, Oggels, and Winters, on the other hand, would ultimately be doomed to disappointment, like the proverbial frog in the kettle as the water gradually heats up. The mid-twentieth-century US Supreme Court decisions limiting or prohibiting Bible reading and prayer in the public schools, based on the doctrine of "the separation of church and state," largely ended their fond hope of free "Christian" education at taxpayers' expense. This further heating of the kettle does not, however, appear to have disturbed the RCA General Synod of 1957, which once again strongly endorsed public schools (as it had in 1892), while largely deprecating Christian schools.[70] The RCA statement reinforced the oft-cited observation of the Unitarian church historian Sidney Mead, that the public school *is* the established church of the United States.[71]

---

apparent deficiency is that he leaves the impression (perhaps because he was of RCA stock) that the Christian schools were populated only by CRC children and not by at least some from the RCA. For a more recent historical sketch of the Sioux County Christian schools, see C. Aue, "Schools for Christian Instruction in Sioux County," in Charles L. Dyke, *The Story of Sioux County* (Orange City, IA: n.p., 1942), 555-58.

[70] "The Relationship of Public and Parochial School Education: A Statement of the Board of Education, Reformed Church in America" (NY: Board of Education, RCA, 1957), 38-40; the General Synod directed that this paper, adopted by the RCA Board of Education, be sent to every RCA pastor "for reading, reference and study." The General Assembly of the Presbyterian Church in the USA adopted a similar statement in this same year. For a negative assessment of the RCA paper by a CRC pastor, see Edwin H. Palmer, "Christian Education and the Reformed Church in America," *Torch and Trumpet* 8, no. 4 (Sept. 1958), 3-4. It took some time before the implementation of the Supreme Court decisions trickled down to the grass roots in Orange City and Sioux County public schools. When the author came to live in Orange City in 1963, prayer and Bible reading were still common practices in the area public schools, but by the time he left in 1998, they had largely been discontinued, although most teachers probably attended local churches (RCA, CRC, and other).

[71] "Of necessity the state in its public-education system is and always has been teaching religion It does so because the well-being of the nation and the state demands this foundation of shared beliefs. In other words, the public schools in the United States took over one of the basic responsibilities that traditionally was always assumed by an established church. In this sense the public-school system of the United States *is* its established church. In this context one can understand why it is that the religion of many Americans is democracy–why their real faith is the 'democratic faith'–the religion of the public schools "; Sidney E. Mead, *The Lively Experiment: The Shaping of Christianity in America* (NY: Harper & Row, 1963), 68.

CHAPTER 3

Wisconsin Memorial Academy

Mary Risseeuw

The public schools in rural Sheboygan County, Wisconsin, at the turn of the twentieth century, were all-graded schools, through grade 8, and the only high school within twenty miles was in the city of Sheboygan. The resources for Christian higher education in this area of Wisconsin were inadequate, and the remoteness of many of the villages made the need for a school more pressing.

In April 1900, Gerrit Kollen, president of Hope College in Holland, Michigan, presented to the council of Hope College a plan to establish an academy in the eastern part of Wisconsin. The Classis of Wisconsin and the General Synod of the Reformed Church in America were enthusiastic supporters. Rev. Jacob Van Zanten, pastor of the First Reformed Church in Cedar Grove, Wisconsin, took the lead in this pursuit and was assisted by Cornelia Walvoord, a resident of Cedar Grove who had graduated from Oshkosh [Wisconsin] Normal School. Egbert Winter, a graduate of Hope College, was appointed the first principal, and by September 1901, thirty-six students from the county were enrolled. Rev. John Sietsema, pastor of the First Reformed Church in Oostburg, Wisconsin, was appointed by the board of trustees to give instruction in English.

Temporary instruction began in 1901 in the chapel of the church. The selection of a permanent location for the school was given to a committee appointed by classis, and Cedar Grove was ultimately chosen. The cornerstone was laid on June 26, 1901, and on June 26, 1902, the building that would house the Wisconsin Memorial Academy was completed. It was valued at $3,000. In 1905 Arend Lubbers donated a valuable piece of land within the village to provide the principal with a residence, and in June of 1914—a particularly important time for supporters of the academy—the debt of the school was eradicated due to liberal donations from "friends in the East."

In the village of Oostburg, in the township of Holland, the public graded school was finally given approval in 1912 to add grade 9; two years later, grade 10 was added. In 1915 it became a full, four-year public high school. The establishment of Oostburg High School provided a great opportunity for more students to attend high school, especially those who lived rurally. But the possibility of a Christian education encouraged many from Oostburg to attend the academy instead of the village high school.

The population of Cedar Grove in 1900 was approximately 327, and Oostburg was about 350. Most of the student population of the academy was from these villages and the rural areas of the two townships that surrounded them. The yearbook for 1908-10 states:

> The academy is continually demonstrating to the people of this community and to the world at large the superiority of Christian education, and already, parents of even distant places, recognizing these advantages, have sent their children to this school.[1]

This comment refers in part to the enrollment in 1908 of William Lammers from Westfield, North Dakota. His father, Rev. Barend W. Lammers, was born in Cedar Grove in 1860 and educated at Hope College and New Brunswick Theological Seminary. Lammers was serving a church in Westfield at the time and chose to send his son back to Cedar Grove for his education. Rev. Martin Flipse made the same choice with his son Martin Eugene. Rev. Flipse was born in Cedar Grove in 1866 and was serving a pastorate at Holland First Reformed Church in Passaic, New Jersey, when he chose to send his son to the academy. Throughout the years of the academy, there was one student from Milwaukee, three from the Friesland/Randolph area, three from Sheboygan (two Dutch

---

[1] Wisconsin Memorial Academy Yearbook, 1908-9.

and one German), and five from Belgium, just south of Cedar Grove. Belgium is a settlement of Catholic Luxembourgers.

Wisconsin Memorial Academy was an institution established for the promotion of science, literature, and religion, and the curriculum was rigorous. As the 1902-3 yearbook states:

> Although it is a denominational school, yet it is nonsectarian, and no religious test is required. All are welcome. The object of the founders has been to safeguard the development of mind and character in its formative period under the best conditions.[2]

College preparatory courses included Latin, Greek, physics, astronomy, botany, civics, and civil government, and some years, French, German, and Dutch were available. A business course was also an option. Extracurricular activities included forensics, drama, baseball, and basketball. The 1904-5 yearbook summarized the driving force behind the curriculum: "In an unobtrusive way, all scholastic work is pervaded by the healthy tone of Holy Writ."[3] Its intent was to educate males to become pastors and females to become teachers. The promotional brochure distributed by the academy explains:

> Its primary purposes are: first, to secure recruits for the needy ranks of the Gospel ministry and prepare them for further training, and secondly, to give to all who desire to prepare for any vocation in life an opportunity to obtain a sound and liberal education in a school where the environment is distinctly Christian.[4]

These objectives were echoed in the 1909-10 yearbook:

> The Wisconsin Memorial Academy offers to all an opportunity to secure a liberal academic course of instruction, and it is well adapted to those who plan to enter college or university. Three courses are offered: the Classical, the Latin, and the Normal, each of which grants a diploma which admits the graduate to a full collegiate course at Hope College or elsewhere. The aim is to powerfully affect the mind and to fit it as a sharp instrument of thought for an avocation in life.[5]

[2] Ibid., 1902-3.
[3] Ibid., 1904-5.
[4] *Do You Believe in Christian Education?* Wisconsin Memorial Academy collection, TeRonde House Museum, Cedar Grove, WI.
[5] Yearbook, 1909-10.

Just like Holland Academy in Holland, Michigan, the Wisconsin Memorial Academy was a classical academy, the equivalent of a college preparatory school. In its early years, it offered three courses: ancient classical, modern classical, and the normal course. The normal course was designed for students who wished to qualify for teaching at the primary and secondary levels.

Publications that were distributed not only were geared toward promotion but also evoked a clear message about the responsibilities of the churches and classis. Rev. Paul Hinkamp, principal from 1908 to 1911, minced no words:

> This is a business proposition—the King's business. The call is an urgent one. The school belongs to the Classis of Wisconsin first of all. It should be supported entirely by the Classis. This the Classis can easily do, though it has been all too negligent of its opportunity and duty in the past. Did your church meet its full apportionment of the expenses last year? Is it going to do so this year? Is it represented by a student on the enrollment list? You know what the answers to these questions ought to be.[6]

Rev. Hinkamp, son of Dutch emigrants who had settled in Milwaukee, attended Hope College and simultaneously received his master's degree from Hope and his divinity degree from McCormick Theological Seminary in 1914. He also taught classical languages at the academy from 1907 to 1911. After serving a pastorate in Sheboygan, he became a professor of religious education at Hope College. Rev. Hinkamp was one of many Hope College graduates who taught at the academy, some of whom were its own graduates.

By 1908 the school had acquired (largely through donations) six hundred volumes for its library, and by 1929, it had doubled that number. The growth of the school was slow but steady. Its humble origins were part of the recollection of the Class of 1917 at their fifty-fourth reunion in 1971. They remembered

> a plain, old-fashioned building, without indoor plumbing, without a lunch room, an entirely inadequate laboratory and library. Yet it was here that new worlds and wide vistas were opened. In that laboratory, consisting of a Bunsen burner, a few beakers, a scale and several test tubes, the students learned about the atom and, under the skilled direction of interested teachers,

---

[6] *Do You Believe in Christian Education?*

about the rudiments of algebra, geometry, and physics—the boys excelled in these subjects.[7]

Between 1904 and 1937, with class sizes ranging from five to twenty-five, the academy graduated approximately 397 students. According to the *Sheboygan Press*, "Large numbers of Academy graduates have entered fields of useful service far and near in numerous professions. Seventy-eight percent of the Academy's alumni have continued their education in institutions of higher education."[8] This historical account highlights a select number of graduates whose careers exemplify the educational rigor and mission of the academy.

Achievements of Graduates

Minister	25
Wife of minister	6
Missionary	15
Professor	8
Principal/Administrator	12
Teacher	78
Doctor	3
Dentist	4
Nurse	18
Lawyer	1
Executive	14
Business	26
Farmer	15
Other	37

Medical professionals

Willis J. Potts (WMA Class of 1914[9]) grew up on a farm outside of Cedar Grove. With money he earned from the farm, he put himself through the academy and also through Hope College. His senior year at Hope was interrupted by World War I, and he enlisted. After the war, he graduated from the University of Chicago, but Hope College awarded him a bachelor's degree as well. He graduated from Rush Medical School

---

[7] "Wisconsin Memorial Academy Class of 1917 Has Reunion," *Sheboygan Press* (5 Aug. 1971).
[8] "Wisconsin Memorial Academy Served Well the Community," *Sheboygan Press* (14 June 1937).
[9] All subsequent dates in parentheses refer to the Memorial Academy graduation date of the person referenced.

in Chicago in 1924 and did postgraduate surgical work in Frankfurt, Germany. Upon joining Children's Hospital in Chicago, he focused on pediatric surgery, and he also had a private surgical practice in Oak Park. When World War II began, he reenlisted and organized the 25th Evacuation Hospital in the Pacific. He was discharged as a colonel and special surgical consultant. On his return, he became the chief surgeon at Children's Hospital and professor of surgery at Northwestern Medical School. Heart surgery—in general—was really in its infancy at this time, and pediatric heart surgery was even less common. Dr. Potts worked with a pediatric cardiologist (Dr. Stanley Gibson) and another surgeon (Dr. Sidney Smith) on the problem of "blue babies" and developed a surgical technique to address the congenital heart defect that was fatal to infants. He and a colleague perfected the technique on thirty dogs—all of whom lived. On September 13, 1946, Potts performed the first aortopulmonary anastomosis on the young patient Diane Schnell. She recovered quickly and left the hospital nineteen days later. Patients came from across the United States and abroad for this life-saving procedure. When Dr. Potts joined Children's Hospital staff in 1930, there was only one pediatric surgeon in the United States, and by his retirement in 1960, there were seventy-five.

Dr. Potts also invented and perfected a number of aortic and vascular clamps that made vascular surgery possible. He is widely known for developing the Potts dissecting scissors, which was somewhat revolutionary in helping to reduce operating time, because it allowed for both the blunt separation of tissue and accurate dissection, without changing instruments. Potts wrote two books, as well as a regular column in the *Chicago Tribune*.[10]

Of the three graduates who chose a career in medicine, only one returned to Sheboygan County to practice—Dr. Wesley van Zanten (1922). He attended Hope College and graduated from Marquette Medical School in Milwaukee in 1931. Shortly after graduation, he and his father, Dr. William van Zanten, established a joint practice in Sheboygan. His father, originally from Allegan, Michigan, had also attended Hope and Marquette. Wesley van Zanten was well known in the county for his service as county coroner from 1938 to 1948, a role his father had also filled.

---

[10] Willis J. Potts, *The Surgeon and the Child* (Philadelphia: W. B. Saunders, 1959), and *Your Wonderful Baby: A Practical Approach to Baby and Child Care* (Rand McNally, 1966).

Harms Bloemers (1925) attended Hope College and Rush Medical School in Chicago. He won a coveted internship at the Henry Ford Hospital in Detroit and established his practice in Staten Island, New York. Dr. Bloemers' wife, Vera Holle (1925), also received a BA from Hope College and was a high school English teacher before their marriage.

All four of the Wisconsin Memorial Academy graduates who attended dental school remained in Wisconsin and practiced in Sheboygan County. Arnie Duenk (1906), Willard Grotenhuis (1932), and Homer Voskuil (1935) all attended Marquette Dental School in Milwaukee. Lester Plekenpol (1919) received his degree from Northwestern University Dental School in Chicago. Dr. Plekenpol's wife, Mabel Weavers (1913), served as a nurse in his practice. After a brief teaching career, she resumed her studies in nursing in Chicago and became a surgical supervisor at Methodist Hospital in Madison. After she married Dr. Plekenpol, they established his practice in rural Cascade, Wisconsin. She also practiced at the Plymouth (Wisconsin) Hospital from 1942 to 1974. She was one of eighteen academy graduates to choose a nursing career.

A well-publicized story in 1936 was that of seven young women who had attended the academy with the intention of becoming nurses.[11] Because there was an age requirement and two of the girls were too young, the others waited a year so they could all enter nurse's training together. Augusta De Master, Dorothy Koskamp, Viola Lewis, Dorothy Droppers, Hazel De Master, Marian Wassink, and Bernice Jentink were all 1932 academy graduates, and they all graduated with honors from Lutheran Hospital School of Nursing in Milwaukee in 1936. Five of them accepted positions at St. Luke's Hospital in Saginaw, Michigan, and two at Memorial Hospital in Sheboygan. Military service and careers that took them to both coasts did not adversely affect their lifelong friendship. The sacrifice their families made during the Depression to make the education of these women possible was not insignificant. Tuition in the early years of the academy was $5 per semester, with reductions for more than one student attending from the same family. Fees rose to $25 per semester by the early 1930s. These costs during the Depression caused many students to continue their education in public schools or to drop out entirely.

---

[11] The eighth member of this group, Esther Gabrielse, received her education at Oostburg High School.

Missionaries, ministers, and the women who supported them

As one would expect from a school supported by the Reformed Church, the emphasis on a life of service to the church was particularly notable. There were twenty-five ministers, six ministers' wives, and fifteen missionaries among the academy graduates. The first church established in Cedar Grove was in 1848 and was incorporated as a Presbyterian Church in 1853. The First Reformed Church in Cedar Grove was organized in 1853. Oostburg's First Reformed Church was established in 1850, and First Presbyterian was organized in 1867. Although a Christian Reformed Church was organized in Oostburg in 1868, it seems to have had little influence on the student population of the academy. The graduates who became ministers and missionaries were affiliated with either the Reformed Church in America or the Presbyterian Church. Those who chose the mission field covered the globe from China to Saudi Arabia to the reservations of the Native Americans in the United States.

Ministers in the Reformed Church in America and the Presbyterian Church

Name	Year
Anthony Haverkamp	1904
William Walvoord	1904
Oliver Droppers	1906
Edward Huibregtse	1906
Raymond Meengs	1906
Benjamin Wynveen	1906
John Lensink	1908
Clarence Blekkink	1909
Edwin Koeppe	1910
Raymond Lubbers	1910
Eugene Flipse	1912
Alwin Ten Pas	1916
DeLloyd Huenink	1919
Daniel DeBraal	1921
Cornelius Dykhuizen	1921
Clarence Hesselink	1922
John Konig	1923
Harold Hesselink	1924
Louis Grotenhuis	1926
Alva Ebbers	1927

Gerald Huenink	1927
David Laman	1932
Reuben Ongna	1933
Reuben Ten Haken	1933
Frederic Dolfin	1937

Rev. Edwin Koeppe and his wife, Elizabeth Renskers, were 1910 graduates. Koeppe and his wife both attended Hope, and he graduated from Western Seminary in 1919. That same year, they joined the mission team in South Fukien province in China. They served there from 1919 to 1951. In 1939 they were joined by Geraldine Smies (1924), a 1932 graduate of Hope. Their experiences during the Japanese invasion and the capture of Amoy in 1941 were well documented at the time. Rev. Koeppe told the story that the Japanese marines took over the international settlement there four hours before the attack on Pearl Harbor and arrested all of the Americans at the point of pistol and bayonet. They were kept under heavy guard even after they were allowed to return to their homes, and all of their property was confiscated.

After almost eight months, they received word of the possibility of an exchange of prisoners. They left on a steamer bound for Shanghai that provided no protection from airplanes or submarines. A month later, they were transported to a ship where 636 people caught in the war in China set sail. At Hong Kong, another 300 people were added. The exchange of prisoners occurred in what at that time was Portuguese East Africa (today's Mozambique) before setting sail for Rio De Janiero. Almost a year after their capture, they finally set foot on US soil at Jersey City. Gerry Smies' account in 1942 mirrored that of Rev. Koeppe, but she concluded her interview with the *Sheboygan Press* by recalling:

> What a thrill we all experienced as the Statue of Liberty came into view! At the time, some of the passengers were eating and some were on the decks, but all stood with hats off and sang first *America* and then the *Star-Spangled Banner*. I am sure I express the feeling of all on board when I say that we are all very happy to be back in the good old United States, our home![12]

Gerry Smies' older sister, Lillian (1924), also chose a career of service as a missionary. She obtained her nursing degree in Chicago and worked in Sheboygan for five years but did not feel challenged

---

12 "Missionary Described Internment by Japanese," *Sheboygan Press* (30 Sept. 1942).

by her job. Meanwhile, Hope College had received a letter that the Christian Medical College and Hospital in Vellore, India, was looking for a nurse, and a few months later, Lillian set sail for India. She was the assistant nursing superintendent at the hospital and was instrumental in assisting in the treatment of leprosy. The school of nursing there was the first to have a degree program. She served in that capacity from 1939 to 1972, and in an interview in 1981, she stated:

> If I was asked tomorrow to do it again, I would, because I gained so many things of importance that India does for the people who visit there, whether it be for weeks, months, or even years. And one of the most important things is that it makes you reflect on who you really are—making you search for your own true identity.[13]

It seems fitting that, after her years of service, on a return trip to India in 1997, Lillian Smies passed away in Vellore. According to her wishes, she was buried there. Six Indian nurses who had known her for fifty years served as pallbearers, wearing white nursing saris. Smies was buried near Ida Scudder and others who had long associations with the Christian Medical College.

Everdene Kuyper (1919) attended the academy during the tenure of her father (Rev. Cornelius Kuyper) as pastor of the First Reformed Church in Cedar Grove, from 1911 to 1934. After graduation from the academy, she attended Hope College and then returned to teach at the academy for four years. During her years at Hope, she met Garrett de Jong of Orange City, Iowa. When Everdene and Garrett were married in 1925, the entire congregation of First Reformed Church in Cedar Grove attended the wedding. In 1926 the couple set sail to begin their mission work in Arabia. When they returned on furlough in 1932, about twelve hundred people from the Cedar Grove church and the surrounding communities welcomed them home. Rev. De Jong assumed the pastorate of First Reformed Church from 1933 to 1938, and then the couple resumed their mission work in Kuwait. During a furlough in 1955, they were interviewed about their work. The *Holland Sentinel* reported:

> During recent years, they have been faced with unusual responsibilities and opportunities. A large income from oil royalties allowed by its benevolent ruler to the development of

---

[13] "Missionary Nurse Would Serve Again," *Sheboygan Press* (24 April 1981).

the town for the public benefit has brought hordes of foreigners to Kuwait—including thousands of Christian groups [sic] which still persist—Syrians, Jacobites, Armenians, and many others of different nationalities. In addition to work among the Arabs, the De Jongs have been attempting to give to these many disperate [sic] groups the necessary Christian leadership. Rev. De Jong built the first Christian church in that part of the Mesopotamian world.[14]

The article also stated that their son, Conrad Keith, was the first American boy born in Kuwait.

Florence Walvoord (1913) attended Hope College and after graduation returned to teach at the academy from 1918 to 1921. Florence's distinguished uncle, Anthony Walvoord, had been a missionary in Japan for many years, until his untimely death in 1919.[15] Following in his footsteps, Florence joined the mission team in Japan in 1922 and served the Baiko Girls School there until 1940. Baiko Jo Gakuin was founded by the RCA in Shimonoseki on the main island of Honshu. During a furlough in 1936, Florence received her master's degree from Columbia University, and when World War II severely interrupted mission work in Japan, Florence shifted her work to India for four years. She returned to Japan in 1947 and served at the Sturgis Seminary in Shimonoseki until 1960. That same year, she was awarded the Order of the Sacred Treasure. This award was established by Emperor Meiji in 1888 for both civil and military merit. In his account of the Japan mission, I. John Hesselink honored Walvoord: "This gracious and devout lady had a powerful Christian impact on young women."[16]

Edna Van De Vrede (1910) chose to serve in Native American Missions for the RCA. In an article on the Reformed Church's mission to Native Americans, E. O'Brock referred admiringly to "the renowned 'Four Misses' of Dulce who contributed 123 combined years of service . . . Hendrina Hospers (1907-46), Edna Van De Vrede (1920-54), Marie Van Vuren (1929-59), and Gertrude Van Roekel (1937-57)."[17] Miss Van

---

[14] "De Jongs Returning to Arabian Mission Field, "*Holland Evening Sentinel* (7 Sept. 1955).
[15] Rev. H. V. S. Peeke, "Sketch of the Japan Mission," Board of Foreign Missions, RCA (1922).
[16] I. J. Hesselink, "Reformed Church Witness in Japan: A Brief History," *The Reformed Review* (2002): 102.
[17] E. O. Brock, "Reformed Church—Native American Missions, Part 1," *The Fourth Focus* (Nov/Dec 2016).

De Vrede wrote numerous articles for the *Church Herald* during the later years of her service.

Rev. John W. Koning (1923) and his wife, Mildred Te Ronde (1925), chose Cameroon, West Africa, for their mission work. Rev. Koning studied at Carroll College in Wisconsin and Princeton Theological Seminary. Mrs. Koning received her nursing degree from Lutheran Hospital in Milwaukee, and they served in Cameroon from 1930 to 1934. On their return, they pastored Presbyterian churches in Wisconsin and Iowa. Rev. Koning also served as a chaplain during World War II.

Those who chose the ministry moved among numerous churches throughout the United States. One notable exception to this practice was M. Eugene Flipse (1912). Although Flipse was born in Albany, New York, his father chose to send him to the Wisconsin Memorial Academy in Cedar Grove for his education. After receiving his divinity degree at New Brunswick Theological Seminary in 1920 and serving two congregations in New Jersey for one year, Rev. Flipse accepted a position at the Douglaston Community Church in Long Island, New York. Flipse served this congregation from 1921 to 1965. The tradition of service to the RCA in the Flipse family has continued with his granddaughter Adrienne Flipse Hausch, who joined the pastoral staff at Douglaston Community Church in 1995.

Academics, educators, and visionaries

Roger Voskuyl (1928) went on to graduate from Hope in 1932 and got his MA and PhD in chemistry from Harvard University in 1938. He had spent his youth assisting his physician father, Dr. Anthony Voskuyl, on house calls. Roger went on to teach at Wheaton College, where he became a prominent professor and was considered an influence on the young Billy Graham. His PhD dissertation led to his invitation to be a group leader on the Manhattan Project, which developed the atomic bomb. He took a two-year leave of absence from Wheaton to work on the project at Columbia University, and he was one of seven people originally from Sheboygan County to work on the Manhattan Project.

In 1950 Voskuyl was recruited to be the president of Westmont College in Santa Barbara, California. Westmont was a failing institution at that time. In the previous decade, two presidents and two interim presidents had come and gone. Almost half of the faculty had resigned in early 1950; student enrollment was down, and the college was in debt. Voskuyl is credited with saving Westmont. A story in *Westmont*

Magazine attests to this fact in a eulogy given by professor emeritus Paul Wilt on the occasion of Voskuyl's death:

> We can say with confidence that in the sovereignty of God, Dr. Roger Voskuyl, with others, "saved" Westmont. He achieved many things in his 18 years as president. He stabilized and then rebuilt the faculty. He reversed the decline in student enrollment and built it to a high of 700 when he resigned. The college received accreditation in 1958. He presided over a building campaign that led to the construction of four dormitories, a dining commons, lecture hall, library, physical education complex, health center, and others. College assets increased from $500,000 to $10 million. It would be hard to overstate the importance of Roger Voskuyl in the history of Westmont.[18]

Robert Voskuil[19] (1933) received his degrees from the University of Wisconsin-Madison and Syracuse University. After the Pearl Harbor attack in 1941, the Office of the Coordinator of Information (COI)[20] rapidly expanded its newly formed cartographer division. Voskuil was the first person hired by new director Arthur Robinson. There were no cartographers as we know them today at that time. Robinson and Voskuil recruited geographers with an interest in mapping, and they all learned on the job. The COI's cartography division produced strategic maps and military operational plans for Naval Intelligence, the Office of Strategic Services (the precursor to the CIA), and the War Department. Following the war, Voskuil spent thirty-one years with the CIA.

John Abbink (1908) continued his education at Hope College and then joined General Electric, where he developed the international operations of the company. After spending time in Argentina, he joined McGraw-Hill Publishing in New York in 1922. By 1947 he was president and director of international operations and held this position until 1957. In his early years at McGraw-Hill, he was instrumental in the development of Business Publishers International Corp., the foreign affiliate of the company. Because of his long involvement in foreign trade affairs, he was asked to be an advisor at the organization of the

---

[18] "Remembers Roger Voskuyl," *Westmont Magazine* (Fall 2005).
[19] "Voskuyl" and "Voskuil" are alternate spellings adopted by different branches of the same family.
[20] On 11 July 1941, FDR established the first peacetime, nondepartmental US intelligence organization, the Office of the Coordinator of Information (COI), and authorized it to collect and analyze all information and data relevant to national security.

United Nations in San Francisco in 1945. He also served as chairman of the National Foreign Trade Council from 1945 to 1949.

Harvey Ramaker (1913) also went on to study at Hope and then embarked on an impressive forty-four-year career at the Country Day School in Milwaukee (MCDS). Country Day was a boys' school founded in 1917. Ramaker taught English and Latin, was the school's first athletic director, and served as headmaster. According to historian A. G. Santer:

> Some students came from families who had sent them to MCDS to be "shaped by Harvey Ramaker," an imposing figure by any standard. Ramaker's voice was as imposing as his towering appearance, and students would find that not getting 100 meant staying after school to make up the grade. A mark of 90 or 95 was not considered acceptable.[21]

Ramaker was also a long-time spiritual leader at Country Day. He took the model of his academy education and transferred it to another institution.

William Verhage (1924) was one of the three students from Sheboygan who attended the academy and boarded in Cedar Grove. Born in the Netherlands, he recalled, "At the age of three, I nearly lost my life in the moat surrounding the city of Middelburg."[22] His family emigrated when he was six years of age; he was forced to begin working at age fourteen and did not enter the academy until he was twenty, but this was not a deterrent to his education. After one year at Hope College, he transferred to Lawrence College in Appleton, Wisconsin. With an excellent academic record, he graduated magna cum laude and won election to Phi Beta Kapa. He received master's degrees from both Oberlin College and Columbia University and a PhD from the University of Minnesota. He also served as a lieutenant commander in the US Naval Reserve and was deputy chief of the military government on Palau Islands. During his tenure teaching economics and political science at Macalester College in St. Paul, Minnesota, he was given the chance to do further studies in China and Japan. The *Winona Republican Herald* reported that "He was at Shanghai at the outbreak of hostilities between China and Japan and was one of those bombed by mistake

---

+ A. G. Santer, "The Squire, the Masters, and their belief in Great Boys," *Whitefish Bay School History* (1996).
22 "W.S.T.C. Notes," *Winona Republican Herald* (20 Jan. 1947).

by Chinese planes."[23] He continued his career as dean of the college at Winona State University in Minnesota and as a political science professor at Boston University.

One family in particular played an important role in the history of Wisconsin Memorial Academy, the family of Anthony and Wilhelmina Lubbers. Like many of his generation in rural Sheboygan County, Anthony was a farmer.[24] Of his ten children, seven graduated from the academy between 1904 and 1923. Anthony's father, Arend, was the one responsible for donating the land for the principal's residence. Jennie Lubbers (1904) and her husband, Anthony Haverkamp (1904), graduated with the first class at the academy, and both attended Hope College. After his graduation from Western Theological Seminary, they served sixteen years at Central Reformed Church in Sioux Center, Iowa, and twenty-three years at First Reformed Church in Pella. Rev. Haverkamp was noted for preaching in Dutch at synod meetings well into the 1920s.

Raymond J. Lubbers (1910)[25] attended Hope College and then taught at Northwestern Academy from 1914 to 1916, before obtaining his divinity degree from Western Theological Seminary. After a six-year pastorate at the Archer Reformed Church in Archer, Iowa, he returned to his Wisconsin roots and served the First Reformed Church in Sheboygan Falls for thirty-four years. His classical education and Dutch classes at the academy served him well, since First Reformed alternated Dutch and English services every week into the 1920s. By 1931 Dutch services were held only once a month, and by 1938, the last service in Dutch had been conducted.

Elmer H. Lubbers (1916) furthered his education at Ripon College in Wisconsin and became a teacher. He served as superintendent of schools in Mauston and Oostburg and spent twelve years as superintendent of the Zeeland, Michigan, schools. In 1944 he stepped down from his educational commitments to take a position with the Public Welfare Department of the state of Wisconsin.

[23] Ibid.
[24] Anthony's father, Arend, was born in Vorden, Gelderland, in 1825, and emigrated in 1847. He was married three times, and he requested to not be buried with any of his wives. His request was granted. Although Arend and his siblings were baptized in the Dutch Reformed Church in Aalten, oral history in the Lubbers family states that they were actually Catholic. When Arend emigrated, he could not find a Catholic church; he began attending a Dutch Reformed Church and later converted.
[25] Not to be confused with Raymond C. Lubbers, pastor of the Gibbsville Reformed Church, 1936-54, who also had a brother named Melvin.

Irwin J. Lubbers (1913) is likely the most well-known of the family. After graduating from Hope College in 1917, he served with the US Air Force before setting off for the Reformed Church Mission in Vellore, India, to teach English at Voorhees College. On his return, he taught English at Hope College and obtained his master's degree at Columbia and his PhD at Northwestern University. He served as president of Central College from 1934 to 1945, and then returned to Holland to assume the presidency of Hope College, a position he held until 1963. He was made an officer in the Order of Orange Nassau from the Netherlands in 1947 and received a Freedom Foundation award in 1953. Irwin Lubbers' legacy of leadership in higher education was passed to his son Arend Donselaar (Don) Lubbers. In 1960, at age twenty-nine, Arend Lubbers became the youngest college president appointed at Central College. He served there until 1969, when he became president of Grand Valley State University, a position he held until 2001.

Harold Lubbers (1918) continued his education at Hope College and initially chose a similar path in education, teaching in Illinois, Missouri, and Wisconsin. Subsequently, he pursued a career as an executive at American Can Co. in Waukegan, Illinois, and Springfield, Missouri. Harold registered for the draft in World War I, and at age forty-two, registered for service in World War II.

Clarence W. Lubbers (1921) graduated from Hope and the University of Michigan before becoming a high school teacher. He also served as the principal of the high school in Grandville, Michigan, for thirteen years and as superintendent of schools in Plainwell, Michigan, for sixteen years.

Melvin B. Lubbers (1923) also graduated from Hope and held the position of superintendent of four different Michigan school districts for over thirty-seven years.

Elmer, Harold, Irwin, and their older brother William all served in World War I, but William died during the Spanish flu epidemic while serving in France. Their older brother, Arthur, also registered for World War I, but did not serve. His missing three fingers on his left hand may have been grounds for an exemption. At age fifty-four, like his brother, Harold, he registered for World War II. Arthur chose not to attend the academy and was employed as the manager and secretary of Cedar Grove Milk Co. and later as a salesman in Sheboygan.

Elaine Lubbers (1933) was the eldest daughter of Arthur Lubbers and Kathryn Huenink. Although her father did not choose the same path as his siblings, the family legacy continued into another generation.

Elaine did her undergraduate degree at the University of Wisconsin-Madison and her master of social work degree at Case Western Reserve University. She joined the Department of Health and Social Services in Green Bay, Wisconsin, and spent thirty years as the supervisor of adoptions. She specialized in hard-to-place and Native American children and was known throughout the state for her dedication to these children.

Elaine Lubbers is just one of many female academy graduates who made a significant contribution in their chosen fields in decades where the education of women and their having careers outside of marriage was not encouraged. Among their ranks are scores of teachers, nurses, missionaries, and ministers' wives. Ministers' wives, in particular, were rarely acknowledged for the contributions they made to their husbands' careers and the culture and stability of the churches they served.

Even the few graduates highlighted here give one an indication of the brain drain that occurred in this community. Many of the best were drawn to Michigan and Iowa and beyond, simply because there were no church-affiliated colleges in Wisconsin. Some came back, but the percentage was not significant. The aspirations and accomplishments of the other graduates, however, are no less exemplary or important. Bankers, businessmen, farmers, and teachers helped create stable and prosperous communities. The Depression ultimately fostered the demise of the academy. The classis and churches no longer had the resources to support it, so it closed its doors in 1937 and became a public high school.

The words of Willard Grotenhuis (1932) in his valedictorian speech are an indication of what the academy stood for and how it influenced generations beyond its closing. This portion of his speech offers a fitting conclusion to the present history of the Wisconsin Memorial Academy:

> Now as we are about to begin a more thorough preparation for our life work, we find ourselves in a world stricken by depression. If we haven't much to live on, we at least have much to live for. We are going forth ready to work with our fellowmen for the welfare not only of the individual but also of the whole social group. For that alone is worthwhile which offers the greatest good for the greatest number. We are launching out realizing that it is more important to make a life than to make a living.[26]

---

[26] Personal papers of Willard Grotenhuis, shared with the author by his family.

CHAPTER 4

Christian Education in the Calumet Region: A Pictorial Memoir[1]

Ken Bult

The Calumet region

Any discussion of the Calumet, Illinois, region must begin with a brief history of early immigrants. Although not as well known as its more popular cousins (Pella, IA, and Holland, MI), the Calumet region was settled at the same time as these regions. The first Dutch settlers in the Calumet region were Hendrik De Jong, his wife, Geertje, and their twelve children. They had arrived in America on April 27, 1847, and lived near Holland for about two months. At some point, Hendrik decided to leave Michigan and go to Wisconsin. The reason is lost to time.

Hendrik built a raft for the family possessions, and the family walked south along the shore of Lake Michigan, dragging the raft behind them, until they came to the mouth of the Calumet River. They followed the river inland until they came to the area that is now called

---

[1] [The following essay by photo journalist Ken Bult provides a vivid portrayal of the types of Reformed schools and their settings that dotted the Midwest landscape in the late nineteenth and early twentieth centuries. Along with their churches, Dutch immigrants planted schools, a notable legacy of their commitments and hopes.–Eds.]

83

Hendrik De Jong
(*courtesy South Holland Historical Society*)

South Holland, Illinois. In the summer of 1847, Hendrik purchased three hundred acres along the Little Calumet River and built a home. He never reached Wisconsin.

Another early settler in the Calumet region was the Widow Paarlberg. In 1847 the widow's ship was blown off course on its way to Holland, Michigan. She ended up in Chicago and went on to buy eighty acres of land on Thorn Creek, a branch of the Little Calumet River that runs along the southern rim of present-day South Holland. Paarlberg is also known for the famous misrepresentation of her in Edna Ferber's 1925 Pulitzer Prize-winning novel, *So Big*, in which she was the model for the lead character, Selina Peake DeJong. Other towns settled by the Dutch in this region include Lansing, Illinois, and Munster and Highland, Indiana.

Munster [Indiana] and Lansing [Illinois] Christian Schools

Once the Dutch had settled in the region, they quickly established their churches, and it was not long before the desire for Christian education began to grow. The Society for Christian Instruction of North Township, Lake County, Indiana, was incorporated in December 1907. They were set up to oversee Munster Christian School, built on the corner of Ridge Road and Hohman Avenue using cement blocks

Munster Christian School (*courtesy Munster Historical Society*)

that the society members had made themselves. The first classes were held on September 16, 1907, with fifty-six children attending the two-room schoolhouse. Two additional classrooms were added in 1914.

In the 1930s, the town of Munster decided to extend Hohman Avenue south of Ridge Road. This municipal improvement would leave very little space for any expansion of the school. Due to the expectation of higher enrollment, it was decided to build a new school on another tract of land in nearby Lansing, Illinois, purchased in 1924 in anticipation of such a problem. In 1942 a new and larger building opened in Lansing, and the name was changed to Lansing Christian School. The building has been expanded several times since 1942.[2]

Highland [Indiana] Christian School

Before Highland Christian School was founded, Highland, Indiana, students made the daily trip down Ridge Road to the Munster Christian School. Ridge Road was not the smooth, four-lane street one would find today. In the early part of the twentieth century, it was a rutted, dirt road, where one's ability to navigate changed with

[2] http://www.lansingchristian.org/explore/history.cfm; accessed 22 March 2019.

John Van der Zee (*left*), principal at the Highland Christian School, listens as Martin Van Dyke, pastor of the Highland Reformed Church, speaks at the groundbreaking for a new school building at 3040 Ridge Road in Highland, Indiana, 1950 (*courtesy Highland Historical Society*)

the weather. Highland Christian School was founded in 1909, and its governing board was formally incorporated on January 10, 1910, as the Association for Christian Instruction at Highland. The first building occupied by the school was a wooden church structure located on Jewett Street that had been converted for school use. A four-room, two-story brick building located on Highway Avenue was erected to serve as the first true school building.[3]

Highland Christian School added a ninth grade to their curriculum in 1936 and a tenth grade in 1940. The current building, first put in use early in 1951, is located right off Ridge Road. The building has been expanded several times since the 1950s.

South Holland [Illinois] Christian School/Calvin Christian School

South Holland Christian School was dedicated on March 19, 1912, and opened its doors to students in September 1913. The first school building consisted of two rooms, in which twenty students and one teacher met. In 1914 the original building was lifted up, and

---

[3] https://www.highlandchristian.org/about-us/our-history/; accessed 30 April 2019.

The "new" Highland school building as it looked soon after completion in 1951 (*courtesy Highland Historical Society*)

a new brick and concrete first floor was built underneath it. In 1917 the school was closed for a short time due to a smallpox epidemic. The year 1921 saw the introduction of Dutch-language classes for the advanced students. A special School Society meeting was held in 1942, the result of which was that the school starting time was changed from 9:00 a.m. to 9:30 a.m. The reason for this change was that, due to other obligations, the owner of the school bus was unable to transport the children to school by nine o'clock. As the student body continued to grow, plans were made for a new building. In 1947 a new building was completed at the school's present location, just north of US Route 6, and the school's name was changed to Calvin Christian School.[4]

Illiana Christian High School[5]

Before the opening of Illiana Christian High School in the border town of Lansing, Illinois, the few students who wanted secondary education commuted about twenty miles to Chicago Christian High School at Seventy-Second Place and Loomis in the Englewood neighborhood of Chicago. As more Calumet-area young people elected to attend high school, some parents found boarding for their children near Chicago Christian, while others banded together to provide transportation back and forth every day.

---

[4] http://www.calvinschool.org/community-alumni/history-of-calvin-christian-school.cfm; accessed 17 May 2019.

[5] "Illiana" is an amalgam of "Illinois" and "Indiana," used to refer to the border towns to the east of the Calumet region.

South Holland Christian School
(*courtesy South Holland Historical Society*)

After much discussion, a meeting of representatives from the five Reformed and five Christian Reformed churches in the Calumet region was held, and a fact-finding committee was formed. Having completed their research, the committee called a meeting on January 19, 1944, at the Munster Christian Reformed Church. Based on their report, the Illiana Christian High School Association was organized with each of the ten churches being represented by an elected board member forming the first Illiana board.

The board had some heavy lifting in front of them. They had to find a suitable site for a new high school and raise funds to purchase the land. At the same time, they were looking to secure temporary classrooms and a teaching staff. At first, classes met in two rooms in the Lansing Christian School and in the basement of the Lansing Christian Reformed Church, with Cornelius Van Beek serving as principal. In the fall of 1946, classes met in two barracks at the former Civil Conservation Corps camp in the Thornton Forest Preserve. The board was allowed to make improvements in order to convert the barracks into classrooms. A student body of 135 filled the six classrooms in one barrack, and the additional barrack was used for recreational purposes. Originally,

Illiana Christian High School (*photo by author*)

September 1947 was announced as the opening of the new building just off of Ridge Road on a piece of land known as Bock's Field, but construction delays led to a January 7, 1948, opening date.

With several additions over the years, the Lansing building served the community well, but in 2018, after years of planning, Illiana Christian High School moved from the building in Lansing that had been its home for seventy years into the new $28 million school that replaced it, located on a forty-acre site at the southwest corner of 109th Street and Calumet Avenue in Hanover Township, Indiana. This location is known locally as "shoe corner," for reasons unknown.[6]

Protestant Reformed Christian School and Heritage Christian High School (Hanover Township)

Right down the road from the new Illiana building in Hanover Township are Protestant Reformed Christian School and Heritage Christian High School. The two schools are a stone's throw away from each other. Not that they do that anymore. The K-8 Protestant Reformed Christian School began life as the South Holland Protestant Reformed Christian School and was one of the three charter members

[6] https://www.illianachristian.org/about/our-history-and-mission/; accessed 8 March 2019.

of the Federation of Protestant Reformed Christian Schools. The other charter members of the federation were Adams Christian in Wyoming, Michigan, and Hope Christian in Redland, California. The present building opened its doors in 1996. The Crete Protestant Reformed Church (formerly South Holland Protestant Reformed Church) located in Crete, Illinois, serves as a major feeder church for the school.[7]

The basis for a Reformed Christian education in the Calumet region, specifically, and in North America, in general, can be summed up in a quote from Dutch American history scholar Henry Lucas: "The theory behind the Christian schools deserves attention. These schools are maintained by Christian parents who, at their children's baptism, have taken on an obligation to bring them up in the Christian faith."[8] Lucas continues: "'The Christian home, the Christian church, and the Christian school constitute the triumvirate to which the training of our covenant youth must be entrusted. This chain ought never to be broken.'"[9]

---

[7] http://www.prccrete.org/Who-We-Are.html; accessed 2 June 2019.
[8] Henry S. Lucas, *Netherlanders in America* (Ann Arbor: University of Michigan Press, 1955), 602.
[9] Quote from the *Banner*, 25 April 1947, in Lucas, *Netherlanders in America*, 602.

CHAPTER 5

Cultivating a Community, Expanding a Church: Religion and Immigrant Education on the Frontier

Andrew Klumpp

"The object of this Incorporation shall be to establish an Institution of learning for the promotion of Science and Literature in harmony with, and Religion as expressed in, the Doctrinal Standards of the Reformed Church in America and to exercise such other and incidental powers as are granted to corporations for Educational and Religious purposes."[1]

On May 15, 1888, six years after the formal incorporation of Northwestern Classical Academy in Orange City, Iowa, John H. Karsten addressed a gathering of the Western Social Conference of the Reformed Church in America (RCA) in Grand Rapids, Michigan. The soon-to-be editor of Holland, Michigan's, *De Hope* presented a talk entitled "Our Educational Institutions." In his address, he identified a trio of aims that informed the RCA's educational endeavors in the West. First, educational institutions "should be the intellectual

---

[1] *Constitution and By-Laws of the Board of Trustees of the Northwestern Classical Academy*, 19 July 1882, Northwestern Classical Academy Collection, Northwestern College Archives.

laboratory where the latent mental forces are called out. The student should there discover what immense possibilities dwell within him."[2] Schools, Karsten argued, should direct young pupils to God, instill sound morals, and encourage a life of worship. These efforts would contribute richly to the growth and development of Dutch churches and communities in the West. Second, "The schools should be the pride of the churches, the centers around which rally their fondest hopes and expectations." In addition, Karsten noted, they "should [be] root[ed] in the affections, love, and sympathies of the masses as much as the local church."[3] Finally, "The establishment of educational centers in the Western States has for its final object the redemption of men from obedience to self to obedience to their creator. . . . Colonization, without college, seminary and academy would simply be to invite failure of the object in view."[4] The RCA's educational development in the West needed to be hubs of community, church, and missionary zeal.

In his address, Karsten outlined three clear goals of education: (1) cultivating upright and godly citizens, (2) equipping the community for prosperous external relations, and (3) evangelizing others throughout the world. And although he was speaking in West Michigan, his vision extended to new institutions like Northwestern Classical Academy in the far reaches of the Dutch colonies in Iowa.[5] In fact, his articulation of the vision for RCA education in the West echoed much of the rhetoric employed by the founders of Northwestern earlier in the decade. Themes of service to the local community and region, support of the church's growth and vibrancy, and the ability to evangelize and influence people throughout the world peppered articles in the *Sioux County Herald* and *De Volksvriend* and reports to and from the RCA's General Synod in the early 1880s. Northwestern fit squarely within this articulation of the denomination's educational vision, and in doing so, it aimed to extend its influence far beyond the community's own boundaries. Orange City never intended to be an isolated, immigrant backwater but instead harbored visions of extending its influence throughout the region and even the globe. In the early settlers' vision, Northwestern

---

[2] John H. Karsten, "Our Educational Institutions," unpublished speech, 15 May 1888, box 1, John H. Karsten, W88-060, Joint Archives of Holland (JAH).
[3] Ibid.
[4] Ibid.
[5] Throughout this chapter, references to Northwestern refer exclusively to Northwestern Classical Academy and not to the later junior and four-year manifestations of the academy.

Classical Academy played a foundational role in realizing these broader ambitions.

At one level, this chapter argues that the founders of Northwestern positioned their new school within the broader project of Dutch immigration, education, and the RCA's efforts to expand westward. Although much of the scholarship about the development of Christian schools within the Dutch immigrant community focuses on the day schools built by the Christian Reformed Church (CRC), this chapter examines how members of the RCA argued in favor of building a school on the frontier, identifying which arguments ultimately proved to be persuasive to supporters and the RCA's General Synod.

At another level, this discussion contributes to developing conversations in the fields of agricultural history and Midwestern and American religious history that challenge the interpretation of nineteenth-century rural communities as isolated backwaters with little interest in events taking place beyond their own communities' boundaries.[6] A careful reading of the sources that discuss Northwestern's early years reveals that the academy certainly aimed to serve the local community, but even more broadly, it also endeavored to engage the church and its mission throughout the world. In keeping with Karsten's vision, the RCA's educational institutions focused well beyond their immediate surroundings.

Schools and the development of Sioux County, Iowa

Schools formed a central pillar of Dutch immigrant life in the United States. The schools, colleges, and seminaries that these immigrants established after their arrival drew from the Dutch community's rich religious traditions and often fell under the purview of church and municipal leaders.[7] Schools went hand in hand with religion. In an 1874 article in *De Volksvriend*, Henry Hospers made this clear as he offered a brief history of the Sioux County colony. Due to the land squeeze in Pella and other Dutch colonies, Hospers feared that Dutch immigrants were likely to send future generations into non-Dutch settlements to attain property. To avoid this, he led a band of settlers farther onto the frontier to ensure that they could continue

---

[6] See, for example, Kristin Hoganson, *The Heartland: An American History* (NY: Penguin, 2019), and Tisa Wenger, *Religious Freedom: The History of a Contested American Ideal* (Chapel Hill: UNC Press, 2018).

[7] Eugene Heideman, *Hendrik P. Scholte: His Legacy in the Netherlands and in America* (Grand Rapids, MI: Eerdmans, 2015), 218.

to cultivate communities centered on their religious and educational institutions. He proclaimed that these earliest arrivals to Sioux County dreamed of developing their new community "under the shadow of the church and school."[8] Although this likely reflected other educational schemes afoot during the mid-1870s, the coupling of the church and school reflected a sentiment that persisted in Sioux County. In the lead-up to the formal establishment of Northwestern, newspapers, letters, and church documents frequently referred to the church and school paired together.

Northwestern's boosters also deftly positioned the new academy as a boon for a variety of constituencies. Throughout the 1870s, plagues of locusts, crop failures, and nation-wide financial stress thwarted early attempts to establish a local academy, to the great disappointment of the community.[9] When the RCA put out a call for the establishment of more academies in 1882, the community in Orange City took up the charge with vigor.[10] By July of 1882, a constitution and bylaws had been approved, and the wheels had started turning for the formation of the new school. Reflecting the close relationship between the church and school, religious and community leaders made up the board, and the charter made Northwestern's Dutch Reformed commitments clear. It was to be "an Institution of learning for the promotion of Science and Literature in harmony with . . . the Doctrinal Standards" of the RCA.[11] According to the founders, this school, like other Dutch academies, offered a distinctively Reformed education for young men and women and promised to be a significant benefit to the community and to the church, both local and universal.

Serving the community

Heralding the benefits of the newfound academy in *De Volksvriend* one week before the formal adoption of its constitution and bylaws, Hospers highlighted Northwestern's benefits for the community. He wrote:

---

[8] Henry Hospers, "Eene beknopte geschiedenis van de vestiging der Hollandsche Kolonie in Sioux County, Iowa," *De Volksvriend*, 25 June 1874. Translations from Dutch are my own unless otherwise noted.
[9] Gerald De Jong, *From Strength to Strength: A History of Northwestern, 1882-1982* (Grand Rapids, MI: Eerdmans, 1982), 15.
[10] Ibid., 16.
[11] *Constitution and By-Laws*.

Those who wanted their sons or pupils to be educated in the higher sciences were forced to send them immediately after leaving primary school to places at a great distance, where they usually have to be wholly among strangers and, against all intentions, a bit of a "temptation" to get rid of the authentic old Dutch character and to be Americanized very soon.[12]

Now, he promised, the academy stood to serve a need in the community. It kept young people closer to their families and guarded the traditions and culture prized by these Dutch settlers. Northwestern promised to continue to cultivate a distinctively Dutch tradition in the next generation and, simply, to keep families together.

Beyond the immediate community in Sioux County, Northwestern offered a particular service to the Dutch Reformed communities strewn throughout the region, a region that they referred to as the Northwest. Hospers boasted, "Sioux County is and will, we believe, remain the middle of the Dutch in the West."[13] A stalwart booster for his colony in northwest Iowa, he gushed about Orange City's accessibility via the railroad and its promising agricultural and economic prospects. He assured readers that Sioux County itself could attract a large number of younger people to the academy. Yet, he also emphasized that its proximity to the Dutch communities that were spreading into Minnesota, portions of the Dakota Territory, and Nebraska would surely help enrollments.[14] Northwestern Academy sat in the center of the nation's frontier and held the potential to become the hub for the region's Dutch population.

Northwestern's early promoters touted its potential to provide an army of teachers for proximate Dutch and non-Dutch communities. In his report to the 1883 General Synod of the RCA, Ale Buursma, then the pastor of Orange City's First Reformed Church and a member of Northwestern's board of trustees, lamented the lack of teachers for schools in Sioux County and particularly the fact that many of the community's teachers were Roman Catholic.[15] He explained to Synod that the region was primarily Reformed, with a sprinkling of German

---

[12] Henry Hospers, "De Academie," *De Volksvriend*, 13 July 1882.
[13] Ibid.
[14] Ibid.
[15] Ale Buursma, "To the Synod convened at Albany, June 6, 1883," *The Acts and Proceedings of the Seventy-Seventh General Synod of the Reformed Church in America*, 6 June 1883 (NY: Board of Publication, RCA, 1883), 308.

Catholics and English Presbyterians in the nearby town of Hospers. Nevertheless, it lacked qualified teachers within the Dutch population, which forced settlers to employ outsiders to educate their youth.[16] The establishment of Northwestern, Buursma explained, would now "be a means of supplying our common schools with such teachers as might again become an influence for good to the Church and to the School."[17] He noted that the same dearth of teachers persisted in communities beyond these Dutch settlements and reminded Synod that the education of teachers to serve in schools throughout the region presented the church with an excellent opportunity to reach out beyond their own communities.[18] By this calculus, the role of the teacher as missionary was not confined to foreign missions.

Within the broader regional context, Northwestern also emerged alongside a rival academy in the neighboring community of Calliope. The history of Orange City and Calliope is a colorful one, complete with electoral malfeasance, a surprise raid by a disgruntled band of Dutchmen, and the consolidation of Dutch control of Sioux County in the early 1870s.[19] Because of growing Dutch dominance in the region, the citizens of Calliope held a grudge, which is most obvious in barbs traded in newspaper articles that appeared for decades after the initial scuffle.[20] One year after Northwestern's formal incorporation in 1882, the Calliope *Independent* announced the opening of Calliope's own academy on October 1, 1883, and trumpeted its educational offerings for the region.[21]

For over a decade, the Dutch had cast themselves as the moral counterweight to their debauched neighbors. They maintained that Calliope officials engaged in financial malfeasance that lined their own pockets at the county's expense prior to the Dutch settlers' arrival in the 1870s. With Calliope Academy ascendant nearby, Northwestern no longer simply offered educational opportunities to Dutch and non-Dutch students. It served as a bulwark against the rival and—

[16] Hospers, "De Academie."
[17] Buursma, "To the Synod," 308.
[18] Ibid.
[19] See Andrew Klumpp, "Colony Before Party: The Ethnic Origins of Sioux County's Political Tradition," *Annals of Iowa* 77, no. 1 (Jan. 2020): 1-35.
[20] "The Holland Conquest of Sioux County," *The Sioux County Herald*, 5 Oct. 1887. This story originated in the *Silverton Democrat* in Silverton, Colorado, whose publisher had previously published the *Sioux County Herald* and resided in Calliope. It also ran directly opposite of the Dutch account, "Sioux County! The Fairest Land Under the Sun."
[21] "Local Siftings," *The Independent* (Calliope, IA), 4 Oct. 1884.

from the Dutch immigrants' perspective—inferior vision of the county being offered by their traditional foes next door. Much like in their early political squabbles, the Dutch prevailed in this duel between academies. Within a decade, not only the academy but also the entire community of Calliope disappeared as populations moved, and the nearby community of Hawarden annexed what was left of the Sioux County Dutch immigrants' traditional adversaries.

Hospers—the primary foe of the Calliope crowd—did not hide his ambitions for Northwestern. At the conclusion of his 1882 article, "De Academie" in *De Volksvriend*, he remarked, "Let us live in peace, and . . . as a powerful Dutch element, [we] can exercise an unprecedented influence in the religious, educational and social spheres."[22] The academy, in his view, played a critical role in the consolidation and exercise of Dutch influence in the region. Northwestern ensured that the next generation stayed close to home and clung to Dutch traditions. It positioned Orange City as a hub for Dutch communities throughout the Northwest, drew in pupils from non-Dutch communities, and equipped Dutch teachers to take over non-Dutch schools. And it also provided a continued check on Orange City's pesky neighbors. In these ways, the founding of Northwestern was about not just a local community but also Dutch and non-Dutch communities well beyond Sioux County.

Serving the church

As Hospers' early writings made clear, the founders of Northwestern envisioned a school that served the community and the church. It was not all politics, schoolhouses, and irritating neighbors. Early advocates for Northwestern envisioned the academy as a valuable endeavor for the church—for the RCA specifically and for the global church. For the RCA, Northwestern would stand as an outpost as the denomination grew in the West. In his 1883 report to General Synod, Buursma stated: "We feel and have felt for some time that such an institution, under the control of our Church, is important for the education of our youth not only, but also indispensable for the extension of our Church in the further [sic] West."[23] In Buursma's words, the early settlers rooted their educational endeavors in their hopes for future growth of the church.

Two years later, the RCA's Committee on Christian Education echoed Buursma's words as it identified the centrality of Northwestern

---

[22] Henry Hospers, "Hope College Gered," *De Volksvriend*, 19 Jan. 1882.
[23] Buursma, "To the Synod," 307-8.

for the extension of the denomination into the frontier. In its report on Northwestern, the Committee on Christian Education noted, "If our Church is to live, it must grow. If it is to grow, its greatest increase must be along the frontier. If it is to hold its own even on the frontier, it must hold and provide for the rising generation."[24] In no uncertain terms, the key to the church's extension rested in the stability of churches and schools and in the cultivation of the next generation. As its westernmost institution, the denomination viewed Northwestern as a crucial outpost. To that end, it was not simply a vital institution in the minds of the men and women living in the vast Northwest but also prized as an outreach platform by members of the RCA throughout the nation.

The Dutch settlers in Orange City rightly believed that young people who hoped to become pastors and missionaries would begin to make their way to Hope College. Hospers promised that Orange City's academy would "supply a good contingent to Hope College every year."[25] Northwestern, therefore, could not only provide an extension of the Reformed Church onto the frontier but also cultivate future pastors and missionaries. They envisioned Northwestern as a dynamic link in the educational pipeline for young people who, after a sojourn at other Dutch educational centers, would head to pulpits on the frontier or to far-flung missionary outposts.

An academy with the ability to produce educated, moral, and religiously orthodox alumni also helped to shore up these new settlements and position them for long-term success. "Though not of first importance, still it is not to be overlooked," remarked Buursma, "our Church in the far West can become strong numerically not only, but also financially. Hence, the churches here may become, and are evidently destined to become, a strong support to our benevolent institution."[26] Presented within his larger apology for Northwestern's significance, Buursma made the case that an academy would not only provide young men and women to fill pulpits, classrooms, and mission fields but also enable these new settlements to begin to fill the denomination's coffers. In doing so, an academy in Orange City, Iowa, would serve the church in northwestern Iowa and the RCA more broadly not only by

---

[24] "Northwestern Classical Academy," *The Acts and Proceedings of the Seventy-Ninth Regular Session of the General Synod of the Reformed Church in America*, June 1885 (NY: Board of Publication, RCA, 1885), 719.

[25] Hospers, "Hope College Gered!"

[26] Buursma, "To the Synod," 308.

the provision of men and women called to leadership roles but also through the faithful support of benevolent causes at home and abroad.

Just two years after incorporation, the RCA's Committee on Christian Education noted that Northwestern acted as "the educational centre of a region now newly settled but destined soon to be a power in its religious, intellectual, and material developments."[27] Written by a board dominated by men hailing from the RCA's eastern churches, these words echoed Hospers' earlier promise in 1882 that Northwestern would become an influence in "religious, educational, and social spheres."[28] The vision of Northwestern was situated clearly within the Dutch educational tradition that Karsten articulated in 1888. This new academy closely wedded the church and school. Its founders envisioned the school as a blessing not only to the local community but also to the entire region, their church, and—through their training and support of pastors, missionaries, and teachers—ultimately to the world.

Conclusion

In 1937 the Women's Conference of the East and West Sioux Classes staged the *Victory of Faith* pageant in Alton, Iowa, just three miles from Northwestern, which was by then a junior college. It was a dramatic affair featuring characters ranging from colonial Dutch leader Jonas Michaelius to a feisty spirit of the prairie. Meant to "inspire a greater interest in missions," the play offered a highlight reel of major events in the development of missionary consciousness among the East and West Sioux classes of the RCA—both rooted in Sioux County, Iowa, at the heart of the Dutch settlements that arose there in the 1870s.[29] As the play progressed, it recounted stories of immigrant settlement, church building, missionary outreach, and—crucially, to the playwright's mind—the story of the founding of Northwestern Classical Academy.

In a scene set in 1882 in a tidy living room, a young boy and girl chatted with one another. They confessed that recently they had both been secretly thinking about a calling. The young boy recounted a sermon preached by the dominie:

---

[27] "Northwestern Classical Academy," *Acts and Proceedings of the Seventy-Eighth Regular Session of the General Synod of the Reformed Church in America*, June 1884 (NY: Board of Publication, RCA, 1884), 508.
[28] Hospers, "De Academie."
[29] Mrs. Jacob Heemstra, *The Victory of Faith*, 1 Oct. 1937, box 9, Western Seminary Pamphlet Collection, W02-1277.5, JAH.

He ... showed how this great country of ours is reaching out farther and farther west ... how people from other countries keep coming to America as though to the promised land, but they do not find God here, because there are not enough men who have dedicated their lives to the service of God."[30]

Convicted by the preacher's sermon, in that very moment, the young lad decided to become a minister. But alas, with no preparatory education to enable him to enroll at Hope, he queries, "What can I do?" The young girl confessed the same concern. She was not headed to the pulpit, though, but to the foreign mission field. "I got to thinking of the children in foreign lands growing up, still ignorant of Christ, because there aren't enough consecrated persons to bring them the message," she confessed. "I too, have decided to dedicate my life to Christ ... and I, too, lack the preparatory training, because there is no school here that I can go to."[31] After the pair declared their intention to serve the Lord for their entire lives and sealed their commitment with a hymn, the young girl announced, "There ought to be a school here with Christian teachers ... so that students may be educated to become Christian doctors, lawyers, teachers, ministers, missionaries, and help to fill the need of the world today for men and women of that type."[32]

After they discussed their dreams with symbolic representations of spirits of sacrifice, progress, knowledge, service, ambition, worship, loyalty, and consecration, the curtain fell. Onto the front stage, a narrator emerged:

> It was just such a spirit ... which prompted the organization of Northwestern Classical Academy. ... Wherever a settlement of Hollanders was to be found, there also was found a church and a school. ... The school played an important part in the program of mission in the Northwest. It has stimulated great interest in mission and made it possible for 120 young men to go into the ministry and about forty more men and women to go as missionaries into the foreign and domestic field.[33]

More than fifty years after the founding of Northwestern, this pageant echoed the enduring vision of Northwestern. The buildings,

---

[30] Heemstra, *Victory of Faith*, interlude 3.
[31] Ibid.
[32] Ibid.
[33] Ibid.

students, courses, and faculty had changed dramatically over half a century. Nevertheless, rooted in the Dutch educational tradition, informed by a worldview that extended well beyond their fledgling communities, and dedicated to serve the community, church, and world, the founding vision persisted that coupled the church and school.

CHAPTER 6

"The Joyous, Jolly Academy days": Northwestern Classical Academy, 1882-1928

Douglas Firth Anderson

B. D. Dykstra[1] emigrated from Friesland with his family in 1882 and became the valedictorian of Northwestern Classical Academy (NWCA) in Orange City, Iowa, in 1892. He later confessed himself "a born student. Knowledge was the hunger and thirst of my life."[2] At the time of his graduation, he characterized his three years there as "the joyous, jolly Academy days."[3]

The thread of jollity at Northwestern persisted into the beginning of the next century. Northwestern principal Philip Soulen quoted Rev. Rollin Lynde Hartt in 1901: "All Scotland may be put in five words: Scott, Burns, heather, whisky and religion. In Iowa you pack the thing tighter. Three nouns are enough: corn, cow, hog." Principal Soulen, however, did not leave things there. He noted that "the Iowa Hollander"

---

[1] Known for most of his adult life as "B. D.," Dykstra's initials stood for Broer Doekeles. As the academy's valedictorian, he was known as "Bert."
[2] B. D. Dykstra, My Apologia, typescript, 23, box 1, B. D. Dykstra Papers, Northwestern College Archives (NCA).
[3] The Classic 1, no. 6 (June 1892): 9, https://nwcommons.nwciowa.edu/northwesternclassics/29/.

B. D. Dykstra, ca. 1900
(*courtesy NCA*)

did not allow "smiling fields and fat porkers... to exclude the claims of the intellect and the soul."[4]

Neither joy and jollity nor corn, cow, and hog precluded the serious claims of the intellect and soul at Northwestern Classical Academy. Spanning four grade levels, which corresponded with grades 9 through 12, and coeducational from its beginnings, the school was "classical" in more than one sense. It not only offered a classical curriculum but was also "to be under the care of, and subject to, the supervision of the Classis of Iowa of the Reformed Church in America" (RCA). The purpose of Northwestern was to be "an Institution of learning for the promotion of Science and Literature in harmony with, and Religion as expressed in, the Doctrinal Standards of the Reformed Church in America."[5]

In the nineteenth century, academies in the United States were serious educational institutions. By midcentury, widespread literacy

---

[4] *Catalogue of the Northwestern Classical Academy, 1901-1902* (Orange City, IA: De Volksvriend Press, 1902), 6.

[5] *Constitution and By-Laws of the Board of Trustees of the Northwestern Classical Academy, as Adopted July 19, 1881, and as Subsequently Amended* (Orange City, IA: n.p., 1882), https://nwcommons.nwciowa.edu/northwesternacademydocuments/3/. The quotations are from the constitution, Articles 3 and 2. The explicit ties of Northwestern to the RCA remain today.

and burgeoning public "common schools" were aspects of American society that natives and visitors alike thought remarkable. A common school education (typically no further than eighth grade), however, did not adequately prepare students for college. But this was not a problem for most Americans before 1900, since few attended college until well into the twentieth century.[6] Yet, even before professionalization made higher education more desirable, those who did want more than an eighth grade education turned to academies.

The academy was "the prevailing institution of higher schooling in eighteenth- and nineteenth-century America," according to historians Kim Tolley and Nancy Beadie.[7] Academies were an adaptation for an American nation of British Latin grammar schools and "public" (actually, private) boarding schools. Schools in the United Kingdom prepared students for higher education within long-standing traditions of an aristocratic class system and an established church. By contrast, in the United States, schooling was shaped not only by informal elites and religious establishments but also increasingly by a populist culture and a market-driven society. Before public high schools became significant in the United States at the end of the nineteenth century, it was private academies that provided secondary-level education for college. Academies also trained many schoolteachers before a college degree became necessary.[8]

Religious groups (Catholic and Jewish, as well as Protestant) arguably sustained most American academies in the nineteenth and early twentieth centuries. Religion, though, was not the only motive for creating academies. Segregation by sex and/or race could also be a factor.[9] There were academies exclusively for boys but also for girls, such as Phillips Exeter Academy (1781; boys only until 1970) and Litchfield Female Academy (1792). There were also academies for young people

---

[6] On the rise of college education in the United States, see Laurence R. Veysey, *The Emergence of the American University* (Chicago: University of Chicago Press, 1965), and Burton J. Bledstein, *The Culture of Professionalism: The Middle Class and the Development of Higher Education in America* (NY: W. W. Norton, 1976).

[7] Kim Tolley and Nancy Beadie, "A School for Every Purpose: An Introduction to the History of Academies in the United States," in *Chartered Schools: Two Hundred Years of Independent Academies in the United States, 1727-1925* (NY: Routledge, 2013), 4.

[8] Tolley and Beadie, "A School for Every Purpose," 4-14, and William J. Reese, *The Origins of the American High School* (New Haven, CT: Yale University Press, 1995), xiii.

[9] Tolley and Beadie, "A School for Every Purpose." For a fascinating and sobering tale of an early, short-lived academy that focused on converting and educating Hawaiian and Cherokee young men, see John Demos, *The Heathen School: A Story of Hope and Betrayal in the Age of the Early Republic* (NY: Vintage Books, 2014).

Henry Hospers, 1872
(*courtesy NCA*)

of color, particularly Native Americans and African Americans, such as Moore's Indian Charity School (1755, which eventually became Dartmouth College) and Tuskegee Normal School for Colored Teachers (1881, which eventually became Tuskegee University). Many academies were unable to maintain long-term support, especially as public high schools proliferated. Nevertheless, private academies still exist, although usually called high schools now. For example, Western Academy of Hull, Iowa, is now known as Western Christian High School. Anecdotally, in April 1923, Northwestern Academy's debate team defeated Western Academy's debate team twice, once in Orange City then again in Hull.

Colonists from Pella, Iowa, established Orange City in 1870. They were largely a second generation from the 1847 colonists who had left the Netherlands' Hervormde Kerk (Reformed Church) in the Afscheiding (Secession) and immigrated to the American Midwest. Henry Hospers (1830-1901), the generally acknowledged leader of the new colony from 1870 until his death, articulated a guiding vision for the Dutch settlers: to make a place where "they might live under the shadow of the Church and School [*kerk en school*]."[10]

---

[10] Henry Hospers, "A Concise History of the Settlement of the Dutch Colony in Sioux County, Iowa, Part 1," *De Volksvriend*, 25 June 1874, trans. Nelson Nieuwenhuis, http://nwcommons.nwciowa.edu/henryhospersdocuments/3/, 3. This article was in

Northwestern Classical Academy, created on July 19, 1882, would have been organized earlier if the Dutch colonists of Orange City had not had to focus their attention on battling grasshoppers and a national economic depression soon after settling in 1870.[11] The school arose out of the faith and aspirations of the Dutch colonists who settled Orange City and the surrounding region.

Church and school would, the newcomers believed, be central in sustaining religious and other traditions. Along with obtaining more affordable land, Hospers and the Orange City colonists were seeking to counter secularizing and modernizing trends, not only in the Netherlands, from which many of them had emigrated, but also in the United States. For the northwest Iowa Dutch settlers, Reformed churches, schools, and piety provided a trinity of institutional, intellectual, and affective anchors for a project of cultural maintenance.[12] Linked to their ethnic territoriality in and around Orange City, this cultural maintenance could be characterized as progressive provincialism.[13] It

---

the inaugural issue of *De Volksvriend*, of which Hospers was the founding editor and publisher. On Henry Hospers, see Douglas Firth Anderson, "'We Are Now Americans': Henry Hospers, Sioux County, Iowa, and Dutch Settler Acculturation," *Northwestern Review* 3 (2018), https://nwcommons.nwciowa.edu/northwesternreview/vol3/iss1/4/.

[11] On the history of Orange City, see Doug Anderson, Tim Schlak, Greta Grond, and Sarah Kaltenbach, *Orange City* (Charleston, SC: Arcadia, 2014).

[12] On piety, see Eugene P. Heideman, *The Practice of Piety: The Theology of the Midwestern Reformed Church in America, 1866-1966* (Grand Rapids, MI: Eerdmans, 2009).

[13] On the cultural maintenance and ethnic territoriality of the Orange City colonists, see Brian W. Beltman, "Ethnic Persistence and Change: The Experience of a Dutch American Family in Rural Iowa," *Annals of Iowa* 52 (1993): 1-49, https://ir.uiowa.edu/annals-of-iowa/vol52/iss1/2/; Brian W. Beltman, "Ethnic Territoriality and the Persistence of Identity: Dutch Settlers in Northwest Iowa, 1869-1880," *Annals of Iowa* 55 (1996): 101-37, https://ir.uiowa.edu/annals-of-iowa/vol55/iss2/2/; Michael L. Yoder, "Anabaptists and Calvinists Four Centuries Later: An Iowa Case Study," *Mennonite Quarterly Review* 67 (1993): 49-72; Larissa MacFarquhar, "Where the Small-Town American Dream Lives On," *New Yorker*, 13 Nov. 2017, https://www.newyorker.com/magazine/2017/11/13/where-the-small-town-american-dream-lives-on. My concept of progressive provincialism adapts ideas from American philosopher Josiah Royce (1855-1916; as a professor at Harvard, he was a colleague of William James and a teacher of George Santayana). See Royce's essay "Provincialism," in *Race Questions, Provincialism, and Other American Problems* (NY: Macmillan, 1908), 55-108; Robert V. Hine, *Josiah Royce: From Grass Valley to Harvard* (Norman: University of Oklahoma Press, 1992), 177-78, 199-200. Royce, while recognizing that a cherishing by local communities of their own "traditions, beliefs, and aspirations" could easily divide one "province" from another, argued that a "wholesome provincialism" made for a local rootedness that could contribute to and enrich a nation; put another way, the local and particular could and should lead to the universal. See Royce's "Provincialism," 61-62.

was provincialism in that it was a religious, agricultural, and small-town set of traditions and sensibilities that was conservative and place-based. Yet it was progressive in that the community was not seeking to merely reproduce a remembered Netherlands but rather to selectively adapt to "progress."

By the time the academy was formally organized, Orange City had become the county seat of Sioux County, and First Reformed Church was not only organized but also had its own building. Henry Hospers was central to both developments. In county affairs, he had become the leader of the board of supervisors. In church affairs, he had helped found First Reformed Church. As a young man in Pella, Hospers had broken religiously with the colony's leader, Rev. Hendrik Scholte. Hospers and many other Pella colonists rejected Scholte's Congregationalist and premillennialist tendencies.[14] Instead, they looked to Rev. Albertus C. Van Raalte, the leader of the Holland, Michigan, colony of 1847, who encouraged Dutch colonists to affiliate with what would become the RCA in 1867. First Reformed Church, organized in 1871, called Rev. Seine Bolks, a protégé of Van Raalte; he arrived as the congregation's first pastor the following year.[15]

Despite the challenges to the Dutch settlers in Sioux County in the 1870s, they held on to the vision of establishing a school to complement their church. Besides the theological commitments informing the vision of *kerk en school*, there were also important cultural sensibilities involved. For one thing, both the 1847 colonies of Pella and Holland had academies—and the Orange City colonists were not prepared to fall behind the midwestern "mother colonies" educationally.[16] For another thing, there was a putative national tradition to emulate. In a 1916 address, academy alumnus and lawyer Anthony Te Paske (1889) reminded the RCA Particular Synod of Iowa of a bit of Dutch history:

> We of our ancestry came from "Brave Little Holland." We know something of her history. We know that when the invading

---

[14] On Scholte, see Eugene P. Heideman, *Hendrik P. Scholte: His Legacy in the Netherlands and in America* (Grand Rapids, MI: Eerdmans, 2015).

[15] Bolks was 58 years old when he came to Orange City. On Bolks, see Earl Wm. Kennedy, *A Commentary on the Minutes of the Classis of Holland, 1848-1876: A Detailed Record of Persons and Issues, Civil and Religious, in the Dutch Colony of Holland, Michigan* (Holland, MI: Van Raalte Press, 2018), 78.

[16] Pella's Central "University" began its preparatory department in 1854; Holland's academy (under several names) started in 1851. Lori Witt, email reply to Doug Anderson, 25 Jan. 2019; Geoffrey Reynolds, email reply to Doug Anderson, 22 Jan. 2019.

Rev. Seine Bolks
(*courtesy NCA*)

Spaniard was stopped at the gates of Leyden and that when finally, after untold suffering and super-human endurance, Alva was foiled, William of Holland asked that famous city what it would take as a reward. You know the answer: not unlike that of young Solomon of old. They asked not for the spoils of war, or wealth, or honor, or the arsenals for future conflicts, but they requested a university. Long will you turn the pages of history for another incident like that. Blind, indeed, must one be, if he has not seen that our people excel in the love of education.[17]

In 1882 Henry Hospers led in finally adding school to church in Orange City. When the new colony was planned, there was agreement in the colony association that a fifth of the proceeds from town lot sales would be set aside for an academy—and Hospers was president of the Orange City town site company.[18] Hospers, Rev. Bolks, and seven other

[17] Anthony Te Paske, *Why the Academy? Address delivered before Particular Synod at Orange City, May the 4th, 1916* (Orange City?), memorial reprint of 1916 pamphlet, https://nwcommons.nwciowa.edu/northwesternacademydocuments/2/.
[18] The rest of this paragraph, unless otherwise noted, is based on Jacob Van der Zee, *The Hollanders of Iowa* (Iowa City: State Historical Society of Iowa, 1912), 280-82, and Nelson Nieuwenhuis, "Henry Hospers: The People's Friend" (Iowa City: published by the author, mimeograph, 1978), https://nwcommons.nwciowa.edu/henryhospersbiography/1/, 101-3.

Academy Hall (the Rink, or Noah's Ark) (*courtesy NCA*)

men drew up the constitution (articles of incorporation) and bylaws for the Northwestern Classical Academy on July 19; on August 1, the group formally began gathering financial pledges. Hospers donated town land and pledged $500—more than anyone else.[19] Rev. Bolks, retired from pastoring due to his health, became the academy board's president, while Hospers became the board's treasurer.

Unofficial private tutoring of a few students by Jacob Van Zanten, principal of the Orange City public school, began as early as 1881; later Van Zanten was aided by two ministers, also Northwestern trustees. Official teaching at the academy started in September 1883, and twenty-five students divided into three levels were enrolled by the end of the second week. The students and the one instructor met in the First Reformed Church's consistory room and in the local public school. In January 1884, Rev. John A. De Spelder took office as principal, and soon thereafter, a two-story frame building was erected

[19] Charter subscription list, 1882, box 1, Northwestern Classical Academy Collection (hereafter NWCA Collection), NCA, https://nwcommons.nwciowa.edu/northwesternacademydocuments/1/. Hospers "sold" two pieces of land in the Southern Addition, the first in 1883 (Block 35 for $1, recorded in 1884), and the second in 1886 (Lot 12 in Block 42 for $125); Village Deed C, 311, 628, Sioux County Recorder records. Probably the land was in fulfillment of the land sales proceeds to be set aside for an academy. There are no further surviving records to clarify this. All monies collected for the academy were to be deposited in Hospers' Orange City Bank, opened in 1880.

Rev. James F. Zwemer

on Northwestern's property. This "Pioneer School" served as the academy's only structure until 1886, when an abandoned skating rink in Orange City was purchased and remodeled. The remodeled structure was officially named Academy Hall, but it was commonly known as the Rink or Noah's Ark.[20]

By 1887-88, the basic academy curriculum was well in place. A chapel service began every class day, and every week there was a class on the Heidelberg Catechism. The classical course of study or curriculum included Latin (four years), Greek (three years), Dutch (four years), English (four years), history (four years), mathematics (four years), geography (two years), physiology (four years), bookkeeping (three years), astronomy (one year), and physics (one year).[21] By 1890 scientific (or modern) and normal (or education) courses of study were added.

Also, by 1890, there was a new principal: Rev. James F. Zwemer. He and his family moved into the Principal's House. On the academy campus, this building was the old Pioneer School, remodeled after the purchase of Academy Hall in downtown Orange City.[22] Bringing a new energy to the school (which probably inspired B. D. Dykstra's "joyous, jolly Academy days"), Zwemer launched the *Classic* in 1891.

[20] Gerald F. De Jong, *From Strength to Strength: A History of Northwestern 1882-1982* (Grand Rapids, MI: Eerdmans, 1982), 18-22.
[21] *Catalogue of the Northwestern Classical Academy, 1887-1888* (Orange City, IA: Herald Print, 1887), 9-10, 16, https://nwcommons.nwciowa.edu/northwesternacademydocuments/8/.
[22] *Catalogue of the Northwestern Classical Academy, 1892-1893* (Orange City, IA: Herald Book, 1893), 2, https://nwcommons.nwciowa.edu/northwesternacademydocuments/7/.

New Academy Hall (*courtesy NCA*)

Published until 1906, the *Classic* was a monthly subscription periodical edited by academy students.[23] In addition to student valedictories, salutatories, and other graduation addresses, such as Dykstra's in 1892, it featured student essays and commentary. The articles ranged from "Our First Woman President" and "The New Woman" to "The Choice of a Profession," "A Christian Training Essential to Good Citizenship," "Piet's Adventure," "Learning to Ride a Bicycle," "Do Animals Think?" "Life on the Farm," "Opium Dreams," "The Ku-Klux Klan," and "Should We Restrict Immigration?"

Although the *Classic* was an important pedagogical and intellectual development for the school, the construction of a new Academy Hall on school property was Zwemer's most visible and material accomplishment. Fundraising for the new building was well underway in 1892, but the national economic depression of 1893 delayed the project. Designed by Pella-born architect George Pass in a Richardsonian Romanesque style, the brick-and-stone hall was dedicated on November 23, 1894, with ceremonies that included a

---

[23] For digitized copies of the NWCA *Classic*, see https://nwcommons.nwciowa.edu/northwesternclassics/index.html. *The Classic* as a title was revived in 1928 for use by the administration of Northwestern Junior College and Academy (NWJC); see https://nwcommons.nwciowa.edu/classic-bulletin/ and https://nwcommons.nwciowa.edu/classic-magazine/.

Academy Hall on the distant horizon, as seen from the north
(*courtesy NCA*)

procession from the old Academy Hall to First Reformed Church and then south to the new building with its hexagonal tower. The total cost of the structure was $16,000.[24] On a stone to the west of the top of the main entrance stairway was inscribed "*Deus est Lux*"—God is Light. Who suggested the inscription is unclear, but after 1928, it began to function as the motto of Northwestern College. The new Academy Hall contained the classrooms, chapel, library, and offices of Northwestern for thirty years. In 1924, when Science Hall was added to the campus, the academy's board of trustees officially renamed Academy Hall as Zwemer Hall.[25]

The new Academy Hall, a monumental building anchoring the south end of Main Street in Orange City, also served to symbolically

[24] Nelson Nieuwenhuis, "Zwemer Hall: A Landmark at Northwestern College," *Annals of Iowa* 43 (1975): 103-12, https://ir.uiowa.edu/annals-of-iowa/vol43/iss2/3/. The building remains standing, remodeled and expanded in 1995, as Northwestern College's administration building. It was placed on the National Register of Historic Sites in 1975.

[25] Minutes, 14 April 1924, 1910-27 ledger, 191, box 1, Board of Trustees Minutes, Northwestern College Collection (NWCA), NCA. Probably this was to honor Principal Zwemer in particular, but the board minutes do not specify that the renaming was for him; it may have been left ambiguous to also give a nod of recognition to the Zwemer family, by then famous in RCA circles, not least for James' younger brother, Samuel M., a founder of the denomination's "Arabia mission" and a missionary statesman and author. On the Zwemer family, see Kennedy, *Commentary*, 764-66, 1568.

Zwemer Hall and Science Hall, ca. 1924 (*courtesy NCA*)

NWCA faculty, ca. 1910-12. Principal Thomas Welmers, *center* (*courtesy NCA*)

NWCA community with *Deus est Lux* discernable, 1898
(*courtesy NCA*)

anchor Northwestern itself as a sustainable educational institution. Not that the academy did not have its challenges. Before Zwemer left in 1898 there was an Orange City public high school.[26] In 1908 academy principal John F. Heemstra noted in his report to the board, "This is the age of high-schools [sic]. . . . To a considerable extent . . . they are our rivals." A few years later, Principal Thomas Welmers expressed ambivalence about the academy versus public high schools. On the one hand, the academy cultivated religious commitment and academic rigor. "In so far as they lend themselves to it," Welmers said to the board in 1912, "we strive to relate all branches [of knowledge] to Christian truth. Responding to student and perhaps parental concerns, in 1917 Welmers dismissed "the objection that it is too hard here"; the academy would, he declared, "maintain as high a degree of scholarship as the material . . . will allow." "We are in this institution," he continued, "endeavoring to inculcate a love for the classics, which we believe affords the best preparation for head, hand, and heart." On the other hand, he acknowledged that public schooling (along with social trends) had its allures, and they were difficult to counter. Too many academy students

---

[26] A new Orange City public school building was opened in 1893. The first notice of a high school graduating class was 1894. See *Sioux County Herald* (Orange City), 22 Feb. 1893 and 24 June 1894. A high school addition came in 1915; *Alton Democrat*, 5 June 1915. In the 1890s, public education in Iowa became more formally organized than before; see Keach Johnson, "Elementary and Secondary Education in Iowa, 1890-1900: A Time of Awakening, Part I," *Annals of Iowa* 45 (1979): 87-109, and "Part II," *Annals of Iowa* 45 (1980): 171-95, https://ir.uiowa.edu/annals-of-iowa/vol45/iss2/2/ and https://ir.uiowa.edu/annals-of-iowa/vol45/iss3/2/.

NWCA baseball team, 1911 (*courtesy NWA*)

were not prepared for academic rigor due to what Welmers in 1915 assessed as "a lack of seriousness borne of and fostered by luxurious living." Further, he admitted ruefully in 1916, "In the immediate future denominational academies will face a hard struggle. This is apparent when we consider the large, beautiful, and well-equipped high schools that are being erected everywhere, also in this vicinity."[27]

Athletics, too, seemed double-edged. Baseball, basketball, and football were popular with early twentieth-century students. As early as 1904, the *Classic* noted that an academy team had beat the Orange City High School team in baseball.[28] Academy Hall, though, had no gymnasium. "Tho [sic] a gymnasium is in many respects a desirable thing, and for some reasons, I would urge [us] to attempt to get one, yet it would not, as some seem to think, be a panacea for all evils of the school," grumbled Principal Welmers to the board in 1915.[29] Not only where and when to practice and play games, but also who could play,

---

[27] Principal's Reports to the Board of Trustees, 1908, Heemstra, 4; 1912, Welmers, 1; 1917, Welmers, 2, 7; 1915, Welmers, 2; 1916, Welmers, 3, NWCA Collection.

[28] *The Classic* 12, no. 8 (May 1904): 11, https://nwcommons.nwciowa.edu/northwesternclassics/38/.

[29] Principal's Reports, 1915, Welmers, 4.

"The joyous, jolly Academy days" 117

Girls basketball team, 1912 (*courtesy NCA*)

had to be decided.³⁰ Despite Welmers' frustrations about a gymnasium, there were academy girls as well as boys basketball teams during his tenure.³¹ Northwestern basketball was played in the town hall until Science Hall was opened in 1924. By 1921, in addition to two basketball teams, there were also football, baseball, track, and tennis teams.³² Basketball, though, dominated the sports coverage in the *Monitor*, the student newspaper between 1922 and 1925.

Athletics, however, were not the only extracurricular activities at the academy.³³ Following morning chapel, regular classes, and afternoon

30 For example, at their 18 April 1913 meeting, the academy faculty decided that an "80% average" was the minimum "required for all who enter contests with teams outside of this institution." Faculty Minutes, Northwestern Classical Academy, 1894-1919 ledger, 137, box 2, faculty, NWC, NCA.
31 Nella Kennedy, "Northwestern Classical Academy, 1910-1920," *The Classic* (Winter 1980-81): 8-9, https://nwcommons.nwciowa.edu/classic1980/20/.
32 *Cullings 1921* (Orange City, IA: Northwestern Classical Academy, 1921), 78-91, https://nwcommons.nwciowa.edu/yearbooks/45/. *Cullings* was something of a cross between a yearbook and a literary magazine; it appeared for only 2 years.
33 For a concise overview of academy extracurricular activities through the 1920s, see Dale Hubers, "A History of the Northwestern Classical Academy, Orange City, Iowa, 1882-1957" (MA thesis, University of South Dakota, 1957), 46-51.

118   DUTCH REFORMED EDUCATION

Chrestomathean Club, 1924 (*courtesy NCA*)

study (either in Academy Hall or at home), activities came after 4:00 p.m. Literary-debating clubs went back to the 1880s. The Philomathean Society, begun in 1896, grew so large that it had to be split in 1914 into the Chrestomathean and Alethean Societies. The Halcyon Club was not a literary society, but an all-male boarding house during the week; on weekends, its members and most other students went home.[34] Music and religious activities engaged many students. By the 1926-27 academic year, YMCA and YWCA groups and the Boys and Girls Glee Clubs were flourishing, along with the literary-debating societies.[35]

What sorts of students attended Northwestern? Limited glimpses come from various sources. Three graduates can give us some sense of academy life and legacy, albeit in fragmentary measure: B. D. Dykstra (1871-1955; Class of 1892), Hendrina Hospers (1880-1968; Class of 1897), and James Muilenburg (1896-1974; Class of 1914).[36]

[34] Kennedy, "Northwestern Classical Academy," 8.
[35] Hubers, "History of the NWCA," 51.
[36] Unless otherwise noted, what follows about Dykstra is from the Dykstra Papers and

"The joyous, jolly Academy days" 119

Hendrina Hospers with unidentified Jicarilla woman
(courtesy NCA)

Dykstra and Hospers were both graduates during the Zwemer years when the academy was young. With no substantive competition from public high schools, the academy was an institutional neophyte that seemed to foster exuberance and expectancy—at least enough so for Dykstra's characterization of it as the "joyous, jolly Academy days." For valedictorian Dykstra, the core of the joy seemed to be faith-informed learning. Hendrina Hospers, third in her class, delivered "The History of the Class of '97"; in it, she provided a couple of hints of some of the school's jollity. In the new Academy Hall, according to Hospers, there was a "'Corner of Wickedness,' where some of the class would frequently be found, devising some sly prank." Further, two groups emerged in her class: the Greeks and the Germans. Besides indicating that the Greeks were more numerous than the Germans, though, Hospers not specify what distinguished the groups.[37]

Beyond the substance and character of academy life, Dykstra and Hospers highlight some important things about the school's students and the academy's impact on their lives. Northwestern was co-educational, as reflected in the fact that Dykstra was valedictorian of

---

D. Ivan Dykstra, "B. D.": A Biography of my Father, the Late Reverend B. D. Dykstra (Grand Rapids, MI: Eerdmans, 1982); about Hospers from Douglas Firth Anderson, "'Are you White or Dutch?': Hendrina Hospers and Living among Apaches," Northwestern Review 4, no. 1 (2019), https://nwcommons.nwciowa.edu/northwesternreview/vol4/iss1/2/; about Muilenburg from James Muilenburg Papers, NCA.

[37] The Classic 6, no. 9 (June 1897): 5, https://nwcommons.nwciowa.edu/northwestern classics/27/.

his class, and Hospers was third in her class. The academy drew from its surrounding region: Dykstra's home was Sioux Center, and Hospers' home was Orange City. Northwestern appealed most to those of Dutch ethnicity: Dykstra, as previously noted, emigrated with his parents from Friesland; Hospers was the youngest child of Netherlands-born Henry Hospers.

Not least, the academy prepared many ministers, missionaries, and schoolteachers. Dykstra went on to Hope College. Before entering Western Theological Seminary in 1897, he taught in a country school for over a year. Ordained in 1900, Dykstra studied ancient Near Eastern languages for one year at Yale (1901-2), but lack of funds prevented his continuing. For ten years, he combined pastoring at Platte Reformed Church and teaching and administering Harrison Christian Academy, both in South Dakota. Married in 1909 and with a growing family, he served as the Dakota Classis missionary, traveling to organize, supply, and encourage small congregations over a wide region between 1913 and 1919. Because he opposed war in general, and the Great War in particular, no congregation would call him. He returned to the Harrison Academy for a second time, then took up the editorship of *De Volksvriend* in Orange City from 1928 to 1934. He left that post, at least in part, because he was not supportive of the New Deal. Except for returning to *De Volksvriend* for its final years (1949-51), Dykstra made a living by self-publishing and peddling his own writings—sermons, essays, hymns, poems—most in Dutch or Frisian. He would travel by train to Dutch settlements throughout the western United States and then get around by bicycle, being a guest preacher, lecturing, and doing readings.

Hospers, like Dykstra, taught school. She, however, remained, at the common school level in the Orange City area until both her parents died. Then in 1907, with her academy diploma and a year of study at Oberlin College (1899-1900), she became a missionary for the Women's Board of Domestic Missions of the RCA. From 1907 to 1913, she was superintendent of the RCA Apache Mission (school and orphanage) at Fort Sill, Oklahoma. In 1913, after the death of Geronimo (Hospers knew him) and the release of the Chiricahuas from their prisoner-of-war status, she traveled with the majority of Chiricahuas who elected to move to the Mescaleros (Apache cousins to the Chiricahuas) on their New Mexico reservation. Upon the invitation of the Mescalero agency trader who intended to become an ordained RCA minister, Hospers moved in 1914 to become the chief field worker of a new RCA mission

James Muilenburg at Union Seminary, 1950s (*courtesy NCA*)

to the Jicarilla Apaches in Dulce, New Mexico. She worked with the Jicarillas for thirty-two years before retiring to Albuquerque.

James Muilenburg, the third academy graduate of our focus, though a generation younger than Dykstra and Hospers, illustrates many of the same things. He was a grandnephew of Hubert Muilenburg, a member of the first survey party from Pella in 1869.[38] Like Dykstra and Hospers, Muilenburg was ethnically Dutch and had grown up in or near Orange City. Like them, he became a teacher. Here, though, some differences need noting. Muilenburg was a student during the Welmers years. By then, Northwestern was facing serious competition with a growing Orange City public high school. Also, these were the years in between the *Classic* and *Cullings* and the *Monitor*, with little to go on for student life.[39]

Yet, Welmers himself remembered Muilenburg. In 1926 Welmers was registrar of Hope College. In a letter that year to Anthony Te Paske, Welmers reflected on Northwestern:

---

[38] James C. Schaap, "Walter J. Muilenburg's *Prairie*: Review Essay," *Pro Rege* 44 (June 2016): 13, http://digitalcollections.dordt.edu/pro_rege/vol44/iss4/3.

[39] James Muilenburg was neither valedictorian nor salutatorian; he was allowed, though, to deliver the class "prophecy." Faculty minutes, 23 Feb. 1914 meeting, 1894-1919 ledger, 142. For some gleanings of academy life at the time, see Kennedy, "Northwestern Classical Academy," 8-9.

I believe it would be difficult to find another institution of learning that has in proportion to its size produced more men and women that have become leaders in almost every profession and calling.... [S]omehow the Academy got into their flesh and bone.... Somehow the boys and girls from the Academy can be depended upon, and consequently are even while students given places of honor. Not every graduate becomes a leading scholar, but they all for the most part give evidence of character which spells success.[40]

After these comments, Welmers mentioned Muilenburg. By then Muilenburg was finishing his PhD at Yale. Before Yale, he had gained his BA at Hope College. Religiously, though, he was moving away from the confessional conservatism of the RCA in Orange City. After Hope, he completed a masters at the University of Nebraska. He was ordained a minister in what became the United Church of Christ. In the fall of 1926, he began many years of teaching religion, Old Testament, and ancient Near East languages, first at Mt. Holyoke College (1926-32), then the University of Maine (1932-36), the Pacific School of Religion (1936-45), Union Theological Seminary (1945-63), and the San Francisco Theological Seminary, which was a partner in the Graduate Theological Union (1963-71). Along the way, for a year, he was director of the American School of Oriental Research in Jerusalem and one of the team of translators who worked on the Revised Standard Version of the Old Testament. He was an exponent of what he called "rhetorical criticism" of the Bible. Although an expert on the book of Jeremiah, he never published a commentary on it. Although he went beyond where any of his academy teachers and northwest Iowa Reformed ministers were prepared to go in biblical criticism, he retained a deep-seated religious commitment that must have had some rootage in the academy and regional Reformed piety. Novelist Frederick Buechner, a student of his at Union Seminary, remembered this about Muilenburg: "With his body stiff, his knees bent, his arms scarecrowed far to either side, he never merely taught the Old Testament but *was* the Old Testament." Buechner continued, "'Every morning when you wake up,' he used to say, 'before you reaffirm your faith in the majesty of a loving God, before you say *I believe* for another day, read the *Daily News* with its record of the latest crimes and tragedies of mankind and then see if you can

---

[40] Thomas E. Welmers to Anthony Te Paske, 10 April 1926, box 4, President Jacob Heemstra Papers, NCA.

honestly say it again.'" He was, said Buechner, "A fool ... for Christ. . . . His prayers, he once told me, were mostly blubbering, and you felt that he prayed endlessly."[41]

Dykstra, Hospers, and Muilenburg are of course only three of many academy graduates. Together, though, they flesh out in their lives important elements of Northwestern's early years and suggest some of its impact as an educational institution: to seek to anchor graduates in Reformed piety and to foster vocational paths into ministry, missions, and education. Another academy alumnus helped bring about a major turn in Northwestern's story: Jacob Heemstra (1888-1958). Heemstra's family farmed near Orange City, and he was a member of the Northwestern class of 1906. After completing a bachelor's degree at Hope in 1910, he returned to northwest Iowa and served a year as Sioux Center's superintendent of schools. Heemstra then attended Princeton Theological Seminary for a year, while also taking courses at Princeton University. He completed his seminary education at Western Theological Seminary in 1914. From 1914 to 1918, he served as pastor of Trinity Reformed Church, Chicago. During his pastorate, he also took courses at the University of Chicago. With his experience in public education, his theological education, and his coursework at Princeton and Chicago, he spent the next ten years (1918-28) teaching Bible, education, and psychology courses as a faculty member and serving as registrar at Central College, Pella.[42]

Then he returned home, in more than one sense. In 1928 Heemstra became president of Northwestern Junior College and Academy (NWJC). The academy continued on after 1928, but largely as a feeder to the junior college. The junior college in turn would become a four-year college in 1960-61; that same academic year saw the last graduating class of the academy.

The goal of creating a college was not new in 1928. As early as 1907-8, a set of first-year, college courses was offered, but there were only three enrolled students.[43] After the First World War, support for Northwestern—financial and otherwise—stabilized enough to add another building on campus. Science Hall opened in 1924, with classrooms, a music room, a laboratory, society rooms, and athletic locker rooms on the first floor and an auditorium and gymnasium on

---

[41] Frederick Buechner, "James Muilenburg as Man and Scholar," in *Hearing and Speaking the Word: Selections from the Works of James Muilenburg* (Chico, CA: Scholars Press, 1984), 7-9.
[42] On Heemstra, see biographical folder, Jacob Heemstra Papers, NCA.
[43] Principal's Reports, 1908, Heemstra, 1, 3.

President James Heemstra
(*courtesy NCA*)

the second floor.⁴⁴ Two years later, the Northwestern board approved adding a junior college program.⁴⁵

Northwestern Classical Academy's solo years ended in 1928. The "joyous, jolly Academy days" were arguably over. Thereafter, it was Northwestern Junior College and Academy. Nevertheless, the academy had set a pattern, lighting a way for students to journey on in what Anthony Te Paske had characterized as the Dutch tradition of "the love of education" while remaining rooted in Reformed piety and confessionialism. In turn, the religiously informed educational road marked by the school meshed well with larger cultural trends, easing the way for the Dutch settlers of northwest Iowa and the greater region to the north and west to accommodate to American society and culture.

"*Deus est Lux*" was the phrase engraved on the Academy Hall in 1894, and in 1932 it became the masthead motto on the Northwestern student newspaper launched in 1928. Given that President Heemstra was an academy alum and, given the motto, it is not surprising that the newspaper Heemstra helped the students start was named the *Beacon*.⁴⁶

---

⁴⁴ *Monitor* (13 May 1924): 1, http://northwestern.advantage-preservation.com.
⁴⁵ Minutes, 30 June 1926, 1910-27 ledger, 221, board, NWCA Collection.
⁴⁶ The *Beacon* is still the Northwestern College student newspaper. Issues are online at http://northwestern.advantage-preservation.com/.

Table 1

NWCA Principals, 1884-1928[47]

Rev. John A. De Spelder	1884-88
Rev. James F. Zwemer	1890-98
Rev. Matthew Kolyn	1898-1901
Philip Soulen	1901-16
Rev. John F. Heemstra	1906-10
Thomas Welmers	1910-20
Gerrit Timmer	1921-25
Rev. John D. Dykstra	1925-28

Table 2

	Enrolled in NWCA[48]	Graduated NWCA[49]		Enrolled in NWCA	Graduated NWCA
1882-83	25		1905-6	N/A	17
1883-84	N/A	0	1906-7	57	12
1884-85	N/A	3	1907-8	64	10
1885-86	N/A	1	1908-9	53	9
1886-87	N/A	7	1909-10	75	9
1887-88	N/A	3	1910-11	77	14
1888-89	74	4	1911-12	77	20
1889-90	56	5	1912-13	64	11
1890-91	66	10	1913-14	70	17
1891-92	77	16	1914-15	73	20
1892-93	N/A	11	1915-16	75	11
1893-94	N/A	15	1916-17	74	12
1894-95	N/A	13	1917-18	86	18

[47] Hubers, "A History of the Northwestern Classical Academy," 94.
[48] Ibid., 88.
[49] Northwestern College Alumni Association, *Northwestern College Alumni Directory*, Centennial Edition 1882-1982 (Dallas, TX: Taylor Publishing Co., 1982), 119-22.

1895-96	77	12	1918-19	90	7
1896-97	N/A	15	1919-20	100	21
1897-98	N/A	14	1920-21	118	16
1898-99	N/A	10	1921-22	122	23
1899-1900	62	16	1922-23	117	21
1900-1	77	16	1923-24	121	30
1901-2	74	17	1924-25	105	26
1902-3	71	11	1925-26	111	25
1903-4	N/A	12	1926-27	92	34
1904-5	N/A	14	1927-28	68	16

Table 3

NWCA Alumni/ae 1885-1921 in Selected Careers or Professions[50]

433		Total names listed
55	(12.7%)	Education (teachers, professors, administrators)
79	(18.2%)	Religion (clergy, missionaries)
14	(3.2%)	Law
45	(10.4%)	Medicine (physicians, dentists, pharmacists, veterinarians)
34	(7.9%)	Baccalaureate students, 1915-21

---

[50] *Catalogue of the Northwestern Classical Academy, 1921-1922* (Orange City, IA: n.p., 1921), 33-43, https://nwcommons.nwciowa.edu/northwesternacademydocuments/5/.

CHAPTER 7

From Dutch Reformed to Nondenominational: Transitions at Timothy Christian Schools of Chicagoland since the 1970s

Robert P. Swierenga

Timothy Christian Schools is a K-12 school system on a twenty-three-acre campus in the western Chicago suburb of Elmhurst that opened its doors in 1911. It is overseen by a parent-run school society founded in 1907 under the auspices of the nearby Douglas Park Christian Reformed Church, also located on Chicago's west side. Church leaders saw the elementary school as the "nursery" of the church and an obligation of parents. The school affiliated in 1920 with the National Union of Christian Schools (NUCS), later Christian Schools International (CSI), but it disaffiliated in 2019 due to CSI pension problems.

In 1927 the school and its mother church both relocated three miles west to Cicero and erected new buildings barely one block from each other. In 1950 a high school was erected nearby. In 1962 the high school relocated to Elmhurst fifteen miles west, leaving the junior high behind until 1970, when it too moved to the Elmhurst campus, followed in 1972 by the elementary school.[1]

---

[1] This chapter is based on Robert P. Swierenga, *His Faithfulness Continues: A History of Timothy Christian Schools of Chicagoland* (Holland, MI: Van Raalte Press, 2020).

128   DUTCH REFORMED EDUCATION

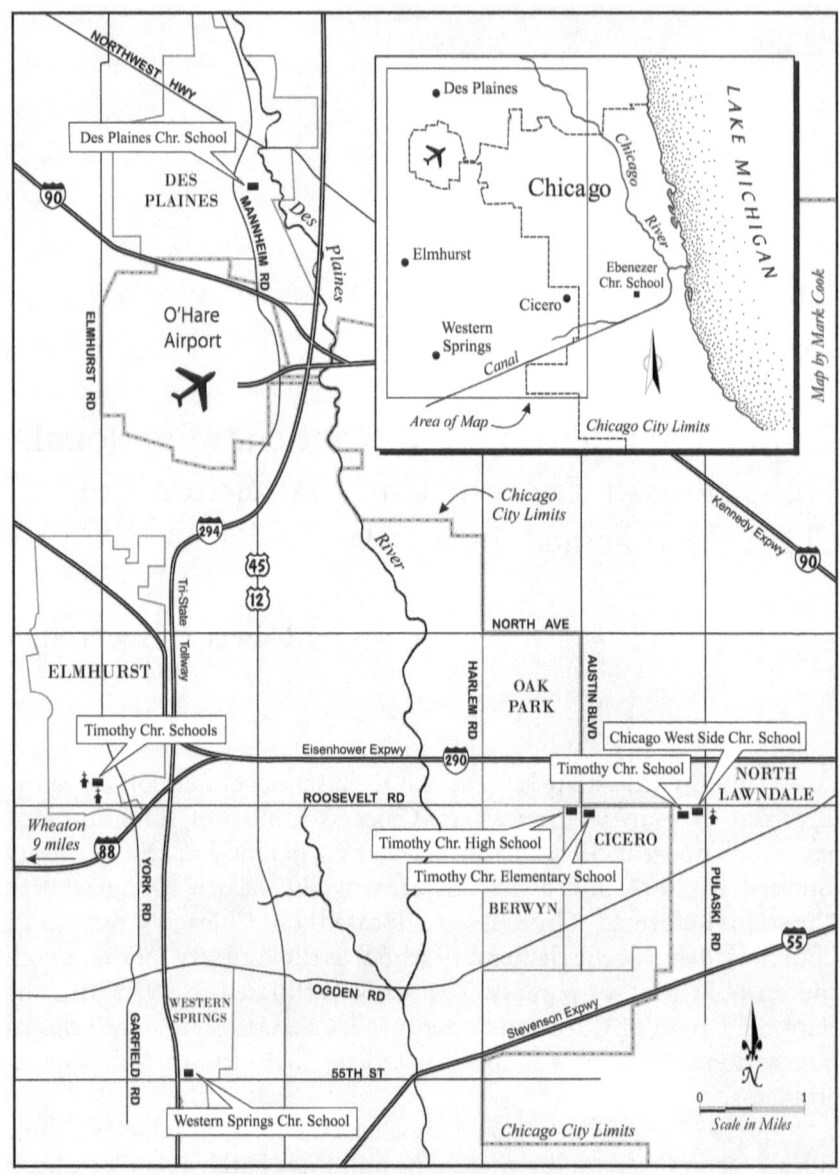

Chicago and Western Suburbs map

This article considers the transformation of Timothy Christian Schools since the 1970s, from its Dutch Reformed ethnic roots into a nondenominational school serving students of diverse backgrounds from several hundred Christian congregations. The proportion of

From Dutch Reformed to Nondenominational   129

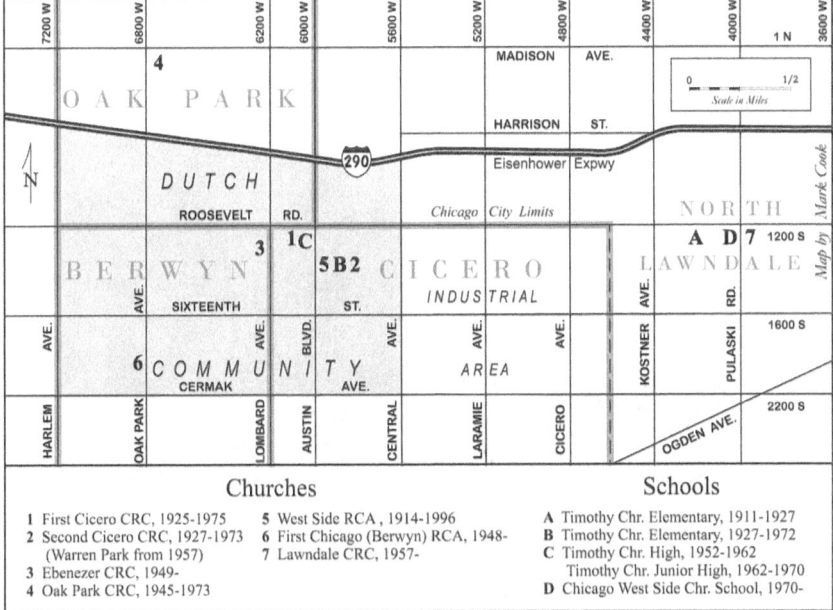

Cicero-Berwyn-Oak Park area

students from Reformed families has fallen in the last fifty years from 90 percent to 35 percent.[2]

Timothy's transformation is mirrored in urban Christian schools across North America. Ontario [Canada] Christian Schools, for example, transitioned in seven short years (2004-11), from 65 percent Dutch Reformed to 15 percent, with three hundred churches represented. The change was deliberate, and the curriculum continued to stress a Reformed worldview.[3] In contrast, Holland [Michigan] Christian Schools, located in a smaller community, dense with Christian Reformed families, has seen its Reformed contingent decline more moderately, from 80 percent to 60 percent, in the last thirty years—less than half of Timothy's decline.[4]

These transitions are reflected in CSI schools across North America. CSI enrollment peaked in 2001 at 107,700 students in 466 schools and has declined sharply since. Nearly three hundred schools have either closed or dropped membership since the 2005-6 school

[2] Board minutes, 20 Nov. 2006, 18 Aug. 2008, 19 Jan. 2009; *Reflector*, Spring 2007, 10 (quote), Spring 2008, Fall 2010.
[3] Len Stob, email, 18 May 2019.
[4] Phone call, James Bultman, acting superintendent, 7 May 2019.

Timothy School for Christian Instruction,
Chicago, 1912-27

year (when CSI began keeping such records).[5] Insiders believe the CSI numbers are worse than reported. And one result of the decline is that the CSI pension plan is deeply underwater financially, and member schools are dropping coverage.

Canadian Christian educator Adrian Guldemond says the CSI statistics are "the harsh reality of school closings and general stagnation in the CSI network across North America since 2010." Guldemond and his ten contributors—almost all educators—warn that the "soul of the Christian school movement ... [is] increasingly at risk."[6] Since the 1970s, CSI schools have reached out to the wider Christian community in order to survive. They may have had no alternative, but what are the risks of reaching out?

One risk is if this broader appeal will in fact stave off the demise of the Christian school movement. A related, salient question is: Does the loss of an ethnoreligious foundation doom a school? Religion and ethnicity are not educational issues, but they pose unique challenges. As

[5] In 2010 CSI enrollment had fallen to 87,000 students in 397 schools, a 20 percent decline. In 2018 the totals had recovered to 89,888 students, an 8 percent decline since 2001. I am indebted to Debra Lantz, CSI executive assistant to the president, email, 4 Jan. 2019, for the 2018 statistics. For 2001 and 2010 statistics, see Adrian Guldemond, *Inspired by Vision—Constrained by Tradition: Conflict, Decline and Revival in Christian Schools in Ontario* [Canada], 1960-2010 (Winnipeg, MB: Monarch Educare Solutions, 2010, 2014), 19-20.
[6] Guldemond, *Inspired by Vision*, ix, x.

From Dutch Reformed to Nondenominational 131

Timothy School of Christian Instruction, Cicero, 1927-72

Guldemond notes, "Ordinary Dutch [Reformed] habits" are important in terms of sacrificial giving, lifestyle, and, one might add, heritage.[7] Another related risk is whether a curriculum based on a Reformed worldview can be sustained when the student body and faculty are mostly non-Reformed.

The mentality of Timothy's founding generations was based on an adage often voiced from the pulpit: "The Christian school is built, not on the soft, moist silt of the wisdom of men; it is built on the solid rocks of God's changeless truth." But little is changeless in today's postmodern culture.[8]

It is time to reassess the Christian school movement built by Dutch Reformed immigrants since the 1880s in the United States and since the 1960s in Canada. Timothy, with 108 years of history, can serve as an example of a school that has transformed itself theologically from Dutch Reformed to nondenominational. Timothy's leaders recognized the reality that the school's Reformed heritage had been supplanted gradually over the last fifty years by a committed Christian faith that is vibrant and deeply rooted. But the curriculum is no longer guided by the Dutch Reformed "world and life view" of the founding generations.

Timothy's founding mission

Timothy's first constitution in 1907 clearly defined its mission: "To provide Christian Instruction for the covenant children, . . . [based

[7] Ibid., 27.
[8] Ibid., 16.

Nellie Van Zanten's 4th-5th grade class, February 11, 1930

High school in Cicero, 1950-62;
junior high, 1962-70

High school in Elmhurst, dedicated 1962

on] the Word of God in accordance with the Confessional Standards of the Reformed Churches, ... that they may be useful members of Church, State, and society." The Confessional Standards are the Three Forms of Unity—Belgic Confession (1566), Heidelberg Catechism (1563), and Canons of Dort (1618-19).

Board members and teachers were required to be confessing members of "a Reformed Church" that honored these confessions. Teachers were subject to dismissal for deviating from "Reformed texts," leading an "un-Christian life," or belonging to a secret society. (The CRC has barred Freemasons since its inception in 1857.) The final article in the school's founding constitution declared that the mission "may not be changed."[9] And it was not changed for 112 years, until 2019, when the dictum to ground the curriculum on the Dutch Reformed Confessions was deleted in favor of one based on the Bible itself. Creedal adherents, it should be added, believe that the Confessional Standards are derived explicitly from the Bible, but this explicit connection was no longer a guiding assumption in the school's reconfigured curriculum.

Although Timothy was founded to educate Christian Reformed youth, from the early days, a few families "outside our circle" were admitted. In 1924—year thirteen—six of eighteen new students were non-Reformed. In the 1940s, several professors at Northern Baptist Seminary enrolled their children. In the 1950s and early 1960s, four Baptists were hired as faculty—a band director (1954), a fourth grade teacher (1955), a junior high math teacher (1957), and a Bible teacher

[9] Constitution and bylaws, adopted 1907; revised 1921, 28 Nov. 1945.

Junior high school in Elmhurst, dedicated 1970

(1961). One Christian Reformed consistory protested engaging the Bible teacher, but the board opined that "churches should not become involved with the hiring of teachers." They promised to make every possible effort to hire teachers of Reformed persuasion. Salaries were low, and Calvin College, the main recruiting ground, was not graduating enough teachers, especially music majors.[10]

Timothy's mission transformed

Beginning in the 1970s, Christian Reformed birthrates declined, due to the birth control pill and socioeconomic changes. Since enrollment was the tail that wagged the dog, the board spoke bluntly to the constituency: "It is easy to see the problem when you realize we are graduating from our High School 80 or more students each year and enrolling an average of 30-40 students in 1st grade." Timothy's viability was at stake. The best solution, in the board's view, was to find families in "evangelical Christian circles in the area served by our schools" who might desire Christian education for their children. The board appointed an outreach committee to identify such families.[11]

Within five years, nearly four hundred students were coming from a plethora of churches—Assemblies of God, Baptist, Bible, Christian, Lutheran, Pentecostal, Presbyterian, and other non-Dutch Reformed congregations. The tent was large and later would include Roman Catholic and Eastern Orthodox students. In general, this move served its intended purpose: to help the bottom line by filling empty seats, and students from non-Reformed churches paid full tuition, not the discounted rate granted to students from Reformed churches.

[10] Board minutes, 15 Apr. 1954, 16 June 1955, 24 Sept. 1957, 4 Oct. 1961, 11 Jan. 1962 (quote).
[11] Ibid., 14 Feb. 1974.

The former were called "affiliated churches," the latter, "supporting churches."[12] Supporting churches had to pledge to contribute the difference between full and discounted tuition for their members' students who attended Timothy.

Since all parents qualified as members of the school society—the ultimate governing body—those from non-Reformed churches could vote for board members, constitutional changes, building projects, and capital campaigns. The resulting transitions gave rise to tension between Reformed members and the newcomers. These transitions had to be managed well, because they risked the loss of vital financial support from the supporting churches, which had given birth to the school.

A large capital campaign in the 1980s to upgrade school facilities brought the issue to a head. Before kicking off the campaign, the board hired an outside company to survey the constituency. Thirty-five intensive interviews with opinion leaders revealed "an extraordinary enthusiasm for, loyalty to, and pride in Timothy Christian schools." But some respondents from Christian Reformed churches, primarily the financial heavy lifters, expressed concerns about losing the Reformed heritage of "*onze* school." The survey uncovered a we-versus-they mentality that worried the board.[13] The board found that there was a fine line between listening to Reformed churches and conforming to their views.

The board insisted that the "outsiders" in the school society would not weaken Reformed perspectives in the classroom. "The constitution of the Society protects this principle and cannot be changed," they averred. They promised to uphold enrollment standards and preserve the mission of the school in administration, staffing, and curriculum.[14] The onus was on the board and administration to manage change without alienating faithful Christian Reformed supporters.

They apparently succeeded, because in 1988, the society voted to fund a building upgrade by a large margin (131-31). The board's implicit trust in Arnie Hoving, long-time superintendent, and Peter Huizenga, board president, was reflected in the decision to build. Indeed, as will become apparent, wise leadership by astute boards and administrators helped Timothy transition from its Dutch Reformed foundations.

---

[12] Arnold Hoving, email, 29 Sept. 2017; secretary's annual report, 18 Sept. 1975; *Timothy Reflector*, Dec. 1972; *Reflector*, Fall 2011.
[13] *Reflector*, Jan. 1988, 3-8, for the entire report.
[14] *Timothy Reflector*, Dec. 1976.

136 DUTCH REFORMED EDUCATION

Arnie Hoving appointed high school principal, 1969 (*Saga*, 1968)

1974 constitutional revision

The board had to square a circle, that is, to admit hundreds of non-Reformed students while maintaining the Reformed perspective mandated by the constitution. Since parents of non-Reformed students were eligible for society membership with full voting rights over board seats, budgets, building projects, and the rest, how could the Reformed foundation be preserved? The leaders tried to walk the tightrope but with increasing difficulty. The two goals were contradictory, and in 2019, the board faced reality and dropped any reference to the Reformed faith.

Opening the school to outsiders, in the first place, required revising the constitution to give them a seat at the table. The main roadblock was the 1907 stipulation requiring agreement with Dutch Reformed confessional standards for society membership, board seats, and faculty. In 1974 the board took the first step by setting aside this requirement in favor of one that opened membership to all parents of an "Evangelical Church." When the society became bogged down over defining the word "evangelical," the board had to find another way to open membership to non-Reformed parents.[15]

Their solution was to single out the oldest of the Reformed confessional standards—the Belgic Confession of 1556. The Belgic

---

[15] For this and the following paragraphs, see *Timothy Reflector*, Aug., Nov. 1974, Oct. 1975, Oct. 1976; board minutes, 19 Sept., 17 Apr. 1975.

Confession, written by Guido de Brés in 1556, had been adopted by Reformed Churches across Europe. Article 29 lists the three marks of a true church: the pure preaching of the gospel, the pure administration of the sacraments, and the faithful exercise of discipline. Membership in a "true church" became the criterion for membership in Timothy's society. Assessing whether or not an individual congregation met the three criteria, however, was beyond the ken of Timothy leaders, so, in effect, all Christian communions would qualify. Directors had to be "members in full communion," and faculty had to be *"regular attenders"* (italics mine). With this 1974 constitutional change, Timothy's leadership and faculty were opened to the widest ecclesiastical diversity within the Christian faith.

But what one hand gave, the other took away. Society members also had to "agree with this constitution," which meant accepting a curriculum based on the "Word of God in accordance with the Confessional Standards of the Reformed Churches." The revised constitution created a disjuncture between non-Reformed membership and a Reformed curriculum. Non-Reformed parents had to be willing for their children to be taught from a Reformed perspective. What this meant in practice was unclear and perhaps irrelevant if it had become a dead letter.

To what extent was the curriculum Reformed in the 1970s? This is difficult to determine since curriculum committee minutes and the teachers' lesson plans are not extant. But it is likely that teachers, faced with students from numerous Christian traditions, treaded lightly on Reformed distinctives, except in Bible class, which often relied on Louis Berkhof's *Summary of Christian Doctrine*, and in literature and social studies, for which CSI textbooks were available. In the sciences, few Christian textbooks existed, so that complicated the teaching of a distinctly Reformed perspective in those areas. To further complicate matters, teachers increasingly were not of Reformed background. So, it is likely that the Bible was more front and center in school life than were Reformed textbooks.

Admissions processes and criteria

The revised constitution required board members to be admissions gatekeepers, seen as essential to maintain the integrity of Timothy's mission. The board faithfully paired off to interview all non-Reformed church parent applicants, guided by five criteria: (1) at least one parent must be an active member of a Christian church, (2) there must be an expressed commitment by the parents to Christian day school education, (3) the student's educational needs must be compatible with Timothy's programs, (4) full tuition would be required, and (5) there must be an acceptable explanation if the parents did not enroll all their school-age children at Timothy.[16]

To ensure confidence in the interview process, the board added the following promise: "It cannot be overemphasized that the parent or family must have a strong Christian commitment, and only those who accept this are accepted." Screening every prospective parent was very time consuming, and not every board member was qualified for the task. Was at least one parent an active member of a true church? Was the motive based on a religious commitment or a desire for an elite private school? It required the wisdom of Job to discern true from false motives. That more than eight out of ten applicants were admitted under the five criteria suggests that interviewing teams were rather flexible in assessing "a strong Christian commitment." The push for enrollment could cloud the judgment of interviewers. Ultimately, they relied on God to send families "whose commitments are genuine and whose love for Christ is sure."[17] When Superintendent Arnold Hoving retired in 1994, he boasted that the student body was spilt 50/50 between Reformed and non-Reformed students.[18]

The faculty also changed after 1974 as more non-Reformed teachers were hired. Bible classes, with few exceptions, were staffed by teachers of the Reformed faith, but that was not necessarily so for classes in the arts and sciences. In addition to Reformed colleges, especially Calvin and Trinity Christian, teachers came from Wheaton College, Trinity Evangelical Divinity School, Northern Baptist Seminary, and public universities.

By the 1990s, just as Christian schools were catching up on faculty salaries and benefits, another crisis developed: the declining commitment to Christian day schools among families in Christian Reformed congregations. With less church support, tuition had to be raised faster than inflation. This increased the need to recruit students from nonsupporting churches who paid the full tuition rate, rather

---

[16] *Timothy Reflector*, June 1981.
[17] The guidelines document was approved at the board meeting of 11 Nov. 1974 and published in *Timothy Reflector*, Mar. 1975 (quotes); secretary's annual report, 18 Sept. 1975. For enrollment statistics of Christian Reformed youth from 1930 to 1970, by decades, see NUCS, *Directory, 1970-1971* (Grand Rapids, MI: 1971), 251.
[18] Hoving email, 29 Sept. 2018; *Timothy Reflector*, Mar., Oct. 1975.

than a "sliding-scale" or discounted rate. The years of growth since 1960 were ending.

Constitutional revisions in 1999

After six years of labor by a constitutional revision committee and many postponements by the board, the school modified its constitution and bylaws in 1999. First, requirements were tightened for supporting-church status, which granted the coveted minimum tuition rate. Supporting churches must actively support the cause of Christian education at Timothy, encourage enrollment there, help parents meet tuition costs, and allow the school to fundraise in the congregation. Most importantly, supporting churches must contribute the difference between the reduced and full cost of tuition for their students.

Board members met with church councils of Timothy families to discuss these revisions and try to increase the number of supporting congregations. But the requirements were almost insurmountable for affiliated churches. So the number of supporting churches remained few—six or seven Christian Reformed churches. By the year 2000, 53 percent of society members belonged to more than one hundred affiliated churches, which gave them a majority vote in elections for board members, annual budgets, expansion projects, and all other vital school decisions.

Second, board membership from affiliated churches was increased to five out of twenty-one directors, or nearly one-quarter, whereas sixteen, or slightly over three-quarters, came from supporting churches. Third, in a nod to diversity, the constitution expanded Timothy's mission to serve students who "possess a wide range of abilities" and "come from diverse economic and cultural backgrounds." The school society approved the new constitution by an overwhelming vote, although turnout was light for such an important issue.[19]

Society membership followed enrollment patterns. In 2000 non-Reformed members comprised a majority, which gave them the upper hand in voting for board members, annual budgets, expansion projects, and all other major school decisions. Board seats were still allocated in favor of Reformed church members by two-to-one. In 1998 a Lutheran was elected board president, followed by a Baptist with a degree from Baylor University. These two were the first non-Christian Reformed

---

[19] Board minutes, 8 Feb., 18 Mar. 1997, 19 Jan., 15 June, 20 July, 14 Dec. 1998, 17 May 1999; Society minutes, 18 Sept. 1997, *Annual Society Meeting Report, 1998-1999*, 4 Mar. 1999; annual society meeting, 28 May 2008, *Annual Society Report, 2008-9*.

board presidents. The Lutheran had grown up in Lombard Christian Reformed Church.[20]

Enrollment trends continued to shift toward non-Reformed students. In the 2004-5 school year, of 140 families interviewed, only 22 percent (30) were Christian Reformed or Reformed; 63 percent (87) were other Protestant, including one from *Unity Church* (*Unitarian*) of Oak Park (italics mine); and 20 (15 percent) were Roman Catholic or Orthodox. Only three families, all Catholic, were denied admittance. Affiliated church families that year outnumbered supporting Reformed families by three to one, and the Catholic percentage was approaching that of Reformed persuasion. These numbers represented new admissions. The total student body was 35 percent Reformed, about the same ratio as it is today.[21]

In 2008 a change in the bylaws granted affiliated churches two additional seats on the board, raising their representation from five to seven seats, or one-third. In short, the ratio of Reformed to non-Reformed board members shifted from 3:1 to 2:1 As Superintendent Dan Van Prooyen noted: "This change would better reflect the church representation shift that is apparent in our student body." The board itself chose nominees from affiliated churches, whereas nominees from supporting churches were chosen by both the board and individual church councils.[22]

Constitutional revision in 2019

In 2019 the board adopted a new mission/vision/values statement dubbed 2.0, which synthesized the results of professional school-wide surveys of parents, alumni, staff, students, and board and represented the thinking of "ALL OF US," according to Superintendent Matt Davidson.[23]

The newly articulated mission was "to uphold Biblical truth, ignite academic growth, and inspire courageous leadership one student at a time." The vision was "to develop life-long learners and servant leaders who fully live out their purpose in the world for Christ." The values—nine in number—were "Christ-centered, Biblically-rooted, excellence driven, growth-oriented, relationship-focused, individually-customized, leadership-minded, opportunity-based, and

---

[20] Board minutes, 17 June 1971; *Timothy Reflector*, Nov. 1974, Dec. 1976.
[21] Calculated from admissions in board minutes, 19 Jan. through 15 Nov. 2005.
[22] Swierenga, *His Faithfulness Continues*, 510.
[23] Davidson email, 6 June 2019.

From Dutch Reformed to Nondenominational 141

Mission/Vision/Values 2.0
(2019)

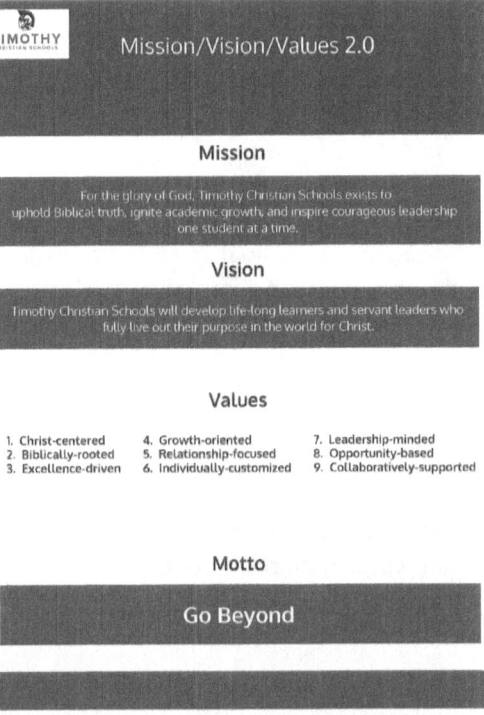

collaboratively-supported." Interested observers might add the values of discernment, discipleship, and cultural engagement.

The new mission statement acknowledges the reality that Timothy serves a wide variety of Christians. The board has officially designated Timothy a nondenominational (or interdenominational) Christian school. After 112 years, the curriculum is no longer based on "the Word of God in accordance with the Confessional Standards of the Reformed Churches"; it is simply "Christ-centered" and "Biblically rooted." This significant change is being incorporated into a new constitution to be ratified by the society in the near future. These steps are likely *pro forma*, since the board approved the statement "unanimously and enthusiastically." This change also led to disaffiliation from Christian Schools International, a Reformed association.[24]

A word on governance

Governance is the key to sustaining the Christian faith in schools like Timothy that have transitioned from a homogeneous Dutch

---

[24] Ibid.

Reformed foundation to diverse nondenominational institutions. Guldemond and Leonard Stob, both Christian school administrators, have studied governance issues carefully. They argue cogently that poor governance is the root problem of failing schools and good governance is the answer for survival.[25]

The model Stob recommends is mission-directed governance, rather than the traditional reactive model in vogue in most Christian schools, in which boards and superintendents deal with issues as they arise. In a mission-directed model, the board adopts a clear mission/vision statement and imbeds it in the authority structure of the school, so that administrators are held accountable in hiring, curriculum design, extracurricular offerings, and school operations, including discipline. School boards are ultimately responsible for honoring mission statements. The board must hold itself, administrators, and staff accountable, and the mission cannot be changed without board or society approval. In short, a strong governance structure is the best way to keep a Christian school true to its mission and values.

Conclusion

For the first sixty years, Timothy was an ethnoreligious island. As late as 1970, it enrolled over 90 percent of school-age children from a half-dozen supporting Christian Reformed churches. The school helped the families and churches to maintain religious homogeneity, notably because high school sweethearts married soon after graduating.

The school culture changed rapidly after Timothy relocated to the Elmhurst campus, and declining birthrates led the board to reach out to Christian families within busing distance. Soon, a third, then half, and now today, two thirds of the student body come from non-Reformed homes. The constitution was amended several times to reflect this new reality. In 2010 the board hired the first non-Dutch Reformed superintendent, Matt Davidson, who grew up in a Lutheran church and came to Timothy from a nondenominational school system in Arizona.

Timothy's gradual evolution from a Christian Reformed school to a broadly Christian institution was due primarily to finances and secondarily to mission outreach. Tuition has been kept within reach

---

[25] Guldemond, *Inspired by Vision*, ix, 15; Leonard Stob, *Mission Directed: Governing Your Christian School with Purpose* (Colorado Springs, CO: Purposeful Design Publications, 2010, 2015), 21-41. Stob is an ACSI (Association of Christian Schools International) consultant and former CSI principal and superintendent. He is also a graduate and former faculty member of Timothy Christian Schools.

of middle-class parishioners, and non-Reformed families with financial need are assisted by the Timothy Foundation. Christian Reformed deaconates assist their member families, and religious diversity promises to be a fertile environment for nurturing the Christian faith on campus.

Healthy schools like Timothy are fighting hard to hold the faith against strong secular forces. George Marsden explains that almost every school of higher learning began as a Christian institution only to fall into apostasy and secularism within several generations. Only mission-driven Christian schools will survive in such a challenging environment, provided they learn how to manage change.[26]

---

[26] George Marsden, *The Soul of the American University: From Protestant Establishment to Established Non-Belief* (NY: Oxford University Press, 1994).

CHAPTER 8

Creating the Third Way in Canada: The Ontario Alliance of Christian Schools, 1952–2018

Adrian Guldemond

On this morning of June 14, 2019, I begin by announcing that last night the Toronto Raptors—that is, the Toronto, *Ontario*, Raptors— defeated the San Francisco Golden State Warriors for the NBA Championship. Let that sink in for a moment. A Canadian team holds the 2019 world title in professional basketball. I mention this "historic" event because it will be a long time before the Raptors win again,[1] and this rare athletic success allows me to highlight yet another Canadian success—the Ontario Alliance of Christian Schools (OACS),[2] one of the few success stories in Canadian educational innovation. Though the odds were stacked against it in 1952, much like the underrated Raptors in 2019, OACS succeeded.

OACS was the premier advocacy organization for independent schools in the province of Ontario from 1960 to 2010. In the beginning, the OACS network rescued the private school sector in Ontario from oblivion. In its heyday—from 1997 to 2007—OACS attained not only government funding for special needs students but also the legislated

---

[1] The Toronto Blue Jays last won the World Series in 1993, and the Toronto Maple Leafs last won the Stanley Cup in hockey in 1967.
[2] [A list of organizational acronyms follows this essay.—Ed.]

Equity in Education Tax Credit (see below) for all private school parents in Ontario. In 2002 OACS had a staff of eighteen and provided fifteen financial and educational programs for its eighty member schools that enrolled 13,500 students. OACS had an annual operating budget of over $1.38 million. These fifteen programs were avant-garde and represented a comprehensive community philosophy of schooling known as the "Third Way."

This essay is a brief account of the development of Christian (Dutch Reformed) education in eastern Canada through the lens of the activities of one of the central organizations of Ontario's educational system. There is currently no complete account of this Christian School movement in print, but it was historically significant from 1955 to 2005. OACS created a professional framework for small Christian schools, thus providing public credibility during a critical time of Dutch immigrant insecurity. This essay outlines the main stages in the enculturation of educational institutions begun in an ethnic subculture.

The Third Way refers to the goal of creating a third educational system, parallel to the two funded school systems—public and Catholic—that existed in many Canadian provinces in 1950. Since then, many Canadian provinces have begun funding a variety of school systems in a variety of ways. But Canadians are mosaic pluralists—some groups are more equal than others.

The Dutch Calvinists who immigrated to Canada from 1947 to 1955 (the big wave) came from an established tradition in the Netherlands that had three fully funded school systems: public, Protestant, and Catholic. And although Dutch Catholic immigrants were happy to send their children to the Ontario Catholic schools free of charge, Dutch Calvinists were surprised to learn that Protestants would have to pay for the privilege of operating schools with a Reformed orientation. They believed this was rank discrimination on religious grounds. They were told that the public schools were Protestant, hence "Dutch schools" were superfluous.

This unfriendly Canadian attitude led to an existential dilemma: either be free of charge and diluted or expensive and undiluted. The dilemma was resolved around 1950 by the pioneers as they considered their religious obligations and political options. The answer was to create the Third Way: begin with the expensive and pure (separatist) approach and work hard to remove discrimination through political and legal means. This political goal (equality) was no pipedream; after all, the previous generation had achieved this same full parity in the

Netherlands by 1917. This epic struggle is part of the family lore of many Dutch immigrant families, including mine. For leading that struggle, Abraham Kuyper, prime minister of the Netherlands from 1901 to 1905, was a demigod in conservative Reformed circles, as well as a household name.

In 1950, that tradition, with Kuyper's central ideas about structural pluralism, was still alive and well among the immigrants landing all over Canada. Kuyper's political philosophy was that civil society is made up of a number of independent but interrelated "spheres" (church, family, education, business, arts, sports, and so forth), each of which has its own "natural" character derived from God's creation order, and neither church nor state should try to control the internal development of these spheres. Schools should be governed by their own "educational" school boards and not church consistories or state inspectors; thus, the importance of the word "societies" in the OACS and Christian school constitutions.

OACS begins, 1952

OACS began at a meeting on March 25, 1952, held at the first Christian Reformed Church in Hamilton, Ontario. Present were nineteen representatives of the seven Christian school societies in the province. They were called together to set up an organization to advance their collective goals. In typical Calvinistic fashion, they spent the day debating the contents of the proposed constitution (bylaws) for this new organization, first called the Ontario Association of Calvinistic Christian School Societies (OACCSS). They agreed on the general purpose:

> The Calvinistic Christian school societies in Ontario wishing to be organized as an Alliance in order to: (1) further the larger cause of Christian education, (2) strengthen individual societies in Ontario, (3) help local societies attain their goals do hereby establish the Constitution.

The "larger cause" was the establishment of a Christian public school system in Ontario. This was to be the third system, parallel to the public and the Catholic systems already in existence and funded by the government. The assumption at the meeting and around the province was that there would also be a network of Christian organizations to assist in this endeavor. There was agreement on the urgent need for Christian organizations in all spheres of life organized around biblical principles. This Kuyperian[3] vision was not at issue, but its implementation in a strange land was daunting.

These folks were not unfamiliar with the hazards involved in this venture. The Reformed section of the Dutch immigrants to Canada had just been through another toxic church split in 1944[4] in the Netherlands, and World War II wounds were fresh and deep in every family. In fact, the (Dutch) minutes[5] of that very meeting prophetically spelled out one of the main debates of the next thirty years, namely the scope and nature of the "Reformed" part of Reformed education: "The discussion around this article took a lot of time. Some were of the opinion that this article needs a broader interpretation; others saw a danger in that approach."

These debates were lengthy; some wanted only the three Creeds of the Christian Reformed Church in the constitution of the schools, whereas others argued for many Reformed creeds[6] and even philosophic statements of Calvinistic principles. As a result of these tensions, the history of the alliance vacillates between broad and narrow interpretations of Kuyperianism.

Right from the beginning, there was a strong cultural engagement spirit in the Dutch Reformed group. The editor[7] of the new magazine *Canadian Calvinist* was clear in his 1949 editorial advice: "Become Canadian citizens so that you can take an active part in the public life of the nation." Abraham Kuyper had said the same thing in Grand Rapids in 1896, but the result there was tepid. In Canada, the result was

---

[3] Kuyperian Pluralism was based on a concept of "sphere sovereignty," which justified a confessional basis for social organizations. Reformed Canadians developed a unique version of it, which I call Kuyperianism.

[4] The schism led to the formation of the Vrijgemaakte (Article 31) Gereformeerde Kerken in the Netherlands. It also led to the establishment of the Canadian Reformed Church in Canada, along with its own group of schools. "De bespreking van Artikel 2 nam veel tijd. Sommigen waren van mening dat dit article een ruimere interpretatie moest hebben, terwijl anderen daarin gevaar zien."

[5] Incidentally, although the minutes in many schools were still in Dutch in the early fifties, English was the language of instruction in all the schools. Fluency in English was also a requirement for Dutch teachers arriving from the Netherlands. Unlike the isolationist practice in the American schools, retaining the Dutch language was neither tried nor even debated. Judging that the members had acquired enough fluency for meetings, OACS switched to English in 1954.

[6] Such as the Westminster Confession or the Philadelphia Confession.

[7] Rev. Paul DeKoek in Edmonton, Alberta.

enthusiastic, with heroic[8] efforts to set up Christian organizations of all kinds.[9] This enthusiasm led to many debates about which organization should be funded first.

The founders of OACS also agreed on another priority: they needed to work together because they could not appeal to any established authority to solve their problems. In a 1953 letter urging everyone to attend yet another meeting, OACS board members were rather direct:

> If you do not show up to help finalize the official bylaws, we are stuck, because we are not infallible popes who can just issue decrees. But, if you do not show up, you do not have the right to criticize us afterwards. So there, get to Hamilton.[10]

And they did "get to Hamilton." They passed the constitution by spring 1956 and adopted the shorter name—Ontario Alliance of Christian Schools—as the official one.

The quiet 1950s

Getting their feet on the Canadian ground was goal number one—high-altitude vision came later. In 1952 there were two "Christian"[11] schools in operation—Hamilton and Holland Marsh—with 222 students and six teachers—three males and three females. Seven school societies were waiting to get started. OACS representatives focused on recruiting the needed teachers for the seven schools in operation by 1956. The OACS board set up the Teacher Recruitment Fund, financed by church collections, to encourage high school graduates to take courses and/or attend Calvin College. In view of the negative publicity the "Dutch" schools were receiving, the board agreed to begin publishing the *Christian School Herald*, a magazine devoted to Christian Schools. It was financed by subscriptions and was an immediate success across the country. With help from the National Union of Christian Schools (NUCS) staff in Grand Rapids,[12] the board also set up a school inspection program in order to encourage common standards of quality.

---

[8] The battle around legal certification of the Christian Labour Association of Canada was indeed heroic, since they were taking on the brutal Teamsters Union in its heyday.
[9] For example, the Dutch Credit Union and Christian Farmers Association.
[10] I summarized the letters which conveyed this urgent tone.
[11] The name "Calvin" was added later in 1958. The original name was "Christian."
[12] John VanderArk had just started as the new executive director of NUCS.

Long-term organizational goals were formulated in strategic stages, such as starting a provincial high school so that its graduates could attend the provincial normal schools, or better yet, a Christian normal school.[13] Hamilton District Christian High School began in a modest church basement in 1959. Board discussions had already noted awareness of the problem with Calvin College and Dort College diplomas: they did not meet Canadian certification standards. Virtually all agreed it was critical that OACS schools employ teachers who could be certified in Ontario. Hence the establishment of the Christian Normal School Committee in 1958.

The radical 1960s

Rapid growth took place in the 1960s. After ten years, in 1962, OACS had thirty-two member schools with 4,277 students, as well as twenty-three member societies. Now that the schools had been operating for a while, the real cost of elementary education had become apparent. There was considerable pressure on OACS to solve financing issues. There were three questions: Did tuition payments qualify as charitable donations? Were the schools exempt from municipal property taxes? When was the provincial government going to give the same subsidies to Calvinists as to Catholic Separate Schools? Committees were set up in 1960, and reports were given to the board. OACS commissioned legal opinions to stickhandle the politicians.

In 1961 OACS agreed to test provincial legal waters by launching a court case on behalf of the Hamilton Christian School Society operating the Calvin elementary school to test the Separate School Act provisions. Did Calvin Elementary qualify as a separate school? The judge said no, it did not. New negotiations took place with several municipalities, and these were favorable on the property tax matter, but only as local exceptions, not as law. In 1965 some OACS board members met with officials in Ottawa to discuss a resolution to the tax reassessment, implemented because the schools did not issue donation receipts properly. A positive outcome was reported: some tuition amounts were deductible—as a matter of local office discretion, not due to a change in the federal law. The pioneers, however, remained optimistic. Comments in the board minutes indicate that it was time to appoint a lobbyist to deal with the politicians. It would be a long haul.

---

[13] Normal schools were the 19th-century institutions for teacher training in North America. These were changed first to teacher colleges after WWI and then to faculties of education in the 1970s.

Organizing school inspections, operating a resource center, processing bulk-buying opportunities, and handling the endless questions from new school societies about teacher salaries and contracts became a burdensome use of board meeting time. In 1963 the OACS board, after rejecting American teacher candidates put forward by NUCS, appointed Albert Hengstman, principal at Sarnia, as the first full-time director of education for OACS. He was required to be a jack-of-all-trades and soon requested secretarial help, especially to handle the growing Teacher Recruitment Fund process of applications, collections, and distribution of funds.

Amid the manifold stressors, there was good news from the province of Alberta in 1967. That provincial government had agreed to provide a subsidy for all private schools. The OACS board immediately extended Hengstman, the Albertan lobbyist,[14] a part-time contract in 1968, with the mandate to lobby the Ontario government in Queen's Park, Toronto. This he proceeded to do very effectively, and pressure mounted at Queen's Park to extend[15] funding for the Catholics and begin funding for the Protestants. At this time, OACS became the voice for alternative schools in Ontario. In 1967 Olthuis also worked part time for the Association for the Advancement of Christian Scholarship (AACS),[16] which had just started the Institute for Christian Studies (ICS), the prototype[17] for a new kind of "people's university" in downtown Toronto. The main organizational goals of the OACS board were thus advancing slowly but surely as new schools were opened, and the Christian school movement seemed to be at the forefront of cultural conversations.

In the 1960s, theological trends in Reformed communities across Canada were influenced by the AACS movement in Toronto. A number of freshly minted PhDs[18] from the Free University in Amsterdam had returned home and started promoting the Cosmonomic philosophy of Herman Dooyeweerd. For Reformed traditionalists, this movement featured a good thing—a more comprehensive and deeper Christian philosophy—and a bad thing—a revolutionary mindset perfectly in tune with the youth rebellion of the late 1960s. These "young fellas" (I was

---

[14] The main lobbyist was lawyer John Olthuis in Edmonton.
[15] Ontario, Quebec, and New Brunswick financed Catholic schools up to the end of grade 10.
[16] The AACS began as the Association for Reformed Scientific Studies (ARSS) in 1955.
[17] A Christian university was a future capstone in the edifice of a Christian school system.
[18] A. DeGraaff, H. Hart, B. Zylstra, Jim Olthuis, and H. VanBelle.

one of them) challenged not only the secular culture but also the more traditional versions of Reformed theology.

The first phase of the "reformation" was benign. It picked up on what was a basic Kuyperian theology—the pluralistic principle of sphere sovereignty and an organic view of society. This meant that official church creeds could not be determinative for deciding school professional matters. As a result of this debate, the OACS board proposed a change to its constitution's Article 2 to add the Education Creed (a set of Christian principles), summarizing the modern Reformed view of education. After two years of intense debate, the membership adopted this principled revision in 1966. That was achieved with no organizational fallout, just some bad temper. This improvement put OACS in a position to consider admitting non-Reformed families to the schools and recruiting evangelical schools to its membership.

The second stage, in the mid-1960s, took its point of departure from the heated discussion in Amsterdam around the views of Prof. Harry Kuitert on evolution. Opinions became more radical, challenging the idea of legitimate authority beyond the Bible. Was the school board's authority based on specific Bible texts, or on a concept of "office," or should it be based on psychology, competence, and insight? Soon the evolution conflict erupted at Calvin College and spread to the pages of the *Banner*[19] and hence to coffee *kletsches* all over Canada.

The inexperienced school boards were not happy about having to deal with this unsettling trend. One of the implications of this philosophy was that parental authority, represented on the board, was limited by professional teacher authority, supported by the provincial organizations. Who should decide the school curriculum—volunteers or professionals? Should there be an insight test before one could serve as a board member? Was this a new view of "office"? Was this view biblical or secular?

This debate came to a climax in the 1969 crisis at Toronto District Christian High School (TDCH) in Woodbridge.[20] One of the teachers had decided to teach a controversial novel in grade 12—*Catcher in the Rye*, by J. D. Salinger. When the board heard about that via the students, its members were upset about not having been consulted on this decision. Over the 1968-69 school year, the heat of the discussion increased. It soon moved from the novel (with bad language and corrupt

---

[19] The official publication of the CRCNA, read all over Canada every Sunday.
[20] See ch. 4 in Adrian Guldemond et al., *"Inspired by Vision...Constrained by Tradition"* (Winnipeg, Canada: Monarch Publications, 2013), for the entire crisis story.

morals) to the matter of authority, about *who* was running this high school. After many meetings, no resolution was in sight, and in April, the annual contracts of the entire staff of twelve were not renewed. The whole staff left in June 1969. The ex-staff of TDCH appealed their fate to the NUCS House of Delegates Convention in August. This assembly merely referred the explosive matter of authority to the NUCS Public Relations Committee to be discussed in the fall. By September 2, 1969, a new faculty was in place at TDCH.

This Toronto crisis left a major impression on the other five Ontario Christian high schools for the next decade. For teachers, the lesson was to cool the reformational[21] rhetoric. For boards, it was that they should not have pastors on the boards and committees of the schools. Schools are their own social sphere, as Kuyper had taught. For reformers themselves, it had also become clear that challenging Reformed doctrine from the inside was a risky "reform" strategy, since they could be confused with popular Canadian authors challenging Christianity itself.[22] Was this stage a reformation or a revolution? That which was exciting to the younger generation was a threat to the older one. The older Dutch Reformed generation, having just immigrated, was in no mood to be told that the North American Way of Death[23] should be denounced from the pulpit. Fortunately, faith in Christian education withstood the fiery internal debates.

The American 1970s

By 1970 the number of OACS schools had grown to fifty-six, with eight thousand students and three hundred teachers, yet OACS was in the middle of an identity crisis. The energetic, young academics with new philosophic theories were also teaching the summer courses for teachers sponsored by OACS. Something had to be done. The OACS board was now in conservative hands, and in 1970, it decided to close down the radical *Christian School Herald* and transfer the promotion of Christian education to the safe, Grand Rapids, Michigan-based *Christian Home and School*, with a promise for a Canadian news "supplement," which did not materialize. In order to contain the increasing pressure

---

[21] "Reformational" was the name for a more radical version of reform stressing the mandate for social justice.
[22] Pierre Berton, *The Comfortable Pew* (Toronto: McClelland and Stewart, 1965), and the reply by William Kilbourn, *The Restless Church* (Toronto: McClelland and Stewart, 1966).
[23] A speech by Dr. H. R. Rookmaaker, a Dutch VU professor touring Canada in 1967.

of the young progressives for change, now fanned by a new publication, the *Vanguard*, the OACS board appointed a twenty-two-member commission "to investigate the unrest in our circles." The commission was representative ideologically as well as geographically, so the report had immediate credibility when it came out in June 1972.

The commission report brought a conciliatory tone to the discussion, noting that the Reformed doctrine of special and general revelation was broad enough to carry the current debate. It was a big tent. The report preferred the traditional position taken by the experienced NUCS staff in Grand Rapids, especially since, by then, they had many fine resources available for the classroom. The "radical" pedagogical position taken by the ICS faculty in Toronto needed to justify its new claims to the schools because the institute professors had not produced anything useful for the school curriculum. The schools supported this cautious approach, and in 1974, removed the radical Educational Creed from the OACS constitution. The report, however, had not recommended this change, thus a new backlash against "American imperialism" developed. Moreover, although many of the radical "young whipper snappers" were graduates of Calvin College, there was a general revulsion against Nixon and the Vietnam War in Canada.

As this ideological conflict played itself out across Canada, the practical business of operating schools soon took center stage. By 1975 the OACS board had approved the appointment of a new executive director to administer the growing resource center, the school inspections, the obvious need for good public relations, and the still-pressing government tax problems. A Canadian solution was desired in order to stop the tax reassessments.[24] In 1976 the board appointed Jack Fennema—an American approved by Grand Rapids—as the second full-time executive director.

Jack was well received in Ontario, and his affable character did a lot to restart the dialogue among the Reformed factions.[25] The workload, however, was heavy and the amount of necessary travel daunting. Fennema resigned in 1977, and the OACS board adopted a temporary tripartite solution. It split the job into administration, curriculum, and promotion and hired three experienced principals on

---

[24] Some schools were treating the entire amount of tuition as a charitable donation, contrary to a 1972 court ruling in the Zandstra v. R. case.

[25] I was president of the Administrators Association (OCSAA) at this time and met with Jack frequently.

Creating the Third Way in Canada 155

a part-time basis—Henk Hultink, John Stronks, and Mel Elzinga. This three-for-the-price-of-one arrangement worked well for OACS but not for the sponsoring school boards. In 1978 Elzinga resigned, and the OACS board decided to appoint a full-time Canadian executive director, without permission from NUCS. In January of 1979, I was appointed and charged with the task of leading the budding movement to greater unity and better quality.[26] The office was moved to Hamilton, Ontario, in the summer of 1979.

The progressive 1980s

Despite internal controversies, OACS schools kept growing. In 1980 there were seventy schools educating 7,290 pupils and employing 510 teachers in Ontario. The schools wanted the reassessments stopped and the income tax status of the schools settled. The technical side of the problem was solved by a new committee of lawyers and accountants who had advised the board that negotiation with the Canada Revenue Agency (CRA) in Ottawa was the route to go. Unfortunately, some of the more radical schools had philosophic reasons for violating the CRA rules set by the Canadian tax courts. It took me two years to get to know the officials, understand the tax problems, and persuade the school rebels that cooperating with the federal government was not the unprincipled destruction of Reformed philosophy. Rather, the new OACS plan was a strategic accommodation around an esoteric philosophy that no one in official Canada had ever heard before.

Once that consensus was achieved, I was able to persuade officials in Ottawa to accept a new accounting system and receipting formula that would end the reassessments. The new system was the beginning of a number of creative financial arrangements that were practical and profitable for all the stakeholders—parents, boards, and OACS itself. This created some financial relief for the sacrificing families and gave OACS authority to rationalize the local school financial formats.

While that reorientation was progressing, the OACS board finally decided to incorporate OACS and thus settle the director's liability problem.[27] That legal move, however, would reopen the constitutional problem of the Educational Creed. But this time around, in 1983, the board decided to be creative and send a questionnaire to the schools.

---

[26] I served as executive director until my retirement in 2009.
[27] The first attempt was made in 1965. OACS wanted to buy the CSH from Guardian Press, but this plan ran aground on personalities and legalities.

It offered three choices: a conservative status quo, the addition of a special Educational Creed, and the elimination of all Reformed Church creeds. The schools picked the second option by a wide margin, and although some debates at membership meetings were still heated, the board knew that, in the end, the schools would approve the modernized version over the old 1966 constitution. The new bylaws also gave the board itself more authority to make financially binding decisions. This was essential if the board was going to hire more staff. In 1984 the board appointed a permanent curriculum coordinator and a finance coordinator.[28]

In 1984 the government of Ontario announced that the Separate Catholic High Schools would receive funding equivalent to the secular public schools. There was a big uproar in the province, and the matter was the subject of two major court cases, in which OACS also participated. The courts sided with the government, and financial equalization for the Separate schools was put into place over the next two years. The courts ignored the OACS appeal for equal funding with the Catholics under the new Canadian Constitution with its equal-treatment provisions. Their claim was that similarly situated groups should receive equal treatment by the government in the provision of universal social services, such as elementary education. Apparently, equality did not trump the historic privilege claimed by the Catholics.

While legal and political advocacy was consuming my time, John Stronks was challenging the NUCS curriculum committees with help from the Alberta and British Columbia curriculum coordinators.[29] After much debate, Christian Schools International (as NUCS was renamed in 1981)[30] agreed to set up two separate national councils to design and process curriculum products for both countries separately. It was hard to get the Americans to understand that "Reformed" did not mean the same thing on the other side of the border—even in Bible materials. After a while, it was agreed that Canadian money should go to finance Canadian projects. This money issue was resolved in 1989 with a new binational "Seattle" agreement. Sharing and cooperation was official while Sheri Haan was executive director of the Grand Rapids-based Christian Schools International (CSI) between 1988 and 1996.

[28] John Stronks and Harry Nieboer.
[29] Harro VanBrummelen and John Vanderhoek.
[30] Another move seen in Canada as paternalistic and imperialistic. There were no other "nations" in the membership, except Canada. There were no differences in membership requirements between the two countries.

Surprisingly, the ten American district organizations flourished when the Canadian federal model was tried in Grand Rapids for some years.[31]

The gung-ho 1990s

The last decade of the twentieth century found the Christian schools doing well despite the recession in Canada at that time. In 1992 OACS membership was seventy-four schools, with 11,400 students taught by 745 teachers, all members of the Ontario Christian School Teachers Association. The leadership of the three Canadian districts[32] pushed expansion of the work of the provincial organizations beyond concerns over good Christian curriculum. To help its new schools, OACS hired a director of public relations in 1991 to encourage the schools to start working on their public image. OACS was also proposing open admissions at its conferences to support the renewed public interest in private and Christian schools. There was a clear trend in the younger schools to admit nontraditional[33] families. Image-conscious leaders wanted to ensure that some customary ethnic habits in the schools would not turn off the interested, Canadian-born evangelicals.

In 1990 the Ontario electorate stunned Canada by electing its first socialist government headed by Bob Rae and the New Democratic Party. This left-wing group was in principle opposed to funding private schools, so OACS decided that this was a good time to take the government to court over the lack of funding. The OACS court cases took place between 1992 and 1996 and were conducted in concert with the Canadian Jewish Congress. Regretfully, the Supreme Court of Canada sidestepped the main issue in 1996 and said that private school funding was a provincial policy discretion, not a legal charter obligation. Still, there were no charter[34] obstacles to funding private schools either.

After that legal clarification, OACS went back to lobbying the provincial government. The membership helped organize a grassroots political network in order to have an impact across the province. In 1995 conservatives under Mike Harris were elected to start their Common

---

[31] The eleven American district offices flourished up to 1998, and then they were undercut by renewed centralization policies from the CSI board.
[32] OACS, Society of Christian Schools in BC (Vancouver), and Prairie Association of Christian Schools (Edmonton).
[33] Not from Dutch and Reformed families who had supported the schools since the beginning.
[34] The Charter of Rights and Freedoms was added to the constitution in 1982. It enumerated such basic freedoms, as association, conscience, and religion.

Sense Revolution.[35] The new government was open to helping both private and independent schools. By 1998 the government had agreed to provide funding for special needs students, but the money came from the health budget. This avoided the direct attack of the teacher unions, who were very aggressive in making sure that not a penny from the education budget would go to "the enemies" of public education.

As the schools began admitting more diverse families, ethnic and doctrinal change was also showing up in the composition of the school boards. The Reformed, tradition-based, cooperative-management style dominating the boards was challenged by the more authoritarian style from the evangelical traditions. OACS decided to formalize the "Christian" management style in a set of manuals around governance. This series not only became the basis for an adult education program for board members but was also the first effort at online seminars.

In the meantime, the OACS curriculum department was progressing under the leadership of Jim Vreugdenhil and Herman Proper, elementary and secondary coordinators. Using creative outsourcing and part-time contracts, OACS was able to produce many, very creative units for a broad spectrum of school subjects. OACS published a book outlining its pedagogical theories[36] so that teachers could see that the curriculum materials were anchored in a coherent philosophic perspective. The only thing holding back the production of more units was money to hire the best educators.

As the potential impact of computers and the internet became clear, the OACS board appointed a director of technologies in 1997 to help switch the resource and publication medium to digital format. The staff set up committees to research classroom use of these new technologies, but many schools were not keen to get ahead of the curve. There was lingering doubt about the long-term viability of new technologies, especially as concerns circulated about the world-wide computer crash predicted for "Y2K"—January 1, 2000. Besides, other moral issues were more important before this new medium could be embraced.

Justice wins in 2001

OACS schools were still growing when the new millennium began. In 2000 OACS membership was up to eighty schools, with

---

[35] The Conservative Party campaigned on a platform of limited government and balanced budgets.
[36] *Hallmarks of Christian Schooling* (Hamilton, Ontario: Guardian Press, 1991).

13,500 students and 876 teachers. Its budget was $1.2 million, and the staff was at sixteen full-time equivalents. The offices were located in a building on the Ancaster Fairgrounds, which had room for portables to house the growing curriculum staff. John Van Asselt was the director of public relations in charge of the lobbying effort, which the board ramped up in 2001 with a part-time, paid team of four "parental school choice" organizers[37] across the province. The Canadian Jewish Congress adopted a similar grass roots political plan in electoral ridings (districts) with Jewish schools around Toronto.

Discussions with the ministry of education and finance officials led eventually to the adoption of a tax credit model for private school support. This suited the government because it was not "education" money, and it suited the conservative factions in the various private school communities who did not like direct grants to the schools.[38] In June 2001, the provincial minister of finance, Jim Flaherty, announced the Equity in Education Tax Credit (EETC) as part of the government's official budget. This program would, when fully implemented, provide a $30 million annual subsidy to parents with children enrolled in private, registered schools. The subsidy was a percentage of tuition paid based on a budget formula.

OACS celebrated its fiftieth anniversary in grand style on November 7, 2002, with a gala banquet attended by 440 school representatives. Although the premier did not attend, cabinet ministers brought greetings. It looked like the sojourn in the educational wilderness was about to end. The ambitious OACS plans for the growth of Christian education would finally be able to access government funds like everyone else. For several years, OACS was treated by government officials like a "real" educational organization. The future was bright as the Third Way vision was looking achievable.

Alas, in a provincial election in 2003, liberals under leader Dalton McGuinty won control of the government from conservative premier Ernie Eves. During the election campaign, McGuinty had promised the teacher unions that the EETC was as good as gone. Their first action in office was to cancel the tax credit, even without a proper budget motion in the House. OACS went to court to stop this improper procedure and thereby extend the tax credits for a year, but the court refused to intervene. Power trumped parliamentary ethics. By 2004 the

---

[37] Barbara Bierman, Tony Kamphuis, Larry Lutgendorf, and Carol Speelman.
[38] That is the private school funding mechanism used in the four western provinces of Canada.

new education minister, Gerard Kennedy, had made it very clear that independent schools were not welcome and that all services and money would go to the public school system. In response to this setback, OACS was instrumental in setting up the Forum of Independent School Organizations, as well as Christian Schools Canada. The Canadian districts worked to consolidate national networks to promote the Third Way, while continuing to monitor the vagaries of provincial politics in Canada.

School life was increasingly dominated by issues raised by the internet, computer technology, and the new social media explosion via cell phone. OACS responded by publishing new protocols for harassment and bullying. For an organization heavily invested in print curriculum materials, however, this switch was a major challenge. Without access to government programs, the cost of the looming transition was prohibitive. OACS set up another foundation[39] to encourage donations for its curriculum work. The Ontario donor network supporting Christian schools was limited and also committed to supporting the growing Redeemer University College.[40] The money required for educational innovation was not plentiful.

Another development strategy adopted by the OACS and the OCSAA[41] boards was to improve the quality of education and so keep the schools competitive with the other private schools. OACS established the Canadian Hallmarks Institute in 2004 in an effort to ratchet up the school evaluation standards. After several years of modest improvements, it became clear that a major advancement in quality would require another major investment in professional development and research. Unlike the investment in political lobbying, the investment in quality did not have immediate payback for the boards. That led to deep discussions about sustainability and long-term planning for the next two decades.

Whereas one group of Christian educators favored academic excellence as an avenue for growth, a larger one was keen on personal faith and social service development, and a smaller, third group remained in the traditional confessional mode, insisting that Reformed doctrine was still the basis for Christian education. Often these factions were within the same school faculty, and this stalemate slowed the curriculum efforts

---

[39] The OACS Foundation in 2006.
[40] Redeemer University had managed to negotiate a BEd degree in 1998 and so finally met the 1957 OACS goal of a certified "Christian Teacher's College" for Ontario.
[41] Ontario Association of Christian School Administrators established in 1967.

of OACS. These factions came to light in the culture war "curriculum" issues.⁴² In addition, increased denominational schisms in the 1990s stymied local school politics, and hence the promotional work of OACS well into the new millennium. Traditional development strategies were undercut by new technological possibilities, such as online courses and even virtual schools. There was plenty of advice, both positive and negative, about the future of schooling.

Strategic retreat at sixty

By 2012, the sixtieth anniversary of OACS, membership had dropped to seventy-one schools, and student enrollment had declined to 11,651. Not a big loss, but a signal that the new, internal community divisions were being solidified. After 2011, a clear, majority liberal election victory, political pessimism set in. This more threatening climate would make a provincial public relations campaign controversial. By this time, gender issues in human resources and sex education had replaced evolution as the litmus test for Reformed orthodoxy. Being conservative on gender, however, destroyed public credibility. Government funding policies and actions became determined by "inclusivity" controversies. Although the centrist Reformed communities were generally tolerant in practice, they were not courageous enough to articulate a clear alternative to the prevailing public school orthodoxy. Hence the reputation of "religious" schools took a hit.

The expansion of OACS membership was no longer a growth engine, especially since CSI staff refused to ease its membership requirements for Canada. American CSI schools had their own serious student decline problems after 2006, and CSI had responded with a centralized organizational model led by a new executive director. This policy led to the rise and consolidation of Christian Schools Canada and the end of the CSI (Grand Rapids) influence in Canada. This situation also led the OACS board to rely more on fundraising from foundations. Unfortunately, the federal government picked this time to crack down on charities with "political" activities.⁴³ The Christian Economic Assistance Foundation was audited in 2013 and had to

---

⁴² The surface issues were homosexuality, abortion, evolution, and the environment. The Canadian debates were more subtle than the American ones, since the Constitutional Freedoms created a restrained legal environment controlled by Human Rights Commissions.
⁴³ The Canada Revenue Agency has long made it illegal for a charity to promote or engage in political activities. Getting caught meant losing one's charitable status.

close down, thus curtailing political lobbying since OACS (itself not a charity) could not afford to fight two years of court cases. Without this source of substantial financial support, many of the innovative OACS programs ran out of money.

The OACS board responded by consolidating several services and reorienting to a professional development model. Train the other leaders, but do not provide the detailed products. Hence, after 2014, OACS went from a comprehensive educational service organization model to a needs-based model. This change reduced the scope of the educational mission from a proactive national leadership role to a coordinating role for professional intervention. The distinctive Kuyperian corporate vision was fading. The classic and distinctive educational creed of OACS was revised in a bylaw revision in 2016, and all references to church creeds vanished.

For five decades, OACS had been the voice for school boards, while administrators (OCSAA)[44] and teachers (OCSTA) had their own organizations. In 2014 the boards of the three organizations began merger discussions for the purpose of designing a more integrated organizational model. It is not clear what principle provided the new organizational vision. OACS was formally dissolved at a special membership meeting in November 2017. The Ancaster office building was sold and the equity gifted to the new Christian Education Foundation. The new replacement organization, Edvance Christian Schools Association, began in August 2018. Some staff members transitioned to the new organization with offices in Burlington, Ontario.

Historical analysis

Many cultural conditions changed over the seven decades of OACS. Schooling principles evolved under the onslaught of technology and radical ideologies. The old Reformed principles for a distinctive Christian education system did not survive into the twenty-first century. Without them, the battle for a Third Way had to be scaled back after 2010. The apt new postmodern metaphor was that the sage on the stage was replaced by some guides on the sides.

The Dutch Reformed communities that had supported the schools across Canada evolved as well. There were several stages in each of these four (religious, ethnic, educational, and political) cultural

---

[44] OCSAA and the Ontario Christian School Teachers Association.

strands, but the net result was major change. The Reformed doctrines changed from Calvinistic to ecumenical. The identity changed from Dutch to global. The philosophy changed from classical to eclectic. The political theory changed from principled outsider to ambiguous insider. These changes have consequences for the viability of a Third Way revival.

In conclusion, OACS was responsible for significant improvements in the larger private school sector in Ontario. Christian schools have a solid foundation and are still providing good, sustainable Christian education across Canada. The success formula of OACS for the 1950-2010 period was simple: clear vision, national network, and excellent leaders. The parallel school success formula was tradition, community, and can-do-ism. What the future holds without these old-fashioned ingredients in the formula remains to be seen.

Glossary of acronyms

AACS	Association for the Advancement of Christian Scholarship
CRA	Canada Revenue Agency
CRC	Christian Reformed Church
CSI	Christian Schools International
EETC	Equity in Education Tax Credit
ICS	Institute for Christian Studies (of Toronto)
NUCS	National Union of Christian Schools
OACCSS	Ontario Association of Calvinistic Christian School Societies
OACS	Ontario Alliance of Christian Schools
OCSAA	Ontario Christian Schools Administrators Association
OCSTA	Ontario Christian Schools Teachers Association
TDCH	Toronto District Christian High School

CHAPTER 9

School as the Vessel of Hope: The Experience of Faith and Dutch Immigrant Culture in Ontario Christian Schools

Phil Teeuwsen

In 1945 the Canadian Army and other members of the Allied forces liberated the Dutch people from five years of German Nazi occupation. The liberation brought much joy and celebration, as well as shed light on the devastating effects of the war on the country and its people. Historian Herman Ganzevoort states that after the war, the Dutch faced "the critical problems of overpopulation, unemployment, and lack of arable land,"[1] a situation that exacerbated an already-exhausted society. Many people began to look for new opportunities and a hopeful future for their children. Given the strong connection the Dutch had with their Canadian liberators, people began to seek out Canada as their new home.

The situation in the Netherlands led to a wave of postwar immigration to Canada. Dutch immigration to Canada rose from 97 in 1946 to 9,866 in 1949 to 20,617 in 1954. Between 1946 and 1954,

---

[1] Herman Ganzevoort, *A Bittersweet Land: The Dutch Experience in Canada, 1890-1980* (Toronto, ON: McClelland and Stewart, 1988), 64.

94,533 people emigrated from the Netherlands to Canada.[2] VanderMey suggests that this number grew to 184,150 by 1982.[3] Large numbers of Dutch Calvinists were included in this wave of immigration. According to Koops, members of the orthodox Calvinist Gereformeerde Kerk were overrepresented in immigration in statistical terms given their population in the Netherlands. Members of the Gereformeerde Kerk made up 7 percent of the postwar Dutch population. In contrast, they accounted for almost 20 percent of postwar Dutch immigrants by 1950.[4] When these Reformed immigrants settled in Canada to remake their lives, they either joined or built Christian Reformed Churches (CRCs), the closest alternative to their home church. Soon after—sometimes prior to—building the church, they established parent-owned Christian school societies. In Ontario, the first Christian school was established in 1943 by prewar Dutch immigrants in Holland Marsh. The rapid increase of Dutch immigration after the war led to the formation of more Christian schools. In 1968 the "Hall-Dennis Report"—a report on learning and education undertaken by the government of Ontario—counted forty-five schools within the Christian Reformed community. Many of these schools joined Edvance Christian Schools Association (www.edvance.ca), whose membership in 2019 counted seventy-five Christian schools. Most of these schools have a heritage that can be traced back to postwar Dutch immigration and settlement.

The Christian schools that these Dutch immigrants built are important for a number of reasons. First, these immigrants established independent schools in an attempt to be faithful to their religious convictions. Second, the schools emerged out of a specific Reformed Christian worldview that integrated religious understanding with ideas of how society should be structured, a worldview found in the teachings of John Calvin and rearticulated in the Netherlands by Abraham Kuyper in the early twentieth century. Third, institution building was consistent with Dutch societal patterns at that time. Johanna Van Dijk states that "The establishment of Christian schools was next in importance to the establishment of churches and local immigration societies. The schools

---

[2] William Petersen, *Planned Migration: The Social Determinants of the Dutch-Canadian Movement* (Berkeley, CA: University of California Press, 1955), 175.

[3] Albert VanderMey, *To All Our Children: The Story of Postwar Dutch Immigration to Canada* (Jordan Station, ON: Paideia Press 1983), 53.

[4] Enne Koops, "Churches Reach Across Borders: 'Emigration Culture' as a Concept to Analyze Religious Aspects of Emigration," in *Across Borders: Dutch Migration to North America and Australia* (Holland, MI: Van Raalte Press, 2010): 19-26.

were the most important organization in maintaining the religious and ethnic identity of Calvinists."[5] According to Van Dijk, between 1946 and 1960, Reformed immigrants started twenty-one Christian schools in Ontario.

The Dutch Canadian immigrants were therefore performing a cultural act when they built their Christian schools. In many ways, they were duplicating in Canada the social structure of their previous homeland.[6] They were seeking to set up their sacred canopy in their new home. According to sociologist Peter Berger,[7] the sacred canopy is a meaning-making structure people apply to their experiences to understand and deal with their life circumstances and their need for social belonging. It is a structure that enables people to connect to something eternal and significant in the face of their own temporal, limited existence. For postwar Dutch Reformed immigrants to Canada, Christian schools were an essential stake in supporting this canopy.

Research design

In this chapter, I explore the intersection of Reformed faith and Dutch immigrant culture through the experiential and professional lens of retired Christian elementary school principals. As is generally the case in schools, Christian school principals are also at the center of school life. They play a key role in the governance and overall direction of Christian schools. As such, they are in a unique position to witness, dwell within, and shape the culture of the schools.

This analysis is based on qualitative research conducted as part of my doctoral studies. Primary data include two open-ended, semi-structured individual interviews with eight retired Christian school principals, four male and four female. Each interview lasted about one-and-a-half hours. The participants had served an average of sixteen years as principals in Christian schools and led an average of two-and-a-half schools. In addition to the sixteen individual interviews, two focus-group interviews were conducted, one with the male participants and the other with the female participants. Additionally, five fiftieth-

---

[5] Johanna Van Dijk, "The Role of Religion in the Settlement Patterns of Dutch Canadians," *The Canadian Review of Sociology and Anthropology* 38, no. 1 (2001): 58-74.
[6] Frans J. Schryer, *The Netherlandic Presence in Ontario: Pillars, Class and Dutch Ethnicity* (Waterloo, ON: Wilfrid Laurier University Press, 1998).
[7] Peter L. Berger, *The Sacred Canopy: Elements of a Sociological Theory of Religion* (NY: Anchor Books, 1967).

anniversary commemorative books published by local Christian schools were analyzed.

This study was conducted within an interpretive, qualitative paradigm that stems from the belief that knowledge and meaning are actively constructed by individuals engaging with each other and with their world.[8] This constructivist approach suggests that reality is open to interpretation and dependent upon the perspective of those involved. Data analysis involved identifying key codes, the clumping of codes into categories, and the distilling of categories into key themes. The analysis of the data involved deliberate triangulation involving the literature, what the participants said, and my interpretation of what they said. In addition, participant response to my interpretation also played a key role in the process as I submitted interview transcripts and my initial analysis to participants soon after each interview and presented my emerging findings to my participants in person during the second round of interviews and the focus groups. Although the interpretation of the data is ultimately mine, the process used in this research was designed to highlight not only what was said but also what was meant in such a way that enabled key meaning and understanding to emerge transparently.

Sacred canopies and third spaces

This study was shaped by the sociological and theoretical work of both Peter Berger and Homi Bhabha.[9] It is helpful, therefore, to comment briefly on their work and the relationship of their work to this study. Berger offers a helpful framework from which to view human society and the role religion plays in social and cultural activities. Humans seek meaning, Berger says. This search for meaning and security provokes society building, including the building of social institutions, which, over time, take on a life of their own and become structures that humans try to fit their lives into. Human-developed institutions—perhaps schools more so than any other—begin to develop human beings. Society begins to determine the life of humans, rather than the other way around. This society provides security for the most part, but this social security has its limits. The human search for meaning, the *nomos*, is continually disrupted by events that serve as reminders of

---

[8] Patti Lather, "Paradigm Proliferation as a Good Thing to Think With: Teaching Research in Education as a Wild Profusion," *International Journal of Qualitative Studies in Education* 19, no. 1 (2006): 35-57.

[9] Homi K. Bhabha, *The Location of Culture* (NY: Routledge, 1994).

School as the Vessel of Hope   169

ultimate, possible meaninglessness: separation from significant others, chaos, and death. In order to deal with this, a sacred canopy, a religious framework, can emerge from human society, under which, ultimate meaning and belonging is maintained. For the Dutch Reformed immigrants to Canada, this canopy included a fairly comprehensive network of schools, churches, businesses, a labour union, and even soccer leagues.

Bhabha provides a framework for understanding the immigrant cultural and religious experience of the participants in this study. Humans and the culture in which they dwell and (re)produce, cannot be defined using binary terms that reinforce ideas of us and them, because there is no pure culture, no pure identity to be found or articulated. Rather, there is a space within which we all dwell, always in between, never arrived. This "third space" is an ambivalent space, "halfway between . . . not defined."[10] It is a space where individual or group identity is not something one simply assumes. Identity is often articulated in a contest of identification. Bhabha writes: "The question of identification is never the affirmation of a pre-given identity, never a self-fulfilling prophecy—it is always the production of an image of identity and the transformation of the subject in assuming that image."[11] Identity—both individual and cultural—is found in between how we might identify ourselves and how others might identify us. Or, as Edward Said writes, "Human identity is not only not natural and stable but constructed and occasionally even invented outright."[12] Such identity is found for the Dutch Canadian Reformed immigrants in between Dutch and Canadian, in between Reformed and evangelical. For them, this third space was found somewhere in "the in between space that carries the burden of the meaning of culture."[13] They were no longer in the Netherlands and would not be going back. They were in Canada, and yet, they did not feel Canadian. They were in between. The Christian schools would provide a home in this space as the immigrants sought to transition from where they started to where they were going.

Findings

In this section, I explore research findings which reveal that the postwar Dutch Reformed immigrants to Canada sought to secure a

[10] Ibid., 20.
[11] Ibid., 64.
[12] Edward W. Said, *Orientalism*, 25th Anniversary ed. (NY: Random House, 1994), 332.
[13] Bhabha, *Location of Culture*, 56.

foothold in Canada through the development of Christian schools. These schools in many ways carried their hopes for a successful and faithful presence in Canada. They also became sites where the identity between Dutch and Reformed/Christian intersected and was contested, with school leaders seeking to highlight the biblical principles of the schools and downplay or counteract Dutch ethnic identifiers that drew attention away from their primary religious purpose.

Being and not being Dutch[14]

The idea of either being or being seen as Dutch, particularly when attached to the identity of the Christian schools, was troublesome for the participants in this study. They were not ashamed of being Dutch, at least not beyond the self-consciousness of any immigrant in a new land, particularly in the early days soon after immigration. They were, however, conscious that their schools were built to be Christian schools, not Dutch schools. This strong desire was rooted in their Kuyperian upbringing in the Netherlands. It was also reinforced for them by influential pastors and academics, chief among them for most of my participants was Evan Runner.

Runner was a professor of philosophy at Calvin College at about the time that young Dutch Canadian immigrants were heading to university. Runner was inspirational to these young Calvinists, particularly in his call to apply the Bible to all areas of life and study. This focus on biblical principles was paramount for Runner and his Canadian students. References to cultural heritage risked masking the essential nature of Christian schools as Christian rather than ethnic institutions. Runner made this clear in his address at the first meeting of the Association of Reformed Scientific Studies in Unionville, Ontario, in 1960, when he warned the "Young People of the Reformation.... [It] is extremely important, of course, that we make clear by our actions that we are not interested in the first place in extending Dutch ways of thinking and Dutch customs and institutions and that we clearly lay the accent on our faith and our principle."[15]

The participants in my study spoke about the Dutch nature of the schools with caution and reluctance. They had all experienced

---

[14] This section is organized using headings that emerged as themes during the research. Names of participants mentioned in this section are pseudonyms, used to protect the confidentiality of the participants.

[15] H. Evan Runner, *The Relation of the Bible to Learning* (Toronto: Wedge Publishing Foundation, 1970), 115-16.

some marginalization in their early years as a result of being Dutch and likely new immigrants as well. They felt the paternalistic attitude of government officials who saw the schools as ethnic institutions that would disappear as the new immigrants got their feet on the ground. But more serious for the participants was the fact that the identification as Dutch hid the primary purpose of the schools. As Rich stated: "It would be incredibly sad after 50 years in the Dutch Calvinist Christian schools that the demise of these schools would hang on the word Dutch."[16] Although this "demise" did not occur, Rich expressed fears that the identification of the schools as Dutch carried with it the risk that non-Dutch people would not enroll and that the primary Christian mission and vision would be lost. Should this primary mission be lost, there would be no reason for the school to continue to exist.

Certainly, the participants understood that the schools had aspects to them that were obviously Dutch, particularly the Dutch last names of the teachers and the close connection to the CRC, to which many Dutch immigrants gravitated. Some of the participants characterized this Dutchness through the experience of being in a close and at times closed community. There were Dutch cultural markers, including the Dutch accents of the teachers and board members, the Dutch treats, and the Dutch cultural symbols, such as Sinterklaas. These stories were accompanied by laughter and smiles during the interviews, as the respondents fell into times of reminiscence.

The participants spoke of the difficulty of trying to hide their Dutchness so that non-Dutch people would not feel marginalized in the schools. This is interesting when considering not only how difficult this would be but also whether it is even desirable to hide one's ethnic identity. The strangeness of the school being Dutch or not Dutch for the participants was found partly in the reality that Christian schools, such as the ones developed by these immigrants, did not "become Dutch" until they came to Canada. In the Netherlands, there were simply Christian schools. Although these immigrants saw the schools they had built in Canada as being no different than what they had experienced in the Netherlands, the schools were perceived as Dutch by those looking in from the outside. It was a contest of identifications, one that the immigrants could really do very little about.

---

[16] Interview 1, Rich.

The struggle

The participants experienced the intersection of faith and ethnic culture in the struggle for Christian schools. This struggle connected them to the past, to prior generations who had fought and won their own school struggles in the Netherlands. It was clear that this struggle was a unifying force. The schools were something they had to fight for, something to which they had to give of themselves. Sectarian schools went against the Canadian cultural grain to varying degrees. Certainly, this was a hard struggle, but it was one they jumped into willingly, almost automatically.

The struggle for parents to have a controlling interest in the education of their own children was so ingrained in the minds of postwar immigrants that they had a word for it: *schoolstrijd*, which refers to the Reformed fight in the first decades of the twentieth century for the right of parents to develop independently owned and operated, faith-based schools, as well as the struggle to have these schools funded on an equal basis as public schools.[17] This was a fight that was won in the Netherlands when Protestant Christian schools were not only permitted to exist but also received government funding equal to that of the public schools.

The struggle for schools in Ontario was linked in the minds of the participants to the school struggles of the past, to their ethnic and religious heritage. As Sue stated:

> The church has a real social aspect and of course doctrine and faith. The school, we were almost fighting for that. I think we fought more for the schools than we did for the church. Because the church, people from the Reformed Christian background who immigrated to Canada, they go to the Christian church. The school you had to fight for, pay a lot of money for, so it's kind of like the fighting spirit, the Abraham Kuyper spirit came out.[18]

The schools required a commitment marked by a significant sacrifice of time and money. The concept of the legitimacy of the struggle emerged in this study as an important part of membership in the group. The first-generation Christian school founders hoped that the new generation would take on this struggle. They were not only passing down the

---

[17] Charles L. Glenn, *Contrasting Models of State and School: A Comparative Historical Study of Parental Choice and State Control* (NY: Continuum International, 2011), 127.
[18] Interview 2, Sue.

schools but were also hoping to pass down to the new generation the desire to continue to struggle and fight for the schools.

The tie that binds

The history of this Dutch Reformed immigrant group prior to their arrival in Canada after World War II is one of institution building, including the establishment of parent-owned Christian schools. It was in their DNA to do so, bred in the bone. This did not mean, however, that they knew how to build schools or for that matter even how to educate children. Even though these immigrants came from the same country, they were beginning again. The early school communities consisted of people who had had diverse school experiences and little-to-no expertise in running a school. Whether or not they had been a part of Christian schools in the Netherlands, they would have to learn how to be a school community in Canada.

The schools had a way of pulling the community together and providing a sense of consistency and a shared identity in the lives of these new immigrants. The common history, a shared ethnic heritage and religious purpose, helped form a cohesive community. From this starting point, immigrant communities began schools. They developed schedules and policies, school calendars and traditions, and governance models and business plans. In the early days, procedures were developed that became routine. Routines turned into traditions, and traditions became definitive of their school communities. This process creates what Berger and Tomas Luckmann refer to as "firmness in consciousness." In Berger and Luckmann's terms, a school's founders are the creators of their own world, to which they give their total commitment, as if the school existed beyond their construction of it.

They understand the world they themselves have made. All of this changes in the process of transmission to the new generation. The objectivity of the institutional world "thickens" and "hardens," not only for the children, but (by mirror effect) for the parents as well. The "There we go again" now becomes the "This is how things are done." A world so regarded attains a firmness of consciousness; it becomes real in an ever more massive way, and it can no longer be changed so easily. For the children, especially in the early phase of their socialization into it, it becomes the world. For parents, it loses its playful quality and becomes "serious."[19]

[19] Peter L. Berger & Thomas Luckmann, *The Social Construction of Reality: A Treatise in the*

Pragmatic decisions define how to do things in school, which in turn become accepted as the right and proper way to do things, perhaps the best and only way to do things. The community, or those who feel most a part of the community, are those who know these routines instinctively. The stories told by the participants reveal a community that knew it would build a school and then figure out what that meant over time. This process and history is one that is remembered fondly in the present. It is a common experience, a common story or narrative that holds the community together. As bell hooks states, "To remember together is the highest form of communion."[20]

The school communities were pulled together by the shared struggle and financial commitment of the immigrants. The schools did provide a community but one that had many demands in terms of time and money. School events, distributed regularly throughout the year, continually brought the community together. The schools were just one institution of the Dutch, Christian Reformed canopy; it also had the Christian Reformed Church, a labour union (the Christian Labour Association of Canada or CLAC), a credit union (Dutch Canadian Credit Union or DUCA), and Dutch import stores that helped round out their social/institutional circles. The institutional completeness[21] of the CRC canopy was comprehensive and demanding on the time and resources of the community. Jim spoke about the comprehensive community that CRC immigrants had developed:

> We didn't integrate as fast. Having our own schools caused us to stay somewhat separate.... Because for many of the Dutch, it was a comfort thing. I don't blame them in that way at all. It was very comfortable. They had left [home] behind and never expected to go back. Some of them, they had left behind a whole life, family, and everything. So to be together in the church, in the school, in all things. You had a grocery store, you had your own butcher, you had your own, you know, all these things. It was really nice. I honestly didn't converse or interact with many [non-Dutch] Canadians until probably in high school. I had no need to. I was extremely busy in the community.[22]

Sociology of Knowledge (NY: Anchor Books, 1966), 59.

[20] Bell hooks, *Where We Stand: Class Matters* (NY: Routledge, 2000), 16.

[21] Raymond Breton, "Institutional Completeness of Ethnic Communities and the Personal Relations of Immigrants," *The American Journal of Sociology* 70, no. 2 (Sept. 1964): 193-205.

[22] Interview 2, Jim.

The ties that bound people together in the school also served to separate school members from the rest of their community. For Jim, growing up in the community, it was a matter of familiarity with his classmates, many of whom were the same people he went to church with, and the time that was devoted to school and church activities.

Involvement in an independent Christian school was no small commitment. The shear cost of tuition often made it necessary for parents to find additional sources of income. This meant additional jobs and, in some cases, starting their own businesses apart from their day jobs. Being a member of the school meant possible service on the school board, including monthly meetings and committee work. If one parent was on a school committee and the other was involved in church council, life was doubly busy. In addition, there were school events that helped raise money for the school budget. It was an all-encompassing life. The kids, like Jim, went to school and church and took for granted the social circle they were a part of.

The school's demand on time and money limited members' involvement in other areas of society. In a sense, this can be seen as an accidental or unintended—yet perhaps foreseeable—consequence of the establishment of Christian schools. The participants could see how the schools had set them apart from their communities. It was interesting to hear how some of the participants had experienced the reaction of people from their communities to their schools. Sue related this story:

> There's a woman once said to me when I spoke to a group in the United Church about being an immigrant kid. And there was a woman there. She was a retired schoolteacher, and she said, "Yeah," she said, "Our country is good enough for you, but our schools weren't." I didn't know what to say to her. I didn't want to get into a big discussion or argument or debate about something. But I thought, wow, "But our schools weren't."[23]

The establishment of schools was a productive undertaking, the founders actively engaged in moving forward in their new country in a way that was faithful to their beliefs. It was not meant to be a reaction against the established Canadian society. And yet, as Sue discovered, some people in the broader community experienced the building of Christian schools this way.

A principled purpose tied the school community together through this common venture. Over time, however, the schools

---

[23] Interview 1, Sue.

themselves became the tie that bound them together as a community. Berger discusses such a process:

> The institution is there, external and coercive, imposing its predefined patterns upon the individual in this particular area of life. The same objectivity belongs to the roles that the individual is expected to play in the institutional context in question, even if it should happen that he does not particularly enjoy the performance.[24]

The newly arrived Dutch Reformed immigrants came together to form school communities. They were bound together by the desire to have a say in the education of their children in accordance with their Christian faith, and this commitment brought them together to build schools. The demands of the school, both in terms of time and money, kept the community circulating around the school. The school itself ultimately became the tie that bound the community together. It was into the school that these immigrants poured their hope for the future, hope that they could remain together and faithful, and hope that they would find their way in the new land.

Cloud of witnesses

The key to understanding both the motivation for building Christian schools and the inspiration for continuing the project six decades after the first schools were built in Ontario is community. A community—a cloud of witnesses—had formed around the schools and still exists as an important element of the experience of the intersection of faith and ethnic identity found in the Christian school experience.

Although the fiftieth anniversary commemorative books analyzed in this study were developed in different independent school communities, they have several similar features. Most striking, at first glance, are the cover pages and the thematic verses that were chosen for the books. Four of the books use Psalm 100:5 as their theme: "For the Lord is good and his love endures forever; his faithfulness continues through all generations." One uses Psalm 78: 4-7, "And we will tell the next generation the praiseworthy deeds of the Lord." The generational theme certainly reinforces an understanding of covenantal theology that is so important in the life experience of Dutch, Christian Reformed immigrants in Canada. The promises are for them and their children,

---

[24] Berger, *The Sacred Canopy*, 13-14.

a phrase heard often at the baptism of children in Reformed churches. It also establishes an understanding of community, a community comprised of significant others who can be relied on to remind the members who they are and where they came from.

The anniversary books serve to remind the community of God's faithfulness through the schools. From a covenantal perspective, this is important, because the CRC community rests on God's blessings; this was made very clear in the conversations I had with the participants. From Berger's sociological perspective, this is also important. Individuals find legitimacy in their relationships with other like-minded, similarly believing people—their significant others. Even the most reliable significant others, however, are prone to forget who they are and where they come from. But God is firm in the hearts and minds of people who find meaning through their religion. God does not forget, and so "God then becomes the most reliable and ultimately significant other."[25] A sacred canopy loses its strength without its God.

The anniversary books are consistent in the way they highlight the words and pictures of founding board members and staff. These individuals represent the first wave of postwar Dutch, Christian Reformed immigrants to Ontario. The books speak to their stories and their struggles with moving to Canada and starting a new life. They are also consistent in highlighting the founders' reliance on their God's faithfulness and their desire that the next generation will remain committed to the cause of Christian schools.

These original board members, teachers, and parents embody the first cloud of witnesses that uphold and encourage the current school members in their own attempt to continue the work that has been started. This older generation connects current members to the principles of Christian education and provides a model for succeeding generations to follow. In some cases, the call to be faithful is subtle, a message that can be inferred from the vast number of pictures of former students shown graduating and original board members staring seriously at the reader; they all present a silent testimony to the value and heritage of Christian schools.

The cloud of witnesses spans the generations and provides a testimony that God is faithful and that Christian schools are worthwhile and necessary. It is important to note that the commemorative books are not neutral documents but are themselves part of the sacred canopy of the Dutch Reformed, Christian school community. David Zwart, in

[25] Berger, *The Sacred Canopy*, 38.

his analysis of commemorative books of Christian Reformed Churches in Canada and the United States, has determined that these books were written for a specific purpose: "While it is clear only a few people in each congregation actually wrote the books, they had to work within the parameters of what would be acceptable to their readers."[26] The same can be said of the fiftieth anniversary books analyzed in this study. The books emerged from the school community to reflect the community in a way that would be pleasing to that community. As such, they can be viewed as part of that culture, an artifact that emerges out of the experience and perspective of the culture, while at the same time contributing to the maintenance and construction of that culture.

The participants spoke of significant others, their own personal cloud of witnesses, who had spurred them on and provided them with the motivation to do the hard work that needed to be done as teachers and as Christian educators. Most of the participants came to Canada as children with their parents and, as such, their initial impressions were shaped by the commitment of their parents to the Christian schools. All of the participants had a story of how and why they had become involved in Christian education. For the most part, these stories involved the commitment and determination of important people in their lives, mainly their parents.

The cloud of witnesses—the group of significant others—spans generations and includes the founding immigrants (and in the background their teachers and preachers), their children, and their children's children. The commemorative books, the school buildings, the stories told during reunions, all point to a remarkable group of supporters who have committed to the cause of Christian schools. This cloud of witnesses, these Dutch and Reformed forbearers, stood as models to follow. They testified to the groundwork that had been laid, and they faithfully passed on to the next generation the task, the cause of Christian education.

Previously, I wrote that new members to the Dutch CRC school communities often found it difficult to feel a part of the schools they had joined. The ties that bound the schools together, both ethnic and religious, could also keep people out, or at least at a distance. New members did not have the common stories of war and immigration to fall back on. They did not participate in the sacrifice originally required to build

---

[26] David Zwart, "For the Next Generation: Dutch Protestant Church Commemorations in North America, 1960-1980," *Tijdschrift Voor Sociale en Economische Geschiedenis* 7, no. 2 (2010): 126-50.

and maintain the schools, at least at the beginning. They did not go to church with many of the other members and, as such, missed out on key conversations and shared experiences that many of the more traditional school members had. People of Dutch descent in the schools possessed a cultural capital that others from outside Dutch circles did not have. They had relatives in the school. They went to church with many other students and teachers, and they understood Dutch jargon and traditions. They knew, on an intuitive level, how the community worked.

The participants indicated a great desire to expand the school community to include more people from different denominational and ethnic backgrounds. They had stories of failed attempts to become more inclusive and stories of great success integrating a diverse cross section of people from the community into their schools. What consistently came through in the interviews was that the participants had encouraged and experienced a change in the makeup of this cloud of witnesses, a change initiated by new people who, although not Dutch in heritage, were interested in and increasingly committed to the religious principles upon which the schools were built.

The language used by school members became a focus for the participants, and as such represents a deliberate attempt to control school identity. Lisa challenged people within her school to explain what they meant when using "insider" language: "And so I will quickly call someone on it and say, 'What do you mean by that? What do you mean by that? Put it in other terms, because we don't want to be that Dutch school, right?'"[27]

The Dutch and Reformed jargon was something the participants sought to weed out in their school communities. In our research, we discovered that this weeding-out process required much more attention on a personal, reflexive level. We found that there may be more to the issue of marginalizing non-Dutch members than using misunderstood words and phrases. There may be a discourse at work that structures language in ways that identify who is on the inside and who is not. In the following focus-group interview, we were talking about non-Dutch people who had become part of the school community:

Sue: And who else is there in our schools? Why do they stay?
Lisa: [name of an individual]
Sue: Ask them if they see Dutch or Reformed or whatever their definitions or what their experiences are.

---

[27] Interview 1, Lisa.

Lisa: But do you see the language you are using? Our schools.
Sue: Well, yes.
Lisa: Not the Christian school, right. It's our school. It's possessive. They have joined us, right?
Sue: Yes, you're right.
Lisa: I don't mean to offend in any way, but I think that's so deeply entrenched in our culture as Dutch Reformed people that it's hard to get outside of that.[28]

It was interesting to see the effect this discussion had on the rest of the conversation. The participants found themselves using the phrase "*our* schools," and then stopping and correcting themselves, seeking phases such as "*the* school" or naming specific schools instead. It was awkward. The participants realized that, through their language, they constructed those to whom the schools belonged and those welcomed as guests.

The cloud of witnesses has represented the intersection of Dutch immigrant culture and Reformed faith in Christian schools. The stories of the past, the pictures in the commemorative anniversary books, the recollections of founding members, all represented aspects of what it means to be Dutch and Reformed in Canada. They represent the heritage of the schools. And yet, the schools were never meant to be Dutch. The founding principle of the Christian schools in Ontario was religious, yet the significant others—those whose examples and wisdom they were following and whose children would immediately attend—were Dutch. The identities came together and intersected in the schools.

Conclusion

The postwar Dutch Canadian immigrants built schools, in addition to other social institutions, as a way of living out their religious and cultural beliefs. The schools can be seen as part of the sacred canopy under which they found meaning and security. This canopy, however, was established in a time of transition, in a type of third space, in which they found themselves dislocated. They were no longer home in the Netherlands, and they could not go back. Yet, they were not yet Canadian; they would struggle to go forward. They found themselves in an unhomely place as immigrants in the New World.

The school, maybe more than any other institution, seemed to carry the hopes and expectations of these Dutch Canadian immigrants

---

[28] Women's Focus Group.

for their new life in Canada. This chapter offers insight into a Dutch Reformed group's experience of carving out a niche for itself in the educational and cultural landscape in Ontario, Canada. It also speaks to the formative power of schools more generally as contested sites of cultural identity. The Dutch Reformed immigrants knew well the formative power of schools. This is in part why they placed so much of their hope, time, and money into the schools. They believed firmly that it was the school more than any other institution that could carry their hopes of making it in the new land. This is what made all of the hard work, sacrifice, and commitment worth the effort.

CHAPTER 10

Calvin Seminary and University as the Full-Size Kampen

George Harinck

The question I will address is a simple one: What are the historical reasons for the Christian Reformed Church having two closely related educational institutions—Calvin Seminary and Calvin University?[1] I will deal first with the nature and Dutch descent of the theological school, then describe the kind of education the school offered, and finally explain the reason for the close relationship between the seminary and university.

Theological education only?

The theological school or seminary of the Christian Reformed Church (CRC), a denomination that seceded from the Reformed Church in America (RCA) in 1857, grew organically out of theological training in the parsonage, first by Rev. W. H. Van Leeuwen (1807-1882), in Grand Rapids, from November 1864, and then by Rev. Douwe J. Vander Werp (1811-1876), of Graafschap, Michigan, from 1865. The CRC was in need of ministers, and since this denomination was a Dutch

---

[1] In the summer of 2019, Calvin College changed its name to Calvin University.

immigrant church, it looked to the Seceder church in the Netherlands[2] to obtain them. When the influx of candidates from the Netherlands became insufficient, the CRC started to train ministers themselves. Vander Werp, who had arrived in Michigan from the Netherlands in 1864, started training students for the ministry the next year, and in 1869, the Holland classis "decided that Vander Werp should do all the training until the church could afford to establish a seminary."[3] He taught in the Dutch language.

Vander Werp himself was trained in the parsonage in Groningen, the Netherlands, by Hendrik de Cock (1801-1842) and Tamme Foppes de Haan (1791-1868), and he began his ministry in 1843 in the Seceder church in the old country as a "student-pastor."[4] As a result, he knew what this kind of more-or-less informal training at home was like. But the practice of training pastors in the parsonage was relatively unfamiliar to the Dutch Reformed community in the United States. The RCA had trained its ministers at New Brunswick Theological Seminary, New Jersey, and from 1866, Hope College in Holland, Michigan. But Vander Werp's colleague and friend Rev. Dirk Postma (1818-1890) had studied in the parsonage of De Haan and become a Seceder minister with whom Vander Werp corresponded when he ran the school in Graafschap.

Postma had immigrated to South Africa in 1858 and soon joined the small, newly founded church, Die Gereformeerde Kerk in Suid-Afrika, or "Dopper Kerk," as a pastor. He trained theological students in Burgersdorp, South Africa, from 1863, in Dutch, just like Vander Werp. Compared to the curriculum Postma offered in his parsonage, Vander Werp's program seems to have been lighter; Vander Werp taught systematic theology, practical theology, Bible history, geography and chronology, church history, Dutch language, exegesis, and preaching.[5]

---

[2] The Christelijke Gereformeerde Kerk was its official name beginning in 1869.
[3] Janet Sjaarda Sheeres, *Son of Secession. Douwe J. Vander Werp* (Grand Rapids, MI: Eerdmans, 2006), 128. His students were J. Schepers (examined and ordained CRC 1868), W. Greve and J. Stad (examined and ordained CRC 1869), L. Rietdijk (examined 1869, ordained CRC 1870), B. Mollema and E. Vander Vries (examination date unknown, ordained CRC 1874), W. Hazenberg (no exam, ordained RCA 1873), Corn. Kriekaard (no exam, ordained RCA 1877), and A. Wiegmink (no exam). Minutes of the Calvin College and Theological School Board of Trustees 1876-93 (with a summary of ministerial instruction prior to 1876). Heritage Hall (HH), archives for the Christian Reformed Church, Calvin Theological Seminary, and Calvin University, is located in Hekman Library at Calvin University. I quote the minutes from the English translation of the original Dutch text, provided by HH.
[4] Sheeres, *Son of Secession*, 69.
[5] G. C. P. van der Vyver, *Uw erfenis is vir my mooi. Gedenkboek by die eeuwfees van die Theologiese Skool van die Gereformeerde Kerk in Suid-Afrika en van die Potchefstroomse*

For systematic theological education, Vander Werp and Postma used the same textbook they had used in their student days with De Haan: Aegidius Francken's *Kern der christelijke leere* (The essence of Christian doctrine) from 1713.[6]

This textbook was mandatory at the Theologische School in Kampen, the Netherlands, founded by the Dutch Seceder church in 1854. Of the four initiatives for the Seceder's theological education in the mid-nineteenth century, two were parsonage training, and two were institutional, although Kampen had developed out of theological education in various parsonages, including De Haan's. Vander Werp and Postma had both been directors of the Kampen School before they left the Netherlands, the former as curator (1860-61), and the latter as treasurer to the curatorium (1855-58).[7] When they started their schools in Graafschap and Burgersdorp, respectively, the Kampen curriculum and De Haan's teaching were their points of reference.

Thus, in the mid-nineteenth century, three Reformed theological schools stemming from the Dutch Seceder tradition were started in the Netherlands, South Africa, and the United States, in 1854, 1863, and 1864, respectively, of which, the Kampen school set the standard.

The education in both Burgersdorp and Graafschap was rather rudimentary at first, but it soon became more rigorous. The synod of the Gereformeerde Kerk in Suid-Afrika, gathering in Potchefstroom in 1869, founded the Teologiese Skool, in Burgersdorp, Cape Province. To promote this founding, Postma had read to the synod parts of the proceedings of the Dutch Seceder synods between 1849 and 1854 regarding the founding of the Kampen theological school.[8] Synod appointed Postma as its first teacher-pastor. The curriculum the synod adopted was a copy of the Kampen curriculum, formulated by the Dutch Seceder synod in 1851.[9] In 1876, the year Vander Werp died, Postma became full-time professor at Teologiese Skool.

Universiteit vir Christelike Hoër Onderwijs (Potchefstroom: Potchefstroom Herald, 1969), 16-17.

6 See D. Postma, *Mijne handleiding voor de godgeleerdheid, volgens de Kern van Aegidius Francken* (Kaapstad: Saul Solomon & Co., 1875); James A. De Jong, "Sometimes Buried Treasure Lies in Plain View: G. E. Boer's Copy of Aegidius Francken," *Origins* 30, no. 2 (2012): 37-42.

7 *Curatorium* was the name used for the board of trustees of the theological school in Kampen. Its members were therefore called curators. The same terminology was used at the theological school in Grand Rapids.

8 Van der Vyver, *Uw erfenis*, 21.

9 Ibid., 30.

From 1869 on, there was one important difference in the character of this South African school, compared with Kampen. When the Kampen school was founded, it was not explicitly stated that the school would offer educational programs for those who did not aspire to the ministry, although, according to some, the synod implicitly held this expectation.[10] Dutch Seceder synods in the early 1850s, however, did not address this issue. This may have had to do with the fact that the educational system in the Netherlands was relatively good, and the majority of children did attend primary schools, although it was not compulsory until 1901.[11] There were Christian free schools, founded since the 1840s by those who had joined the Seceder church and the Réveil movement, and as of 1849, there was a Christian teachers academy in Nijmegen.[12] Among Seceder churches, many of these free schools were founded by local consistories.[13] The issue of secondary education in general may also not have been addressed by the synod because of the relatively short distances in the Netherlands. A school was almost always available, and the Christian school movement grew rapidly after the new Dutch Constitution of 1848 guaranteed freedom of education—within a decade, about sixty primary schools were founded,[14] and secondary schools would soon follow, including teachers academies in Nijmegen and Utrecht (1857) and *gymnasiums* in both Zetten (1864) and Doetinchem (1878).

Whatever the reasons for not dealing with secondary education in general at Seceder synods, in the years after the founding of the Kampen school, it seemed wise to consider broadening and diversifying the curriculum, for many students lacked the level of education required for theological studies, and their general education required a significant

---

[10] Lucas Lindeboom defended this interpretation of Kampen's founding history in 1876. See George Harinck and Wim Berkelaar, *Domineesfabriek. Geschiedenis van de Theologische Universiteit Kampen* (Amsterdam: Bert Bakker, 2018), 97.

[11] Michael Wintle, *An Economic and Social History of the Netherlands, 1800–1920: Demographic, Economic and Social Transition* (Cambridge: Cambridge University Press, 2000), 270.

[12] Anton van Renssen, *Het wezendorp Neerbosch. De protestants-christelijke weesinrichting Neerbosch en haar stichter Johannes van 't Lindenhout* (Nijkerk: Nabij producties, 2015), 125-26.

[13] A. C. Roosendaal, *Naar een school voor de gereformeerde gezindte. Het christelijk onderwijsconcept van het Gereformeerd Schoolverband (1868-1971)* (Hilversum: Verloren, 2006), 21.

[14] L. C. Stilma, *De School met den Bijbel in historisch-pedagogisch perspectief. Ontstaan en voortbestaan van het protestants-christelijk lager onderwijs in Nederland* (Nijkerk: Intro, 1987), 205.

amount of time. In Kampen, this problem was dealt with in the "literary department," where students were taught and prepared for theological study. Teaching theology in the literary department was for four decades a burden to the theological professors. The study for the ministry remained the core business of the Kampen Theologische School—of the professors and the church. To lift the teaching load for the professors, a special teacher for the literary department was appointed in 1866. Was this enough to solve the need for general education? In 1866, 1872, and 1875, the synods of the Christelijke Gereformeerde Kerk considered ways to develop the literary department into an independent secondary school that would give access to academic studies (in the Dutch system, this would be a gymnasium), but not enough funds were raised.[15]

The situation in South Africa was different: distances were long, and the level of literacy was lower than in the Netherlands. The Potchefstroom synod therefore decided in 1869 to organize the school in Burgersdorp in such a way to educate not only ministers and schoolteachers but also those whose future plans were yet undetermined. This was the nucleus of the Potchefstroomse Universiteit vir Christelik Hoër Onderwijs, founded in 1919 and separated at that time from the Teologiese Skool.[16]

Orientation Kampen

When Vander Werp died in 1876, the CRC started an institution of theological education. Given the examples of Kampen and Burgersdorp and the differences between both institutions indicated above, what kind of school would this be?

In 1876 Kampen alumnus and Christian Reformed minister G. Egberts Boer (1832-1904) was appointed by the synod as the first full-time docent. The school now moved from the parsonage in Graafschap to the second floor of the Christian primary school in the white-washed building at Williams Street, in downtown Grand Rapids.[17] The only formal relation with the Christian primary school at the ground floor was a cleaning agreement: "For keeping the lecture hall clean,

---

[15] Harinck and Berkelaar, *Domineesfabriek*, 38-39, 62.
[16] Van der Vyver, *Uw erfenis*, 23; Harinck and Berkelaar, *Domineesfabriek*, 67.
[17] Minutes of the curatorium of the theological school gathered in the lecture hall [of the school in Williams Street] in Grand Rapids, 22 March 1882, art. 1: "The question is raised whether the lecture hall should be white-washed at the expense of the school. Answer, yes." HH. I quote the minutes from the English translation of the original Dutch text, provided by HH.

the assembly allows a yearly honorarium of $20.00 to Mr. J. Hoekstra, elementary teacher in Williams Street."[18] Twice a week, students had come to the parsonage in Graafschap, but now a real school, with daily classes, opened its doors.

The Dutch descent and nature of the CRC and its education at the theological school in Grand Rapids was omnipresent. The opposing theological systems taught in the classroom were not American. Students were taught Groningen theology, the modern theology of Leiden, and sometimes the Seceder's own tradition, as taught in Kampen. Language classes were in Dutch, and history classes were partly on Dutch history.[19] The focus of the CRC was on the Netherlands, and in the first decade, the Grand Rapids school used the Dutch language.

The ties that bound the Reformed immigrants in the Midwest with the motherland were strong. In 1851 Helenius de Cock (1824-1894), Hendrik de Cock's son, at that time a minister in 's Hertogenbosch, was called by the Reformed Church of Graafschap, Michigan.[20] In 1871 Simon van Velzen (1809-1896) received and declined a call to emigrate to Holland to teach at Hope College (established three years before the Kampen school).[21] In 1873 Kampen professor Van Velzen and Christelijke Gereformeerde minister Jan Bavinck (1826-1909) were called to come over to Michigan to strengthen theological education in the CRC.[22]

The synodical committee that ran the school became the curatorium, just like in Kampen. Part of the 1876 reorganization was the curatorium's request to Boer "to see if he has some framework for operating,[23] and if not, then to request them from [the theological school in] Kampen in the Netherlands."[24] Boer was not successful in

---

[18] Minutes curatorium, 31 Aug. 1882, art. 5.
[19] Ibid., 1877, art. 6. In the meeting of 26 June 1888, art. 2, it was decided "that the study of the Dutch language thus far placed under rubric of Letter A, to be moved under rubric of Letter B, and the history of America be put in its place."
[20] Elton J. Bruins and Karen G. Schakel, eds., *Envisioning Hope College. Letters Written by Albertus C. Van Raalte to Philip Phelps Jr., 1857 to 1875* (Holland, MI: Van Raalte Press; Grand Rapids, MI: Eerdmans, 2011), 415.
[21] *Handelingen der zes-en-twintigste vergadering van de kuratoren der theologische school der Christelijke Gereformeerde Kerk in Nederland* (Kampen: S. van Velzen Jr., 1871), 12.
[22] *Handelingen der dertigste vergadering van de kuratoren der theologische school der Christelijke Gereformeerde Kerk in Nederland* (Kampen: G. Ph. Zalsman, 1874), 16.
[23] In Dutch, the term is *"reglement,"* and infers guiding principles or a framework for conducting business.
[24] Minutes *curatorium*, 4 Aug. 1876, art. 16; Harinck and Berkelaar, *Domineesfabriek*, 66.

providing such a framework,²⁵ so four years later, curator Rev. Gerrit K. Hemkes (1868-1915) was charged to develop a framework for the school, "and to use as a basis for this that being used in Kampen."²⁶ In every aspect, the theological school of the Christelijke Gereformeerde Kerk in Kampen was the model for the new school in Grand Rapids.

In 1883, after the departure of Grand Rapids alumnus Geerhardus Vos (1862-1949), the assistant docent for a year and a half, Christelijke Gereformeerde minister Anthony Brummelkamp Jr. (1839-1919), of Groningen, the Netherlands, was called as the second docent in Grand Rapids, hoping "to serve the interests of the school according to our abilities by increasing the faculty and to follow in this way the [Kampen] example set by the Mother Church in the Fatherland of old."²⁷

Brummelkamp replied to this call with an inquiry about the conditions of his employment and a series of questions, to which the curatorium responded:

Question: Which subjects are taught at the school?
Answer: We try to follow as much as possible the example of the Theological School in Kampen in preparatory subjects as well as theological and related subjects.

Question: Will each Docent have his own subjects, for example, one the literary [subjects] and the other theology?
Answer: That is not the intent. The curators judge that both Docents have to be able to teach in both fields, but if they think this is difficult, then they hope you can accept the appointment, and after you get here, a mutual discussion between the curatorium and docent can be held concerning the division of the subjects.

Question: What preparatory studies are required before somebody can enter the school?
Answer: This happens here as it did in the past in Kampen; some have had education such as one of the five now starting the next semester who has studied at Hope College for

---

²⁵ Minutes *curatorium*, 4 Nov. 1880, art 6: "It is proposed to develop [a set of] regulations for the school as quickly as possible and present it to the first possible synod assembly."
²⁶ Ibid., 30 Nov. 1880, art. 1: "Since we have a need for [a set of] regulations for the school. Rev. G. Hemkes is charged to develop one, and to use as a basis for this that being used in Kampen, with the necessary changes."
²⁷ Ibid., 7 Aug. 1883, art. 3.

a few years, one in Doetinchem, the Netherlands, for a few years, and a third has been an assistant teacher. However, two have to start at the very beginning, and this last sort is the most common.

Question: How many years of study do you require?
Answer: As a rule, four years for literary and two years for the theological subjects.[28]

Brummelkamp declined the call, but he was not the last alumnus from Kampen who was asked to come over to Grand Rapids. Douwe K. Wielenga (1841-1902) was also called several times, but he never accepted.

After Brummelkamp and Wielenga declined, still other Kampen-affiliated ministers were called, like Jan Bavinck and Kampen alumnus and professor at Western Theological Seminary in Holland, Michigan, Nicolaus M. Steffens (1839-1913).[29] After pursuing further studies in Princeton, Berlin, and Strasburg, Professor Geerhardus Vos returned to the Grand Rapids school in 1888 but left it in 1893, partly because of objections to his neo-Calvinist teachings.[30] Following Vos' departure, a curator visited the Netherlands, searching for a successor. He made inquiries regarding six ministers, all Kampen alumni.[31] The trustees and curators did not look elsewhere either in the Netherlands or the United States; Kampen was their only resource. This focus matches Robert Swierenga's observation that the Christian Reformed settlers in the New World acted as colonists, whereas members of the RCA acted as immigrants.[32]

---

[28] Ibid., 7 Aug. 1883, art. 3.
[29] Ibid., 29 June 1892, art. 28: "The curatorium stipulates that if Dr. N. M. Steffens declines the appointment as professor, the clerk will send a call letter to Doctor D. K. Wielenga."
[30] See George Harinck, "The Michigan Years (1888-1893) of Geerhardus Vos," in *Dutch Muck—and Much More: Dutch Americans in Farming, Religion, Art, and Astronomy* (Holland, MI: Van Raalte Press, 2019), 253-74.
[31] Minutes curatorium, 4-5 April 1894, art. 15: "Rev. Vos submits a report about the mandate to search in the Netherlands to see if a suitable docent can be found there. Among other things, he has made inquiries with and regarding docent Wielenga and the ministers [T.] Bos, [G.] Elzenga, [P.] Biesterveld, Ten Hoor, [T.] Noordewier."
[32] Robert P. Swierenga, "True Brothers: The Netherlandic Origins of the Christian Reformed Church in North America, 1857-1880," in *Breaches and Bridges: Reformed Subcultures in the Netherlands, Germany, and the United States* (Amsterdam: VU Uitgeverij, 2000), 79: "The CRC increasingly reflected the orthodox mentality of the northern Netherlands."

In examining the history of the theological school in Grand Rapids, one can clearly see the central role of Kampen, considering that all the docents or professors appointed in the first twenty-five years had been educated in Kampen. The first appointed professor educated elsewhere was Ralph Janssen (1874-1942), and he arrived in 1902. Boer, Hemkes, Henricus Beuker (1834-1900), Foppe M. ten Hoor (1855-1934), and William W. Heyns (1856-1933) had all been educated in Kampen. All trustees and curators of the theological school in the first twenty-five years of the school had also studied in Kampen. The only exception was Geerhardus Vos, who had studied at the theological school in Grand Rapids. If, however, his father, Kampen alumnus Rev. Jan H. Vos (1826-1913), had not accepted a call in 1881 from Spring Street Christian Reformed Church in Grand Rapids and immigrated with his family to the United States, Vos would likely have been sent to Kampen.

This singular focus does not mean Grand Rapids always agreed with what happened in Kampen; the ministers who founded the CRC were theologically more conservative than the average minister in the Christelijke Gereformeerde Kerk in the Netherlands.[33]

Vander Werp was rather critical of the Theologische School in Kampen, because the young professor Helenius de Cock expressly deviated from Francken's *Kern* by also using sixteenth-century, Reformed theologians like Calvin in his teaching. For Vander Werp, the *Kern* text stood for Reformed theology as defined in the eighteenth century once and forever. To him, the dynamics De Cock introduced by using additional sources was like introducing the historical critical method of modern theology into Reformed theology. Related to this stance, Vander Werp also rejected the fact that De Cock paid more attention to the covenant then to election. Vander Werp denounced De Cock's teachings as Remonstrant. Postma, however, in Burgersdorp, does not seem to have been that critical of developments in Kampen.[34]

This conservatism was also true of docent Boer. Whereas Kampen professor A. Brummelkamp Sr. (1811-1888) considered Francken's *Kern* outdated systematic theology, and in the classroom, instead, relied on his education at Leiden University, Boer kept on using *Kern* as the dogmatic textbook at the school in Grand Rapids.[35]

---

[33] Swierenga, "True Brothers," 79.
[34] Sheeres, *Son of Secession*, 134.
[35] Harinck and Berkelaar, *Domineesfabriek*, 31.

Conservatism gained some ground with appointments after Geerhardus Vos left the school in 1893. Both of Vos' successors, Beuker and Ten Hoor, had left the Netherlands in the mid-1890s, seemingly critical about the ecclesial and theological developments in the Netherlands, where Herman Bavinck (1854-1921) and Abraham Kuyper (1837-1920) had developed a neo-Calvinist theology that, in Beuker and Ten Hoor's opinion, was not in every aspect in line with classical Reformed theology.[36]

The way Boer taught was outdated compared with Kampen standards. Herman Bavinck, a Kampen professor from 1882 on, did not dictate his lessons but used free speech. Boer stuck to the catechetical method of his own student days in Kampen. "The students recited, often in rote fashion, the exact words of the text. There was no opportunity for discussion ... there was still an unusual emphasis upon the memory."[37] This method did not satisfy the students, and they criticized Boer's teaching method. Therefore, in 1883, he was asked by the curators "to consider whether it might not be better to change the catechetical form of instruction with an acroamatical [conversational] form," that is, in the form of a more lively communication. Boer replied "that this new form of teaching will be a new experience," but he would give it a try.[38] For this and other reasons, docent Geerhardus Vos was much more appreciated by the students: "His material was more sophisticated and scholarly."[39]

Toward separating the departments

From the start of the theological training of the CRC in 1868 by Vander Werp, the curriculum, and consequently the exams, were not merely theological. The students arrived at the school with different levels of education, and quite a few applicants were rejected for their lack of knowledge. But many of those who were admitted still needed general education before they could start their theological studies, which were in Dutch, as in Burgersdorp and Kampen. How fluent in Dutch were those Dutch American boys? "The older folk that came here were for the most part not very literate and, for a large part, people

---

[36] J. Faber, *Amerikaanse Afscheidings-theologen over verbond en doop* (Barneveld: De Vuurbaak, 1995), 12.
[37] John J. Timmerman, *Promises to Keep. A Centennial History of Calvin College* (Grand Rapids, MI: Calvin College and Eerdmans, 1976), 15-16.
[38] Minutes curatorium, 2 May 1883, art. 18.
[39] Timmerman, *Promises to Keep*, 16.

from the countryside, who were brought together in this country from different provinces in the Netherlands. They hardly could understand each other."[40] Initially, the teachers had a hard time educating these young men, even in the Dutch language. Once a week, docent Boer, just like the professors in Kampen, held a more informal *krans*—a Kampen name for circle or gathering—in which seminary students were required not only to present and socialize but also to become more civilized.

In time, teaching in the Dutch language became problematic since more and more students were fluent in English. In 1880 a student asked to withdraw from the theological school for a year, "to be totally exposed to English, with the goal of learning the English language better." The curatorium hesitated, handed the request over to the synod of that year and noted "that this matter is not without danger for the students."[41] With this warning, they betrayed their colonist mindset.

Language was an identity marker for the first generations in the Christian Reformed immigrant community and therefore also for the school, but of course, theology was at the heart of the curriculum. Systematic theology was part of it, as well as exegesis, homiletics, biblical history, and church history. More generic subjects were also part of the curriculum and exams: geography, chronology, history, Dutch language, and mythology, and from 1876 on, also logic, psychology,[42] Greek, Latin, and Hebrew.[43] At examination time, according to the minutes of the exam committee in 1871, "An evaluation is made in theology and all the other subjects necessary to be able to [attain] the ministry."[44]

When more students and teachers came, the curriculum became more diversified, and the need to distinguish between a literary and a theological department became more pressing. In 1879 the curatorium for the first time distinguished explicitly between literary and theological students and issued literary and theological diplomas.[45]

Over the years, the literary and theological sections were distinguished more clearly. The course was divided into two parts.[46]

---

[40] Rev. N. H. Dosker in his Dutch American monthly, *Huisvriend* (16 Aug. 1876): "De ouderen, die herwaarts overkwamen, waren meerendeels ongeletterden, en voor een groot deel platteland-bewoners, die uit de verschillende provinciën van Nederland hier samenvloeiden; te nauwernood kunnen ze elkander verstaan."
[41] Minutes *curatorium*, 22 June 1880, art. 8.
[42] Ibid., 1879, art. 11.
[43] Ibid., 1879, art. 8 mentions Hebrew as well.
[44] Ibid., 23 May 1871, art. 8.
[45] Minutes *curatorium*, 26 June 1879, art. 7.
[46] Ibid., 25 June 1879, art. 5, 7.

The first years of the approximately four-or-five-year curriculum were devoted to literary education and the final two years to theology proper. Both sections had the same teachers. In 1880 the theological school had ten students, in 1883 fifteen,[47] and gradually the school grew. The work load for Boer became too heavy. He was asked by the curators "to preach as little as possible and to exclusively dedicate himself to the needs of the school, to do it no more than once on one Sunday per month, and as much as possible to decline the invitations of vacant congregations."[48]

In 1889 the question was raised in the curatorium "whether we should not start [to] investigate about obtaining our own building."[49] A committee was appointed to develop a plan for the synod concerning the location and the building itself. A new building would come in 1892, when the school moved to the campus at Madison Avenue and Franklin Street in Grand Rapids.

In previous publications on the bi-educational aspect of the history of the theological school in Grand Rapids, the desire to educate youth is usually mentioned as the reason to extend the literary department. Not only those who wanted to become ministers had to be educated in a Christian atmosphere but also the other young people of the CRC. According to Henry Zwaanstra, "Boer [in 1892] was the first to propose the separation of the two departments so that those not intending to enter the ministry could also study at the school."[50]

The synod of 1894 rejected several proposals to separate the departments, but it did allow the admittance of students in the literary department of the theological school "who do not wish to be prepared for the ministry."[51] J. Rooks and John J. Timmerman concluded this decision was "the harbinger of a new era";[52] this resolution "opened the way to the making of Calvin College."[53] In 1894 Albertus J. Rooks (1869-

---

[47] Ibid., 7 Aug. 1883, art. 3.
[48] Ibid., 16 March 1880, art. 5; 4 Nov. 1880, art 2.: "The president asks Docent G. E. Boer about the amount of time [days and hours] set aside for instruction, and the answer given is 5 days and 21 hours of instruction and two more for the Circle [krans]."
[49] Minutes *curatorium*, 21 June 1889, art. 31.
[50] Henry Zwaanstra, *Reformed Thought and Experience in a New World: A Study of the Christian Reformed Church in its American Environment, 1890-1918* (Grand Rapids, MI: Eerdmans, 1974), 157n72.
[51] Ibid., 24.
[52] A. J. Rooks in *Semi-Centennial Volume. Theological School and Calvin College 1976-1926* (Grand Rapids, MI: n.p., 1926), 51.
[53] Timmerman, *Promises to Keep*, 24.

1958)—the first docent born in the United States—and K. Schoolland (1851-1938) were appointed by the Christian Reformed synod as teachers exclusively for the literary department. Rooks had studied at Hope College and Schoolland at Groningen University, after studying for two years at the Kampen theological school. Any influence of the Vrije Universiteit, founded in 1880 in Amsterdam, the Netherlands, and its ideal of education free of the church, seems absent at that time.[54] Schoolland, a staunch Kuyperian, realized this shortly after he was appointed in Grand Rapids.[55]

The Seceder tradition goes abroad

This development in Grand Rapids of a two-pronged educational approach resembled what had been decided about the school in Burgersdorp in 1869. But what if we compare these developments with what was happening in the mother institution in Kampen? Kampen also had a literary department, which also developed into an independent school, the Gereformeerd Gymnasium. In Grand Rapids, this separation started in 1894, in Kampen in 1896, and—to mention South Africa once more—in Potchefstroom, it was realized in 1919. Although these developments may look the same, in Potchefstroom and Grand Rapids, a college developed out of the literary department of the theological school in an organic way, but this did not happen in Kampen.

Kampen professor Herman Bavinck recalled in 1896: "In previous days, from several sides, the proposition had been defended, that the Theological School should be extended over time into a university."[56]

---

[54] Contra Gert van Klinken's suggestion in "Tussen Grand Rapids en Groningen. Een briefwisseling tussen twee kuyperianen, 1914-1924," *Documentatieblad voor de Nederlandse Kerkgeschiedenis na 1800* 85, no. 2 (Fall 2016): 44-45.

[55] K. Schoolland aan F. J. Albracht, 27 mei 1923: "Wat mij vóór ruim 30 jaren, toen ik hier voor 't eerst in de geestelijke atmosfeer ademde en uit gebrek aan geestelijke oxygeen dreigde te stikken, zoo diep trof, gevoelde ik thans weer: wat is er in Nederland veel meer geestelijke actie, ook op kerkelijk gebied, maar vooral op het breede sociale en politieke terrein, - actie voor de bewuste, alles-omvattende souvereiniteit Gods -, dan in dit land." (What struck me here when I arrived 30 years ago, when I breathed the spiritual atmosphere for the first time and almost choked by lack of spiritual oxygen, I have felt time and again: what a lot more of spiritual action there is in the Netherlands, in the church, but also in the broader social and political domain—action for the conscious, all-encompassing sovereignty of God—than in this country.) Collection Gert van Klinken, Protestantse Theologische Universiteit, Amsterdam.

[56] H. Bavinck, P. Biesterveld, M. Noordtzij and D. K. Wielenga, *Opleiding en theologie* (Kampen: J. H. Kok, 1896), 31: "Van verschillende zijde ... werd vroeger de stelling verdedigd, dat de Theol. School zich allengs moest uitbreiden tot een universiteit."

In the 1870s, the synod of the Christelijke Gereformeerde Kerk in the Netherlands hesitated about extending the Kampen school in that direction but in the end rejected a proposal to develop the literary department into a gymnasium because of a lack of financial resources.[57] In the 1880s, however, Seceded ministers like Beuker still wanted the church to found a college or gymnasium to replace Kampen's literary department.[58] Beuker had the same idea that Boer of Grand Rapids had, and Herman Bavinck and Beuker had hoped in this way to also elevate the theological department to a more academic level. The synod of the Christelijke Gereformeerde Kerk in the early 1890s in the end did create two new teaching positions in the literary department but still did not found a gymnasium. In sum, Die Gereformeerde Kerk in Suid-Afrika in 1869 and the CRC in 1894 had both decided to consider the possibility of literary education by the church. Although the Christelijke Gereformeerde Kerk had at first decided the same in 1896, after a decade, it concluded that secondary education was not the task of the church.[59]

The Christelijke Gereformeerden had decided in this way for two reasons: unlike the situation in the United States or South Africa at that time, the church was reluctant to found schools. According to the emerging neo-Calvinist view, schools were the responsibility of parents or, more generally, citizens, not the church. The Christian primary schools in the Netherlands were—with some exceptions—founded by associations of parents, not the church. The Vrije Universiteit was founded by an association of citizens, not a church. And second, after the Vrije Universiteit opened its doors in 1880, members of the Christelijke Gereformeerde Kerk tended to support that university, and the impulse to develop the literary department at Kampen into a gymnasium

---

[57] Bavinck, *Opleiding en theologie*, 12: "Zelfs hadden de curatoren in datzelfde jaar den stouten moed, om op de synode te Groningen te komen met een voorstel tot oprichting van een ... gymnasium, en zelfs niet alleen ten dienste van hen, die straks aan de School theologie, maar *ook ten behoeve van zulken, die later elders in andere wetenschappen zouden gaan studeeren*. En de synode schrikte zoo weinig voor dit voorstel terug, dat zij het met algemeene stemmen aannam. Alleen om financieele redenen werd later het plan helaas prijs gegeven." (The curators had the strong courage in that same year to come to the synod of Groningen with a proposal to found a gymnasium, not only for them who would study theology at the School *but also for those who would study in other academic disciplines later on*. And the synod was shocked so little by this proposal that it was accepted with one accord. It was only for financial reasons that, later on, the plan was given up regrettably.)

[58] Gerrit Jan Beuker, *Abgeschiedenes Streben nach Einheit. Leben und Wirken Henricus Beukers 1834-1900* (Kampen: Mondiss; Bad Bentheim: Hellendoorn, 1996), 138-50.

[59] Harinck and Berkelaar, *Domineesfabriek*, 92-97.

waned.⁶⁰ The Christelijke Gereformeerde tradition originally had a different opinion, and Kampen theologians like Beuker and Herman Bavinck saw no problem in a gymnasium run by the church.⁶¹ But the neo-Calvinist opinion became dominant in Christian Reformed circles in the Netherlands. For this reason, Kampen's literary department never developed into an independent college, although this would have been in line with the Christelijke Gereformeerde tradition.

Conclusion

What are the historical reasons why the CRC has two closely related educational institutions, Calvin Seminary and Calvin University? In a nutshell, the answer is that these institutions are the result of the embeddedness of the CRC in the Dutch Seceder tradition, with a leaning to the conservative side of this tradition. In the Netherlands, this tradition was largely adapted and became integrated with the neo-Calvinist tradition and its notion of sphere sovereignty, which designated the founding of schools as a task not of the church but of citizens, especially parents.

The Seceder ideal was at times close to realization in Kampen, but in the end, it did not materialize there. It was, however, realized in Grand Rapids and in Potchefstroom. In South Africa and in the United States, the ties between the church and schools for general education were not severed. Interestingly, this ideal was realized in Grand Rapids just before the neo-Calvinist ideals began to take hold in the CRC and change the educational scene in such a way that education there also became in large part the responsibility of citizens, not the church. The theological school in Kampen never developed the strong relationship with a college like the Siamese twins in Grand Rapids did. Calvin University and Calvin Theological Seminary embody the educational ideals of the Christelijke Gereformeerde tradition, and that is why they can be considered the full-sized, pre-Kuyperian Kampen.

---

[60] H. Bavinck, *Theologische School en Vrije Universiteit. Een voorstel tot vereeniging* (Kampen: J. H. Bos, 1899), 30: "De meesten zien de noodzakelijkheid niet in, dat de kerken er een gymnasium op na houden en dit nog voor anderen dan aanstaande predikanten open stellen. De stroom beweegt zich duidelijk in de richting van losmaking van het gymnasium." (Most don't see the necessity for the churches to run a gymnasium and for it to be open for anyone but prospective ministers. The current is clearly running in the direction of severing ties with the gymnasium.)

[61] Beuker, *Abgeschiedenes Streben*, 87-112.

Part II

Race- and Gender-Based Legacies

CHAPTER 11

Members Only: The Founding of Erasmus Hall Academy, 1786-1813

Stephen Staggs

Mae West, Sid Luckman, Neil Diamond, and Barbara Streisand are just a few of the famous and accomplished alumni of Erasmus Hall, a public high school located in the Flatbush neighborhood of Brooklyn, New York. Founded in 1786, Erasmus Hall was originally established as a private academy. Named after the Renaissance scholar Erasmus of Rotterdam, Erasmus Hall Academy was the first secondary school granted a charter by the twenty-one members of the board of regents appointed to provide oversight to colleges and academies incorporated in the state of New York after 1784. Almost half of the regents were prominent Dutch Americans. But if you visit the original academy building or read about its history, you will not hear about the racism that was poured into its foundations. It has been hidden beneath its white-washed clapboards.

In order to uncover the white supremacy embedded in the foundations of Erasmus Hall, it is useful to dig into the roots of the Dutch community of Midwout. In the 1640s, the leading inhabitants of New Amsterdam began dividing up the western half of Long Island into farms and farming communities. In the middle of that part of the island, however, was a *vlackebos*, a wooded plain that was difficult to clear for farming. Around 1650, families from Ruinen, in the impoverished county of Drenthe, arrived in New Netherland and set to work clearing the *vlackebos*. By 1652 they had established the village of Midwout, which, following the English takeover, was renamed Flatbush.[1] The administration of Midwout mirrored the administration of villages in the Dutch Republic, with an overlap in religious and secular entities. This overlap continued until well after the English takeover in 1664. Indeed, half the people in the town's administration were, at one time or another, also members of the consistory of the Flatbush Reformed Protestant Dutch Church.[2]

Four years after the English takeover—in 1668—Flatbush was declared the seat or administrative center of what would become Kings County. It was predominately a Dutch agricultural county, with the highest concentration of enslaved Africans in the colonial North. Enslaved black labor was central to the day-to-day survival and economic life of these Dutch Americans. In fact, by 1698, over 40 percent of the households included enslaved people from sub-Saharan Africa and the West Indies. As slavery became the core legal, economic, and social system in colonial New York, the rights of free blacks were eroded as the number of enslaved Africans steadily grew.[3]

As the laws increased restrictions on black liberties, so did black resistance. During the night of April 1, 1712, for example, some enslaved blacks killed nine inhabitants of New York City, including the prominent Dutch American merchant and landowner Adrian Hooglandt, who was also a member of the Collegiate Reformed Protestant Dutch Church. The local authorities quickly convened special courts, which ultimately resulted in the conviction and execution of eighteen blacks through a variety of tortures. Later that year, the New York Assembly responded

---

[1] Russell Shorto, "A Tour of New Netherland: Long Island: Midwout (Flatbush)," New Netherland Institute, accessed 24 May 2019, https://newnetherlandinstitute.org/history-and-heritage/digital-exhibitions/a-tour-of-new-netherland/long-island.midwout/; Jaap Jacobs, *New Netherland: A Dutch Colony in Seventeenth-Century America* (Brill: Leiden, 2005), 76. In 1662 sixty-two more emigrants from the southwestern corner of Drenthe arrived in New Netherland, most of them settling in Midwout.

[2] Jacobs, *New Netherland*, 286.

[3] Graham Russell Hodges, *Root & Branch: African Americans in New York & East Jersey* (Chapel Hill: University of North Carolina Press, 1999), 45, 47-53, 68; "Slavery Here. Right in Brooklyn and Out on Long Island," *The Brooklyn Daily Eagle*, 29 Dec. 1891, 2; Leslie M. Harris, *In the Shadow of Slavery: African Americans in New York City, 1626-1863* (Chicago: University of Chicago Press, 2003), 11. By 1703 there were 343 enslaved blacks in Kings County, 207 of whom were male.

by passing a more restrictive black code. The new "Negro Act" reiterated sanctions against entertaining, trading with, or selling liquor to slaves. It also gave enslavers permission to privately correct the people they claimed as property, except in capital offenses. It also forbade free blacks from selling liquor to the enslaved and ordered: "No Negro, Indian or Mallattoo [sic], that hereafter be made free, shall enjoy, hold or possess any Houses, Lands, Tenements, or Hereditaments in this colony." Finally, the act stated: "[Since] it is found by Experience that the free Negroes of this colony are an Idle Slothful people and prove very often a charge on the place where they are," any European wishing to free a person they had enslaved must first post a £60 surety and provide £20 annually to ensure the former slave's maintenance.[4] In so doing, the Euro-American assemblymen defined blacks as slaves, blocked blacks from the path to freedom, and echoed the racism articulated in one of the most popular travelogues ever written: the *Nauwkeurige beschrijving van de Guinese Goud- Tand- en Slavekust* (Accurate description of the Guinean gold-, ivory-, and slave coast).[5]

This description of the West African coast was written by Willem Bosman, an *opperkoopman*, or head merchant, in the Dutch West India Company (WIC). Published in Utrecht in 1704, it became an immediate bestseller and was translated into both English and French the very next year. Dedicated to the directors of WIC, *Nauwkeurige beschrijving* took the form of twenty letters addressed to one of Bosman's good friends.[6] The racist bias in Bosman's book is patently obvious. At the outset of the ninth letter, Bosman identifies the *inboorlingen* (natives) by the color of their skin, equating Africans with blackness. Bosman explained to his readers that he used *Negros* to identify the peoples of West Africa because *neger* or *niger* means *zwart* (black) and *Negers* were clearly *zwarten* (blacks). Having equated Africans with blackness, he went on to describe their *aangebooren Aart* (inborn nature). According to Bosman, Negers were born and raised in a stinky environment. By nature, he continued, Negers are hypersexual, dishonest, and deceitful. They are a lazy, carefree, and devilishly stingy race who love strong drink and put no care into the construction of their villages, houses,

---

[4] Hodges, *Root & Branch*, 65, 67; Francis J. Sypher Jr., ed., *Liber A of the Collegiate Churches of New York, Part 2* (Grand Rapids, MI: Eerdmans, 2015), 466.
[5] Hodges, *Root & Branch*, 68; Albert van Dantzig, "Willem Bosman's New and Accurate Description of the Coast of Guinea: How Accurate is It?" *History in Africa* 1 (1974): 105.
[6] Dantzig, "Willem Bosman's *New and Accurate Description*," 105-6. In less than 30 years, Bosman's *Nauwkeurige beschrijving* went through five Dutch editions.

and roads. As for their parenting and religion, Bosman characterized them as bad parents and dumb Gentiles.[7] In sum, Bosman asserted that blacks were inferior to the Blanken (whites).

Bosman's conclusions would be echoed by none other than Thomas Jefferson eighty-three years later. In *Notes on the State of Virginia*, Jefferson asserts that blacks are "inferior to whites in the endowments of both body and mind."[8] Jefferson then went on to present a lengthy list of black attributes similar to those set forth by Bosman. Blacks, Jefferson asserted, are sensual, irrational, unimaginative, and short-sighted. According to Jefferson, they also produce a strong disagreeable odor.[9] The fact that Jefferson's description of Africans mirrored that of Bosman's, it turns out, is not surprising. A search of Jefferson's 260-page catalog of the books in his library, ca. 1783, shows that he owned a copy of the French edition of Bosman's *Nauwkeurige beschrijving*. There, on page 164, in his own hand, Jefferson recorded the French title: "Voiage de Guinee de Bosman."[10] In 1788, five years after Jefferson cataloged his own library collection, an English edition of his *Notes on the State of Virginia* was published in Philadelphia and widely circulated in the North.[11]

Meanwhile, some "pious and well-informed Negro men" were requesting membership in full communion in the Flatbush Reformed Protestant Dutch Church. But according to the dominie of Flatbush, Peter Lowe, their request was met with a "singular kind of

---

[7] Willem Bosman, *Nauwkeurige beschryving van de Guinese Goud- Tand- en Slave-kust: nevens alle desselfs landen, koningryken, en gemenebesten, van de zeeden der inwoonders, hun godsdienst, regeering, regtspleeging, oorlogen, trouwen, begraven, enz.: mitsgaders de gesteldheid des lands, veld- en boomgewassen, alderhande dieren, zo wilde als tamme, viervoetige en kruipende, als ook 't pluim-gedierte, vissen, en andere zeldzaamheden meer, tot nog toe de Europeërs onbekend* ('t Utrecht: Anthony Schouten, 1704), 105, 107, 113-20, 131.

[8] Thomas Jefferson, *Notes on the State of Virginia* (Chapel Hill: University of North Carolina Press, 1954), 143.

[9] Jefferson, *Notes*, 139; Nicholas E. Magnis, "Thomas Jefferson and Slavery: An Analysis of His Racist Thinking as Revealed by His Writings and Political Behavior," *Journal of Black Studies* 29, no. 4 (March 1999): 491, 494.

[10] Thomas Jefferson, "1783 Catalog of Books, ca. 1775-1812," 164, Coolidge Collection of Thomas Jefferson Manuscripts, Massachusetts Historical Society.

[11] Coolie Verner, *A Further Checklist of the Separate Editions of Jefferson's Notes on the State of Virginia* (Charlottesville, VA: Bibliographical Society of the University of Virginia, 1950), 5, 7-9. Jefferson wrote *Notes* to respond to questions posed to him by the secretary of the French delegation in Philadelphia in 1780. First completed in 1781, it was updated by Jefferson in 1782 and 1783. The first edition of the *Notes on the State of Virginia* was anonymously published in Paris in 1785.

opposition."[12] In October the General Synod—the highest authority for the Reformed Protestant Dutch churches in North America—met in New York City under the leadership of Lowe's mentor, Dominie John Livingston, who, at the time, claimed three black people as property.[13] During the meetings, Synod passed its first resolution on the subject of the "reception of slaves as members of the Church." Ultimately, Synod determined that "overseers of congregations should exercise all proper prudence by receiving the testimony of masters and mistresses in relation to the subject [of membership]; and likewise, by attending to everything which may subserve the promotion and establishment of peace of the household."[14] As a result, the reception of slaves as members of the church was left up to individual congregations.

The very next month, Dominie Lowe—who, at the time, claimed two black people as property himself—wrote a letter outlining some of the objections expressed by those opposed to the admission of the "worthy" black men who wanted to join the Flatbush congregation. The objections of the leaders in the Reformed Protestant Dutch Church—most of whom claimed black people as property—reiterated the same racist view of Africans as expressed by Bosman and Jefferson. "Negroes," the Dutch Reformed supremacists asserted, "have no souls." "They are," the white supremacists continued,

> accursed of God. . . . They are a species very different from us—witness their nauseous sweat, complexion, [and] manners . . . I would be ashamed to commune with them. . . . If these should be admitted who have now applied the whole community of blacks will flock, too, and what a terrible congregation shall we have. . . . [their] pretended zeal is nothing else than vain parade and ostentation. . . . If many Negroes be admitted . . . adieu order and harmony in the Dutch Church . . . [N]egroes will at length summon their masters before the Consistory, nay will

[12] Peter Lowe, *Peter Lowe to Unidentified/Anonymous, November 1788*, ArMs 1974.008, box A0027, folder 34, Peter Lowe Correspondence 1782-1818, Brooklyn Historical Society.

[13] 1790 United States Federal Census (USFC), NYC West Ward, National Archives and Records Administration (NARA) microfilm publication M637, roll 6, p. 18, image 523, Family History Library Film (FHLF) 0568146.

[14] *The Acts and Proceedings of the General Synod of the Reformed Protestant Dutch Church in North America, Vol. I: Embracing the Period from 1771 to 1812, Preceded by the Minutes of the Coetus (1738–1754) and the Proceedings of the Conferentie (1755–1767) and followed by the Minutes of the Original Particular Synod (1794–1799)* (NY: Board of Publication, RPDC, 1859), 183.

constitute a Consistory themselves. What an awful sight negro elders, deacons, Church masters.... They will intermix with white people at the Lord's Table to their great offense.[15]

In the end, the pious men were denied membership.

Meanwhile, the influential dominie of Collegiate Church, John Livingston, was spending the summer in Flatbush with his theology students. During the summer of 1786, Livingston and John Vanderbilt, a New York state senator and member of the Flatbush congregation, convinced the prominent families in and around Flatbush to support the establishment of an institution of higher learning in their village. Soon forty male heads of households signed and circulated a subscription paper. The signatories, who pledged a sum of £915, counted men of means and power in the early republic and the state of New York, including John Jay, US secretary of state; Peter Lefferts, US senator; George Clinton, governor; Aaron Burr, state attorney general; and Alexander Hamilton, state assemblyman. In the end, the largest pledges came from three of the most prominent members of the Flatbush congregation, John Vanderbilt, Peter Lefferts, and Johannes Lott, who donated one hundred, sixty, and fifty pounds respectively. Not coincidentally, these men were also three of the largest enslavers in Kings County. Among the three of them, they held thirty-eight blacks in bondage in 1790, reflecting the fact that their economic wealth, social status, and political power rested on claiming black people as property. In 1786 and 1787, they and their fellow members of the Flatbush congregation donated money, timber from their farms, and a plot of land on which to construct the school building. One can imagine that the enslaved blacks from the surrounding Dutch American-owned plantations pitched in to construct the one-hundred-by-thirty-six-foot structure.

Granted a charter, the fifteen members of the board of trustees gathered for their first meeting in the newly constructed hall on December 17, 1787. All but one of the trustees who sat down in Erasmus Hall that evening claimed people as property. Among them, they enslaved a total of 106 black people. At least eight of the trustee

---

[15] Peter Lowe, *Peter Lowe*, ArMs 1974.008, box A0027, folder 34, Peter Lowe Correspondence 1782-1818, Brooklyn Historical Society; 1790 USFC, Flatbush, Kings County, NY, NARA microfilm publication M637, roll 6, p. 8, image 369, FHLF 0568146; 1790 USFC, NYC West Ward, NARA microfilm publication M637, roll 6, p. 18, image 523, FHLF 0568146.

enslavers were members of the Reformed Protestant Dutch Church. In fact, two of them were dominies in the church. These were the men entrusted with the task of shaping the first chartered secondary school in the state of New York. They decided to design an academic institution superior to English grammar schools and, consequently, resolved that "no scholars be admitted into the Hall but such as have begun to write."[16]

The founders also determined that Erasmus would include an English department, offering courses in English language, reading, writing, arithmetic, and bookkeeping, and a classics department, with courses in Latin and Greek, as well as surveys of the geography and history of Western Civilization. In order to gain entrance for classical instruction, families paid one guinea, with tuition set at six pounds. For English instruction, families paid an entrance fee of a half guinea and three pounds ten shillings for tuition. In setting such standards and costs, the trustees effectively placed a "Whites Only" sign above the Erasmus entrance. Not only was the cost prohibitive, but because most Dutch American slaveholders did not provide religious instruction—let alone literacy education—to the blacks they claimed as property, there was little chance a nonwhite candidate would be accepted. The Dutch Americans often justified the decision to refuse education to enslaved blacks on the assertion that Africans had no souls.[17]

In 1788 the parents of twenty-six Euro-American boys took advantage of this newest step toward the upper echelons of society. Although there appears to have been some bias favoring students from the prominent families of Flatbush, the students who walked through the doors came from near and far. By 1790-91, the student body included seventy-two sons of prominent families from New York, Pennsylvania, Maryland, North Carolina, South Carolina, Georgia, and Louisiana. The student body also included sons of prominent families

[16] Willis Boughton, *Chronicles of Erasmus Hall Academy, 1787-1896* (Brooklyn: The General Organization, Erasmus Hall High School, 1906), 29-34, 37; 1790 USFC, Flatbush, Kings County, NY, NARA microfilm publication M637, roll 6, p. 8, image 369, FHLF 0568146; 1790 USFC, Fishkill, Dutchess County, NY, NARA microfilm publication M637, roll 6, p. 82, image 186, FHLF 0568146.

[17] Lowe, *Peter Lowe to Unidentified/Anonymous*; Hodges, *Root & Branch*, 87, 124, 181; Boughton, *Chronicles*, 37-38, 43-44; Peter Lindert and Jeffrey G. Williamson, "American Incomes before and after the Revolution," *Journal of Economic History* 73, no. 3 (Sept. 2013): 742. According to Lindert and Williamson, the gross total income for Euro-Americans in New York ca. 1774 was around $38.28 million in current dollars ($4.44/£ sterling). In 1800 their gross total was around $134.4 million ($4.44/£ sterling).

from France and Portugal, as well as the sons of the planter class from the British, Danish, and Dutch West Indies.

Upon arrival, students were welcomed by the first principal of Erasmus, Dominie Livingston, who served in that capacity until 1792. As principal, Livingston selected and closely supervised the first teachers, James Tod and Brandt Schuyler Lupton—whose father, William, lived in New York City's North Ward and claimed one black person as property. Tod was put in charge of the Classics Department and therefore considered first in rank. As the chief teacher, he was given the right to inspect the progress of all students in their respective branches as often as he deemed necessary. He was also appointed custodian of the nine scientific instruments and 115 books donated to Erasmus by the state board of regents in 1791.[18]

Among the most popular and influential of these books were Samuel Johnson's *A Dictionary of the English Language* (London: 1755) and Oliver Goldsmith's *A History of the Earth and Animated Nature* (London: 1774). It is instructive to look at the racial assumptions regarding blacks that students were likely to find in the standard textbooks used at Erasmus. If Erasmus grammar students looked up the word "black" in Johnson's *Dictionary*, they learned that it was a noun, which in the third instance, meant "blackamoor." A quick scan down that same page and students learned that the word "blackamoor" was a noun that described "a man of a black complexion; a negro." Johnson then provided the word in context by quoting *Some Thoughts Concerning Education* (1693), by John Locke: "They [newborn babies] are no more afraid of a *blackamoor* or a lion, than of a nurse or a cat." In this instance, Johnson cited a manual for the education of young gentry boys by the revered English Enlightenment philosopher, which intimated that, like fear of lions, fear of black men had to be learned by infants.

When those enrolled in the survey of the geography and history of Western Civilization turned to Goldsmith's *A History of the Earth and Animated Nature* to learn about the differences among humans, they learned that the chief difference was the "tincture of his skin." In other words, Goldsmith presented a quasi hierarchy of race that included six "human species." At the apex of his hierarchy were the Europeans and the nations bordering them who, according to Goldsmith, "generally agree in the colour of their bodies, the beauty of their complexion, the largeness of their limbs, and the vigour of their understandings." The

---

[18] Boughton, *Chronicles*, 37-38, 44-45; 1790 USFC, NYC North Ward, NARA microfilm publication M637, roll 6, p. 8, image 369, FHLF 0568146.

subordinate races in his hierarchy were the "Southern Asiatics," living in India, who most "resemble the Europeans in stature and features"; the "Tartars," who live in the "greatest part of Asia"; the "Laplanders," living in the polar regions, who proceeded from the Tartars; the "natives of America"; and the "Negroes of Africa."[19]

In his description of the "Negroe nations," Goldsmith reinforced the racist attitudes toward blacks that had become so prevalent in the West Indies and the Early Republic. According to Goldsmith, the "Negroes of Africa [are] a gloomy race [that] blackens all the southern parts of Africa." Although he did differentiate the "Negroe nations," noting that those of "Guinea, for instance, are extremely ugly, and have an insupportable scent," but "those of Mozambique, are reckoned beautiful, and have no ill smell whatsoever," he nonetheless asserted that "Negroes, in general, are of a black colour, with a smooth soft skin." "They are," he continued,

> said to be well shaped; but of such as I have seen, I never found one that might be justly called so; their legs being mostly ill formed, and most commonly bending outward on the shin bone. But it is not only those parts of their bodies that are obvious, that they are disproportioned; those parts which among us are usually concealed by dress, with them are large and languid. The women's breasts, after bearing one child, hang down below the navel; and it is customary, with them, to suckle the child at their backs, by throwing the breast over the shoulder. As their persons are thus naturally deformed, at least to our imaginations, their minds are equally incapable of strong exertions. The climate seems to relax their mental powers still more than those of the body; they are, therefore, in general, found to be stupid, indolent, and mischievous.[20]

Clearly, books such as these explicitly reinforced an assumed supremacy of whites. Indeed, Goldsmith closed his comparison of the human species with the following declaration:

> Of all the colours by which mankind is diversified, it is easy to perceive, that ours [Europeans] is not only the most beautiful to

[19] Samuel Johnson, *A Dictionary of the English Language: In Which the Words are deduced from their Originals, And Illustrated in their Different Significations By Examples from the best Writers. To which Are Prefixed, A History of the Language, And An English Grammar* (London: J. & P. Knapton, 1755), 249; Oliver Goldsmith, *A History of the Earth, and Animated Nature* (London: J. Nourse, 1774), 2: 211-13, 219, 223, 226-31.

[20] Goldsmith, *A History of the Earth*, 2: 226-27.

the eye, but the most advantageous. The fair complexion seems, if I may so express it, as a transparent covering to the soul; all the variations of the passions, every expression of joy or sorrow, flows to the cheek, and, without language, marks the mind. . . . The colour, therefore, most natural to man, ought to be that which is most becoming; and it is found, that, in all regions, the children are born fair, or at least red, and that they grow black, or tawny, as they advance in age. It should seem, consequently, that man is naturally white.[21]

A number of the students who graduated from Erasmus took such lessons to heart and applied them in their positions of power. In 1906, ten years after the academy was turned over to the New York public school system, an Anglo-American English teacher at the renamed Erasmus Hall High School highlighted four of its most "distinguished" graduates in the *Chronicles of Erasmus Hall*: John Blair Linn, William Alexander Duer, John MacPherson Berrien, and George McIntosh Troup. Born into a Scotch Irish family in the backcountry of Pennsylvania in 1752, Linn's father, William, served as a chaplain of the Continental Army during the Revolutionary War, associate dominie of the Collegiate Dutch Reformed Church, first chaplain of the US House of Representatives, and president of Queen's College (present-day Rutgers University). After completing his studies at Erasmus, Linn began studying law with Alexander Hamilton but soon quit those studies and moved to Schenectady to study theology at Union College with his father's friend, Dominie Dirck Romeyn. At the conclusion of his studies with Romeyn, Linn became the pastor of the First Presbyterian Church in Philadelphia. Since Philadelphia was the nation's capital at the time, First Presbyterian counted President John Adams, members of Congress, and distinguished members of the American Philosophical Society among its congregants. The black Presbyterians living in Philadelphia, however, were not welcome at First Presbyterian, and so John Gloucester—a former enslaved man from Tennessee who had received religious instruction from the Presbyterian pastor who had claimed him as property—founded the First Colored Presbyterian Church in 1807.[22]

---

[21] Ibid., 2: 232-33.
[22] Boughton, *Chronicles*, 46-47, 51, 55; Lewis Leary, "John Blair Linn, 1777-1805," *The William and Mary Quarterly* 4, no. 2 (April 1947): 159, 162; Euell A. Nielsen, "John Gloucester (1776-1822)," Black Past, last modified 5 March 2015, https://www.blackpast.org/african-american-history/gloucester-john-1776-1822-2/; Euell A.

Like Linn, William A. Duer was the son of a patriot. Indeed, his father, William, was a member of the Continental Congress. Born in Rhinebeck, New York, in 1780, following his studies at Erasmus, Duer went on to study law in Philadelphia and New York City. Admitted to the bar in 1802, Duer began practicing law with Edward Livingston who, at the time, was the United States attorney for the district of New York and mayor of the city. In deep financial debt to the federal government, Livingston moved to New Orleans in 1804, the year after his older brother had helped to negotiate the Louisiana Purchase from Napoleon. Once there, Livingston established a large law practice, which Duer eventually joined.

Duer arrived in New Orleans at a time when the new American territorial government was scrutinizing the legal recognition between the large population of free blacks and slaves in French Louisiana. This was because many of the Euro-American inhabitants of the Territory of Orleans, including the legislators, associated free blacks with slave revolts and the "contamination" of the "White race." As a result, the Territorial Legislature asked Livingston's firm to conduct a study of the legal system that had governed French (1682-1762, 1800-1804) and Spanish (1763-1800) Louisiana, including the provisions in the French Code Noir and the Spanish Coartacion that addressed the legal status of slaves. The legislature also asked Livingston—who, by 1820, had claimed one young black male between the age of fourteen and twenty-five and three black females under the age of fourteen as property—to draw up acts regulating legal practice and procedure relative to slaves. These were adopted by the legislative council on April 10, 1805. These and subsequent acts not only excluded free blacks from many of the new American institutions but also deprived them of many of the freedoms previously provided under the French and Spanish legal systems.[23]

Nielsen, "First African Presbyterian Church, Philadelphia, Pennsylvania (1807-)," Black Past, last modified 24 Feb. 2015, https://www/blackpast.african-American-history/first-african-presbyterian-church-philadelphia-pennsylvania-1808/. According to the independent historian Euell Nielsen, First African Presbyterian Church was "the fourth of the first five African American churches founded in Philadelphia."

[23] Boughton, *Chronicles*, 46; John Fiske and James Grant Wilson, eds., "Duer, William," *Appletons' Cyclopædia of American Biography* (NY: D. Appleton and Company, 1900), 2: 245; Lynn Stewart, "Louisiana Subjects: Power, Space, and the Slave Body," *Ecumene* 2 (1995): 228, 230; Ferdinand Stone, "The Law with a Difference and How It Came About," in *The Past as Prelude: New Orleans, 1718-1968* (Gretna, LA: Firebird Press, 2008), 59; 1820 USFC, New Orleans, New Orleans City, LA, NARA microfilm publication M33, roll 32, p. 31, image 43; Territory of Orleans, *Acts passed at the first session of the Legislative Council of the Territory of Orleans: begun and held at the Principal,*

Duer's political persuasions were shared with the other "distinguished graduates" of Erasmus Hall, celebrated by Boughton. George McIntosh Troup and John Macpherson Berrien were, like Duer, members of the Democrat-Republican Party formed by James Madison and Thomas Jefferson in 1792. Unlike Linn and Duer, however, Troup was born south of the Mason-Dixon line. In fact, he was born in one of the earliest European settlements in what is present-day Alabama: McIntosh Bluff. When he was old enough, his parents sent him off to Flatbush. Upon completion of his studies at Erasmus, Troup entered the prestigious halls of the College of New Jersey (Princeton). Following graduation, he moved to Savannah, Georgia, where he was admitted to the bar. Having established his reputation, he threw his hat into the political ring.

A Jacksonian Democrat, like his Erasmian classmate and friend John Macpherson Berrien, Troup was subsequently elected to the Georgia Assembly, the US House of Representatives, and the US Senate, where he became a political ally of an ardent defender of slavery from South Carolina, John C. Calhoun. A believer in Manifest Destiny, Troup also supported the construction of roads, canals, and railroads; entrance into the War of 1812; and the removal and relocation of Native Americans. In fact, while serving as governor of Georgia, he helped negotiate the removal of the Muscogee (Creek) people from Western Georgia in 1825.[24]

---

in the city of New Orleans, on Monday the third day of December, in the year of our Lord one thousand eight hundred and four, and of the independence of the United States the twenty-ninth (New Orleans: James M. Bradford, 1805), 166, 168, 172, 174, 176, 178, 234, 238, 240, 242, 244, 246; Liza Treadwell, "Louisiana," in *A State-by-State History of Race and Racism in the United States* (Santa Barbara: ABC-CLIO, LLC, 2019), 351. Duer eventually returned to New York, where he married and opened a law office in Rhinebeck. In 1814 he was elected to the New York State Assembly. As a state assemblyman, he chaired a committee on colleges and academies and promoted canal legislation. At the end of his term, he served as a judge on the New York Supreme Court from 1822 to 1829 and, subsequently, president of Columbia College (present-day Columbia University) until 1842. As for Livingston, the legislature of the state of Louisiana later appointed him to a commission to compose a new civil code for the state. Adopted in 1825, the code established anti-miscegenation laws, denied property rights to slaves, prohibited slaves from receiving religious instruction, segregated militias, restricted employment, and made it a crime to teach slaves and freed blacks to read.

[24] Boughton, *Chronicles*, 55; Theodore Bowling Pearson, "Early Settlement around McIntosh Bluff: Alabama's First County Seat," *Alabama Review* 20 (Oct. 1978): 243; Brian Schoen, *The Fragile Fabric of Union: Cotton, Federal Politics, and the Global Origins of the Civil War* (Baltimore: Johns Hopkins University Press, 2009), 98; Edward J. Harden, *The Life of George M. Troup* (Savannah: E. J. Purse, 1859), 4, 11-12, 115, 121-

Troup's classmate and friend, John Macpherson Berrien, was born in the Berrien family home in Rocky Hill, New Jersey, in 1781. His grandfather, Judge John Berrien, a former surveyor and land agent from Long Island, had purchased the home overlooking the Millstone River sometime in the 1730s; he had counted George Washington among his close friends and served as a justice of the Supreme Court of New Jersey and trustee of the College of New Jersey. John Macpherson's father served as a major in the army of General Lachlan McIntosh during the Revolutionary War. During the war, Major Berrien served in Georgia for a time and, a year after the birth of his son John, moved the family to Savannah.

Like the Troups, Major Berrien and his wife, Margaret Macpherson, wanted their son to have the best educational advantages, so when he came of age, they sent him off to the preparatory school on Long Island. After completing his studies at Erasmus, Berrien went to the College of New Jersey (Princeton), graduating a year earlier than his classmate Troup. Like Troup, Berrien headed to Savannah to study law and was admitted to the bar the same year as Troup. Berrien then began practicing law in Louisville, Georgia. After serving as the solicitor of the Eastern Judicial Circuit in 1809 and captain of the Georgia Hussars during the War of 1812, he was elected to the state senate in 1822. Two years later, he ran for the US Senate as a Jacksonian Democrat and won.[25]

During his freshman year in the US Senate, he found himself representing the vice consul of Spain before the US Supreme Court. The vice consul claimed ownership of some of the three hundred chained Africans found aboard the *Antelope*, discovered adrift off the northern coast of Florida by federal authorities. Francis Scott Key—author of *The Star-Spangled Banner*—opened the case for the federal government by arguing that it was philosophical and constitutional hypocrisy to declare that all men were created equal, while operating under the assumption that all Africans were slaves. In his rebuttal, Berrien argued

---

32, 160, 170, 174-86, 188-89, 197-99; David E. Johnson, *John Randolph of Roanoke* (Baton Rouge: Louisiana State University Press, 2012), 146.

[25] Boughton, *Chronicles*, 47; Alexander R. MacDonnell, "John MacPherson Berrien," the *Georgia Historical Quarterly* 17, no. 1 (March 1933): 1-5. The Berrien home served as General George Washington's final headquarters during the Revolutionary War. It is here, wrote Alexander MacDonnell in the *Georgia Historical Quarterly* in 1933, "that he is said to have written his famous farewell address [to the armies of the United States], a fact which has caused the old Berrien home to be fittingly preserved as one of the patriotic shrines of the Republic." In 1970 the home was added to the United States National Register of Historic Places.

that slavery "lay at the foundation of the Constitution."[26] In the end, the Supreme Court decided that the Spanish and Portuguese had the right to engage in the slave trade. As a result, many of the Africans were sold to American slave owners and the proceeds given to the Spanish and Portuguese claimants as restitution for their losses. A couple of months after the court decided in his favor, Berrien was back in Georgia's capitol building when he ran into his friend of twenty years, Governor George McIntosh Troup. Before the legislature convened, the friends conversed "on the subject of our slave property, and the danger it was exposed by the repeated attacks of other States and of the United States."[27] Indeed, the two Erasmus alums had a lot to lose. Between them, by 1840, they had claimed 299 fellow humans as property, seventy-five of whom were under the age of ten.[28]

The original, white-washed Erasmus Hall Academy founded, funded, and built by the Dutch Reformed community in and around Flatbush was constructed to prepare the sons of prominent Euro-American families to ultimately assume positions of authority in institutions meant to preserve and protect their own power, privilege, status, and wealth. And the graduates of Erasmus Hall High School lived up to those historic objectives well into the twentieth century.

As for Erasmus Hall's recent fortunes, much has changed. It did not remain an all-white school. The popular perception is that an influx of minorities into the Erasmian student body was due to the immigration into the surrounding community of middle-class Jews in the 1960s. This brief encounter with diversity, however, did not

---

[26] Edward Hatfield, "*The Antelope*," National Archives, accessed 7 June 2019, http://www.archives.gov/files/atlanta /finding-aids/antelope.pdf; Jonathan M. Bryant, *Dark Places: The Voyage of the Slave Ship Antelope* (NY: Liveright Publishing Corporation, 2015), xi–xii; Allen C. Guelzo, *Fateful Lightning: A New History of the Civil War and Reconstruction* (NY: Oxford University Press, 2012), 46.

[27] Hatfield, "*The Antelope*"; Harden, 299-311.

[28] 1840 USFC, Savannah, Chatham, Georgia, NARA microfilm publication M704, roll 50, p. 61, FHLF 0007047; 1840 USFC, District 8, Chatham, Georgia, NARA microfilm publication M704, roll 38, p. 140, FHLF 0007042; 1840 USFC, Laurens, Georgia, NARA microfilm publication M704, roll 45, FHLF 0007045; William W. Freehling, *Prelude to Civil War: The Nullification Crisis in South Carolina 1816–1836* (Oxford: Oxford University Press, 1992), 1-3. Nine of the people enslaved by Berrien in 1840 lived in his home in Savannah. The rest lived and worked on his plantations in Chatham County. In 1829 President Andrew Jackson appointed Berrien attorney general of the United States. As attorney general, Berrien was an outspoken supporter of states' rights during the Nullification Crisis that emerged after a state convention declared the Tariffs of 1828 and 1832 unconstitutional and, therefore, null and void in the state of South Carolina.

last long. Janelle Peterkin, a student at Macauley Honors College at Brooklyn College, uncovered a significant factor in the resegregation of Erasmus Hall in the last quarter of the twentieth century. In 1976 New York State's education commissioner reversed his initial ruling that all necessary steps be taken to integrate Erasmus. The commissioner's ultimate ruling regarding attendance zones excluded nearby white neighborhoods from Erasmus Hall's zone of recruitment. The number of students from low-income, minority families has increased over time to the point that they now predominate. But that is a story for another occasion.[29]

---

[29] Janelle Peterkin, "Erasmus Hall," *Uncovering the Secrets of New York City's Streets*, last modified 25 March 2019, https://macaulay.cuny.edu/seminars/wills09/articles/e/r/a/ErasmusHall1279.html. In the spring of 2009, professor Jocelyn Wills gave the students in her "The People of New York" seminar at the Macauley Honors College at Brooklyn College a project assignment: select an intriguing site in one of New York's five boroughs that holds personal significance. An immigrant from the island country of Grenada in the West Indies, Peterkin chose Erasmus Hall because she attended Science Technology and Research Early College High School at Erasmus and wanted to learn more about its history.

CHAPTER 12

The Integration of Grosse Pointe Christian Day School

Douglas J. Vrieland

At its monthly meeting on June 28, 1967, the president of the Grosse Pointe Christian Day School (GPCDS) board, Gerrit Van de Riet, gave the report, "Negro children from Community Christian Reformed Church." According to the minutes from this meeting, a separate meeting had been held on this matter on June 22. The board had received a copy of the minutes from that meeting "to acquaint them with the action being contemplated."[1] The action being contemplated was admitting black[2] children from Community Church to GPCDS. Community Church was a joint outreach effort of First Christian Reformed Church (CRC) of Detroit, Dearborn Christian Reformed Church, and the recently formed Classis Lake Erie. The minutes of the board meeting continue:

[1] Minutes of the Grosse Pointe Christian Day School Board, 28 June 1967, held at First Christian Reformed Church of Detroit, Grosse Pointe Park, MI (hereafter cited as minutes).
[2] The appropriate way to refer to African Americans has changed over the years. In 1967 the term "Negro" was commonly used. Later "black" became more common and then "African American." I have maintained the term "Negro" in quoted sources; otherwise, I use the term "black" or "African American."

A long discussion was held on the subject, during which, each board member expressed his feelings on the matter. At the end of the discussion, the chair instructed the Education Committee to look into the matter of teacher attitudes and pupil testing and report back at the next board meeting. The Finance Committee was requested to investigate the financial problems which might be encountered. . . .[3] If necessary, the next school board meeting will be held on July 26.[4]

But no meeting was held on July 26—other events undoubtedly were the focus of the board members on that day.

On Sunday, July 2, 1967, just four days after the June school board meeting, Rev. Franklin Steen was installed as the pastor of First CRC of Detroit, the congregation that started the school and provided the majority of its support. First CRC is located in Grosse Pointe Park, one block from Detroit city limits, and its building was adjacent to GPCDS. Three weeks after Rev. Steen's installation, on July 23, the city of Detroit erupted in a weeklong riot that stunned the nation and remains one of the worst civil disturbances in the history of the country.[5] The rebellion began when police raided an unlicensed drinking establishment catering to blacks, located on Twelfth Street and Clairmont on Detroit's west side. Community Christian Reformed Church was located on Fourteenth and Pingree, just six blocks from Twelfth and Clairmont.

A segregated city

"Grosse Pointe" (or "the Pointes") refers to five of Detroit's oldest and most exclusive suburbs. These five independent cities—Grosse Pointe Park, Grosse Pointe Farms, the city of Grosse Pointe, Grosse Pointe Woods, and Grosse Pointe Shores—are all on Detroit's east side, along the shores of Lake St. Clair. In 1967 Grosse Pointe was generally referred to—in the language of the day—as a "lily white" community.

In April 1960, Grosse Pointe drew national attention with the revelation of the so-called "point system," in place since 1945 to keep

---

[3] Minutes, 28 June 1967.
[4] Ibid.
[5] The question of how to label the July 1967 disturbance in Detroit is the subject of ongoing discussion, as is the question of whether it was truly a "race" uprising or an uprising of a broader coalition of poor and disenfranchised citizens of the city. See Ken Coleman, "Rebellion, Revolution, or Riot: The Debate Continues," in *Detroit 1967: Origins, Impacts, Legends* (Detroit: Wayne State University Press, 2017), 158.

property values high.[6] According to this system, used by the Grosse Pointe Brokers Association and the Grosse Pointe Property Owners Association, prospective residents of Grosse Pointe were screened by a private detective as to their desirability on the basis of race, religion, nationality, and employment, as well as more subjective criteria, to determine if their way of living was "typically American."[7] Michigan's Democratic governor, G. Mennen Williams—himself a resident of Grosse Pointe—called the system "odious," and the attorney general called it "morally corrupt."[8] He ordered the abandonment of the system within thirty days and announced that, if his order was violated, the state would "impose all sanctions possible."[9] The point system was dropped, but discrimination continued. Realtors did not make follow-up calls to black clients as they did for white clients,[10] and when potential black renters tried to look at vacant apartments, they would be met with such excuses as "It's been rented already. . . . It's not ready. . . . The landlord had to check out a faulty [this or that]. . . . The apartment is not for rent."[11] In March 1967—three months before Gerrit Van de Riet gave his report—an estimated eighteen million viewers saw a report on integration efforts in Grosse Pointe on the Huntly-Brinkley Report on ABC News. Open housing in Grosse Pointe was in the national spotlight, and the exclusive community was a symbol of racial segregation.

It is important, however, to see the racial struggle of Grosse Pointe in the context of the history of Detroit, of which the Pointes are but one part. Detroit has always been a segregated city. With its proximity to Canada, Detroit was one of the final stops of the Underground Railroad. And, although many runaway slaves made it to Detroit, and both the black and white populations of the city willingly offered their assistance, the Fugitive Slave Act of 1793 required runaway slaves to be apprehended in free states or territories and returned to their owners. At least six fugitive slave riots occurred in the city before the Civil War as runaway slaves fought back against the slave catchers.[12]

---

[6] "Michigan: Grosse Pointe's Gross Points," *Time* (25 April 1960): 25.
[7] "Elaborate Screening Test Used in Detroit Suburb," *New York Times*, 24 April 1960.
[8] "Michigan Fights Real Estate Ban," *New York Times* (5 June 1960): R1.
[9] "Michigan Orders Point System End: Screening of Prospective Home Buyers Denounced by Attorney General," *New York Times* (15 May 1960): 81.
[10] Kathy Cosseboom, *Grosse Pointe, Michigan: Race Against Race* (Lansing, MI: Michigan State University Press, 1972), 16.
[11] Ibid., 24.
[12] Roy E. Finkenbine, "The Underground Railroad and Early Racial Violence," *Detroit 1967*, 24.

After the Civil War, blacks in Detroit made gradual progress toward complete equality and lived not only in the predominately black neighborhoods of Black Bottom and Paradise Valley but also throughout the city in other predominately white neighborhoods.[13] But things changed on January 5, 1914, when Henry Ford announced that he would pay five dollars a day to anyone who would work in his factories. Soon, African American and poor white farmers from the South began flocking to the city to work in the factories, bringing with them their Jim Crow experience and mentality, if not the laws. Whites began to complain that African Americans degraded their neighborhoods, "making them less clean, less safe, less desirable, and less valuable."[14] The claim that black residents brought down property values was the same claim that the Grosse Pointe Brokers Association and the Grosse Pointe Property Owners Association would use to justify the point system twenty-five years later.

In 1917 the Supreme Court ruled that municipalities could not pass laws for the purpose of segregating neighborhoods.[15] But segregation persisted by other means, namely violence, which became the main way to keep blacks out of Detroit's white neighborhoods. During the summer of 1925, there were five separate incidents of white mobs violently removing blacks from their neighborhoods. The final incident resulted in the death of a white protester, Leon Breiner, because of a shot fired from the home of Dr. Ossian Sweet, an African American who had moved into an all-white neighborhood. The incident occurred as the Sweet family was attempting to defend themselves from an all-white crowd, which had gathered for the second night outside their home. Some in the crowd were throwing rocks at the house, breaking an upstairs window in the process.[16] Dr. Sweet, defended by Clarence Darrow, was acquitted by an all-white jury in a second trial in April 1926. The trials became known as the "Sweet Trials."[17]

By 1950 neighborhood covenants had replaced violence as a means of segregating black and white neighborhoods. In January of that year, Albert Cobo (after whom Cobo Hall and Cobo Arena are named) was installed as mayor of the city of Detroit, elected on the promise

---

[13] Kevin Boyle, "The Rages of Whiteness: Racism, Segregation, and the Making of Modern Detroit," *Detroit 1967*, 43.
[14] Boyle, "The Rages of Whiteness," 43.
[15] Buchanan v. Warley, 245 US 60 (1917).
[16] Herb Boyd, *Black Detroit: A People's History of Self-Determination* (NY: Harper-Collins, 2017), 110.
[17] For the complete story of Ossian Sweet, see Phyllis Vine, *One Man's Castle: Clarence Darrow in Defense of the American Dream* (NY: HarperCollins, 2004).

to uphold Detroit's restrictive racial covenants and oppose the "Negro invasion" of white neighborhoods.[18] Ten years after Albert Cobo was installed as mayor of Detroit, the point system in Grosse Pointe was exposed to a national audience.

The Grosse Pointe Real Estate Association defended the practice, suggesting that 95 percent of Grosse Pointe residents approved of the system, since it effectively kept property values high. But many residents disapproved of the practice and formed the Grosse Pointe Human Relations Council in response to the revelation of the point system.[19] Several members of First CRC were members of that council. On June 29, 1963, the council sponsored a march down Kercheval Avenue in Grosse Pointe's exclusive "Village" shopping district.

This local action followed the Detroit "Walk to Freedom" march the previous Sunday down Woodward Avenue. On that occasion, Martin Luther King Jr. gave the first rendition of his famous "I Have a Dream" speech, which he later delivered on the steps of the Lincoln Memorial. Republican governor George Romney, a devout Mormon, refused to participate in political activities on Sunday, but the following Saturday, he unexpectedly appeared and led the six hundred marchers in Grosse Pointe calling for open housing. According to the *Grosse Pointe News*:

> [A]s they walked, it became increasingly clear that Pointe residents intended to extend a friendly welcome.
>
> Interested watchers in the village looked on peacefully, breaking into spontaneous applause at many points. Flags were hung on poles along Kercheval. Many homes displayed flags as well, all along the route.
>
> A good number of Pointe spectators joined the ranks of the marchers as they progressed, and soon, the parade stretched at least three blocks....
>
> Along the route of march, demonstrators stopped in front of two real estate offices for a few brief minutes. The firms were singled out as "ringleaders" in the alleged Pointe discrimination.[20]

---

[18] Michael R. Glass, "Cities during World War II and in the Postwar Period, 1941-1952: Detroit," in *Cities in American Political History* (Los Angeles: CQ Press, 2011), 514.

[19] *Grosse Pointe Civil Rights Organizations: Papers, 1963-1973* (Detroit: Archives of Labor and Urban Affairs, Accession Number 1456). https://reuther.wayne.edu/files/UR001456.pdf (accessed 19 April 2019).

[20] "Whites and Negroes Join in Demonstration against Housing Discrimination," *Grosse Pointe News*, 4 July 1963. http://digitize.gp.lib.mi.us/digitize/newspapers/gpnews/1960-64/63/1963-07-04.pdf (accessed 20 April 2019).

The demonstration was followed by a rally at Grosse Pointe High School, with attendance from eleven hundred to two thousand people, 70 percent of whom were white and 30 percent of whom were black.[21]

Three years later, twenty-six pastors, representing all but two of the churches in Grosse Pointe, signed a statement calling for open housing in Grosse Pointe. It began:

> As ministers of churches in the Grosse Pointe community, we believe the time has come for a clear statement of religious conviction and democratic principle on the matter of race relations in our community and in the metropolitan area of which it is a part. We cannot separate ourselves from the currents of change and the new patterns of human relationships that are moving forward in America and throughout the world today. To attempt to do so is to betray our common democratic heritage and Judeo-Christian ethics which our churches, through their respective denominations, represent.[22]

With the statement, "Every person has the moral as well as the legal right to purchase or rent a house anywhere without limitations based on race, color, religion, or national origin,"[23] the pastors pointed out that their stand "is supported and sanctioned by the teaching of the several churches and denominations to which we belong."[24] And further, "The churches and their members should lead the way in making sure that this right of every person is not violated in our own community either by accepted practices or community prejudices."[25] Rev. John Groenewold, who at the time was pastor of First CRC of Detroit in Grosse Pointe Park, was one of the clergymen who signed the statement.

Getting to "yes" on the question of integration

The June 22, 1967, meeting that brought the report, "Negro children from Community Christian Reformed Church," to the full board of GPCDS was not the first time that the question of admitting a

---

[21] Ibid.
[22] "Opening Doors: Grosse Pointe Committee for Open Housing Newsletter" 1 (no. 3): 3, folder 5, box 4, Grosse Pointe Civil Rights Organizations Records, Walter P. Reuther Library, Archives of Labor and Urban Affairs, Wayne State University.
[23] Ibid.
[24] Ibid.
[25] Ibid.

black student from Community Church to the Grosse Pointe school had been raised. Mel Vander Brug, a member of First CRC who worshipped at Community Church, was serving with the Big Brothers program to mentor Lamar Germany, one of the young men of the church. He spoke with Gerrit Van de Riet about enrolling Germany in the Christian school. When Rev. Harold Botts heard about this, he called Vander Brug and said it was not fair to the other Community Church children if only one of them could attend the Christian school. Vander Brug responded that his interest in Germany's admittance to the school was due to a request from Germany's mother Louise. Botts and Vander Brug agreed to work toward a plan to make Christian School education available for all the children of the congregation. Germany never attended GPCDS but instead was enrolled in the Friends school in downtown Detroit.[26]

After their June 22 meeting, the school board did not meet again until August 30. According to the minutes of that meeting, "A report was received for information concerning the negro [sic] children from Community Chr Ref Church entering our school."[27] Presumably, the report came from the education committee, tasked in June to look into the matter of teacher attitudes and pupil testing and report back at the next board meeting. According to Curtis Vrieland, placed on the education committee at the June 28 meeting, the teachers understood the challenge of getting the black children up to grade level and that, if they took on this extra work, the board would not be able to increase their pay. The teachers indicated their willingness to take on this challenge anyway.[28] One of the teachers, Shirley Verspoor, was the wife of a law student at Wayne State University. During the summer months, she would catch a ride downtown when her husband had to attend class and volunteer at Community Church as a tutor. The teachers understood firsthand the needs of the black students. Still, their openness to take on this challenge was impressive. GPCDS was a small school, with four classrooms serving eight grades. The teachers already had the challenge of two grade levels in each classroom, and although they were overworked and underpaid, they were willing to take on this additional responsibility.

The minutes of the school board meeting of August 30 continue:

---

[26] Oral interview with Mel Vander Brug, Naples, FL, 26 March 2019, and follow up email, 30 April 2019.
[27] Minutes, 30 Aug. 1967.
[28] Curtis Vrieland, interview by author, Gun Lake, MI, 28 April 2019. Curtis Vrieland is the father of the author of this paper.

"The decision to entering [sic] our school is being considered for the 68-69 session after Rev. Botts of the Community Chr Ref Church has conducted proper testing with the prospective students."[29]

One other entry to the minutes of the August 30 meeting, although not directly related to the question of integration, is nevertheless significant. It is from a parent who "thought that a $600 total pledge was required to enroll children. It was explained that this was not correct, as no covenant child would be refused a Christian education because of monetary considerations."[30] A "covenant child" is the child of a believer, a member of the church community. According to the Heidelberg Catechism, one of the doctrinal statements of the Christian Reformed Church, "Infants as well as adults are included in God's covenant and people."[31] Because of this, they must be baptized and "distinguished from the children of unbelievers."[32] The church believed it had a special responsibility to these children; they took a vow at the children's baptisms to train them in the Christian faith. Christian Day School education was one concrete way the church kept this vow, along with Sunday school and catechism classes. The concept of covenant children would prove very important in the board's considering whether to admit the Community Church children to GPCDS.

The financial implications of admitting the Community Church students remained a concern. According to the minutes of the September 27 meeting, the "suggestion was made [to] check into Federal subsidies for Negro children entering parochial schools under the General Welfare clauses of the Federal Government."[33] Five months later, at the February 28 meeting, the Aid to Non-Public School Education Bill was discussed. According to the minutes, "Representative Waldron visited our school concerning this. He was very favorably impressed. Information concerning this proposed bill will be disseminated to the school mailing list."[34]

On November 29, 1967, Rev. Botts, pastor of Community CRC, along with Dave Cooke and Mel Vander Brug, representing the two families from the Grosse Pointe church who attended Community Church weekly, met with the board. At that time, as many as twenty-five

---

[29] Minutes, 30 Aug. 1967.
[30] Ibid.
[31] Heidelberg Catechism, Question and Answer 74. https://www.crcna.org/welcome/beliefs/confessions/heidelberg-catechism (accessed 2 May 2019).
[32] Ibid.
[33] Minutes, 27 Sept. 1967.
[34] Minutes, 28 Feb. 1968.

children from Community Church were potential students for GPCDS, with the following grade level breakdown: grade one—four students; grade two—two students; grade three—five students; grade four—four students; grade five—five students; grade six—three students.[35] The mind of the board at this point is clear from the following entry:

> The discussion was centered in three areas:
> A. It was the feeling that educational standards would not and could not be compromised and that negro [sic] parents must be made fully aware of this.
> B. Concerning tuition and cost of education, the Board would be most helpful—but basically this is a parental responsibility.
> C. There is a defined need for a process of education for our present Christian School constituency to facilitate the acceptance of Negro children in our school.
> Discussion of the subject was closed for the evening after thanking Rev. Botts for his time in visiting us.[36]

From this entry, it appears that the board was open and willing to admit African American students. Across town, however, things were different. At the January 31 board meeting, members were informed by Dr. Phil Feringa—who by this time had replaced Van de Riet as board president—that "Dearborn is out as far as educating Negro children."[37] The reference is undoubtedly to Dearborn Christian School, located in a city nationally known at the time for its racist mayor, Orville Hubbard, who was quoted as saying he was "for complete segregation, one million percent."[38]

In contrast to the Dearborn school, the GPCDS board throughout the entire process struggled with the question of how to get to "yes" in answer to this request. There was no concern expressed by the board, either on November 29 following Rev. Botts' visit, or at any other time, that community acceptance of African American students in the school might be a concern. The only indication that the board ever considered this came the following summer, after the decision was made to admit

---

[35] Minutes, 29 Nov. 1967.
[36] Ibid.
[37] Minutes, 31 Jan. 1968.
[38] "Hubbard, Orville." *The Detroit Historical Society Encyclopedia of Detroit*. https://detroithistorical.org/learn/encyclopedia-of-detroit/hubbard-orville (accessed 1 May 2019).

black students. On that occasion, board member Robert Melling was tasked with giving "a resume to the Grosse Pointe Human Relations Committee concerning the children of the Community Church coming to our school."[39] Melling apparently fulfilled his assignment and reported back to the August board meeting:

> Bob Melling informed us that the Human Relations Committee of Grosse Pointe will discuss the children from Community Church coming to our school at their Executive Board Meeting. It was recommended the Secretary write a letter to the Mayor's office of the City of Grosse Pointe Park and to the Human Relations Committee formally informing them of the acceptance of the Community Church children to our school.[40]

The board may not have been concerned about the Grosse Pointe community's acceptance of black students, but it was concerned about the broader GPCDS constituency and took proactive steps to facilitate the constituency's acceptance of black students in the Christian school. At the April 24, 1968, meeting, board member John Batts was given the responsibility of devising "a questionnaire to help determine the reaction of the people of the school society to the Community Church children entering our school."[41] The results were discussed "in detail" at the following meeting.[42]

The teachers also were proactive in working to prepare students for the possible arrival of black students. Shirley Verspoor included activities in her fifth and sixth grade classroom emphasizing the equality of people, regardless of race, and the arbitrary nature of racial prejudice. In one exercise, when dismissing the class for recess, on one day, she would dismiss the blue-eyed children first, making those with brown eyes wait, and on another day, she would dismiss children with shoelaces first, insisting that those with Velcro straps remain in their seats.[43]

At the May 29, 1968, meeting, a final decision had to be made. "A letter was read from the parents of the Community Christian Reformed Church making applications for 11 children in the Grosse Pointe

---

[39] Minutes, 26 June 1968.
[40] Minutes, 21 Aug. 1968.
[41] Minutes, 24 April 1968.
[42] Minutes, 29 May 1968.
[43] Oral interview with Shirley Verspoor, Grand Rapids, MI, 22 May 2019. I was in her fifth grade class that year, and her lessons on race made a deep impression on me.

Christian School."⁴⁴ Rather than the twenty-five students identified by Rev. Botts on November 29, the letter included only children at the fourth grade level and below, likely a concession to the concern for academic standards and the difficulty of older students to get caught up to grade level. The decision was clearly a difficult one for the board, and the members did not take it lightly.

> A two-and-one-half-hour discussion ensued in which scholastic standings were discussed. It was brought out that a difficulty would be the children's short attention span, but it was felt that this was a correctible situation. The possibility of starting a Community Christian School was discussed, but it was considered unadvisable and unworkable. The questionnaires sent to the School Society members were also discussed in detail.
>
> A motion was then made and supported to accept the covenant children of inner-city on the same basis as children from other backgrounds based on the conditions set forth by the School Board and applicatory letter.⁴⁵

Note the way the motion was worded. These may have been "Negro" children, but the board saw them first and foremost as "covenant" children. The motion refers to these black children as "covenant" children. They had been baptized. They were to be "distinguished from the children of unbelievers." What distinguished these children was not their skin color but their baptism. GPCDS was a school for "covenant" children, and the board believed, as indicated by their earlier decision, that "no covenant child would be refused a Christian education because of monetary considerations." The board had no choice but to vote "yes," based on their deeply held theological convictions. The result of a secret ballot was unanimous. Covenant children from Community CRC would be admitted.⁴⁶

A broader discussion

It is helpful to look at the board's decision in the context of the broader discussion about race within the CRC in the late 1960s. The church's General Synod, the annual meeting of representatives from across the United States and Canada where business and theological

---

⁴⁴ Minutes, 29 May 1968.
⁴⁵ Ibid.
⁴⁶ Ibid.

concerns are addressed, convened one month after the board's final decision. Four items on Synod's agenda that year dealt with either racism or Christian education for minority students within the denomination and together give a good picture of the struggle within the denomination.

The first item came in a report entitled "Analysis of Original Mandate of the C.R.W.R.C. [Christian Reformed World Relief Committee, tasked with providing diaconal response efforts at the denominational level]." According to the report, "The church in Miami, Florida, approached the CRWRC for financial aid for the Christian education of children of Cuban refugees in that area."[47]

The denomination's Board of Home Missions also addressed the racial concerns of the nation in its annual report. The report gives clear insight not only into what the nation and church were facing in 1968 but also what they would face in the coming years:

> The third feature of the late '60s is revolution. John Gardner, who is resigning as head of the U.S. Department of Health, Education, and Welfare, has said recently, "It does not seem to me that either the congress or the public is fully aware of the alarming character of our domestic crisis. We are in deep trouble as a people, and history will not deal kindly with a rich nation that will not tax itself to cure its miseries." The Christian Reformed Church is not fully aware of the rapid social change in Canada and the United States. In a sense, we fail to understand the forces and currents which swirl around us. In some instances, we see the problem, but we try to solve it with outdated tools and programs. There is a revolution in progress. The church must meet these turbulent times with the relevant message of the gospel, willing to be an agent of God's purpose in the crowded by-ways of the world. The Inner-City may well be the scene in which the church will demonstrate its greatest triumph or its ignominious abdication.
>
> The favorable feature of this period is diversity. In religion, this is the day of pluralism. The image of the small town with a Presbyterian church, a Methodist church, a United church, and a Catholic church, is gone. Today the religious pattern is shattered by the sects. Mormonism and Spiritualists vie for a place on the university campus. Students are becoming intoxicated with

---

[47] CRC *Acts of Synod* (Grand Rapids, MI: Christian Reformed Publishing House, 1968), 319.

the heady wine of Eastern Mystics. Even the Hippies gather a following because of their religious emphasis on "love and prayer." Historians have said that the rise of the weird religious groups is a commentary on the failure of the Christian Church to provide a relevant ministry. In any case, the Church of the Reformation must take its stand, speak clearly concerning Christ, and act as His representative. May the Head and King of the Church make us strong to do His will.[48]

The third item on the agenda of Synod in 1968 came from Classis Lake Erie (the regional body of churches that included eastern Michigan and the state of Ohio). The Detroit-area members of this classis—First CRC in Grosse Pointe Park, Community CRC, Farmington CRC, Dearborn CRC, Cherry Hill CRC in Inkster, North Hills CRC in Troy, and Roseville CRC—were particularly hard hit by rioting during the "long, hot summer of 1967." Seven other churches in Classis Lake Erie were also in cities that experienced rioting that summer: Flint, Saginaw, Lansing, and Jackson, Michigan, and Toledo, Akron, and Cincinnati, Ohio. The three congregations in Cleveland and the Dayton congregation experienced riots in 1966 (and Cleveland again in 1968). Columbus did not see riots until 1969. Only Ann Arbor, which is very close to Detroit but not considered a part of the metropolitan area, and the rural congregations in Imlay City, Michigan, and Willard, Ohio, experienced no rioting in their communities during the decade of the 1960s.

In response to so much turmoil, the Lansing church sent an overture (an official request) to classis requesting classis send an overture to Synod. The classis agreed and forwarded to Synod what became Synodical Overture 5, entitled "Implementation to Eliminate Racism."[49] The overture called for the church:

> to appoint a committee and full-time staff person to design, organize, and implement programs through which the denomination, individual churches, and members can effectively use all available resources to eliminate racism, both causes and effects, within the body of believers and throughout the world in which we live.[50]

---

[48] Ibid., 331.
[49] Ibid., 563.
[50] Ibid.

The first of four grounds for this overture said that the "denomination, churches, and members have, apparently, failed to translate the principles of Christian faith and morality into meaningful Christian works with respect to race relations."[51] The apparent failure with respect to race relations referred to in Overture 5 was likely, at least in part, a reference to the refusal by the board of Timothy Christian School in Cicero, Illinois, to allow black students from the nearby Lawndale Christian Reformed Church in Chicago to enroll. The history of the Timothy board and the Lawndale parents has been well documented elsewhere.[52] When Classis Lake Erie submitted its overture, this tension had been going on, unresolved, for three years.

The fourth item on Synod's agenda in 1968 was Overture 4 from the consistory (board of elders) of Ebenezer Christian Reformed Church in Berwyn, Illinois. Ebenezer CRC was one of the supporting churches of Timothy Christian School. The overture made reference to the "volatile conditions of our times and the subtle indications of prejudice and fear existing in the Christian Reformed community"[53] and called Synod to "appoint a day of prayer and fasting early in the summer"[54] for repentance by members of the CRC and for "a renewal of our society,"[55] so that "men of different races may be cleansed of their sinful antagonisms through the atoning blood of Jesus Christ and live together in the fellowship of love under the discipline of His lordship."[56] The overture went on and called Synod

> to declare that members of the Christian Reformed Church ought freely to receive as brethren, regardless of race or color, all who repent of their sins and make a credible profession of faith in Jesus Christ as Savior and Lord; that exclusion from full Christian fellowship on account of race or color is sinful; and that if members are judged responsible for such exclusion, they must be dealt with according to the provision of the Church Order regarding Admonition and Discipline.[57]

---

[51] Ibid.
[52] See Christopher H. Meehan, *Growing Pains: How Racial Struggles Changed a Church and a School* (Grand Rapids, MI: Eerdmans, 2017); [Robert P. Swierenga, *His Faithfulness Continues: A History of Timothy Christian Schools of Chicagoland* (Holland, MI: Van Raalte Press, 2020), ch. 11.—Ed.]
[53] *Acts of Synod*, 561.
[54] Ibid.
[55] Ibid.
[56] Ibid.
[57] *Acts of Synod*, 561.

According to the overture, "fear of persecution or any other adversity arising out of obedience to Christ"[58] was no excuse. Such fear "does not warrant denial of full Christian fellowship and privilege in the church or in related organizations, such as Christian colleges and schools,"[59] and CRC members who advocated denial of such fellowship "must be reckoned as disobedient to Christ and be dealt with according to the provisions of the Church Order regarding Admonition and Discipline."[60]

John Vander Ploeg, editor of the denomination's weekly magazine, the *Banner*, wrote that the overtures from Classis Lake Erie and Berwyn were "clearly reflecting the tenor of our times and also evincing a conscientious and vigorous effort to bestir our constituency to address itself to the current crisis in race relations."[61]

The two overtures were successful in "bestirring the constituency." Classis Hamilton sent Overture 29, endorsing the Berwyn consistory's overture and urging its adoption.[62] Classis Chicago North, of which the Berwyn church was a member, sent an endorsement of the overture with several amendments, the most significant of which deleted the reference to the Church Order's provisions for admonition and discipline, substituting the words "a censurable sin" and "ought to be considered disobedient to God's Word and ought to be dealt with accordingly."[63] The consistories of four churches in Classis Chicago North that were in the Timothy school district (Warren Park CRC of Cicero, Elmhurst CRC, First CRC of Cicero, and Western Springs CRC[64]) all sent overtures either objecting to or protesting the Ebenezer overture.

The Lawndale Council (governing board made up of both elders and deacons) sent an overture in response to Classis Lake Erie's overture. The Lawndale overture stated, "Although many in our denomination would argue that racism is not a problem of any great proportion in our membership and institutions, we are in a position to testify that it is a real problem and issue."[65] The Lawndale Council suggested that, rather than setting up a committee with a full-time staff person, which the Lake Erie overture called for, "A wholehearted evangelism

---

[58] Ibid.
[59] Ibid.
[60] Ibid.
[61] John Vander Ploeg, "Preview of Synod," *The Banner* (24 May 1968): 8.
[62] *Acts of Synod*, 584.
[63] Ibid.
[64] *Acts of Synod*, 589-92.
[65] Ibid.

in the ghetto would be a better means to attack the problem if that evangelism is done in terms of the newly arising need and spirit of the ghetto."[66] They recommended to Synod a proposal that Rev. Harry Boer had made in an address to the Christian Reformed Minister's Institute, a continuing-education meeting of ministers from across the denomination that met the week prior to Synod. Boer's proposal was to "appoint a commission to study the whole question of appropriate evangelism in the ghetto."[67] Boer recommended the Board of Home Missions undertake such a study. The Lawndale overture said, "It would be better if the commission were more independent and answerable to synod, so that its recommendations are addressed to the church as a whole and not the responsibility of its Mission Board."[68] The issue of racism, according to the Lawndale Council,

> is of such a size and scope that nothing will be effective against the evils of racism in our denomination unless our ghetto evangelism program arises out of the bosom or "soul" of the entire denomination. It may be implemented by a Board but it must be synod's program given to a Board to implement and not a Board's program adopted by a synod.[69]

The pastor of the Lawndale church, Rev. Duane Vander Brug (brother of Mel Vander Brug), grew up in First CRC of Detroit and received nine years of primary school education at GPCDS. In the same issue of the *Banner* in which John Vander Ploeg commented on the effort to bestir the constituency to address race relations (and, interestingly enough, whose front cover featured a silhouette of three soldiers in Vietnam, with the words, "Thou art with me," in honor of Memorial Day that week), Vander Brug published the first of two articles on the Lawndale/Timothy Christian School situation. In his article, Vander Brug insisted that race was not the issue for Lawndale and Timothy Christian. "*The issue was Christian discipleship*—whether we had the courage of faith to do the right thing in the face of opposition."[70] Vander Brug's article was published five days before the final GPCDS board voted to admit the Community Church students.

[66] Ibid.
[67] Ibid.
[68] Ibid.
[69] Ibid., 192.
[70] Duane Vander Brug, "Up the Up Staircase," *The Banner* (24 May 1968): 4 (italics in the original).

Two schools, different outcomes

The question remains, why did Community Church's request to admit children to the Christian school in Grosse Pointe receive a positive response, whereas Lawndale Church's similar request to the Timothy board received a negative answer? I would suggest five things that might account for the different outcomes in the GPCDS situation.

The first and primary reason for the different outcomes in the two attempts at integration is the difference between the two communities—specifically, the difference in social class. Cicero was a blue-collar town, similar to Dearborn in the Detroit area, where the request to admit black students was also initially declined. Strong blue-collar racism that threatened to erupt in violence had a powerful effect on the constituency of both Cicero and Dearborn.[71] Grosse Pointe was more like Elmhurst and Des Plaines, white-collar communities, where violence was less likely to be employed as a means of settling disputes. Integration was simply less of a risk in these white-collar communities than it was in Cicero and Dearborn.

One example of the differences between blue- and white-collar communities can be seen in the Cicero Race Riot of 1951. The cause of the riot was an African American family moving into an apartment building in Cicero. Angry residents surrounded the apartment building and burned it to the ground. The governor of Illinois called in the National Guard to end the violence.[72] In contrast, the governor of Michigan led a group of residents of Grosse Pointe on a march down a major street in support of open housing. When the question came up of integrating Timothy Christian School, the Cicero churches had to contend with a group calling themselves "Concerned Citizens," a hate group that threatened violence should the board allow the school to be integrated.[73] The Grosse Pointe integration initiative included no such organized opposition.

---

[71] The integration of Dearborn Christian School in the years following Grosse Pointe remains a topic for another paper. On 17 May 1968, the Dearborn consistory sent an overture to Classis Lake Erie "to appoint a committee to draw up a suggested list of reference materials (books, articles, pamphlets, tapes, films, etc.) for use by churches and individuals of Classis to assist them in studying and facing the racial problem with Christian objectivity and involvement." Clearly, the members of Dearborn Christian Reformed Church were also struggling with how to minister in an environment marked by racial hostility.

[72] Meehan, *Growing Pains*, 61-62

[73] Ibid., 143.

A second reason is the influence of organized crime at that time. Both Cicero and Grosse Pointe were communities with a strong mob presence. In Cicero, however, the mob had power in city hall, which they did not have in Grosse Pointe.

> For most of the twentieth century, there were direct links between town hall [in Cicero] and the mob.... [T]own hall didn't hesitate to strong arm anybody. If city officials decided they didn't like you, you obeyed, you suffered, or you got out of town.[74]

In Grosse Pointe, the mob had never had that kind of power (although they did exert a great deal of power in Detroit). The pastors in both Cicero and Grosse Pointe sought to give moral leadership to the community, but mob influence was a major factor in the pastor's effectiveness. In Grosse Pointe, the pastors issued a ministers' statement, which became a major influence in the community's view of racial segregation. Contrast this with Cicero where, in 1948, the pastors made an all-out effort to get John Stoffel elected as mayor in an effort to "clean up" the city, thereby eradicating the influence of organized crime.[75] Although Stoffel was indeed elected, the mob exerted pressure against implementing the ministers' demands, and Stoffel eventually resigned. The ministers in Cicero were simply not as successful as the ministers in Grosse Pointe in their attempts to influence the political process because of the powerful influence of the mob.

A third reason for the different outcomes in Cicero and Grosse Pointe is that the Grosse Pointe board maintained the identity of these students as covenant children and not Negro students. The original request from the Lawndale Council to the Timothy Christian School board was based on the fact that these were baptized, Reformed, covenant children and as such should be availed of the opportunity for a Christian school education.[76] The Cicero community surrounding the Timothy school was able to reframe the question as admitting black children, rather than admitting covenant children. Once race became the focus, fear took over.

Fourth, the timing of the Grosse Pointe board's decision was much different than that of the Timothy board. In Grosse Pointe, the decision came on the heels of the "long, hot summer of 1967," a summer

---

[74] Ira Glass, radio program, *This American Life*, quoted in Meehan, *Growing Pains*, 60.
[75] Meehan, *Growing Pains*, 61.
[76] Personal email to author from Rev. Duane Vander Brug, 7 May 2019.

that saw 159 race riots across the country, including the weeklong riot in Detroit. President Johnson's Kerner Commission Report, published on February 29, 1968, made clear the frustration within the black, inner-city communities across the nation, and a riot-weary nation was open to new approaches to race relations. Although Rev. Frank Steen of First CRC never took the lead in the decision to integrate the school, his behind-the-scenes influence (which was his style) was unmistakable. According to his daughter, Stacy, he had made integrating the Christian school a priority of First CRC's response to the riots.[77]

The Grosse Pointe board also had the advantage of the experience of the Timothy board. The overture from the Berwyn consistory had already been distributed throughout the denomination in the 1968 *Acts of Synod*, although the overtures from Classis Hamilton, Classis Chicago North, the four overtures from the Chicago suburban churches, and the Lawndale overture would not appear until after Synod met. The board's own Classis Lake Erie's overture, also published by this time, contained language that was clearly applicable to the board's decision:

> Our denomination, its members, and the organizations and institutions which they support and shape can exert a strong Christian influence in the religious, educational, economic, social and governmental spheres. Our inescapable participation in a wide variety of activities means that we either support actions which endorse and perpetuate racism, or we use every available resource to overcome racism. We must choose the later course.[78]

The *Banner* issue, in which editor John Vander Ploeg spoke of efforts to "bestir our constituency to address itself to the current crisis in race relations" and which included the first of the two articles under the title "Up the Up Staircase," was dated May 24, just five days before the Grosse Pointe board's final vote. The Timothy board was pioneering new territory. They did not have the advantage of the broader church discussion, and once they did, they were put in a defensive position.

Finally, in Grosse Pointe, there was strong lay leadership pushing for integration. A number of members from First CRC were active in the Grosse Pointe Human Relations Council and its daughter organization, the Grosse Pointe Committee for Open Housing. One of the members of First CRC, Jack Nyenhuis, was the landlord for one

---

[77] Oral interview with Stacy Steen, 6 Dec. 2018.
[78] *Acts of Synod*, 563.

of the first African Americans to move into Grosse Pointe.[79] Board member Bob Melling contacted the Grosse Pointe Human Relations Council once the decision on integration was made. The relationship between the Grosse Pointe Human Relations Council and First CRC was a strong one, and it had the support not only of the pastor but also of prominent lay persons.

The story of Timothy Christian School and Lawndale Church is part of the history of race relations in the CRC. But it is not the whole story. The story of the Grosse Pointe Christian School and Community CRC is also part of the denominational story, but the outcome was much different. This chapter is an attempt to have the whole story told and to offer material for further reflection on the CRC's history regarding race relations.

---

[79] Telephone interview with Jack Nyenhuis, 22 April 2019; Cosseboom, *Grosse Pointe*, 29.

CHAPTER 13

Educating the North American Indian: Dutch Christian Reformed Contributions and Their Legacy

Peter Hovens

Beginning in the 1840s and continuing through the remainder of the nineteenth century, seceding and other Dutch Reformed emigrants settled in Michigan, Iowa, and Wisconsin. Population growth and chain migration from the Netherlands increased their numbers and drove westward expansion into the northern plains states and the Pacific Northwest. Emphasizing doctrinal purity and cultural preservation, the Christian Reformed Church (CRC) separated from the Reformed Church in America in 1857. The new denomination was small and needed to firmly establish itself in its New World setting. For a long time, it was preoccupied with internal theological and organizational matters and with building its Dutch American home base.

Awakening missionary zeal required decisive action.[1] Occasionally, financial contributions were provided to Indian missions, but it took until 1906 before the CRC established Indian missions and schools. In

[1] John Bratt, *The Missionary Enterprise of the Christian Reformed Church of America* (PhD thesis, Union Theological Seminary, 1955). Richard DeRidder, *The Development of the Mission Order of the Christian Reformed Church* (MA thesis, Hartford Seminary Foundation, 1956).

1888 Synod charged its new Board of Heathen Missions with carrying out missionary work by preaching the Gospel to children and adults and building schools. Although the board's motto was "Teach and Preach and Heal," the "teach" referred primarily to religious instruction within the context of formal academic education. It took six years to identify a potentially profitable mission field among Native American tribes and to find a suitable missionary candidate.[2]

Rehoboth: the Navajo boarding school, 1903-1940

A thorough survey by the CRC concluded that there was a potential opportunity for a main mission with a chain of outstations to reach many Indians on the Navajo Indian Reservation in New Mexico and Arizona. The Navajos were a nation of seminomadic herdsmen, roaming over large areas with their flocks of sheep and goats. In late 1896, two CRC missionaries—Rev. Herman Fryling and his assistant, Andrew Vander Wagen—began work at Fort Defiance, Arizona. At the government boarding school, they were allowed to give religious instruction. But relations between the missionaries and the Indian agent, George Hayzlett, soured when the latter voiced criticism of Fryling's rigid manner and lack of religious results. When Episcopalians and Franciscans also obtained permission to give religious instruction at the government school, Rev. Henry Beets, on behalf of the CRC mission board, protested to the commissioner of Indian affairs, William Atkinson Jones, in Washington, DC. He was told, however, that all churches had equal rights and that Indian parents would decide which denomination they would allow to instruct their children.[3]

The CRC decided to look elsewhere to continue their mission work in an environment that was less competitive and less constrained by federal oversight. Church authorities were convinced that, in order to be successful, they needed as much control as possible over the daily lives of potential converts. That could be achieved only by independent mission stations and mission schools. In a school setting, church authorities and administrators had vast control over the daily lives of

---

[2] Henry Beets, *Toiling and Trusting: Fifty Years of Work of the Christian Reformed Church among Indians* (Grand Rapids, MI: Grand Rapids Printing Company, 1940), 16-33. Bratt, *Missionary Enterprise*, 103-17. DeRidder, *Development*, 51-61. Robert Groelsema, "Christian Assimilation: The Pioneer Christian Reformed Indian Mission," *Origins* 5, no. 1 (1987): 43-44.

[3] Beets, *Toiling and Trusting*, 33-36, 42-49. M. J. Warner, *Protestant Missionary Work with the Navajo Indians* (PhD thesis, University of New Mexico, 1977), 412-15.

the Indians. The scope of control was naturally greater in boarding schools than in the day schools. The authorities also realized that combining an academic curriculum with domestic and vocational training could make such an institution self-sufficient to a certain extent, thus making the running of schools an affordable undertaking. Student labor could be used to clear building plots, for construction (carpentry, brick making, plastering, painting), and to make furniture, and a school farm could provide food for staff and pupils, with the surplus sold in regional markets. Girls could do general housekeeping, run the kitchen and dining hall, and make and repair clothes. In 1901 Synod adopted the plan for which Rev. Beets began collecting funds.[4]

In 1903 the CRC bought a ranch east of Gallup, New Mexico, and established its main Navajo Indian mission station just outside the reservation borders. It was christened Rehoboth, "The Lord Has Made Room." Many of the first generation of ministers, camp workers, teachers and matrons who worked in the CRC Indian missions in the southwest were born in the Netherlands; they came to the United States with their parents and grew up in Dutch American communities in the Upper Midwest. By 1940 about twenty mission stations had been established by the CRC for the Navajos in New Mexico.

The CRC needed to raise its own funds to operate schools for Indian children. Support for missions and schools was mustered during Sunday services, lectures at churches, addresses at "mission fests," and through the publication of articles, pamphlets, booklets, commemorative books, and a mission periodical. In many Dutch American communities, Women's Missionary Unions organized to promote mission work by informing congregations about the progress in the various missions and encouraging church members to work in missions in various capacities, to collect clothes and gifts, and to raise funds. Periodicals like *De Wachter*, *The Banner*, *The Christian Indian*, and *De Heidenwereld* (later, *Missionary Monthly*) informed church members about the current state of affairs. Some publications were in Dutch to solicit support in the Netherlands for Indian missions and schools.[5]

Rev. L. P. Brink was put in overall charge of the Rehoboth project. He defined a mission boarding school as:

> An institution for heathen children of either or both sexes, where they are wholly supported a certain number of months or the

---

[4] John Dolfin, ed., *Bringing the Gospel in Hogan and Pueblo, 1896-1921* (Grand Rapids, MI: Van Noord, 1921), 238. Beets, *Toiling and Trusting*, 46-48.
[5] Beets, *Toiling and Trusting*, 296-98.

whole year. The exalted purpose of such a School is to give the children a Christian training and education, that they may, by the grace of God, grow up to be Christians and honorable citizens, showing forth the redeeming love of God in Christ Jesus, thru the Holy Spirit, and serving as means in the providence of the Lord and in obedience to His Great Commission.

The emphasis of the Rehoboth project was the school; it was expected that the pupils would attract parents to the school and mission and that, through the pupils, the Gospel would make its entry into many Navajo homes.[6]

The Rehoboth Mission School taught eight grades and eventually accommodated children between the ages of six and fifteen. The school year lasted from nine to ten months, without weekend breaks but with a one-week Christmas holiday. Early academic teaching staff at Rehoboth included Nellie Noordhoff, Mattie van Dyken, Fanny Leys, Carrie Ten Houten, Cocia Hartog, Anna Derks, and Catherine Venema, who also taught domestic subjects to the girls. Renzina Stob, who obtained a degree in education at Calvin College, became principal in 1919, a position she held for a remarkable forty-six-year tenure, until her retirement in 1965. Industrial arts teachers included Dick Vander Wagen, Lee S. Huizenga, Henry Schram, Mark Bouma, and John Spyker. Jacob Bosscher arrived in 1913 and stayed almost four decades.[7]

At Tohatchi, New Mexico, Rev. L. P. Brink trained Navajo assistants. One of them, Jacob Casimero Morgan, aided Brink with translations of the Bible, hymn texts, and stories used for religious and educational purposes. These texts were used at the Rehoboth school not only for religious instruction but also to teach English and aspects of natural history, emphasizing creationism rather than evolution.[8]

The first official act that took place when pupils arrived at Rehoboth was to give all children an English name. Next, their hair was cut short. Then all new arrivals were bathed and clad in clean, Western clothes, often secondhand, donated by CRC congregations in the Upper

---

[6] L. P. Brink in *Bringing the Gospel*, 102. Lee S. Huizenga, *Leonard Peter Brink: Thirty-Five Years Among the Navaho Indians* (Grand Rapids, MI: Zondervan, 1937), 27, 37.

[7] J. W. Brink in *Zuni and Navaho Mission Work of the Christian Reformed Church* (Muskegon, MI: privately printed, 1918), 7-14. Beets, *Toiling and Trusting*, 51-52, 64. Bosscher's career was the subject of popular articles by Marian M. Schoolland, "Our Pioneer Mission to the Native Americans," *The Banner*, Jan.-May 1977.

[8] Dolfin, *Bringing the Gospel*, 135-36, 224-25; John DeKorne, ed., *Navaho and Zuni for Christ: Fifty Years of Indian Missions* (Grand Rapids, MI: Christian Reformed Board of Missions, 1947), 61-62, 73, 76, 104, 204.

Staff and Indian pupils at Rehoboth Mission School, ca. 1909-10; staff (*l-r*): Suzanna Dieleman and Katherine Rosbach (matrons), Anna Derks, Mark Bouma, Mrs. Bouma, and Cocia Hartog (*courtesy Heritage Hall [HH], Calvin University*)

Midwest. When funds were available, school uniforms were supplied. These were either sewn by women's groups or purchased in bulk. Boys' uniforms tended to emulate military styles.

Rehoboth sought and obtained recognition of their curriculum and exams by McKinley County and the state of New Mexico. This was achieved by using the federal curriculum guidelines and submitting to periodic inspection by government agents. By 1940 all graduates received a state diploma.[9]

The curriculum consisted of academic subjects taught in the morning and practical learning in the afternoon. Academic subjects included English, reading, writing, arithmetic, geography, and music. Older boys were often keen on learning arithmetic, because they appreciated its practicality. J. W. Brink used his stereopticon to teach geography. Children were forbidden to speak Navajo during classes or training sessions. Discipline was strict.[10]

Practical teaching aimed to provide vocational training for boys and to prepare girls for domestic work. The instruction was meant

[9] Stob in *Toiling and Trusting*, 65. Bosscher in *Bringing the Gospel*, 243. Cocia Hartog, *Indian Mission Sketches* (Gallup, NM: privately printed, 1910), 21.
[10] Stob in *Bringing the Gospel*, 230-31.

Navajo Indian boys at the Rehoboth Boarding School, ca. 1915 (*courtesy HH*)

to equip the boys for work in a mostly rural economy and to enable girls to become efficient homemakers and possibly domestic servants in white households. In addition, this practical part of the curriculum contributed to the material survival of the school itself.

The girls received instruction in food preparation, cooking and baking, sewing and mending clothes, housekeeping, and health and hygiene. In practice, they prepared food for pupils and staff; cleaned dormitories, the kitchen and dining hall, and classrooms; and mended clothes for the pupils. Thus, they also learned the skills required to manage Western-style households of their own, as well as to work as servants in the homes of middle-class whites. No other vocational skills were taught, and by 1920, some within the CRC wondered what could be done for girls to equip them for the market and cash economy that was eliminating traditional means of subsistence at a fast pace. The CRC, however, elected not to train girls for employment in traditional Navajo industries, such as weaving, even if adapted to contemporary market conditions, something Catholics and some Protestant denominations specifically promoted to make Indian families self-sufficient. Acceptance of elements of Navajo culture, even with the purpose of providing income opportunities, went against the fundamentalist grain of divesting Indians completely of their cultural and social heritage, and turning them into civilized, orthodox Protestant Christians.[11]

Navajo boys at Rehoboth also faced a vocational curriculum based on both the practical requirements of the mission and school and engagement with the wider community. Industrial arts teachers taught carpentry, painting, and construction, and with these acquired skills, the boys could improve and maintain the existing buildings. They also learned how to repair leatherwork—principally shoes, harnesses, and saddles. The boys were put to work on the farm, where they learned

---

[11] Dolfin, *Bringing the Gospel*, 237-38. For a dissenting voice, cf. L. P. Brink, "The Future of Our Indian Graduates," *The Banner* (11 May 1916): 304-5.

animal husbandry. They took complete care of the cows and goats--feeding, milking, breeding, and even butchering them. Fields were laid out and planted with potatoes and vegetables, and the boys mastered skills relevant to their future lives as stockmen and farmers. Some might become employed in a variety of other professions, and a few might even set up their own businesses. It soon became apparent, however, that the semiarid wild desert was not conducive to agriculture. Rehoboth had to buy food at competitive prices on the regional market. Funds to purchase a farm with arable land in the region were not forthcoming. The school farm never became the training ground for civilization as envisioned, and in the early 1930s, the farming program was abandoned.[12]

Industrial superintendent Jacob H. Bosscher regarded many Navajos as industrious, either as traditional herdsmen of sheep and horses or in the market economy, where they worked for wages on road and railroad construction and maintenance. But he believed they needed different attitudes and more skills to advance themselves in their quickly changing environment on and off the reservation. Frugality and thrift, initiative and perseverance, planning and organization, effectiveness and efficiency, and responsibility and leadership were all required. Therefore, Bosscher was an outspoken advocate of providing thorough general academic and vocational training at Rehoboth. This was aimed at improving conditions of everyday life in the Navajo communities, as well as increasing opportunities for employment both on the reservation and beyond.[13]

About the intelligence and personality of Navajos, teacher Cocia Hartog observed:

> It is generally acceded [that] Indian children are difficult to teach and require an untold amount of patience on the part of the teacher. On the other hand, they have not the vices of white children and are much more easily governed. They like written work much better than oral and excel in drawing and painting.

According to Rev. Brink, the Navajos generally did not show their feelings. Only approval and displeasure were readily displayed. Some interpreted the seeming lack of response as apathy, but those more familiar with Navajo character knew that the Indians reflected on what

---

[12] Jacob H. Bosscher, Memoirs, Bosscher Papers, col. 312, B1F1, 48-50, 60 (HH). Henry Ippel, "Making Room for Rehoboth," *Origins* 21, no. 1 (2003): 10-11.

[13] Bosscher in *Bringing the Gospel*, 241-49.

they saw and heard and discussed it with kin and friends. Brink was convinced that the intelligence of the Indian children was on a plane equal to that of white children, and Cornelius Kuipers confirmed this in a scientific study.[14]

Religious instruction and practice in the school took the form of daily prayers and Bible reading before breakfast and daily catechism lessons in class. On Sundays, Indian children attended church services and Sunday school. In the execution of the academic curriculum, much use was made of learning aides based on Christian ideology. Thus, reading and writing were done by using religious stories and texts from hymns or the Bible. In addition, the dormitory matrons regularly tested the children during the early evening hours and on weekends. The attitude of Navajo parents toward Christianity, however, remained cautious. Frequently, they told their children to learn as much as possible at school but ignore religious instruction.[15]

At times, truancy was a problem because children were scared in their unfamiliar and restrictive new environment. Some ran away, while others hid in the dormitories under beds and in closets. Rehoboth had a "jail" for children who had attempted to run away. Virtually no truancy occurred in the 1930s, because Indian parents urged their children to stay at the school where the institution provided clothes and food that Indian families could ill afford during those difficult times.[16]

Dorothy Dykhuizen, who taught at Rehoboth in the early 1940s, showed understanding and sympathy for the young Indian children that enrolled for the first time:

> There are a host of complicated customs that the tiny Navahos at school for the first time must learn all at once: sleeping in a bed instead of on a sheepskin thrown on the dirt floor of a *hogan* [traditional Navajo dwelling]; sitting on chairs instead of on the ground; eating at a table and using silverware instead of the ever-so-much-more convenient fingers; feeling their bodies constricted

---

[14] Hartog, *Indian Mission*, 21-22. J. W. Brink in *Bringing the Gospel*, 106, 117. Cornelius Kuipers, *Results of an Intelligence Test Based on Indian Culture* (MA thesis, University of New Mexico, 1934), 5, 42-43.

[15] J. W. Brink in *Bringing the Gospel*, 108-16. Julia Ensink, *Rehoboth Memories, 1948-1983* (Grand Rapids, MI: privately printed, 1996), 5. Bonny Mulder-Behnia, "Rehoboth Christian School Celebrates Century of Faithfulness," *The Banner* 138 (2003): 30-32.

[16] Bosscher, Memoirs, 57, 77. Ed Oppenhuizen and John Klein, *Introduction for New Missionaries on the Indian Field* (Grand Rapids, MI: Christian Reformed Board of Home Missions, 1968), 22. Henry Ippel, "Twelve Rehoboth Mission Pioneers," *Origins* 21, no. 1 (2013): 17.

by tight clothes and shoes instead of the casual native costume; going to bed by the clock—dressing, playing, working, attending school and church, all at designated hours, instead of roaming the hills at will and coming home when convenient. No wonder their little heads whirl, and they sometimes long bitterly for home during those first weeks when the *Biliganah's* [white man's] slavery to convention seems too strange and hard for them. The matrons who preside with motherly devotion over the dormitories are required to be wells of comfort and encouragement during the first few weeks at school. They must quiet with loving sympathy the nostalgic fears of the lonely little children away from home for the first time.... Many children, before they start school, have never seen, much less used, such implements and materials as scissors, crayons, paper, pencils, chalk, or paste. They must not only become skilled in the use of these tools but must also learn the names for them as well as the written symbols. Unless they have a fairly large speaking vocabulary before they try to read, reading itself proves impossible.... For that reason, almost the entire first semester for the beginners is devoted to learning the language.[17]

Zuni: The day school, 1908-1940

After the failure of the CRC to work satisfactorily with the Bureau of Indian Affairs authorities at Fort Defiance, Andrew Vander Wagen visited Zuni Pueblo, New Mexico, a large village of sedentary, horticultural Indians south of Gallup. Their culture differed substantially from that of the Navajos and essentially was a theocracy in which priesthoods regulated many aspects of life. Vander Wagen called Zuni Pueblo a "citadel of Satan" and decided that an industrial school was needed to make successful inroads into the hearts and thoughts of the Zunis.[18] Rev. Herman Fryling moved to Zuni in 1906 to carry out the religious work in the pueblo. In 1908 a day school was established.[19]

---

[17] Dorothy Dykhuizen, *Go Quickly and Tell* (Grand Rapids, MI: Eerdmans, 1946), 105-7.
[18] Beets, *Toiling and Trusting*, 199, 206. Interview of Rev. Kuipers by Rev. J. H. Brink, Cornelius Kuipers Papers, HH, undated. Andrew Vander Wagen, "At the laying of the cornerstone of the Mission Church at Zuni," ms. of speech, 31 Aug. 1926, HH.
[19] DeKorne, *Navaho and Zuni*, 53-54. Benson Tong, "The Hindrances are Many: Zunis and Missionaries at the Christian Reformed School," *New Mexico Historical Review* 70, no. 3 (1995), 335.

Rev. Fryling regarded all vestiges of Zuni culture as expressions of paganism. In his way of thinking, a school was needed to separate Indian children from their heathen environment for at least several hours most days of the week. The chapel at the CRC mission was therefore converted into a school building. In a new parsonage, space was made available for a YMCA reading room, where students returning from off-reservation boarding schools could gather in order to prevent them from completely reverting to Zuni ways. Rev. Meindert van Beek and later Rev. Calvin Havenga were in charge of the YMCA work.[20] Despite all efforts, many Navajo children returned to traditional ways after they left school.[21] Disagreement with church authorities on the way to evangelize the Indians soon led to the resignation of Vander Wagen.

When Zuni Indian elders visited the day school, they expressed their satisfaction to Fryling. The Zunis were especially impressed with the mild manner of teacher Nellie De Jong. It was a burden to keep the pupils and their clothes clean, and contagious diseases frequently took their toll. In 1910 Nellie de Jong wrote to Rev. Beets:

> Our Own Christian school now numbers twenty pupils, and so far, the children come more regular this year than two previous years. It is not unlikely, if we had the room, that we could bring, with the help of our truant officer, the number up to thirty. But the room we do not have, we are too crowded already.... The school room is twenty-two by sixteen. In this, we daily instruct twenty pupils, and in this same room, we have in one corner a cupboard containing the school supplies and some of the children's clothes. In another corner, we have the needed apparatus for the children's daily bath. ... We also have to have the children's wraps and a box for fuel in this same room as we have no hall and no shelter whatever for the wood. There is no laundry or bathroom, so Miss Neyenhuis is compelled to give the children their weekly bath in the chapel and do the washing outdoors. We hope that, before long, the board may see the way clear for erecting a new school building.

---

[20] Herman Fryling, "Our Mission in Zuni: Day Schools and Religious Instruction," *The Banner*, 4 May 1911. Fryling in *Zuni and Navaho*, 3. Ralph Terry, *A Church Growth Study of the Zuni Indians* (PhD thesis, Abilene Christian College, 1971), ch. 4. Henry Beets, ed., *Navaholand and Zunitown: Christian Reformed Missions A.D. 1934* (Grand Rapids, MI: Grand Rapids Printing, 1934), 39-40.

[21] Stob in *Bringing the Gospel*, 227-28. Hartog, *Indian Mission*, 20-22. J. W. Brink in *Bringing the Gospel*, 119. Groelsema, "Christian Assimilation," 47.

Through the 1925-26 school year, the teachers at the Zuni Day School included Anna Van der Riet, Alice Aardsma-Hoekstra, Sophia Fryling, Dena Brink-Vander Wagen, Cora Elhart, Anna Goudberg, Wilhelmina Brink, Joanna Van Dyken, Cora Brandt, and Cornelius Kuipers.[22]

Principal Cornelius Kuipers arrived in Zuni Pueblo in 1927 and characterized the Zuni child in language that revealed his frustration:

> The Indian child is reticent. He must be led, not driven. He manifests no outward thrill upon achievement and shows no regret when he fails.... They wish to please the teacher, and they will cheat and lie in order to gain the 100 percent the teacher wishes them to have. The personal element is a great factor in teaching Indian Children.

About Zuni parents, Kuipers was also uncharitable: "His folks at home deride all schooling.... The older Zunis do not take kindly to education.... What we sow, Zuni destroys.... Zuni is sold to the Devil." Kuipers, however, was convinced that by 1927 the mission endeavor had reached a tipping point toward success with the new generation in school and some former students becoming church members.

Matron Nellie Hamming reported about working with women and children at the school, providing a rather factual account:

> Monday morning at daybreak girls come flocking for their baths. After the girls have finished, the boys come in for theirs.... [E]ach of them receive[s] an outfit of clean clothes furnished by the Mission. Thereupon they are a very presentable group of children ready for another week of schoolwork. After the morning devotionals in their classrooms, there are certain girls and boys who I desire to be sent down to help me wash their dirty clothes. The boys are sent down to turn the washing machines, and the girls do the rubbing and rinsing, and then hang out the clothes. By Monday noon, the washing of my large family, an average of sixty-five, is finished, besides having the laundry floor scrubbed and cleaned.... In the afternoon, I teach the boys to iron the shirts and the overalls, and the girls are taught to iron the dresses and slips. Oftentimes, while at work like this, we sing gospel hymns.

---

[22] De Jong to Beets, Zuni, NM, 16 Dec. 1910, general Zuni file, HH. Bert Sprik, letter, To Whom It May Concern, Zuni, NM, 31 Aug. 1926, HH. John Dolfin, ed., *Thirty Years Among the Zunis* (Muskegon, MI: Classis of Muskegon, 1927), 3, 72.

> The Zuni children surely enjoy singing.... [T]he remainder of the week... the children come down a little while before the nine o'clock bell rings to brush their teeth, wash their hands and face, and comb their hair.... After the Tuesday morning devotionals, the girls come down and help me mend the clothes and help me put the clothes in their individual lockers, so by Tuesday noon, the clothes are in order for the next week. While the children are at work, I have a fine chance to tell them a Bible story or converse about Jesus... I can tell them why we are working here, why we have left our own people and our homes and why we have come to tell them the only way of salvation.

About the work at the school in the late 1920s, Kuipers related:

> The Zuni children... for the greater part did not communicate English too easily.... We never had any strict rule that they could not speak Zuni in the classrooms... but we did encourage them to speak English.... We tried to achieve the same standard of the other Indian schools... [W]e were trying to approach better standards each year.... [W]e had not only prayer and Bible study, and like any typically Christian school, we tried to meet the principles of Jesus Christ in each subject and the application of arts and crafts and sports... and evangelism was at the thrust of the whole program.

In 1927 the total enrollment of Zuni children was 150 at the federal day school, 80 at the sanatorium, 100-plus at the Catholic school, and 60-plus at the CRC day school. Enrolment at the CRC mission school rose slowly, and a third teacher was appointed in the 1930s.[23]

In 1930 missionary staff at Zuni consisted of Rev. C. Havenga and assistant Andrew Vander Wagen. The teachers were Cora Brandt, Jean Memmelaar and Bessie Reed. Cornelius Kuipers was the principal of the school and manager of the mission. George Cheeko, a Zuni man, was employed as truant officer. Academic studies and vocational training dominated the daily schedule, with devotionals at the start and finish of the school day. Bible class took place every Thursday. The school band practiced twice weekly. Art classes were devoted to beadwork, pottery, and music. The weekend was occupied with bathing, Sunday school, group prayers, socials, and picnics.

---

[23] Kuipers and Hamming in *Thirty Years*, 87-89, 92-95. Cf. Dykhuizen, *Go Quickly*, 154-56, about Rehoboth. Interview of Rev. C. Kuipers by Rev. J. Herbert, undated, Kuipers Papers, HH. Tong, "Hindrances," 138-39.

Kuipers stayed as principal of the Zuni Day School until 1932. At that time, Marie Vos and Nellie Lam taught the children. The government boarding school at Black Rock closed in 1934, adding students to the CRC school. Rev. George Yff was appointed as CRC missionary in 1938. The school enrolled ninety-six children in the fall and another twenty-two during the school year. In 1939 Synod granted a fourth teaching position.[24]

Depression, New Deal, and World War II

President Franklin D. Roosevelt is widely credited for his enlightened and effective policies to combat the Depression in the 1930s. His New Deal for America also included progressive political, economic, and cultural policies specifically for American Indians. The CRC, however, became one of the most vehement critics of plans for strengthening self-government, even on democratic principles.[25] The CRC railed against support for traditional arts and crafts, even as a means for economic progress. The CRC further objected to the inclusion of Indian culture and history in the curriculum, and the church was against legal protection of Indian religious traditions. On the latter, J. D. Verplanck noted that "Many Protestant missionaries of the old school taught and still teach their converts to condemn them all indiscriminately."[26] Rev. William Goudberg characterized the new approach to Indian Affairs "like a cold blast." CRC lay worker James C. Morgan, of Navajo parentage and a strong advocate of Western education, was also a vocal opponent of the new policies and called for the dismissal of commissioner of Indian affairs John Collier.[27] But the New Deal for Indians went through.

[24] Activity calendar of the Zuni Christian Reformed Mission, 1930, folder 820.3, box 25, E. 65, correspondence files, RG 75, BIA, Zuni Indian Agency, Federal Archives, Denver. Cornelius Kuipers, *Zuni Also Prays: Month-by-Month Observations among the People* (Grand Rapids, MI: Christian Reformed Board of Missions, 1946). CRC 1939 *Acts of Synod*, 43, 164, 169, 176.

[25] Historian Kenneth Philp noted that the CRC, Presbyterians, and Baptists were the staunchest opponents of the New Deal policies for Indians. Kenneth Philp, *John Collier's Crusade for Indian Reform, 1920-1954* (Tucson: University of Arizona Press, 1977), 151.

[26] J. D. Verplanck, *A Nation of Shepherds* (Boston: Ruth Hill, 1934), 15.

[27] L. P. Brink Collection, various papers in B1F7 and B1F11 (HH). L. P. Brink, "Are We a Christian Nation?" *The Christian Indian* (July-Aug. 1934), 35-36. Donald Parman, "J. C. Morgan: Navajo Apostle of Assimilation," *Prologue* 4, no. 2 (1972), 83-90. Philp, *John Collier's*, 173. James B. LaGrand, "The Changing Jesus Road: Protestants Reappraise American Indian Missions," *Western Historical Quarterly* 27 (1996), 494-504. Bruce J. Gjeltema, *Jacob Casimero Morgan and the Development of Navajo Nationalism* (PhD thesis, University of New Mexico, 2004).

A 1939 report by the Phelps-Stokes Fund[28] on the Navajos commended the sincerity, generosity, and devotion of the CRC to promote the welfare of the Indians. It also noted, however, that almost all efforts were directed at Christian teaching and conversion in the Dutch Calvinist tradition and that schools were regarded only as a means to that end. The missionaries tended to work *for* the Indians rather than *with* them, following their own ideology and program exclusively, not engaging the Native community in a meaningful way. The Phelps Stokes Fund expected that the CRC would be slow to adapt any of their programs to the unique conditions and realities of the Navajos and their environment. A year later, another research project concluded that the regional and cultural needs of the Navajos should be considered in curriculum development to enable schools to offer education relevant to their everyday lives.[29]

In 1940 Rehoboth industrial superintendent Jacob Bosscher and principal Renzina Stob noted that Indian children were being sent to the Rehoboth school at a younger age than previously. About half of their parents were Christians, and three-quarters had previously attended denominational or government schools. Funds for a much-needed ninth grade were not available. One encouraging factor was that a number of Rehoboth graduates were employed in reservation day schools, mostly in manual jobs, housekeeping, and maintenance and that several had jobs as interpreters. Rehoboth employed five alumni, and they believed that in time the school would be supported and run by Christian Indians. In 1946 Mission Board chairman Rev. Henry Beets concluded: "The work is difficult, but far from hopeless; in fact, it is encouraging, witnessing the fruit already reaped."[30]

World War II not only fundamentally changed the world order but also had a major impact on the Indian mission field. The first and older generation of Protestant and Catholic missionaries had either retired or passed away. Young Indians who had served with the American army in the Pacific and Europe returned home and demanded equal treatment and the right to self-determination, and this also applied to the field of education. If the mission denominations were to be relevant, they had to adapt to new realities. Not all clergy, however, were in agreement

---

[28] The Phelps-Stokes Fund is a private, nonprofit agency intent on promoting Native American interests, among other benevolent objectives.

[29] Thomas Jones, *The Navajo Problem* (NY: Phelps-Stokes Fund, 1939), 98-99. Alan Hulsinger, *Region and Culture in the Curriculum of the Navaho and the Dakota* (PhD thesis, Teachers College, Columbia University, 1940).

[30] Bosscher in *Navaholand and Zunitown*, 6. Bosscher and Stob in *Toiling and Trusting*, 60, 65-66. DeKorne, *Navaho and Zuni*, 196.

with the new shift in emphasis. For example, in 1945, Rev. A. A. Koning criticized the CRC because missionaries had given priority to education rather than salvation. A year later, however, Synod emphasized formal education as auxiliary missionary work and allowed Rehoboth to add a high school. Its construction took five years to complete.[31] The CRC's attitude toward elements of Indian culture also changed in the postwar period of cultural pluralism, when tribal languages and Native arts and crafts were gradually included in the curriculum.

Legacy

In looking back on the history of CRC contributions to the education of Native Americans in the United States, several conclusions emerge. Euro-American territorial expansion sparked Protestant and Catholic churches to undertake a spiritual crusade to combat and conquer the minds of the aboriginal populations. Scholar Tim Giago makes the case that the missionary and educational work of denominations made these churches complicit in the cultural genocide of Native peoples. Government and churches often became partners in what scholars and Native leaders have termed "an unholy alliance."[32] The CRC story fits the pattern that Giago describes.

The CRC maintained the position that, to become a real Christian, the Indian must abandon all tribal traditions and even any association with non-Christian families. This has historically strained Indian-CRC relations, hampered growth of the CRC, and contributed to intracommunity divisions and tensions, especially in Zuni Pueblo. Determination and perseverance for over a century has resulted in the emergence of a distinct CRC congregation in the pueblo. The CRC school in Zuni Pueblo has played a major role in this development. Among the Navajos, the number of CRC congregations and members has grown since 1945. Navajo members come principally from the more acculturated tribal members.[33]

---

[31] Henry Beets, *The Christian Reformed Church in America* (Grand Rapids, MI: Baker Book House, 1946), 148-50. DeKorne in *Navaholand and Zunitown*, 161-62. *The Christian Reformed Mission to Reservation and Urban Indians: A Sociological Analysis* (Grand Rapids, MI: Social Research Center, Calvin College, 1977), 1:30. Groelsema, "Christian Assimilation," 49.

[32] Tim Giago, *Children Left Behind: The Dark Legacy of Indian Mission Boarding Schools* (Santa Fe, NM: Clear Light, 2006).

[33] Terry, *Church Growth Study*, 86, 88-89, 113-14. Sally Southwick, "Educating the Mind, Enlightening the Soul: Mission Schools as a Means of Transforming the Navajos," *Journal of Arizona History* 37, no. 1 (1996): 59-63. *The Christian Reformed Mission*, 1:24-25.

Faced with Native demands for Indian rights and self-determination, the churches were obliged to transform their approach to missions and education. During the 1970s, the CRC emphasized its commitment to "indigenization," making Indian missions self-sustaining both organizationally and financially and maintained by Native American leadership. At Rehoboth, responsibilities were gradually transferred to Indian parents. During the 1990s, the Rehoboth school transitioned from a boarding establishment to a day school when a school bus system was introduced. In 2001 the Rehoboth school adopted a course on the Navajo language into its curriculum.[34] After a disastrous fire in 1971, the CRC Zuni Day School struggled until the 1990s when Indian parental involvement was successfully promoted. In 2014 the new mission and school opened. Rebuilt on a grand scale, the complex dominates the center of the pueblo, albeit in an irreverent or a neocolonial way, according to some residents.[35]

In 2003 Rehoboth commemorated its centennial. The event became an occasion for reflection and reconciliation. The CRC and the school authorities seemed to have come to terms with their past and the now vastly changed sociopolitical environment. Director Ron Polinder confessed to the church's role in undermining Indian culture and traditions:

> We have talked too much ... therefore we listened too little. ... We didn't read enough, and still don't. We don't know enough about Native religion, cultural patterns, history or tradition. ... How unfortunate it is that most of us did not learn Dine Bizaad. How we regret showing dishonor to languages other than English. We apologize for what were, at times, heavy-handed disciplinary methods. We are sorry for not building more friendships with Native American people. We were so caught up in the arrogance of Western culture. A cultural superiority prevailed. ... [This was] institutional racism, ... we acknowledge it. It took on a Dutch tint and tone at Rehoboth. Our comfortable, cloistered

---

Thomas Dolaghan and David Scates, *The Navajos are Coming to Jesus* (South Pasadena, CA: William Carey Library, 1978), 42, 93-94, 149-50. David Scates, *Why Navajo Churches Are Growing* (Grand Junction, CO: Navajo Christian Churches, 1981), 71, 120-28, 146.

[34] Tom Claus and Dale Kietzman, eds., *Christian Leadership in Indian America* (Chicago, IL: Moody Press, 1976), 61, 97. Gerrit Haagsma, *A Plan for the Growth of the Christian Reformed Church in Classis Red Mesa* (PhD thesis, Fuller Theological Seminary, 1985), 153.

[35] Personal comments to author, Zuni, NM, 2014-16.

community has not been very good at welcoming those different from ourselves. Our miscalculations regarding language, culture, and the boarding school [have] left a scar on our history and on some of our students. It was likely not intentional, but painful nonetheless. Can you find it in your heart to forgive us? I hope you will extend us that grace!

In 2016 Synod recognized the suffering of Indian children at the Rehoboth boarding school, repeated apologies for mistreatment of pupils, and confirmed its commitment to mutual learning, encouragement, and healing.[36]

Today many Indian nations operate their own schools and monitor public schools on their reservations to assure that the curricula include tribal language, culture, and history. This is the case on the Navajo and Zuni reservations. If the CRC mission schools at Rehoboth and Zuni keep renewing themselves periodically to adapt to changing conditions, they will contribute to improving the daily lives and futures of their Navajo and Zuni congregations.[37]

[36] Mulder-Behnia, "Rehoboth Christian School," 30-32. www.rcsnm.ork/confession.pdf (accessed 11 Dec. 2018). CRC 2016 *Acts of Synod*, 923. Also cf. James C. Schaap, *Rehoboth: A Place for Us* (Grand Rapids, MI: Faith Alive, 2010) about Rehoboth alumni.

[37] For assistance in gathering the materials on the CRC Indian missions and schools, the author wishes to thank the staff at the following institutions: Heritage Hall; the Center of Southwest Research at the University of New Mexico, Albuquerque, NM; the Octavia Fellin Library in Gallup, NM; the Federal Records Center in Denver, CO; and the library of the Theological University at Kampen, the Netherlands.

CHAPTER 14

Writing about Education: Gendered Visions in Dutch American Letters and Memoirs from the Turn of the Twentieth Century[1]

Suzanne M. Sinke

What did Dutch immigrants at the turn of the twentieth century write about education in the United States? What image of Dutch American education did they paint for their relatives and friends in the Netherlands? How did that image compare to Dutch education models, particularly in terms of gender ideals? These themes appear to a limited degree in my book on Dutch immigrant women,[2] which relies extensively on the letters of the Dutch American population. Since that publication, I have worked more broadly with letters of other— not exclusively Dutch— migrants, highlighting techniques for working with correspondence as sources.[3]

---

[1] The author would like to thank Justin Vos and the editors of this volume for their comments on a draft of this paper, as well as staff members at Heritage Hall, Calvin College, particularly Hendrina Van Spronsen, for her assistance.
[2] Suzanne M. Sinke, *Dutch Immigrant Women in the United States, 1880-1920* (Urbana: University of Illinois Press, 2002).
[3] Bruce Elliott, David Gerber, and Suzanne M. Sinke, eds., *Letters across Borders: The Epistolary Practices of International Migrants* (NY: Palgrave Macmillan, 2006); Suzanne M. Sinke and Babs Boter, "Adjusting and Fulfilling Masculine Roles: The Epistolary Persona in Dutch Transatlantic Letters," *The History of the Family* 21, no. 3 (2016): 337-49; Suzanne M. Sinke, "Mapping the Limits of Travel Writing:

The 2019 AADAS conference theme, Dutch Americans/Canadians and Education, provided incentive to revisit the topic of Dutch immigrant correspondence using the Dutch Immigrant Letters Collection (DILC), as well as a few other published collections.[4] Although Dutch people of various religious backgrounds migrated to North America, the DILC tends to include those of Protestant background, particularly those of Christian Reformed Church affiliation, who brought with them from the Netherlands a strong sense of the importance of Christian education. Hence, my inquiry in this paper centers on Protestant Dutch migrants, with a focus on the period from 1870 to 1920. The research for this paper includes my examination of a variety of letters and memoirs, looking for patterns of information about education as they relate to gender.

The findings replicate much of what scholars have already suggested but with some nuances.[5] As an historian with a social scientific inclination, I appreciate confirmation studies—ones that demonstrate the validity of past work—using a slightly different perspective or set of sources. For *Dutch Immigrant Women*, I oversampled both letters by women and family collections that included letters by women; for this study, I used a broader base, which includes more letters or memoirs by men.[6] The letters most often traveled between a Dutch migrant in the

---

A Dutch American Example," in *Tracking Female Trails: Reisverhalen in boek en brief* (Amsterdam: Vrije Universiteit, 2013), 26-31.

[4] Note on translations: where the DILC offered a translation, unless otherwise noted, I used it. I cite where I translated the text myself. The DILC is kept in Heritage Hall, Calvin University. The webpage allows access to some letters.

[5] Sinke, *Dutch Immigrant Women*, 113-16, 118-21. Similar shifts to public school teaching among ethnic populations appear in Lori Ann Lahlum, "Women, Work, and Community in Rural Norwegian America, 1840-1920," in *Norwegian American Women: Migration, Communities, and Identities* (St. Paul: Minnesota Historical Society Press, 2011), 80; Jon Gjerde, *The Minds of the West: Ethnocultural Evolution in the Rural Middle West 1830-1917* (Chapel Hill: University of North Carolina Press, 1997), 299; and Hasia Diner, *Erin's Daughters in America: Irish Immigrant Women in the Nineteenth Century* (Baltimore, MD: Johns Hopkins University Press, 1983), 96. On other ethnic denominational groups that shared similar hesitation toward women in teaching, see Linda Schelbitzki Pickle, *Contented Among Strangers: Rural German-Speaking Women and their Families in the Nineteenth-Century Midwest* (Urbana: University of Illinois Press, 1996), 82-83; Carol K. Coburn, *Life at Four Corners: Religion, Gender, and Education in a German-Lutheran Community, 1868-1945* (Lawrence: University Press of Kansas, 1992), 73; Christiane Harzig, "Creating a Community: German-American Women in Chicago," in *Peasant Maids—City Women* (Ithaca, NY: Cornell University Press, 1997), 217-18; Ingrid Semmingsen, *Norway to America: A History of the Migration* (Minneapolis: University of Minnesota Press, 1980), 93.

[6] As an historian, I know to question my sources and to recognize that I need corroboration for much of the information. Moreover, any immigrant letter

Writing about Education 257

United States and family members in the Netherlands, though I did examine a few going in the opposite direction when they specifically dealt with educational themes. My findings illustrate how Protestant Dutch immigrants to America during this timeframe described and explained gendered elements of US education to their Dutch correspondents.

Dutch newcomers reported to the Netherlands one major difference in the educational system—most teachers in the United States were women. Letter after letter notes this. One wrote in 1908: "Here in our little city of Zeeland, for example, we have a school in which there are 14 teachers, of which 13 are women, and only one man, namely the principal."[7] Another immigrant described his first school in Kalamazoo in a memoir: "To our great surprise, all the teachers including the principal were ladies."[8] By contrast, memories of the Netherlands generally included primarily men as teachers. One man's autobiography describing education in the province of Groningen at the beginning of the century explains that he had attended school for seven years, until age twelve, and in that time, all the teachers were male, except for one woman who taught first grade.[9] Joseph Mol, writing in 1905 to a male relative in the Netherlands who had shown interest in a teaching position, made it clear: "There is no demand for Dutch [language] teachers, because it is used only in Christian education, and those are mostly women teachers, just like in all the other public schools. There are a few schools where the head teachers are *men*."[10]

The correspondents were not simply imagining this gender imbalance. According to US statistical reports, in US schools overall, roughly 60 percent of teachers in the 1870s were female, and that percentage rose steadily from 1880 to 1920, when it reached over 80 percent.[11] In 1900, when women outnumbered men in teaching almost three to one, an immigration commission report noted that 7.5 percent

---

collection, regardless of size, cannot fulfill the standard of being representative. Rather, they provide insights. On this theme, see Wolfgang Helbich and Walter D. Kamphoefner, "How Representative are Emigrant Letters? An Exploration of the German Case," in *Letters Across Borders*, 29-55.

7   H. J. Everhard, Zeeland, MI, to relatives, Lochem, Gelderland, 6 Dec. 1908, DILC.
8   George Bos, "Memoirs of a Schoolmaster," manuscript, 23, DILC.
9   Jacob Koenes, autobiography (1907-75; Grootegast, Groningen, to Cascade, MI), DILC.
10 Joseph Mol, Grand Rapids, MI, to Abraham Mol (nephew/cousin), Rilland, Zeeland, 17 Nov. 1905, DILC.
11 Thomas D. Snyder, ed., *120 Years of American Education: A Statistical Portrait* (National Center for Education Statistics, 1993), 38, fig. 10, "Percentage of elementary and secondary school teachers, by sex: 1869-70 to fall 1990."

of teachers came from the second generation (US-born children of immigrants), compared to a mere 2 percent of foreign-born women.[12]

A quick look at the *Yearbook of Schools for Christian Instruction* from 1918 to 1919, also confirms that in many communities Christian independent schools in the United States employed more women than men—but not everywhere. For example, several one-room schools in Iowa had a lone male teacher for the entire school, and men filled the ranks of teachers in a couple of urban locations. More common, though, was the pattern that the Mol letter identified—a mixed population with a man as principal.[13] Few female principals appeared in the yearbook.

Whether public or independent, the proportion of women serving as teachers in schools in the United States stood in stark contrast to immigrants' memories of the Netherlands. Other historical sources support the lower proportions of women teachers in Dutch schools.[14] One report from the Netherlands notes that, as late as 1898, women could rarely teach above grade two and up to 1948 generally taught only up to grade three.[15] This kind of contextual or background research can verify the insights of immigrant letters. Even without the academic studies and hindsight, however, the letters I consulted regularly disseminated information back to the Netherlands about this gender distinction of many more women in teaching staff.

In the United States, schools began hiring more women as teachers—at least for the early grades—much earlier in the nineteenth century as the association of women with domestic ideology, including caring for children in most capacities, gained popularity. Under this cultural vision, teaching through the grammar school level became a domain primarily for women. Although school boards later questioned the unique qualifications of women—that special "nurturing ability"—

---

[12] William P. Dillingham et al., *Abstracts of reports of the Immigration Commission: with conclusions and recommendations, and views of the minority* (Washington, DC: G.P.O., 1911), 818-19.

[13] B. J. Bennink, ed., *Yearbook of Schools for Christian Instruction* (Alliance of Christian Schools in Michigan, 1918-19).

[14] In the Netherlands, the shift to primarily women teachers for elementary (*primair*) education took place in the 1980s, and at that point, men still predominated for upper-level instruction. Marjolein van Dijk, Karin Jettinghoff, Miranda Grootscholte, "Feminisering van het primair onderwijs," 2; https://www.arbeidsmarktplatformpo.nl/fileadmin/bestanden/bijlagen_nieuws_agenda/feminisering_van_het_primair_onderwijs.pdf (accessed 19 June 2019).

[15] This did not apply to Catholic schools, where nuns held prominent roles. On the trends, see M. G. Schenk, *Vrouwen van Nederland 1898-1949* (Amsterdam: Scheltens & Giltay, 1948), 92.

they continued to find the lower wages they could pay women attractive.[16] As in other fields, women earned significantly less than men, sometimes half as much, for the same work. A Dutch immigrant in Blendon, Michigan, reported to his relatives in Gelderland in 1903 that "education is expensive here," noting that a male teacher in his community earned $50 a month, whereas a woman teacher would make from $25 to $30.[17] Clearly, if costs figured heavily into the decision, hiring women was more practical for many communities. To the degree that teaching was an honored profession for women—one of a limited number of options available for paid employment—it became more difficult to convince men to join the profession. Men had more lucrative employment options.

Dutch immigrants sometimes identified a difference in teacher training between the two countries as one cause of the gender imbalance. As Willem de Lange, a teacher whose formal education took place in the Netherlands, explained in 1873:

> Concerning your question about my becoming a schoolteacher so easily here, I must tell you that America is a free country, and everyone does what they want! Even if I wished to declare myself a physician, no one would stop me. But it is also certain that those with evidence of training have the most credibility. It is difficult to find accredited teachers here.[18]

Standards did rise over time, but not to a level comparable to the requirements in the Netherlands in the eyes of some immigrants. Klaas Hoekema, a young immigrant in Washington, when writing to his family in Friesland in 1913, echoed the difference in training required to be a teacher.

> Houkje, I hope you will become head of the sewing and knitting school, then you will not have to come here. Otherwise you must come here and become a schoolteacher. . . . Last year, we weren't

---

[16] See, for example, Jo Anne Preston, "Domestic Ideology, School Reformers, and Female Teachers: Schoolteaching Becomes Women's Work," *New England Quarterly* 66, no. 4 (Dec. 1993): 531.

[17] Harm Avink, Blendon, MI, to R. W. Bouwmeester Family, Lochem, Gelderland, 3 Dec. 1903, in Herbert J. Brinks, ed., *Dutch American Voices: Letters from the United States, 1850-1930* (Ithaca, NY: Cornell University Press, 1995), 69. The Brinks edited collection draws from the DILC.

[18] Willem Hendrik de Lange, Grand Rapids, MI, to H. Houck, Deventer, Overijssel, 22 Dec. 1873, Brinks, *Dutch American Voices*, 409. De Lange died a couple of months later after a bobsled hit him.

able to celebrate your graduation, but we hope you will pass the exams this time. If you do, I'll get a bottle of beer.[19]

In the United States, qualifications for teaching depended on the state. Preparation standards typically required a high school education. These state regulations increased over time, but one or two years beyond a high school curriculum often sufficed. In Michigan, at the turn of the century, a high school diploma and being eighteen years old were adequate to teach. The next level of preparation involved normal schools or normal classes, designed specifically for those planning on going into teaching. In 1903 the Michigan state legislature set up county normal classes, which took place in conjunction with local high schools. Certificates for teaching depended on a student's level of high school education, along with additional normal school classes. For the many rural, one-room schools, however, Michigan did not require any normal school preparation.[20] Other areas required some normal school certification. In South Dakota, a state normal school provided the basic training in the 1910s. This was the educational route taken by Jessie Eringa, who began teaching at age eighteen in Tyndall, South Dakota.[21] Like many of the Dutch American women who went into teaching during this period, Jessie came from the second generation—born in the United States to Dutch immigrant parents.

Normal schools developed specifically for the purpose of training teachers. They sprang up in the late nineteenth century as stand-alone institutions, most notably in areas of the Midwest. Dutch Americans, who lived in various concentrations in these areas, therefore, had access to these schools. Normal education, however, soon faced challenges—it had to compete with a broader movement for the professionalization of education, which had gained traction from the turn of the century. Under this banner, states shifted to promote a college education based on what they considered "modern" curricula for potential teachers.[22] The turn of the century, however, remained a heyday for

---

[19] Klaas A. Hoekema, Sunnyside, WA, to parents, brothers, and sisters, Wommels, Friesland, 26 Feb. 1913, DILC.

[20] Ernest Burnham, "Michigan's Preparation of Teachers for Rural Schools," *The Elementary School Teacher* 9, no. 3 (1908): 138-45.

[21] Brian W. Beltman, *Dutch Farmer in the Missouri Valley: The Life and Letters of Ulbe Eringa, 1866-1950* (Urbana: University of Illinois Press, 1996), from the reminiscences of Ulbe Eringa, 162.

[22] David Diener, "The Intellectual Climate of the Late Nineteenth Century and the Fate of American Normal Schools," *American Educational History Journal* 35, no. 1/2 (Spring/Summer 2008): 61-79.

Teacher's County Certificate, issued in 1913 (Origins *37*, no. 1, 2019)

normal schools, where women (and men) could gain certification for teaching positions without necessarily completing a full college degree program. Normal school preparation, however, qualified one for only certain levels of instruction, and often the certificate one earned had to be renewed (as opposed to a permanent teaching credential). Still, normal schools offered opportunities for women to get credentials and begin teaching at a relatively young age, especially if they were unsure of whether the time and cost of college would be worthwhile. Families that might not want to invest in a daughter's college education might support a shorter course of study leading to quick employment. The kind of credentials one would earn appears in the image above of a certificate for teaching in the first grade, good for three years in the state of Kansas. Gertrude Vande Riet, the recipient, taught all grammar school grades (1st through 8th) in a one-room schoolhouse.[23] Vande Riet remained in teaching for most of her life, but many women left after a few years to marry. Not all left voluntarily. Compounding the transience of the teaching force, employment typically went from year to year, so a school governing board might close a class or choose another teacher (especially if a woman got married).

For potential teachers, family negotiations about getting an education could be fraught. Nellie De Jong, writing from the Normal School in Flagstaff, Arizona, in 1913, explained to her siblings: "I am afraid that at home they are of the opinion that I have now gathered

---

[23] John Timmerman, "A Woman's Voice from the Plains: The Diary of Gertrude Vande Riet," *Origins* 35, no. 1 (2019): 14.

enough knowledge to do my job properly, but I think that they cannot pass judgement on this, as well as somebody who is actually working in this field. . . . More is gradually being demanded from teachers, and if we fall behind, we shall soon be excluded."[24] The goal in De Jong's case was to combine more knowledge with higher certification. She recognized that continuation, let alone advancement, as a teacher required increasing qualifications.[25] Both men and women who sought advanced positions recognized the need to go beyond the normal school preparation. The results were significant, as Elizabeth Furens, a teacher and principal in Florida, reported to her cousins in the Netherlands: "I have a first class certificate for life, and I can teach anywhere and won't ever have to take another examination for teachers."[26]

The Eringa family demonstrated a range of advanced education for teaching among their four daughters. All four attended the rural school (with one teacher) in Running Water, South Dakota, and then went on for more advanced education. Jessie attended the South Dakota Normal School in Springfield, plus one year at Northwestern Classical Academy.[27] Thryze and Alys also attended Northwestern Academy and earned teaching accreditation. Thryze taught in rural schools for a year, then went to Central College and finished a degree there. She spent two years teaching high school but quit after she married. The fourth daughter, Dora, felt called to missionary service. She earned a college degree from Central College in Pella and took a three-month course from Moody Bible Institute in Chicago. Trained to teach and evangelize, Dora set out for Japan. She started her career by helping to form a new Christian congregation in one location, but then the Reformed Church transferred her to Yokohama to teach young women.[28]

---

[24] Nellie De Jong to sister and brother, Normal School, Flagstaff, AZ, 11 Aug. 1913, in Ulbe B. Bakker, ed. *Zuster, kom toch over: Belevenissen van een emigrantenfamilie uit Friesland. Brieven uit Amerika in de periode 1894-1933* [Sister, please come over: experiences of an immigrant family from Friesland/the Netherlands. Letters from America in the period 1894-1933] (Winsum, NL: Ulbe B. Bakker, 1999), 333.

[25] On De Jong and her family, see also Justin Vos, "The 'Many Children of God': The Role of Religious Community in Dutch American Migration," in *Dutch Muck—and Much More: Dutch Americans in Farming, Religion, Art, and Astronomy* (Holland, MI: Van Raalte Press, 2019), 153-76.

[26] Elizabeth M. Furens, Sanford, FL, to Cousin Antone and sisters, Netherlands, 17 Nov. 1922, DILC.

[27] Northwestern Classical Academy in Orange City, IA, was the precursor to Northwestern College, though the academy functioned more as a high school.

[28] Beltman, *Dutch Farmer*, 159-62, 226-27. After a time in Yokohama, Dora suffered a nervous breakdown. When she returned to the United States, she ended up institutionalized and died of pneumonia.

Teacher training as a component of missionary service applied to a number of Dutch American women at the turn of the century, both Reformed and Christian Reformed. Effie Hofman received diplomas in both teaching and nursing, as well as additional training at the Moody Bible Institute prior to her placement at the Christian Reformed mission to the Navajo.[29] A mix of training also applied to Nellie Noordhoff who worked at Rehoboth mission from 1903 to 1905 and who shows up in records as matron, cook, and teacher.[30] The timing of migration means that in the period from around 1900 to World War I, "the halcyon years" of women's mission activity for the United States, a Dutch American base existed to support this movement.[31]

Young men also required either high school or academy training to pursue various careers, including teaching. With the expectation of a lifelong career, young men tended to gain more training that would open possibilities for both career paths and advancement within those fields. As one correspondent noted: "One of [your sister's sons] is now at the Academy studying Greek and Latin. Also Bernard Rensink [Weelink] had already been at the Academy 2 or 3 years."[32] A number of letters in the Heritage Hall collection include information on people attending academies tied to denominational institutions such as Hope College, Northwestern Academy, Calvin College, and Central College. Typically, the people attending were either the children of immigrants or perhaps the 1.5 generation—born in the Netherlands but arrived with their parents and grew up to a significant degree in the United States.[33] Even if their training came in a normal school, scholarship suggests that men, to a greater degree than women, had instructors who prepared them for supervisory roles as principals and school superintendents.[34]

[29] Sinke, *Dutch Immigrant Women*, 120.
[30] Christian Reformed Board of Missions, *Navaho and Zuni for Christ: Fifty Years of Indian Missions* (Grand Rapids, MI: Christian Reformed Board of Missions, 1947), 39.
[31] Patricia R. Hill, *The World Their Household: The American Woman's Foreign Mission Movement and Cultural Transformation, 1870-1920* (Ann Arbor: University of Michigan Press, 1985), 122.
[32] John Beijer, Hull, IA, to G. J. Geurkink, Winterswijk, Gelderland, 28 Jan. 1901, DILC.
[33] On this concept, developed primarily among sociologists, see Rubén G. Rumbaut, "Ages, Life Stages, and Generational Cohorts: Decomposing the Immigrant First and Second Generations in the United States," *The International Migration Review* 38, no. 3 (2004): 1160-1205; S. Karthick Ramakrishnan, "Second-Generation Immigrants? The '2.5 Generation' in the United States," *Social Science Quarterly* 85, no. 2 (June 2004): 380-99.
[34] For example, Barbara Speas Havira, "Coeducation and Gender Differentiation in Teacher Training: Western State Normal School, 1904-1929," *Michigan Historical Review* 21, no. 1 (Jan. 1995): 49-82.

Men tended to predominate in those positions, if they were present on the teaching staff at all.

A few collections in DILC include information on people who had trained in the Netherlands for teaching and then came to the United States. Gerhardus Bos, who fit that profile, shows up in the memoirs of his brother George. George had consulted Gerhardus after receiving a request from his minister to restart a Christian school in Kalamazoo. George had enjoyed his education in the United States but was now working for good wages and moving into higher positions in a local shop. According to the memoir, Gerhardus, who at that point was teaching in a Christian School in Paterson, New Jersey, offered rather cautionary advice: "Teaching is often a thankless job, the wages are small, and there are many in our circles that oppose Christian Education."[35] George, nonetheless, took up the call, and like many men, in time, moved into school administration.

What did immigrants write about the schools that Dutch Americans attended? Not surprisingly, education appears most often in the letters of those with school-age children. At the minimum, the migrants might report to their relatives in the Netherlands that their children "go to school."[36] Parents—both fathers and mothers—would write these messages. At times, news focused on which children attended school, since the age range might vary (particularly if the parents sought English-language instruction for Dutch-born offspring). Teunis van den Hoek wrote to his relatives in South Holland that all his children would be starting school the following week "except our oldest daughter, Willempje, because she is past school age."[37] The 1.5 generation might have to retake grades in order to manage the work in English. George Bos, a 1.5er who had come with his parents from Woldendorp, Groningen, to Kalamazoo, Michigan, described spending a few months in each grade from first grade on up. That way, he gained sufficient English-language skills in various subjects to make the transition to the next level. He could then pick up with others of his age and grade with sufficient linguistic skills to succeed.[38] In this same vein, letters regularly suggested that parents would have their children attend school, even if they were a bit older, in order to learn English.

---

[35] Bos, "Memoirs of a Schoolmaster," 32, DILC.
[36] Geert Becksvoort, Saugatuck, MI, to relatives, Gieten, Drenthe, 13 Feb. 1906, DILC.
[37] Teunis van den Hoek, Orange City, IA, to relatives, Goudriaan, Zuid Holland, 26 Nov. 1887, in Brinks, ed., *Dutch American Voices*, 144.
[38] Bos, "Memoirs of a Schoolmaster," 23, DILC.

Some writers noted that, during the slack winter months, they could use the opportunity to learn English: "Almost every winter, there is instruction in English given by Hollanders, but that is free. It is offered by one or the other charitable organization. It is also offered for free in a few of the schools."[39] This also applied to rural areas, where a break in farm work in winter meant an opportunity to attend school if the weather allowed.[40]

Within the context of rural communities in the United States, where many of the Dutch moved and where much instruction took place in either one- or two-room schoolhouses in this period, mixed-age and coeducational groups with differing skill levels allowed flexibility for shifting grades. The letters also hint at attendance irregularities for teenagers who fell at the borders of the regular school age range. The letters provide no particular division based on gender for children missing or leaving school in early grades in order to go to work. Thus, Willem Brouwer wrote to his grandfather: "I attend school, but I had to dig potatoes now. I am at school to learn English."[41] Likewise, Dina Beijer, after a lengthy description of her household and farm work (e.g., milking cows, washing clothes), explained that she and her siblings had learned English "good enough that we can manage well to talk and write. During the first winter, we four older ones went to school for a few months." She then noted the younger siblings "go to school all the time."[42] The implication was that she no longer attended, at least not regularly.

Compulsory school attendance laws varied state by state and over time, but for this *fin-de-siècle* period, they remained somewhat limited.[43] The Iowa state legislature did not pass a school attendance law until

---

[39] Joseph Mol, Grand Rapids, MI, to Abraham Mol, Rilland, Zeeland, 17 Nov. 1905, DILC (author's translation).
[40] Teunis van den Hoek, Harrison, SD, to Goudriaan, Zuid Holland, 1891, in Brinks, *Dutch American Voices*, 107.
[41] Willem Brouwer, Orange City, IA, to Pieter Kooiman and family, Andijk, Noord Holland, 24 Sept. 1888, DILC.
[42] Dina Beijer, Hull, IA, to Dora Geurkink (friend), Winterswijk, Gelderland, 4 March 1901, DILC.
[43] Mark Groen, "Literacy and the Meaning of Citizenship in American Education," *American Educational History Journal* 41, no. 1/2 (March 2014): 80. For a quick overview of when states passed compulsory attendance laws, see Stephen John Provasnik, "Compulsory Schooling, From Idea to Institution: A Case Study of the Development of Compulsory Attendance in Illinois, 1857-1907" (PhD dissertation, University of Chicago, 1999), 332, app. E.

1902.[44] By 1918 all states had some measures on the books, but they differed both in form and enforcement. These laws targeted children either up to a particular age, for a set number of years, or through a particular grade, and they applied only to basic schooling. High school remained optional. When in place, compulsory school laws did make it more likely that children of less educated parents would finish a grammar school course of study, which in turn meant better chances for more highly skilled employment for both males and females.[45] Many Dutch immigrants looked critically at the increased cost of education and the lost work or wages in gaining education beyond a basic level.[46] Harm Avink included a number of comments about education in his letters from Michigan back to Gelderland: "Much is done here to prevent raising ignorant children. They start school when they are five years old, and the law requires that all children must attend school for a certain length of time. The government always pays a portion of the cost."[47] This actually corresponded quite closely to Dutch laws, which in 1900 required children to attend school from age six to twelve.[48]

State laws that impinged more on the immigrant population related to command of English and whether public school authorities had control over private schools. For example, in Wisconsin, the Bennett law of 1890 required twelve weeks of schooling and instruction in English.[49] In Illinois, the Edwards law of 1889 required private schools be approved by public school officials; this requirement lasted until the legislature repealed it four years later.[50] Even more draconian, the Babel proclamation, passed during World War I in Iowa, stipulated: "Only

---

[44] "Compulsory Education in Iowa, 1872-1919," *Annals of Iowa* 49, no. 1/2 (Summer/Fall 1987): 58-76.

[45] Emily Rauscher, "Educational Expansion and Occupational Change: US Compulsory Schooling Laws and the Occupational Structure 1850-1930," *Social Forces* 93, no. 4 (June 2015): 1397-1422.

[46] For comparison with the period beyond this paper, see Stephen A. Lassonde, "Should I Go, or Should I Stay?: Adolescence, School Attainment, and Parent-Child Relations in Italian Immigrant Families of New Haven, 1900–1940," *History of Education Quarterly* 38, no. 1 (Spring 1998): 37.

[47] Harm Avink, Blendon, MI, to R. W. Bouwmeester Family, Lochem, Gelderland, 10 Jan. 1888, in Brinks, *Dutch American Voices*, 69.

[48] Dutch law shifted to add one year, from six to seven, in 1921. Centraal Bureau voor de Statistiek, *Jaarboek onderwijs in cijfers, 2010* (The Hague: Centraal Bureau voor de Statistiek), 7.

[49] Thomas C. Hunt, "The Bennett Law of 1890: Focus of Conflict between Church and State," *Journal of Church & State* 23, no. 1 (Winter 1981): 69-93.

[50] Charles Shanabruch, "The Repeal of the Edwards Law: A Study of Religion and Ethnicity in Illinois Politics," *Ethnicity* 7, no. 3 (June 1980): 310-32.

English was legal in public or private schools, in public conversations, on trains, over the telephone, at all meetings, and in all religious services."[51]

Writers typically included the language of instruction for their children when describing schools. For example, Ante Gorter-Brouwer wrote her family in Noord Holland that her daughter Betje "attends the English school."[52] Some correspondents simply seemed to accept or at least resign themselves to the new status quo. This was the case with Arie van den Hoek who wrote: "There is no Dutch school here. English is the primary language of America."[53] At the turn of the century, this linguistic distinction—Dutch or English—coincided with religious and, to a degree, denominational lines; that is, if instruction was primarily in English, the school tended to be public, and if instruction was primarily in Dutch, then writers might interchange "Holland School" with "Christian school." Over time, Christian schools introduced more English, but the association of the Dutch language with Christian instruction remained strong for many, at least up to World War I. Even if some schools switched to English, instruction in Dutch tended to take place more often in Christian schools.

The distinction also had implications for who would teach. The more orthodox Calvinists who advocated for Christian schools tended to prefer men in teaching positions beyond the early years. Some based their views on biblical passages from I Timothy or I Corinthians about the role of women in the church. Some based their opposition on other grounds. In any case, the debate about allowing women as teachers included several versions: (1) women as teachers at all, (2) women as teachers for younger grades, (3) women as teachers for adult women, and (4) women as teachers for all grades.[54] Women might become teachers for all female groups, for example, in mission settings or

---

51 "Babel Proclamation, May 1918," at: https://iowaculture.gov/history/education/educator-resources/primary-source-sets/immigration-regulation-response-and/babel-proclamation (accessed 19 June 2019). I did not find reports on the Bennett, Edwards, or Babel measures in the letters, but that could be the result of sampling.
52 Antje Gorter-Brouwer, Orange City, IA, to Pieter Kooiman and family, Andijk, Noord Holland, 12 May 1889, DILC.
53 Arie van den Hoek, Harrison, SD, to Brother and Sister, Goudriaan, Zuid Holland, 3 Jan. 1894, in Brinks, *Dutch American Voices*, 149.
54 Sinke, *Dutch Immigrant Women*, 118; Robert P. Swierenga, *Faith and Family: Dutch Immigration and Settlement in the United States, 1820-1920* (NY: Holmes & Meier, 2000), 165; Steven Vryhof, "Between Memory and Vision: A Brief History of Reformed Christian Schools," *Journal of Presbyterian History* 77, no. 2 (May 1999): 99; on a comparable debate among the Missouri Synod Lutheran congregations, see Pickle, *Contented Among Strangers*, 82-83.

handwork classes, but leaders of Christian Schools tended to advocate for male teachers, especially for older students.

The divide between Dutch Americans who favored public as opposed to private education mapped onto the two major Calvinist denominations: the Reformed Church and the Christian Reformed Church. Actually, the distinction between those favoring private, Christian education and those working to provide moral instruction through the public schools went even further back, to the midcentury migration of Seceders. The division took on even greater strength toward the turn of the century when the Neo-Calvinist movement gained political power in the Netherlands under Dutch theologian Abraham Kuyper.[55] Writing about this distinction in the 1920s, Jacob van Hinte described the orthodox Netherlanders who came to America:

> [T]hey too were convinced that education was not the exclusive concern of the state or of the church but rather of the parents. In other words, independent Christian schools should be established by specially created associations not limited to Christian Reformed members but also open to other orthodox Reformed and Presbyterian believers.[56]

As historian Robert P. Swierenga has noted, the shift away from church control to independently controlled groups sometimes required adjustment, especially when parents found the minister to be the person best suited to run the organization.[57]

By contrast, Van Hinte wrote that those who were connected to the Reformed Church in America "feel that it is their duty to see to it that there is a Christian atmosphere in the public schools" and that not to do so would be civic neglect.[58] In 1892 the National Synod of the Reformed Church in America endorsed the model of having Christian youth remain in public schools in order to influence the broader

---

[55] On the relationship of the Seceders to education, see Janet Sjaarda Sheeres, "The Struggle for the Souls of the Children: The Effect of the Dutch Education Law of 1806 on the Emigration of 1847," in *The Dutch in Urban America* (Holland, MI: Joint Archives of Holland/Hope College, 2004), 34-47; Vryhof, "Between Memory and Vision," 99.

[56] Jacob Van Hinte, *Netherlanders in America: A Study of Emigration and Settlement in the 19th and 20th Centuries in the United States of America* (Grand Rapids, MI: Baker Book House, 1985 [1928]), 870.

[57] Robert P. Swierenga, "For God and Country," *Michigan History Magazine* 100, no. 6 (Nov. 2016): 28-32.

[58] Van Hinte, *Netherlanders in America*, 871.

culture.⁵⁹ This fit with the idea of becoming American while remaining Calvinist, which Kuyper had also supported in his writings and which had gained resonance with some Reformed Church leaders.⁶⁰

The lines of connection to the Netherlands supported these religious divisions. For example, the Heritage Hall collection includes a letter to Klaaske Bewulda in the United States from a former teacher and classmates in Schettens, Friesland:

> We noted with satisfaction that all goes well with you, and that soon you will be going to a Christian school. That pleases me greatly, for I would regret it if you didn't continue your education in the way to which I directed you.⁶¹

Mutual reinforcement of Christian education regularly graced the pages of immigrant letters from the more orthodox Calvinists. As one father of three children who attended a Christian school in Grand Rapids explained:

> [Dutch schools] are maintained by the congregations in order to impress the Dutch language and pure Biblical truths upon the minds of the children. There is also in this town a Dutch Academy with 5 or 6 professors and 50 students.⁶²

The geography of public schooling came up often in the letters of migrants, particularly in rural areas. Herman Beijer, of Hawarden, Iowa, wrote to his family about the system of surveying the land into sections and having a school at regular intervals: "Now each four sections have a school, so no one can be farther from a school than two miles."⁶³ Other correspondents added distance into the "sacrifice" they made to send their children to Christian schools: "The public school is only half a mile from here, and the Christian school is at two and a half

---

[59] Robert P. Swierenga, *Dutch Chicago: A History of the Hollanders in the Windy City* (Grand Rapids, MI: Eerdmans, 2002), 355.

[60] George Harinck, *"We live presently under a waning moon": Nicolaus Martin Steffens as Leader of the Reformed Church in America in the West in Years of Transition (1878-1895)* (Holland, MI: Van Raalte Press, 2011), 61-62.

[61] Classmates (children) and Teacher, Schettens, Friesland, to Klaske Bewulda, United States, 31 July 1912, DILC.

[62] Krijn Goudzwaard, Grand Rapids, MI, to relatives, Oud Vossemeer, Zeeland, 15 March 1898, DILC.

[63] Herman Beijer, Hawarden, IA, to Geurkink Family, Winterswijk, Gelderland, 23 Jan. 1896, DILC.

miles distance."[64] Bad weather could render that distance impassible to children.

Most writers who discussed public education stressed that it was "free." So, for example, Arie van den Hoek wrote to his brother and sister that two of his children were working in Harrison, South Dakota, and attending the English school. "The school and the books are free." Yet others noted there were costs associated with public education. "Our tax last year was $6.00, which gives free education to all children."[65] Monetary charges for education appeared more often in the letters of those whose children attended Christian schools. From Paterson, New Jersey, in 1902, where the letter writer reported paying twenty cents a week for one child, to Chicago in 1904, where another writer noted paying $1.50 a month for three children, immigrants sought to let their Dutch counterparts know the costs.[66] This fit the pattern of sharing cost-of-living information more generally.[67] Other sources not only confirm some of this information but also indicate some variations. In the 1918-19 report on Christian independent schools, every school reported their tuition, which varied by duration as well as amount. In some locales, it cost $.25 per week for a child. Others required from $1.00 to $2.50 per month, and another sought $20 for a full academic year.[68]

What does this foray into the personal writings of Dutch immigrants from the turn of the century suggest about gender and education? First, the feminized teaching force at the lower levels of schooling in the United States surprised Dutch immigrants. Many adapted to and rapidly accepted this element of US gender roles—a significant shift. Female teachers became a staple in many Dutch American schools, including some of the Christian schools, though the tendency to employ men for supervisory positions continued. Second, a number of Dutch American women embraced opportunities for further education to go into teaching themselves, finding this professional

---

[64] Teake and Maggy DeJong to brother, sister, and family, Harrison, SD, 26 Dec. 1916, in Bakker, ed., *Zuster, kom toch over*, 339.
[65] Harm Avink, Blendon, MI, to R. W. Bouwmeester Family, Lochem, Gelderland, 30 March 1884, in Brinks, *Dutch American Voices*, 67.
[66] Maartje Zondervan, Paterson, NJ, to Sijds Lautenbach (brother and sister-in-law), Tzummarum, Friesland, 25 March 1902, and Klaas Niemeijer, Chicago, IL, to Pieter and Jantje Niemeijer Family (parents, brothers and sisters), Middelstum, Groningen, May 1904, in Brinks, *Dutch American Voices*, 299 and 309.
[67] See Sinke, *Dutch Immigrant Women*, 121-29: section, "pinching and saving a penny."
[68] Bennink, ed., *Yearbook of Schools for Christian Instruction, 1918-1919*.

outlet attractive for either a few years of employment prior to marriage or a longer-term career. Women teachers faced few challenges from the broader US community, though they sometimes needed the approval of their denominations for more specialized roles, such as teaching in mission settings. The era around the turn of the century offered young single women of Dutch background an increase in opportunities both for teaching and for missionary work. Third, male teachers faced the difficulty of making a career in a feminized occupation, one where school boards could pay female teachers significantly less. On the other hand, a largely female teaching force also assisted in providing opportunities for men in school administration, since these roles tended to remain in male hands. Fourth, the religious division between public and independent private schools, which had developed earlier in the United States and accelerated at the turn of the century in the Netherlands, played a major role in the lives of Dutch Americans in the United States. The field of education provided a central site for Protestant Dutch Americans to observe and sometimes embrace shifting gender roles.

I leave the last word to Klaas Hoekema, who sometimes encouraged his sister to stay at a school in the Netherlands and at other times suggested she could become a teacher in the United States: "What a fuss the people make over Houkje's wish to become a schoolmistress. We wonder why. It is too bad because teachers are about the most important people to society."[69]

---

[69] Klaas A. Hoekema, Sunnyside, WA, to parents, brothers, and sisters, Wommels, Friesland, 2 May 1913, DILC.

CHAPTER 15

Women in Higher Education: The Case of Five Reformed Institutions

Rhonda Pennings

Throughout history, women have met many obstacles in their pursuit of an equal, high-level education: inferior standards of education for young girls, the belief that women were intellectually inferior to men, and even concern that education would not adequately prepare them for their "natural" role as wives and mothers.[1] In fact, prior to the Civil War, few colleges even admitted women.

At the beginning of the Civil War, when many college-age males left home to fight, more opportunities arose for women to enroll in colleges, and gradually, more and more educational institutions opened their doors to them. Since then, positions and opportunities for women in the educational sphere have continued to increase. In the past fourteen years, the majority of post high school degrees in the United States, from bachelor's to doctoral, have been awarded to women.[2] Women in higher education today have opportunities for

[1] Sherry Penney, Jennifer Brown, and Laura McPhie Oliveria, "Numbers are Not Enough: Women in Higher Education in the 21st Century," *New England Journal of Public Policy* 22, no. 1 (21 March 2007): 167-82.
[2] Patsy Parker, "The Historical Role of Women in Higher Education," *Administrative Issues Journal: Connecting Education, Practice, and Research* 5, no. 1 (Spring 2015): 9.

advancement more than ever before in history.

This paper will examine the plight of women and education in five Dutch Reformed institutions of higher education: Hope College, Calvin University, Northwestern College, Dordt University, and Trinity College. My research focus is an historical overview of the experience of women in each of these institutions. I will examine the year each college began to include women, the reasons surrounding their inclusion, and the roles of key women within each institution. I will further explore how these women made a significant impact on the advancement of women more generally.

Research questions

I will first sketch the overall history of women in higher education, drawing on a recognized five-stage outline, and then examine four key questions:

1. What was the first year these colleges and universities admitted women?
2. When did these colleges and universities begin to hire female faculty?
3. When did they hire the first dean of women or female administrator?
4. What obstacles did these women face?

According to Linda Kerber,[3] the history of women in higher education can be divided into five distinct stages, and each stage highlights the increasing progression of women's roles in institutions of higher education.

Stage 1

The first stage is called the "Early Stage," from 1700 to 1775. A key characteristic of this time period is the skepticism of the culture of women's efforts to participate in higher education. Although women's literacy grew through the three Rs ("reading 'riting, and 'rithmetic"), there were no institutions of higher education open to women. Thus, women who aspired to higher education sought mentors. The onus was

---

[3] Linda K. Kerber, "'Why Should Girls be Learn'd and Wise': Two Centuries of Higher Education for Women as Seen through the Unfinished Work of Alice Mary Baldwin," in *Women and Higher Education in American History* (NY: W. W. Norton & Company, 1988), 20.

on the women to receive education from others, primarily, their male counterparts.[4]

Stage 2

Stage 2 is the "Era of Great Debate over the Capability of Women's Minds," from 1776 to 1882,[5] during which, an emphasis was placed on the continued improvement of literacy for women. During the 1800s, a cultural revolution erupted that outlined the need for education for moral citizenship, with an emphasis on religious instruction for both males and females. This led to questioning the claim that women could not succeed in higher education and, ultimately, to accepting that women should pursue higher education.[6]

During this second stage, women's colleges were established in response to the need to advance education for women who were not allowed into most existing higher education institutions. A key objective for these institutions was to recruit and maintain a high percentage of female faculty members. Due to the segregation of men and women and the predominance of males at higher-education institutions, female professors were excluded from faculty positions at men's colleges, but they did become the leaders of these new women's colleges during this historic time.[7]

In addition, two private colleges, Oberlin and Antioch, allowed coeducation beginning in 1837, although many classrooms were still exclusively male. Extracurricular activities were segregated, and male-female relationships were closely monitored. Female students at both colleges resisted the segregation, wanting freer access to classes and activities. The clearly defined roles required that men study Greek and Latin and prepare for the ministry, and women cook, wash, and clean. In fact, administrators at Oberlin dismissed women from Monday classes so they could do laundry for the male students.[8]

Stage 3

Stage 3 is the period of "Continuing Opportunity for Women," from 1888 to 1930.[9] During this time, more and more colleges became

[4] Ibid.
[5] Ibid., 20.
[6] Ibid., 35.
[7] Parker, *Historical Role*, 6.
[8] Ibid.
[9] Kerber, "Why Should Girls," 35.

coeducational institutions; it also marks the beginning of coeducational state universities. The hallmark of this time period is the increased accessibility of women to higher education. Women were given more choices of which college to attend, as well as greater opportunities to participate in extracurricular activities. The first generation of female college graduates demonstrated their dedication to academics by serving as professors, deans, and administrators at coed institutions.[10]

Despite these advances in opportunities, it was a controversial time in the history of women and higher education. The desire of women to attend institutions of higher education created a great debate that lasted over a century. On the one hand, conservatives claimed that it would destroy the role of women in the household as homemakers, wives, and mothers. Progressives, on the other hand, claimed that a college-educated woman would be a better homemaker, wife, and mother. At a time when most Americans received only a primary or secondary education, a college education was seen as something that warranted separation between males and females.[11]

Stage 4

The fourth stage is the "Women's Right to Be Educated," which lasted through the balance of the twentieth century.[12] The prevailing belief was that women were fully entitled to all levels of education and that they should be given more options in choosing a career. Since 1979 women have earned more than half of all bachelor's and master's degrees and one-third of all doctorates.[13]

The push in the 1960s and 1970s toward equality in the work place and in education changed the role of women in higher-education administration and on college and university faculties.[14] Colleges had no choice but to decrease the attention they had previously given to men's campus needs and attempt to treat men and women as equals.

From 1950 to the present, males have occupied the majority of presidencies, vice presidencies, deanships, and other top administrative positions on college campuses.[15] There are a substantial number of women in education and administration graduate programs, but a

---

[10] Parker, *Historical Role*, 7.
[11] Parker, *Historical Role*, 6.
[12] Kerber, "Why Should Girls," 41.
[13] Parker, *Historical Role*, 9.
[14] Ibid.
[15] Ibid., 7.

predominantly male population is filling the offices that manage higher education.

Stage 5

The fifth stage, "Women Striving for Progress," encompasses the twenty-first century.[16] Despite the high representation of women as students in higher education, by 2016, about 70 percent of all college and university presidents were male, as were 62 percent of the tenured professorships. Additionally, data indicate that female professors, when compared with males, move up the career ladder more slowly, are less productive in their research and scholarship, and have heavier teaching loads and lower salaries.[17]

In response to these issues, the American Council on Education has launched the Moving the Needle initiative. This collaborative initiative seeks to increase the number of women in senior leadership positions to achieve gender parity by 2030.[18]

Women administrators

Historically, women have not held positions in higher-education administration. The first administrative position offered to females in coeducational institutions was the dean of women position. Women were employed as deans of women as early as the 1890s.[19] These positions became necessary because of the sharp increase in the female population on college campuses. College presidents began to hire females to serve as advisors and counselors for the female students, and "dean of women" was the new title assigned to these leaders.

The responsibilities of these deans from 1890 to 1930 were wide ranging. The deans were to oversee the relatively new minority population of women, which involved insulating the men from the women and protecting and guiding the women.[20] Most of the deans were also faculty members, so their primary responsibility was teaching. These deans had the academic rigor and scholarly development of

---

[16] Daryl Smith, "Progress and Paradox for Women in US Higher Education," *Studies in Higher Education* 42, no. 4 (2017): 812; Penney, Brown, and McPhie Oliveria, *Numbers are Not Enough*, 176.
[17] Parker, *Historical Role*, 6.
[18] Ibid., 9; "Moving the Needle: Advancing Women in Higher Education Leadership," www.acenet.edu. (accessed 2 June 2019).
[19] Parker, *Historical Role*, 5.
[20] Parker, *Historical Role*, 10.

women at the forefront of their concerns. Female students found how advantageous it was to have women faculty and administrators on campus who went to great efforts to improve curriculum and extracurricular activities for them.[21]

The case of Reformed institutions of higher learning

Historians have praised Calvinistic colleges for being more welcoming to women students due to Calvin's views on women and education.[22] Calvin believed that women were equal to men in that both possessed the image of God, which included their mind and intellect. Thus, both should be educated in order to receive religious training.[23] This study will examine five Calvinistic colleges and universities to ascertain if this assumption is true.

Hope College was founded in 1866 and Calvin University in 1876, during stage 2 of women in higher education—the Era of Great Debate over the Capability of Women's Minds. Northwestern College was founded during stage 3—Continuing Opportunity for Women from 1888 to 1930. During this time, more and more colleges became coeducational institutions with the beginning of the coeducational state universities. Next, Dordt University and Trinity College were founded in 1955 and 1959, respectively, during stage 4—Women's Right to Be Educated in the Twentieth Century.

Table 1 includes information concerning women students and administrators for the five colleges and universities affiliated from their founding with either the Reformed Church of America (RCA) or the Christian Reformed Church (CRC). Institutions are listed from oldest to youngest in terms of years of existence. Information about women in these higher-education establishments was obtained through the archives or library of each institution.

The historical context of these colleges and universities may correlate with the types of challenges and obstacles that women faculty and administrators faced. As indicated in table 1, the hiring of the first female administrator ranged from 1907 at Hope College to 2007 at Dordt University. This one-hundred-year span shows that progress for women is still being made. All female leaders from colleges affiliated with the RCA and CRC were hired in stage 3, although it has been

---

[21] Ibid.
[22] Sam Arts, *Calvin, Nature, and Women*, www.cbeinternational.org., 15 May 2019.
[23] Ibid.

documented that women were employed as deans of women as early as the 1890s (stage 2) in some institutions of higher learning.

Table 1

	Year Founded	Year Women Admitted	1st Female Faculty	1st Female Administrator
Hope College	1866	1878	1904	1907
Calvin University[24]	1876	1901	1926	1926
Northwestern College	1882	1882	1882	1950
Dordt University[25]	1955	1955	1961	2007
Trinity College	1959	1959	1959	1991

Note: Central College was not included in the study, since it was founded as Baptist College in 1853 and did not become affiliated with the RCA until 1916.

Hope College

After Holland, Michigan, was first settled, Pioneer School, the predecessor to Hope College, was opened by Dutch immigrants in 1851. Hope College received its state charter in 1866 and first admitted women in 1878.[26] Four years later, two women were listed in the graduation records, including a daughter of Hope president Philip Phelps, Frances Few Christie Phelps Otte.[27] Two more women, including Eliza Phelps, graduated in 1885, two in 1887, and one in 1891; and although women were enrolled continuously after 1902, Hope remained "very much a man's college until the erection of Voorhees Hall [1907]."[28]

---

[24] In 2019 Calvin College became Calvin University, https://calvin.edu/about/history/.
[25] In 2019 Dordt College became Dordt University, https://www.dordt.edu/about-dordt/college-history.
[26] https://hope.edu/about/hope-college-history.html.
[27] Jacob Nyenhuis *et alii, Hope College at 150: Anchored in Faith, Educating for Leadership and Service in a Global Society*, 2 vols. (Holland, MI: Van Raalte Press, 2019), 265.
[28] Ibid.

Hope College hired Amy Yates (later, Amy Yates Kremers), its first female faculty member, in 1904, and Christina Van Raalte Gilmore, its first dean of women, in 1907. Before serving as dean of women from 1907 to 1909, Gilmore served as lady assistant and matron from 1887 to 1891 and lady principal from 1898 to 1907.[29] Thus, it appears that, like other private colleges, Hope had hired Gilmore to assist females in the early years of it existence.

Christina Van Raalte Gilmore was the fifth child of Rev. Albertus C. and Christina de Moen Van Raalte. She was born on March 30, 1846, in the Netherlands and immigrated to America with her family when she was six months old.[30] She enrolled in a ladies preparatory course at Olivet College from 1863 to 1866 but apparently did not graduate. In 1869 she married William Brokaw Gilmore, who was part of the first graduating class at Hope College. Upon his ordination as a Reformed minister, he assumed positions as a minister and teacher. After his death in 1884, Christina moved to Holland, Michigan, and three years later was hired by Hope College in various roles to support female students.[31]

By all accounts, Gilmore was highly esteemed as the dean of women. According to Jacob E. Nyenhuis, "Since she was a Van Raalte, and since Van Raalte was highly regarded, I think that that also gave her an advantage. . . . I have seen no evidence that Dean Gilmore was not accepted by the male teachers. Rather, they recognized the need for women to work with all the female students who were coming in, once Voorhees Hall was open to accommodate them."[32]

Hope Academy, in which Hope College was established in 1862, was a coeducational institution when Rev. Phelps became principal in 1859. Phelps was known for his strong support of women during his tenure at Hope Academy; this continued throughout the early years of Hope College,[33] and now for over 150 years.

Later in the history of Hope, however, there were obstacles in the hiring of women faculty. In the 1970s, there was resistance to women in graduate school and on the faculty. Nyenhuis wrote, "When I came to Hope in 1975 as dean for the humanities, only 17 percent of the faculty was comprised of women, and when I became provost in 1984, it was only 20 percent. I worked hard to change those statistics, and by the

---

[29] Ibid., 917.
[30] Ibid., 350.
[31] Jacob Nyenhuis, email, 31 May 2019.
[32] Ibid.
[33] Ibid.

time I retired seventeen years later, women made up almost 40 percent of the faculty."[34]

Today, Hope College is actively supporting women in academics and extracurricular activities. Founded on the principle of hope as described in Hebrews 6:19, "We have this hope, a sure and steadfast anchor of the soul,"[35] Hope's vision is for both males and females.

Calvin University

Calvin College (now University) of Grand Rapids, Michigan, was the first college affiliated with the CRC. It was founded in 1876 as a school of ministry (Calvin Seminary), which began with seven students. In 1900 Calvin College began offering preprofessional programs, and preprofessional education programs would became a popular career choice for women.[36]

In 1901 Calvin first admitted women. In 1905, more than a decade before women's suffrage was affirmed, Anna Groendyk-Houtman became the first woman to graduate from Calvin.[37] In 1926 Johanna Timmer became the first female faculty member and dean of women. Timmer had graduated as class valedictorian from Holland High School at age seventeen. She taught in New Jersey for one year and then returned to Grand Rapids to attend Calvin and earn a bachelor's degree.[38]

Richard Harms, retired curator of Archives in Heritage Hall, said Timmer's appointment "marks a change in the history of higher education . . . Throughout the country, more women were attending college. Calvin's programs in nursing and teaching drew a growing number of female students—and the administration decided that they, like many other institutions, should hire a dean of women."[39]

One of Timmer's legacies to Calvin was to write a code of conduct for female students; it gave instructions on attire, curfews, dating policies, and household responsibilities. These rules were mandatory for all female students, both on and off campus. Timmer read the

---

[34] Ibid.
[35] https://hope.edu/about/hope-college-history.html.
[36] https://calvin.edu/about/history/.
[37] Ibid.
[38] Jessica Folkema, "First Faculty Member: Johanna Timmer," http://calvin.edu/news/archive (9 March 2011).
[39] Ibid.

policies of other colleges in the Midwest and used them as templates to construct Calvin's own code of conduct.[40]

In addition to her duties as dean of women, Timmer taught classes in English and German, wrote articles, gave speeches, earned her master's degree from the University of Michigan, and took graduate courses at two seminaries and a divinity school.[41]

According to Harms, "I don't think anyone had reason to dispute her credentials, but sexism was very prevalent in the 1920s. A number of her male colleagues truly thought she couldn't do the job simply because she was a woman. She refused to be marginalized. If someone pushed, she pushed back."[42] By all accounts, Timmer was an excellent educator and administrator.

Johanna Timmer's letters and correspondence to female students, parents, and staff show that she had great compassion for the female students under her care. In the estimation of Harms, she wanted to do everything possible to help them succeed. She approached her role at Calvin with grace and determination. She proved that being a woman had no impact on her ability to do the job well.[43]

Her legacy lives on at Calvin University through her writings and work in advancing women and their studies in higher education. Many people consider Timmer a pioneer in promoting high academic standards for women and an example of upholding Christian virtues in her work as dean of women and faculty member. She was able to transcend the discrimination of her time and help women grow as people and as academically successful students.

Northwestern College

Founded in Orange City, Iowa, in 1882, Northwestern Academy began as a high school with the enrollment of both men and women, thus, women were admitted to Northwestern at its inception.[44] There were several female faculty members teaching at Northwestern Academy in 1882. Female faculty and students were also active in extracurricular activities in the early years of the college.[45]

---

[40] Ibid.
[41] Ibid.
[42] Ibid.
[43] Ibid.
[44] https://www.nwciowa.edu/about/history-and-heritage.
[45] Greta Grond, email, 30 May 2019.

In 1950, after Northwestern had become a two-year junior college, the position of dean of women was created to address the increase in female enrollment. For the next decade, three women held that position: Marion Hull from 1950 to 1953, who continued as faculty member until 1955 when she left to attend classes at Northwestern University in Evanston, Illinois; Clara Van Til started in the fall of 1953 and left in 1955 to take a one-year teaching appointment in the Netherlands; and Fern Smith was appointed acting dean in June 1955. Clara Van Til returned in 1956 and assumed the role of dean of women but left at the end of the year. In 1957 Fern Smith became dean of students and continued in this role until 1961.[46]

According to Doug Anderson, archivist at Northwestern College, "Fern Smith was an imposing and influential personality in the life of Northwestern Junior College."[47] Smith and other female faculty members were key to the success of the college.

Fern Smith was born in 1898 to Clarence K. and Amanda McAdams Smith near Pullman, Nebraska. She was the fourth child born in a three-room sod house built by her father for his bride in 1892.[36] Smith loved music and took piano lessons from Karl Hillyer at a music school in Delta, Colorado. Hillyer suggested that Smith go to college and major in music; she was musically talented and an excellent scholar. He introduced Smith to George Sadler, a music professor at Central Academy in Pella, Iowa. Fern Smith and her sisters, Leona and Clarice, attended Central Academy.[48]

In 1928 Northwestern Junior College was established and needed a music teacher. President Jacob Heemstra at Northwestern College had taught at Central Academy and knew of Fern Smith's talent, so he invited her to take the music position. It was a good fit for both Northwestern College and Fern Smith. In the early years, the music department put on operettas, such as Victor Herbert's *Babes in Toyland*.[49] Smith was also talented in set and costume design for the operettas.

In the 1930s, Northwestern Junior College and Central Academy formed choirs to present concerts in out-of-state Reformed churches. This was done to attract prospective students and to raise money for the institutions. Since choir members were housed in private homes on the

---

[46] Doug Anderson, email, 30 May 2019
[47] "Fern Smith Story," M. Fern Smith 1895-1982, Northwestern College Archives.
[48] Ibid.
[49] Ibid.

tour, Smith taught her students guest etiquette and proper manners as goodwill ambassadors for the college.[50]

When Northwestern Junior College needed a dean of women to be approved by North Central Association, Smith took the required courses to enable her to fill the position.[51] For five years, Fern Smith was dean of women at Northwestern College; she was an avid supporter of academics for women and a role model for the Christian faith.

Fern Smith is undoubtedly remembered as a pioneer in supporting female students and coeducational extracurricular activities (especially music) at Northwestern College. Her accomplishments have left a legacy for future generations.

Dordt University

Dordt College (now University) was founded in 1953 in Sioux Center, Iowa, as Midwest Christian Junior College. It began as an attempt to fill the need for qualified Christian schoolteachers. Two years later, in 1955, Midwest Christian became a four-year college and changed its name to Dordt College, in honor of the Synod of Dordt, the momentous seventeenth-century meeting of Reformed Churches, which took place in Dordrecht, the Netherlands.

When the college began in 1955, there were thirty-five students enrolled, both men and women, with five male faculty members. Dordt's first four-year BA degrees were awarded to a graduating class of fifty-eight in 1965.[52] Women had been admitted to Dordt College from the first year of its existence, and the first female faculty member was hired in 1961, six years after the college was founded. Charlotte Lothers was hired as assistant instructor in art.[53]

Dordt College did not have a dean of women position in its early years; it hired its first female administrator in 2007. Bethany Schuttinga assumed the position of vice president for student success and supported both male and female students at the college. Records show that the first female board member, Mary Poel, from New Mexico, was elected in 1987.[54]

Throughout its history, Dordt University's foremost mission has been "to equip students, alumni, and the broader community toward

---

[50] Ibid.
[51] Ibid.
[52] https://www.dordt.edu/about-dordt/college-history.
[53] Ingrid Mulder, email, 5 June 2019.
[54] Ibid., 31 Oct. 2019.

Christ-centered renewal in all aspects of contemporary life."[55] It appears that Dordt has fulfilled this mission by providing faith-based education for both men and women throughout its years of existence.

Trinity Christian College

Trinity Christian College is the youngest institution of higher learning included in this study. It was established in 1959, with no direct affiliation with either the RCA or CRC, though it has emphasized a Reformed theological heritage. Trinity has been a coeducational institution since its founding in 1959. In fact, the first class at Trinity College included sixteen female and twenty-one male students.[56]

The first female faculty member was Gerda Bos, hired in April 1959 as one of the original faculty members, and she went on to complete her doctoral degree. One of Bos' job responsibilities was to attend to the concerns of female students.[57] Trinity did not have an official dean of students, but female faculty in the early years were responsible for supporting women on campus in both academics and extracurricular activities.

There were female board of trustee members at Trinity College in the mid-1980s, including Carol Voss (1984-87). The first female administrator, however, was not hired until the 1990s.[58] In 1991 Ginny Carpenter served as assistant dean of students. She held that position until being promoted to dean of students in 1996. Carpenter became vice president for student development in 2001, when the college switched to the VP model. She remained in that role until 2014. Carpenter was the only senior female administrator from 1996 until Dr. Liz Rudenga became provost in 2000. Rudenga served as provost for fourteen years, until becoming interim president for one year.[59]

Thus, Trinity College has been active in supporting women throughout its short existence by admitting women students and hiring women administrators. Trinity includes a statement emphasizing diversity and inclusion: "Trinity acknowledges that inclusivity, diversity, and openness in the context of a Reformed, Christian worldview enhance the preparation our students receive for life and service in a

---

[55] Ibid.
[56] Cathy Mayer, email, 4 Sept. 2019.
[57] Donald Sinnema, *If We Begin with Christ: The Founding of Trinity Christian College, 1952-1960* (Palos Heights, IL: Trinity Christian College, 2009), 10.
[58] Cathy Mayer, email, 4 Sept. 2019.
[59] Ibid.

multicultural and global world."⁶⁰ Thus, throughout its history, Trinity has embraced women and other diverse groups as integral parts of its academic community.

Findings

This examination of women in higher education for five RCA and CRC colleges and universities shows that, although women have made advancements in the area of higher education, there is still work to be done. All colleges and universities in this research project admitted female students to their institutions early in their existence.

It appears that most chief executive officers were supportive of women on their campuses. Many of them were Calvinist ministers who subscribed to Calvin's views that women were equal to men and should receive religious training. They also would have adhered to Calvin's theory that men and women should have complementary relationships, although most CEOs regarded women as weaker than men.⁶¹ This view may account for the varying efforts to hire women in leadership or administrative positions.

There are differences among the five colleges and universities in regard to the dates they hired female professors and administrators. This may be largely due to the historical time period in which they were founded. It took many years for women to assume academic and administrative positions in colleges and universities founded in the 1860s and 1880s. Institutions founded in the 1950s were established as coeducational institutions, so there were more opportunities for women from the outset. The 1950s and 1960s were years of struggle for women, but with that struggle came an attitude of greater equality between men and women and an acceptance of the changing role of women.⁶²

Women who assumed dean of women positions left a legacy for those who came after them. Johanna Timmer, Christina Van Raalte Gilmore, and Fern Smith were all champions in supporting, promoting, and advancing women in their institutions. Their legacy is still evident today. By the 1960s, many institutions were no longer hiring a dean of women but subsuming that role under a dean of students. There was a greater perception that males and females should be treated equally. This is also reflected in the fact that Dordt College and Trinity Christian

---

60 https://www.trnty.edu/about-us/who-we-are (30 Sept. 2019).
61 Sam Arts, *Calvin*, www.cbeinternational.org.
62 Parker, *Historical Role*, 8.

College did not have a dean of women, apparently seeing no need to make the deans gender related.

The climate of acceptance of women at these schools also varied by institution based on its historical context. The reception of women on campus was at times both warm and chilly, based on the societal expectations and historical context of each era. But like most institutions of higher education today, although women in these five institutions now comprise the majority of the student population, they still lag behind men in professorships and administrative positions.

Thus, from an historical perspective, progress for women in higher education in RCA and CRC colleges and universities is occurring, and positive changes have been made. CEOs are promoting women on campus, and programs exist to help women advance their careers in higher education. Steps are indeed being taken to help women achieve parity with men in the future.[63]

Conclusion

Women now comprise the majority of students in institutions of higher learning in the United States, and over the years, women as both students and administrators have seen progress in their advancement in higher education.

There is, however, still a need for women in higher education to move up the career ladder. Training opportunities in leadership positions in higher education may help women obtain more tenured faculty and administrative positions. Through additional training and support from these institutions, women will continue to advance and achieve their career goals.

For RCA and CRC institutions of higher education, the advancement of women has been enhanced by the Calvinist view of equality of the sexes, but barriers still exist due to societal expectations. The key to success for these women has been the support of influential men and women who have paved the road for them.

Throughout history, Reformed and Christian Reformed Church-affiliated colleges and universities have shown their commitment to the advancement of women. It is clear that they have focused on providing excellent, rigorous, faith-based learning for all students, and this philosophy has reinforced their mission to advance God's kingdom on earth.

---

[63] "Moving the Needle," www.acenet.edu.

CHAPTER 16

The Development of Diversity at Western Theological Seminary

Donald J. Bruggink

Diversity, as used in this paper, refers to nationality, ethnicity, and gender. The latter is included because, for eighty-eight years, not one graduate of Western Theological Seminary in Holland, Michigan, was female, and for ninety-eight years, not a single faculty member was a woman. LGBTQ and persons with disabilities are not included in this study, not because of lack of importance, but because of a complete lack of data about them.

Why write about diversity at Western Theological Seminary? At its base, this question is about the ability of the seminary to remain true to the Gospel mandate to "make disciples."[1] Back in the 1950s, it was considered a truism among some who sought to establish new Reformed Churches in the suburbs of the Midwest, that if those new churches attracted too many Dutch, it would limit growth among "Americans." If the biblical command to make disciples includes all people, should not the seminary reflect the diversity inherent not only in that command but also in America?

---

[1] "Therefore, go and make disciples of all nations," Matt. 28:19 (NIV).

Western Theological Seminary was founded for the specific purpose of maintaining the religious perspective of nineteenth-century Dutch immigrants to the Midwest. Although the Dutch in America already had a seminary in New Brunswick, New Jersey, with a reputation as a bastion of conservative orthodoxy, that seminary and its cultural milieu were feared by many immigrants to be corrosive to the faith of the secessionist Dutch. A seminary on the western frontier, therefore, was necessary for their particular needs, theological and cultural. A. C. Van Raalte urged his followers to become American. Nevertheless, the need for ministers who understood the Christian perspective of their Dutch immigrant congregants meant that, in this context, diversity was not highly valued.

The Gospel, however, calls to be spread, and even the immigrant Dutch were not immune to the missionary movement of the nineteenth century. The subject index in the Kennedy commentary on the minutes of Classis Holland from 1848 to 1876 carries the entry "missionary vision of immigrant churches and commitment," and there follow twelve references.[2] The vision was such that even Van Raalte volunteered to answer the call to be a missionary to South Africa, but the classis dissuaded him.[3] Despite the commitment to mission, Western had failed to attract any foreign nationals, even though, in 1872, three Japanese students attending Hope College were baptized in Holland's Hope Church. Two of them, Kumaji Kimura and Motoichiro Oghimi, graduated in 1879 but enrolled in New Brunswick Theological Seminary, graduated, and were ordained by the Classis of Albany in 1882.[4]

Although it was established to provide ministers for the midwestern Dutch immigrants, Western's vision was broader. In the first extant reference to admissions (1889) is the invitation: "The Seminary is open for the admission of students from every denomination of Christians."[5] Although the invitation was open to all, for the first half century, the only non-Dutch/German student at Western appears to be William Brokaw Gilmore (Class of 1869). But even he had Dutch roots,

---

[2] Earl Wm. Kennedy, *A Commentary on the Minutes of the Classis of Holland 1848-1876*, 3 vols. (Holland MI: Van Raalte Press, 2018), 2063.

[3] Kennedy, *Commentary*, 1202n73.

[4] Jacob E. Nyenhuis *et alii*, *Hope College at 150: Anchored in Faith, Educating for Leadership and Service in a Global Society*, 2 vols. (Holland, MI: Van Raalte Press, 2019), 592-98.

[5] *Catalogue of the Western Theological Seminary of the Reformed Church in America, Holland, Michigan. 1889-1890*, W88-0733, Joint Archives of Holland (JAH). This is the first reference to admissions for theological studies in any known source.

The Development of Diversity at Western Theological Seminary   291

for his mother was Margaret Van Nostrand, and he was the son-in-law of Van Raalte. Until World War II, there had been among the student body no more than five students whose surnames were not of Dutch or German ancestry.

This paucity of ethnic diversity was also true of the board of superintendents, who controlled the composition of the faculty. From the inception of the seminary until 1895, all board members were ordained ministers of the Reformed Church. In that year, the Synod of Chicago added the first of three Reformed Church elders. In 1920 that number rose to four out of a total of twenty-seven superintendents—the high point prior to 1939. Diversity among the governing body was provided only in terms of those three or four laymen mixed in with the clergy, all of the superintendents being members of the Reformed Church in America.[6]

Of the faculty, all were also members of the Reformed Church in America. The only faculty members who were not of Dutch or German ancestry until 1975 were John Walter Beardslee and his son John Jr. The elder John Walter was of Connecticut English ancestry (although he was born in Sandusky, Ohio) and a graduate of Rutgers University and New Brunswick Theological Seminary. Two of Western's professors were born in the Netherlands, and the rest grew up in the Midwest, with thirteen of the seventeen having attended Hope College and three at Rutgers. Seven had received their theological education at New Brunswick and eight at Western. All were ministers of the Reformed Church with college and seminary educations, and subsequent to seminary professorships, *all* were given honorary doctorates.[7] Nonetheless, the lack of a professional degree, with its inherent multiple perspectives, could be a limitation to educational diversity.

A notable exception to that rule was Prof. Nicholas M. Steffens (1884-95). When only twenty and a member of the Altreformierte Kirche in Emden, Steffens travelled to Constantinople to teach at the Scottish Free Church's Italian School for Jews. It was there that he met a Scottish lady missionary, Jane Graham Sutherland, whom he married. During his four years of teaching and studying in Constantinople,

---

[6]   W88-0733 catalogs, JAH.
[7]   Kennedy, *Commentary*, 1417n97. Russell L. Gasero, *Historical Directory of the Reformed Church in America, 1628-2000* (Grand Rapids, MI: Eerdmans, 2001), 20. The *Historical Directory*, from which much subsequent data has been taken, lists all ministers serving the RCA and its predecessors since 1628, as well as presidents and theological professors.

he also experienced a call to ministry.[8] Being largely self-taught (an accomplished autodidact), when he returned to Emden, he enrolled in the theological seminary in Kampen and was allowed to begin with the final year's courses, at the end of which, he successfully took the literary exam and the theological exam in the same week. After having served three congregations of the Altreformierte Kirche, Steffens accepted a call to the Reformed Church of Silver Creek, Illinois. This was followed by a call to the Reformed Church of Zeeland, Michigan, and a professorship at Western (1884). His honorary doctorate was received from the University of Jena, Germany, in 1886.[9]

From Western's inception in 1866 until 1939, only John W. Beardslee Jr. had a PhD, and he taught at Western from only 1913 to 1917, after which, he taught at New Brunswick Theological Seminary, becoming its president in 1935 and serving there until 1947. Rev. Winfield Burggraff, ThD, was a lector in systematic theology from 1931 to 1934. That was the limit of diversity in advanced professional degrees in over a half-century of professorates.

There was an incipient portent of change when in 1939 the three new members of the faculty all had professional degrees: Rev. Lester J. Kuyper arrived with a ThD from Union Seminary in New York City, Rev. William Goulooze with a ThD from the Free University in Amsterdam, and Rev. George H. Mennenga with a PhD from Southern Theological Seminary in Louisville, Kentucky.

It was also in 1939, as World War II broke out in Europe, that formerly cohesive Dutch immigrant communities began to come under assault. In particular, major movements of populations had a lasting impact on Dutch enclaves. One result was the diversification of Western's student body. I came to Western as a student in 1951. The graduating class of that year bore the first fruits of the diversifying effects of WWII. Antonio Moncada from Siracusa, Italy, a graduate of the Royal Magisterial in Tripoli, received his BD from Western and accepted a call to a church in Saskatchewan, Canada. That same year, several other non-Dutch students graduated from Western: two African Americans, Wilson Duke Richardson and Samuel Williams; one Korean, Young Chang Chun; and one Native American, Wendell Chino. During my first year, I benefited from the presence of "diverse" students. Peter

---

[8] George Harinck, *"We live presently under a waning moon": Nicolaus Martin Steffens as Leader of the Reformed Church in America in the West in Years of Transition (1878-1895)* (Holland, MI: Van Raalte Press, 2013) 9.

[9] Harinck, *"We live presently,"* 9-11, 79.

Hsieh and Wesley Shao were of the Chinese diaspora. Two more were from Germany: Reinhard Koester from the city of Hamburg was a student at the University of Marburg and came on a World Council of Churches Fellowship, and Paul Diez came from Nuremberg and graduated with Western's BD in 1954.[10]

I became especially close to Reinhard. Having been raised in a very traditional Reformed, theologically orthodox background, I had never encountered what I then perceived to be a "heretical" seminarian. Reinhard was a follower of Rudolph Bultmann, a proponent of "demythologizing" the Bible, an approach in sharp contrast to my orthodox Calvinist background. Reinhard never insisted I believe as either he or Bultmann, but he did defend the latter's Christian faith, which saw this brilliant theologian going to church every Sunday to listen to rather simple sermons. Although I never strayed from my professor's admonition to not believe everything Bultmann said, I nonetheless benefited from and began to enjoy living with diversity. Unfortunately, only two more foreign students graduated during the decade of the fifties, Paul Shih from Taiwan and Paul Hayashi from Japan. Except for the occasional "special," non-degree-seeking student, there was no further diversification of Western's student body during the 1950s.

As for my formal theological education, I found it excellent in many respects. At the head of the seminary was Rev. John R. Mulder, who had come in 1928 to teach practical theology; he moved to systematic theology in 1936 and in 1942 was named president. During my student days at Western, Mulder was a superb teacher of homiletics. He saw the seminary through the war years and the influx of students that came at the war's end. His faculty consisted of Simon Blocker, William Goulooze, Lester Kuyper, and George Mennenga. Rev. Richard C. Oudersluys arrived in 1942 with a ThB and as a candidate for a PhD from the University of Chicago. In 1953 Rev. M. Eugene Osterhaven came with a PhD from Princeton Theological Seminary, and in that same year, Elton M. Eenigenburg arrived with a PhD from the University of Chicago. All were ministers of the Reformed Church in America but with considerable diversity in their professional backgrounds.

[10] Over the decades, since inception, graduation records were variously printed in faculty minutes and/or catalogs. Registrar records involving names were denied access. The most consistent records are the graduation photos, of which, two (1977 & 1978) have been lost. Faculty minutes seldom give information as to how foreign students came to Western.

Mulder's leadership promoted diversity in the student body and in the professional education of his faculty. At the same time, he was very aware of the inadequacy of the seminary's physical presence. But welcoming a new and enlarged faculty, plus successfully planning the building of new structures, left little time or energy to deal with questions of curriculum. A prince of the pulpit, President Mulder's stature in the church was such that in 1955 he dedicated a splendid, debt-free, architecturally cohesive, Georgian colonial structure, embracing a chapel, a commons, a kitchen, faculty offices, and classrooms.

Only five years later, however, lapses in Mulder's memory resulted in the board of trustees terminating his role at the seminary in favor of Rev. Harold Englund, pastor of Second Reformed Church of Zeeland. Of Scandinavian descent, Englund was part of the post WWII student diversity at Western, having graduated in 1950.

Changes began to take place immediately. The first faculty meeting under the new president was held on September 6, 1960, and the second was barely three days later, on September 9. Englund presented a plan "to have foreign students on our campus."[11] Faculty meetings were convened weekly, and the curriculum came under review. Englund began to actively recruit students, including those from outside the RCA; this was perhaps the first intentional attempt to further diversify the student body. Even the appearance of the seminary catalog underwent a major change. More substantively, however, although women had been permitted to enroll in BD classes as non-degree-seeking students from time to time, for the first time, a woman, Elsie Wen-Hua Shih Law, was allowed to enroll in studies leading to a BD.

Reforms proceeded with alacrity, and on February 10, 1961, the decision to grant a master of theology (ThM) degree passed unanimously. To further prepare the way for a proposed master of religious education (MRE) degree, Rachel Henderlite was invited to speak, becoming the first woman in a professional capacity to lecture at Western Seminary. On March 23, 1961, President Englund interviewed a woman, "Mrs. Egbert Lubbers," for the position of professor of religious education, and on August 13, 1962, he welcomed "Mrs. Elaine Lubbers" to the faculty.[12]

At the same meeting in which Elaine Lubbers was introduced, laudatory resolutions were passed in support of Englund, who had announced his intention to resign. Then president of Grand Valley

---

[11] Unfortunately, the plan is unrecorded in the faculty minutes.
[12] Faculty minutes of 23 March and 13 Aug. 1962, respectively.

State College (now University), Arend Lubbers observed that "Harold Englund was not a plow horse but a race horse."[13] It might be inferred that the faculty had grown tired of trying to keep up with their president.

Diversity in both ethnicity and gender was evident at Western before Englund left. In May 1963, BD degrees were received by Stanley H. K. Lin, Moses Keng, Jeremy Chung Hian Law, and his wife, Elsie Wen-Hua Shih Law. As far as the evidence shows, Elsie Law was the first woman allowed to study for—and be granted—the degree of master of divinity (MDiv). That the road was opened for the ordination of a woman to work among the Chinese offers two rather diverse perspectives on the Chinese and American churches. As early as 1916, "the South Fukien Synod upheld the right of churches to appoint women as deacons," and in 1936, the Reformed mission district conferences for consistory members were composed of one third women "including not only deaconesses but also several elders."[14]

On September 13, 1963, Herman J. Ridder (WTS 1952) was installed as president of Western. The faculty, exhausted by the rigors of Englund's presidency, was not to be given a rest by this young president. The catalog of 1965-66 includes a supplement on the pending "Century Two Curriculum," but that of 1967-68 touts this new curriculum as established fact. By the catalog of 1970-71, Western had agreed to the invitation to merge with New Brunswick. Together they produced the novel "Bi-Level, Multi-Site Curriculum," utilizing both campuses, faculties, and student bodies.

Ridder was open not only to curriculum and administrative diversity but also to innovation in teaching. Accordingly, when I proposed teaching church history in Europe—where it had happened—the idea was supported. And although this initiative did not bring foreign students into the seminary, it did take seminary students into foreign environments, where they could experience something of the development of the faith and its complexities. Ridder's support was evidenced by a full-page spread in the catalog promoting the program, as well as by subsequent photographs, including those of Western Seminary students meeting Pope Paul VI.[15] The success of the program was proven by thirty-one further Western Christendom Travel Seminars

---

[13] Personal conversation with the author.
[14] Gerald F. De Jong, *The Reformed Church in China 1842-1951* (Grand Rapids, MI: Eerdmans, 1992), 206-7.
[15] *Student Guide, 1967-68*, 10; *Century II, Western Theological Seminary 1969-70*, 15, W88-0733, JAH.

(later, Intercultural Immersion Experiences), each from two to six weeks in length. Overseas study continued to live on, and during the Western Seminary presidency of Dennis Voskuil, it was seen as so desirable that overseas study was made mandatory. Taking place during the January term, the immersion experiences have ranged from Chiapas and the Mexican borderlands to Oman and India.

On September 4, 1963, the master of religious education (MRE) was changed to the master of Christian education (MCE). One would have anticipated an influx of MCE students under the leadership of the gifted Elaine Lubbers, but her contributions were primarily in improving the BD course offerings. And although many of the students rejoiced in her creative contributions to the rapidly changing curriculum, others were unable to transcend their heritage of patriarchy and accept that a "woman" could teach them anything. Family concerns with her late husband's aging parents, for whom she was the only caregiver, resulted in Elaine's resignation in 1965 to take the position of minister of Christian education at the Eastminster Presbyterian Church in Grand Rapids.[16] In her place, Rev. Hugh Koops, from the University of Chicago Divinity School, was appointed assistant professor of Christian education.

The impact of the MCE program on diversity within the halls of Western Seminary during the 1960s and 1970s was not what one might have expected. Charlotte Heinen was the first woman to graduate with an MCE in 1965, and Ruth Kleinheksel followed in 1968. Of men of color was Hsi Ming (Andrew) Hsieh in 1969; the other ten MCE graduates during the 1960s were Caucasian males.

In 1963 the seminary had approved the establishment of the MCE degree to meet the perceived need of the churches. In the 1969-70 catalog, however, the Christian educator is five times referred to as "he" and not once as "she."[17] The first professor employed in the program is named in the 1974-75 catalog as "Mrs. John Stewart." In the 1960s, two women were granted the MCE, whereas eleven males received theirs. In the 1970s, the number of male graduates was eight, and six white women and four of color received the MCE.

As with the MCE, the inception of the ThM initially had little effect on the diversity of the student body at Western Seminary. It offered pastors an opportunity to improve their scholarship while earning an

---

[16] George Brown, "Finding a Place at the Table" [Elaine Lubbers at WTS], in *Tools for Understanding, Essays in Honor of Donald J. Bruggink* (Grand Rapids, MI: Eerdmans, 2008), 31-65.

[17] *Century II* (catalog), 2-3, W88-0733, JAH.

advanced degree. The catalog description made this very clear with its emphasis on the writing of a thesis on a subject approved by the faculty in its conception and completion. In 1961 six pastors, all white males, enrolled in the ThM. The first to receive the degree in 1962 was Rev. Harry Buis. The second in 1963 was Ronald T. Smith, with nine more Caucasian males enrolled. In 1965 Stanley H. K. Lin received his ThM, but at the same time, there were fourteen Caucasian males enrolled in the program. Following the graduation of Indian students Thotathill Mathai George (1968) and L. V. Azariah (1969), there remained twenty-three white males enrolled in the program in 1970.

The pattern of few non-white, non-male graduates from the large pool of candidates continued, so that, in the midst of the pressure on faculty from two rapidly changing curriculums, it was decided to bar the admission of new ThM students beginning with the 1973-74 academic year. The description of the ThM disappeared from catalogs until the 1989-91 edition. Nonetheless, during these thirteen years, students continued to enroll and graduate with ThM degrees upon completion of their work. In total, eight students graduated with ThM degrees, of whom four were white males, together with Mahamimai Rufus of India, Soo Am Park of Korea, and Makomoto Suzuki and Katsuhiro Itoh of Japan. The fact that John H. Piet had been a missionary in India from 1940 to 1960, and that I. John Hesselink had been a missionary in Japan from 1953 to 1972, assured a warm and knowledgeable welcome for Indian and Japanese minister-students.

In the RCA, the issue of women being ordained to the office of Minister of Word and Sacrament was becoming increasingly heated during the 1970s.[18] For the issue of diversity in the seminary, it meant that, in anticipation of ordination, ever-increasing numbers of women were opting for the MDiv, rather than the MCE. In 1971 Charlotte Assink was granted the MDiv degree, and in 1976, three more women—Nancy Van Wyk, Joyce Borgmann De Velder, and Elaine Kay—received their MDivs, followed by four more in 1977 and another four in 1978. The 1979 Synod, after considerable wrangling, ratified the ordination of women, thereby catching up with Western Seminary's graduates.

During these years, there was also increased diversity in faculty background, training, and governance. On the faculty side, in the 1960s were Gerrit ten Zythof, with theological studies in the Netherlands and a PhD from the Divinity School of the University of Chicago; myself,

---

[18] For a detailed account, see Lynn Japinga, *Loyalty and Loss: The Reformed Church in America, 1945-1994* (Grand Rapids, MI: Eerdmans, 2013).

with a PhD from the University of Edinburgh, New College; John H. Piet, with his PhD from Union Theological Seminary, New York; and James I. Cook, with his ThD from Princeton Seminary. There was also the appointment of the first woman, nonordained, in the person of Elaine E. Lubbers. In 1966 Hugh Koops, a candidate for a PhD from University of Chicago Divinity School, came to the faculty before moving to New Brunswick in 1971. Sonja Stewart arrived in 1971 with an MRE from Pittsburg Theological Seminary and as a candidate for a PhD at Notre Dame.

Under President Hesselink (1974-84), who himself had his PhD from the University of Basel, new faculty included William L. Schutter, with a New Brunswick Seminary MDiv and a PhD candidacy at Cambridge University, England. Also showing greater diversity in his undergraduate work, Christopher Kaiser arrived with a bachelor's degree from Harvard, from whence he matriculated for his MDiv at Gordon Conwell and PhDs from the University of Colorado in astrophysics and New College, Edinburgh, in theology; and in 1983, Dr. Virgil Cruz, an Hispanic African American, with a Dutch wife (both of whom spoke Dutch), joined the faculty with a bachelor's degree from Houghton College, an MDiv from Pittsburgh-Xenia, and a PhD from the Free University, Amsterdam.

Before leaving the 1970s and 1980s, something should be said about the tension sometimes created by diversity. Since I do not know the extent to which this illustration is totally factual or largely apocryphal, I will not divulge names, dates, or locations. It involves both Hope College and Western Seminary, insofar as a very gifted African American student who, while attending these institutions, met a young woman from one of the Dutch suburbs, and they fell in love. As the relationship grew ever more serious, the young woman felt it necessary to introduce this handsome man to her parents—which she did with fear and trepidation. Her parents, however, dealt with the shock with amazing calm, and as the young couple left the house, the husband commented to his wife: "Well, at least he's not Christian Reformed."

Under President Marvin D. Hoff (1985-94), a graduate of Hope College and Western Seminary and holding a *doctorundus* from Kampen Seminary in the Netherlands, diversity continued to grow among the faculty. New members included Thomas Boogaart, with his PhD from the University of Groningen, the Netherlands; Paul Smith, with master's degrees from the University of Iowa and the University of Toronto; John Schmidt, a doctoral candidate at Western Michigan University; Charles

Van Engen, an MDiv graduate from Fuller Seminary with a ThD from the Free University of Amsterdam; Robin Mattison with degrees from the University of Delaware and the University of Chicago Divinity School, as well as being a PhD candidate at Vanderbilt University; Richard A. Rhem with a PhD from Leiden University, the Netherlands; George Brown Jr., with advanced degrees from Princeton Seminary and Michigan State University; James V. Brownson, with a PhD from Princeton Seminary; George R. Hunsberger, also with a PhD from Princeton Seminary; Diane Maodush-Pitzer, with a bachelor's degree from Northern Illinois University, along with her MDiv from Western Seminary; Jay R. Weener, with an honorary DD from Hope College.

In terms of all of the degree programs, in the 1970s, there were seventeen "diverse" graduates, of whom sixteen were women, earning seven MCEs and ten MDivs (one high-achieving woman earned one of each). In the 1980s, there were fifty "diverse" graduates, of whom, forty-seven were women, together holding twenty-four MDivs, twenty-two MCEs, and three ThMs. But the statistics get even more impressive upon entering the 1990s, when 110 women graduated, among whom, fifty-six earned MDivs, thirty-six MCEs, and thirteen ThMs. Among them were fifteen women of other nationalities and ethnicities, with five earning MCEs and ten ThMs. In total, between 1963 and 2019, Western Seminary awarded either a BD or an MDiv degree to 163 women.

These remarkable statistics require interpretation, crucial to which is the context of the seminary. Under President Hoff (1985-93), the ThM was rewritten and appears in the 1989-91 catalog as a twelve-month program, with the stipulation that at least half of the students be from "outside North America ... based on their intent and ability to relate theological study to the social, cultural and historical contexts of their ministries."[19] The program was not only for their intellectual and experiential enrichment but also for the enrichment of Western Seminary faculty and students. Scholarships were also to be provided when necessary. That the program was a success is witnessed to by the number and diversity of origins and its continued success into the present. In 1989 four ThMs were conferred on a diverse constituency, including to Mercy Rani Bai of India, Sayuri Okazaki of Japan, and Stephen Shu and Samuel Tiniyiko Maluleke of the United States. In the 1990s, fifty-two foreign nationals received ThMs. In the first decade of the new millennium, fifty-one were granted ThMs, and in the second decade, thirty-one. In all, the ThM program attracted ministers from

[19] *1989-1991 Catalog, Western Theological Seminary*, 19, W88-0733, JAH.

thirty-five countries, from Azerbaijan to Zambia. It is without a doubt that the ThM as rewritten during the Hoff presidency has contributed the most to an international presence at Western Seminary, which continues right into the present. It should also be noted that the residential housing on Thirteenth and Fourteenth Streets (also initiated by Hoff), available to international students, has also contributed to the success of the program.

Sonja Stewart assumed the post of director of the MCE program in 1971. Under her leadership, there was a gradual increase in the program into the 1980s and 1990s, when it enjoyed major growth with more than eighty graduates, all but ten of whom were women. Nonetheless, during more recent years, the fact that women may enroll in the MDiv and be ordained, combined with an ample supply of ordained personnel to fill educational roles, has resulted in a gradual reduction in candidates for the MCE both at home and abroad. And the reality that MCEs or MREs are well below the ordained graduates on the pay scale does not help to make those degrees attractive.

During the presidency of Dennis Voskuil (1994-2008), the seminary took a major step toward continued growth in the establishment of the distance-learning MDiv, which allows men and women to earn the degree with minimal time away from family and employment. It, too, has contributed to the growing diversity at Western Seminary by allowing those employed in widely diverse geographical and urban areas to obtain an MDiv online. This is a challenging program, in part, because it can hamper the student-to-student and student-to-faculty dynamic that reinforces diverse perspectives as personally held, rather than as abstract notions on term papers.

During the presidency of Timothy Brown (2008-19), the move toward the diversity that is America continued. In 2010 the Faculty Fellows Program was instituted with the successive appointments of three African Americans: Eric Williams with a BA from the University of Illinois at Chicago, an MA from McCormick Theological Seminary, an MDiv from the Divinity School of Duke University, and a PhD candidacy at the University of Birmingham, UK; Chris Dorsey, with an MDiv from Garrett Evangelical Theological Seminary, a graduate certificate in African studies from Northwestern University, and a PhD from the University of Chicago; and Brian Madison, assistant professor of theology, who earned his BSA at Drew University, his MDiv from Princeton Seminary, and is pursuing doctoral work at Duke University.

With an eye to the future, in 2016 Brown brought Alvin Padilla to Western to serve as vice president of strategic initiatives, director of advanced degrees, and professor of New Testament. Padilla earned a BS at Villanova University, an Mdiv at Gordon-Conwell Theological Seminary, and a PhD from Drew University. In 2017, under his auspices, the Hispanic Ministries Program was launched.

Brown has left Cook Library in the capable hands of the seminary's first Hispanic professor, Daniel Flores, director of Cook Library and assistant professor. Flores earned his bachelor's degree at Southeastern College, his MA at Gordon-Conwell Theological Seminary, his MDiv from Princeton Theological Seminary, an MSLIS at Drexel University, and his MPhil and PhD degrees from Drew University.

In 2019 Felix Theonugraha became president of Western Seminary. Of Indonesian parentage and Chinese ethnicity, he is a graduate of the University of California, Berkeley, with an MDiv and PhD from the Trinity Evangelical Divinity School.

A final observation

From its founding in 1866 until 1939, the student body of Western Seminary was all male, with only five students whose surnames did not seem Dutch or German. During those years, the faculty was of similar ethnicity, as was the board of superintendents. But much has changed. Of the last five classes to graduate, four saw the combination of women and people of color outnumbering white males. The three top administrative positions are now held by non-Caucasians. Rev. Albertus Christiaan Van Raalte wanted his *kolonie* to become Americanized. I wonder if he would be pleased that Western Seminary is beginning to look more like America. If it involves a more effective mission to the world, I suspect that he would.

Part III

Other Legacies

CHAPTER 17

Dutch Immigrants and Education: Where Winning Meant Losing[1]

Robert Schoone-Jongen[2]

On November 22, 1900, Thanksgiving Day, the SS *Amsterdam* eased into the Holland America Line pier in Hoboken, two weeks out of Rotterdam. The ship's company included fourteen second-class passengers who, as real paying customers, avoided the Ellis Island ordeal. Eight of the passengers belonged to one family, the Minnemas. The ship's clerk recorded their destination as 50 Clinton Street, Paterson, New Jersey, the home of Rev. Frederick G. Dekker, pastor of the First Holland Reformed Church.[3]

The family did not emigrate to escape poverty or persecution but to dodge the military draft. Their oldest son, an apprenticed carpenter, was just shy of his seventeenth birthday. The father, John Minnema, an

---

[1] The keynote address at the AADAS conference in Grand Rapids, MI, 16 June 2019.
[2] At the outset, I want to express my gratitude to the Van Raalte Institute, Hope College, Holland, MI, for a generous research grant that enabled me to assemble the materials that made this paper what it is and to two individuals who opened the archives of the Eastern Christian School to me during a visit in April 2019: Tom Dykhouse (executive director and head of school) and Nancy Knyfd Hemrick (records management assistant).
[3] Passenger manifest, SS *Amsterdam*, departed Rotterdam, 8 Nov. 1900.

305

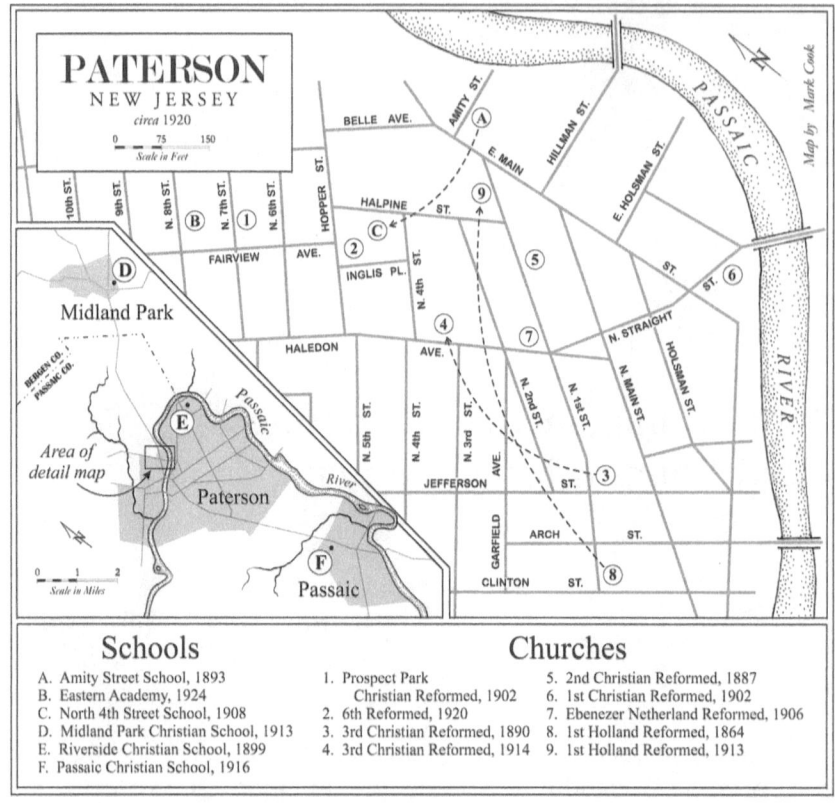

Paterson, New Jersey, ca. 1920

ardent Kuyperian and a faithful member of the Plantage Gereformeerde Kerk in Amsterdam, owned the neighborhood grocery store, and he dreaded the thought of his son being led away into the debauched life of a soldier.[4]

Years later, the oldest daughter, fifteen when the family arrived in Hoboken, recalled that no one had met them at the pier that day because there was a rumor that the ship had foundered somewhere in the North Atlantic. More likely, it being a holiday, Rev. Helenius Nies, pastor of Paterson's Union Reformed Church and denizen of the Hoboken docks, was conducting a service. But, somehow, the family ran the gauntlet of railroad facilities that lay to the south of the dock

---

[4] Baptism notation on birth certificate of Teunis Minnema (in the author's collection). Frances Greydanus, "History of John and Frances Minnema," 2, typescript in Heritage Hall, archives for the CRC, Calvin Theological Seminary, and Calvin University, in the Hekman Library at Calvin University.

John Minnema family, ca. 1904

and located the Jersey City passenger terminal of the Erie Railroad Company. From there, if they had taken the midafternoon local, they would have arrived in Paterson in about one hour.[5]

Clinton Street was about a mile through a maze of streets from the Erie station. Minnema could communicate enough with an Irish barkeep to prompt him to send someone to summon Rev. Dekker, and as they awaited his arrival, the Irishman beckoned the rest of the family into his establishment and gave them their first American meal, free of charge. According to Greydanus, John's daughter, "When the minister arrived, John and Frances asked about the location of the Christian school. The minister said, 'That poor Dutch School!'"[6]

Although he had won the struggle to find Rev. Dekker, the immigrant newcomer immediately lost esteem in the dominie's eyes. John Minnema never joined Rev. Dekker's congregation but opted for the Second Christian Reformed Church located several blocks farther up North First Street, a congregation that ardently supported "that poor Dutch school."

Amity Street Christian School is emblematic of the topic the AADAS conference was considering. It was organized by religiously inclined immigrants determined to do two things: train their children to be Dutch Calvinists and prepare them to live in the United States

[5] Ibid.
[6] Ibid., 3.

Amity Street Christian School

without losing that heritage. Which begs the question: can cultural artifacts endure, intact, in a different environment? The school's founders believed the answer was an emphatic "yes," but we know it was not that simple. Was successfully building a private school really the success its supporters sought? The Dutch were not the only immigrants in Paterson hoping to directly control what their children learned. In 1900 the Paterson board of education maintained eighteen primary and grammar schools, a high school, a technical school, a commercial department, and a normal school. In addition, Paterson supported two Dutch Christian schools, one German Lutheran school, two Hebrew schools, and a dozen Catholic schools, including Our Lady of Lourdes, which catered to Dutch Catholics.[7] But the price for establishing these schools was isolation and suspicion in the eyes of the broader community and dissention within each of the immigrant communities. Victory came at a cost.

The Vereeniging voor Gereformeerde Middelbaar Onderwijs voor Paterson en Omgeving (Society for Reformed Higher Education for Paterson and Vicinity) was organized on August 17, 1892. The driving force behind the school was Rev. Peter Van Vlaanderen, pastor of First Christian Reformed Church, with an assist from Rev. Roelof Drukker

---

[7] *Griffith's Paterson and Passaic Directory, 1900* (Washington, DC: Joshua Griffith, 1900), 66, 931. Raymond J. Kupke, *Living Stones: A History of the Catholic Church in the Diocese of Paterson* (Clifton, NJ: Diocese of Paterson, 1987), 139. Annita Zalenski and Robert J. Hazenkamp Jr., *Ecclesiastical History of Paterson, NJ: A History of Paterson's Churches, Synagogues, and Missions, 1792-1942* (Paterson: Passaic County Historical Society Genealogy Club, 2011), 39-40.

Rev. Peter Van Vlaanderen

of the recently organized Second Christian Reformed Church. First Church had staggered into the Christian Reformed fold in 1864, after successively operating as a Reformed, an Independent, and an Under the Cross congregation in the span of eight years. Thereafter, for almost thirty years, the congregation's leaders, both ordained and lay, were badgered at classis and synod meetings in Grand Rapids and Chicago about Paterson's lack of a Christian school. For almost thirty years, the delegates had pleaded poverty. Van Vlaanderen's arrival from the Netherlands in 1889 broke the cycle.[8]

Van Vlaanderen was born in 1850 in Oost Souburg, Zeeland, and graduated from the Kampen theological school in 1879. He was ordained in the Gereformeerde Kerk that same year and installed as minister in Westmaas. Four years later, he accepted a call to Yerseke. In 1889, when the call he had solicited from Paterson came, he accepted. As a devotee of Abraham Kuyper, the dominie immediately took steps

---

[8] "Rededication of North Fourth Street Christian School" (1933), 8-20, Eastern Christian School Archive (hereafter EC Archive), North Haledon, NJ. *Seventy-Fifth Anniversary: First Christian Reformed Church of Paterson, 1856-1931* (Paterson, n.p., 1931), 22. *History of First Christian Reformed Church*, HH. "Rev. P. Van Vlaanderen, In Memoriam," *The Banner* (5 Nov. 1908): 714. "Rev. Van Vlaanderen Expires at Rochester," *The Morning Call* (31 Oct. 1908): 1, 16. Richard H. Harms, ed., *Historical Directory of the Christian Reformed Church* (Grand Rapids, MI: Historical Committee of the Christian Reformed Church in North America, 2004), 369.

Midland Park Christian School

to start a proper school. First came Dutch language classes that were held in the two Christian Reformed churches during the summers of 1890 and 1891. In 1892 the school society was organized with Van Vlaanderen and Dekker as the president and vice president of the board. Classes began in Second Church's basement (because it had one) and in November 1893, the students paraded two blocks from the church to the school on Amity Street. Two years later, an addition doubled the size of the building, and in 1899, a second school—"Building B"—opened across the Passaic River in the Riverside section, where yet another Christian Reformed congregation had been organized in 1896. Eventually two more Christian schools would open in Midland Park and Passaic in 1913 and 1916, respectively.[9]

A major motive behind the Amity Street School was the Dutch language. The Christian Reformed Church, from its earliest days, regarded Dutch as essential, not just for liturgical reasons, but for educational purposes as well. The hallowed theologians and devotional writers dating back to the seventeenth century had all written in Dutch. Then there was the Statenbijbel, the Dutch equivalent of the King James for English readers. Their faith had been formulated in Dutch.

---

[9] "Celebrating God's Faithfulness: Midland Park Christian School, West Wing Dedication and 75th Anniversary Celebration, October 23, 1988." "History of Passaic Christian School," EC Archive.

Passaic Christian School

The dominies had been educated in it. The laymen had been catechized in it, memorized the questions and answers in it, and sang the psalms in it. Some folks actually believed God's first utterance had literally been, "*Daar zij licht!*"[10] If the faith was to be conveyed to the next generation, Dutch was essential, not just for the here and now, but for eternity. And the Amity Street School devoted all but forty-five minutes of every school day to instruction in the Dutch language.[11]

The first teachers were sought from the Netherlands to ensure linguistic, theological, and pedagogical purity. Luring them to Paterson proved impossible. The Dutch community and its schools stood amid the stench, soot, and noises of dye houses, a gas works, slaughterhouses, the river, and two railroads. Eventually—and reluctantly—the board of directors began to look to Grand Rapids for teachers.[12]

The school suffered from perception problems in the community. Their adoption of the exclusive "Christian school" label seemed presumptuous to the Lutherans and Catholics, who also maintained

---

[10] "Let there be light." Gen 1:3.
[11] Richard Ostling, "In thy Light shall we see Light: Eastern Christian Schools, 1892-1992" (Eastern Christian School Association of North Haledon, NJ, 1992), 8, kept in author's personal collection.
[12] For one account of how the school recruited teachers, see Ed Gerritsen, "Adrianus G. D. Gerritsen Jr.," *Origins* (Spring 2010): 28-33.

DUTCH REFORMED EDUCATION

Riverside School

separate schools. The community had other names for the school on Amity Street. The 1900 city directory named it the Holland-English school, with School "B" in Riverside listed as the English-Holland school. Though Dutch was gradually de-emphasized in the schools (to the great consternation of Rev. Klaas Van Goor, one of the Christian Reformed ministers), the Dutch label stuck.[13] In 1915 the New Jersey state census asked that respondents specify the schools their children attended. Even in the very neighborhood where the Christian school stood, the census taker, a son of Dutch immigrants, recorded "Holland School" for the children who attended the school. Prospect Park's census taker and the school's attorney, Peter Hofstra, listed the students as attending the "Christian" school. John Walchenbach, another longtime board member, also insisted on the "Christian School" label when a non-Dutch census taker visited his home in Paterson.[14]

[13] In 1907 the board appointed a committee to consider the language issues, with Rev. Klaas Van Goor, minister of Second Christian Reformed Church, as a conspicuous presence on it. This followed on the heels of a split vote on the board regarding the stone inscription that would be placed over the front door of the new school. On a vote of 5-7, the members rejected "School for Christian Instruction." "Christian School" was adopted 7-4. Board minutes, 30 July 1907, 24 April 1907, EC Archive.

[14] *New Jersey State Census, 1915.* Manuscript schedules for City of Paterson, County of Passaic (Wards One and Three); Borough of Prospect Park, County of Passaic; Borough of Midland Park, County of Bergen.

The language issue also helped alienate potential supporters in several Dutch immigrant congregations, especially those whose pastors had graduated from New Brunswick Theological Seminary. Among them, Rev. Frederick G. Dekker (who had sneered at John Minnema's choice of schools), an 1892 Kampen graduate, who had enrolled at New Brunswick Seminary and graduated in 1896.[15]

The leaders of the Reformed Church in America in the New York metropolitan area tended to view the hidebound Christian Reformed minsters and congregations as embarrassing, what with their refusal to shift swiftly toward English and their self-righteousness defense of the exquisite beauty of a foreign tongue. Sixth Reformed, the largest Reformed church in Paterson (and third largest in the entire denomination) was more sympathetic to the separate school, as long as the congregation was led by a Dutch-educated, Dutch-speaking minister. When Rev. Elbert van Hetloo retired in 1906 and the consistory voted to replace him with an English-speaking Dutch immigrant, that support dwindled. A substantial number of members, repulsed at this Americanization move, walked out of the fateful congregational meeting and organized the Ebenezer Netherland Reformed Congregation, a group that provided significant support to the school. Although the support of Sixth Reformed for the Christian school diminished, it did not disappear.[16]

Paterson's ecclesiastical history caused a rift among the Christian Reformed churches. There were the immigrant congregations—First, Second, Fourth, and Prospect Park—organized into Classis Hudson. Then there were the churches that had once been part of the True Dutch Reformed Protestant Church that joined the Christian Reformed in 1890 as Classis Hackensack. These were English-speaking congregations, with roots reaching back to the days of New Netherland. Paterson's Third Christian Reformed Church was at the core of this group, and they had to be coaxed into supporting a school that taught in Dutch. Their support would be reluctant, at best, until the arrival in

---

[15] Peter N. VandenBerge, *Historical Directory of the Reformed Church in America, 1628-1978* (Grand Rapids, MI: Eerdmans, 1978), 42.

[16] *Ebenezer: 100 Years of God's Mercy & Faithfulness, 1906-2006* (Ebenezer Netherlands Reformed Church of Franklin Lakes, NJ, 2006), 1-18, kept in author's personal collection. Zalenski and Hazenkamp, *Ecclesiastical History of Paterson*, 172-73. When the Christian school board sent a delegation to urge Rev. Arnold J. Van Lummel, the new minister at Sixth Reformed, to endorse the school, he declined. Board minutes, 21 May 1907, 13 June 1907, EC Archive.

1928 of a new minister, Rev. John J. Hiemenga, the former president of Calvin College.[17]

If the separate school was supposed to keep the Dutch immigrants from blending in with Paterson's cultural environment, it certainly did not happen. Paterson had a very long and turbulent labor history of strikes and pitched battles between strikers and mill owners and strikers versus scabs going back at least to the 1870s. When the graduates of Amity Street school ventured away from the Dutch enclave into the factories and foundries, they rubbed shoulders with a wide assortment of decidedly nonsympathetic coworkers. Education on Amity Street tended to see the non-Dutch world not as a place to be redeemed but as a hostile place filled with ideas and actions to avoid. Most prominent were the Catholics and Jews who formed a major segment of the labor force. In the case of the Catholics, Italians formed an increasing presence in the city and factories. They were often closely related to the inhabitants of East Harlem whom Robert Orsi described in *The Madonna of 115th Street* as people who displayed their faith parading statues in the streets on feast days and holding fundraising carnivals featuring games of chance.[18]

Among these devout Italians dwelled another, decidedly not-so-devout group—anarchists on the run from the Italian government. King Umberto I's assassin (and later Franklin D. Roosevelt's would-be assassin), came from Paterson, which functioned as a hideout for Italian radicals. In Paterson, they joined forces with home-grown American Marxist radicals, the Industrial Workers of the World. To the politically conservative Dutch, this was very dangerous stuff. Another thing that added to the Dutch aversion to the political radicals was the presence of a vocal minority within the local Dutch community that espoused socialism and eschewed church affiliations.[19] With the Dutch churches viewing labor union membership as very sketchy at best or anti-God

---

[17] Bethel Christian Reformed Church and Third Christian Reformed Church histories (HH).

[18] Robert Anthony Orsi, *The Madonna of 115th Street: Faith and Community in Italian Harlem, 1880-1950* (New Haven, CT: Yale University Press, 1985).

[19] Annemieke Galema, *Frisians to America, 1880-1914: With the Baggage of the Fatherland* (Groningen: REGIO-PRojekt Uitgevers, 1996), 164-77. Anne Huber Tripp, *The I.W.W. and the Paterson Silk Strike of 1913* (Urbana: University of Illinois Press, 1987). Kenyon Zimmer, *Immigrants against the State: Yiddish and Italian Anarchism in America* (Urbana: University of Illinois Press, 2015), 49-87. Robert Schoone-Jongen, "Fighting on the Borders: Dutch Americans and the Paterson Silk Strike of 1913," in *Across Borders: Dutch Migration to North America and Australia* (Holland, MI: Van Raalte Press, 2010), 199-209.

at worst, when strikes beset the textile mills and dye houses, the North Ward and nearby Bunker Hill and Riverside became a major source of strike breakers. The neighborhood that housed the Holland school was known as Scab Hill.

And yet, the insular Dutch could not remain immune to the city's raucous side. While the faithful considered the future of their overcrowded Christian school, they also attended other public meetings that required police presence to maintain order. The Holland Mutual Burial Fund provided the match that lit the fuse that burned through the Passaic Valley's Dutch enclaves. An insurgent faction of Amity School's teachers demanded larger payouts; the board stood fast for fiscal restraint. The debates turned to shouting matches, and the meetings (held often at Paterson's Helvetia Hall, a favorite venue for labor union meetings) bordered on brawls. This spectacle inspired a jeremiad from the local correspondent to the Christian Reformed Church's publication, the *Banner*, that ended with the lament, "The spirit for which Paterson is known thruout [sic] our whole land seems also to have found lodgement [sic] in some of our Dutch people."[20]

Nineteenth-century travel narratives about remote places, like the Pyrenees Mountains, often remarked about how the past endured as living fossils in locations like Andorra. One visitor observed that along the French-Spanish frontier:

> Each valley is still a little world which differs from the neighbouring [sic] world as Mercury does from Uranus. Each village is a clan, a kind of state with its own form of patriotism. There are different types and characters at every step, different opinions, prejudices and customs.[21]

This sounds a lot like the Dutch-immigrant enclave that supported the Amity Street Christian School. They were people who stood apart from the common national narratives in both the United States and Canada. Especially for those optimists who believed Christian schools

---

[20] "War Still On In Holland," *Paterson Evening News* (12 Feb. 1908): 1-2. "All Quiet in Holland," *Morning Call* (12 Feb. 1908): 1. "First Blood for the Insurgents," *Morning Call* (14 Feb. 1908): 1. "Gag Rule Prevailed, So 'Insurgents' Said," *Morning Call* (6 March 1908): 1. "Holland Burial Fund before the Chancellor," *Paterson Evening News* (11 Nov. 1908): 1. "Insurgents' Nominations," *Passaic Daily News* (19 Nov. 1908): 10. "'Insurgents' to Organize," *Passaic Daily News* (26 Dec. 1908), 1. E. Bartson, "Eastern Notes," *The Banner* (29 Oct. 1908): 802.

[21] Matthew Carr, *The Savage Frontier: The Pyrenees in History and the Imagination* (NY: The New Press, 2018), 209 (quoting Michel Chevalier).

John C. Van Vlaanderen

could redeem the world, winning the struggle to start these schools usually meant isolating themselves from the very world they wanted to redeem. And for those who supported the schools to keep their children from evil influences, they too lost when those influences seeped into the school with the experiences and ideas the children and teachers carried with them from the streets beyond the neighborhood.

But the Amity Street Christian School thrived. It began with about one hundred students. With the influx of immigrants to Paterson from the Netherlands in a tidal flow that endured for thirty years, there were always new students to add to the attendance rolls. When John Minnema founded the school in 1900, he immediately enrolled three more children, then eventually a fourth and a fifth. Since there were so many others also doing this, within three years, the school board considered relocating the school. With enrollment approaching five hundred students, the society bought land a few blocks to the west (and "up the hill" as the locals would have said), a location in the center of the growing Dutch community and above the Passaic River's floodplain, at the corner of Halpine Street and North Fourth Street.

Enter the Dutch American contractors, excavators, masons, carpenters, tin ceiling installers, painters, plumbers, and electricians, plus Paterson's resident Dutch American architect, John C. Van Vlaanderen (who was serving as the president of the Christian school board). In a matter of months, they had graded the site, erected retaining walls that made the playground level and kept the neighboring houses from sliding onto said playground, and erected the school itself. The

Dutch Immigrants and Education 317

North Fourth Street Christian School

retaining walls are still in place, doing their duty 111 years later, even though the school building came down in the 1970s.

On October 23, 1908, the 446 students marched from Amity Street to North Fourth Street to occupy the building that would house the Passaic Valley's largest Christian school for the next sixty-one years. The children marched with American flags in hand, and Louis A. Patmos, a local druggist (an American-born Dutch American) donated a large flag that flew from the staff attached to the roof of the school.[22]

The program held to commemorate this Dutch American milestone is an interesting study in the cultural ambivalence that underpinned the school and its community of supporters. The printed program's language ratio leaned heavily in the Dutch direction. Most of the songs were sung in Dutch, both by the audience and the students. Most of the speeches were in Dutch, with the exception of the address by Rev. John Westervelt of the English-speaking Third Christian Reformed Church. The offices held by board members were listed in English, except for the all-important post of treasurer. The lyrics for the songs

---

[22] "Dedicated New School," *The Morning Call* (26 Oct. 1908): 9. *The Banner* (29 Oct. 1908): 696. "Program van de Ingebruikneming der Christelijke School No. 4th en Halpine Sts., Paterson, NJ, Zaterday, 24 Oct. 1908," EC Archive.

printed in the program were in Dutch. The title of *The Star-Spangled Banner* appears on the page with the Dutch songs, but not the lyrics. The advertisements, from both the Dutch and non-Dutch contractors, were all in English.[23]

The school would physically dominate the neighborhood for precisely two years. Then this Dutch American triumph would be dwarfed when the Paterson board of education erected a new School No. 12 directly across the street. Symbolically, the public school's backside faced the North Fourth Street Christian School. To some in the neighborhood, that little school and its separated supporters smacked of what a nineteenth-century English visitor to the Pyrenees remarked about tiny, isolated Andorra, "What profit is there in such independence? This is no idyllic peasantry, children of Hellas and of light, but just the rude Catalan in his primitive state."[24] Soon after acquiring the property, the board adopted a motion to erect a sign, "No dumping allowed onder [sic] penalty of the law." Vandals were breaking windows in the school, even before the student body occupied the premises. Confrontations between students of the rival schools were not unheard of, right up until the day the Christian school students moved on to Midland Park and Wyckoff, and the Paterson board of education rented the vacated building as an annex to No. 12.[25]

If the North Fourth Street School was intended to anchor the Dutch Americans in place in the North Ward and the adjacent boroughs, it did not succeed. If anything, the education the school afforded provided the means, over time, for the graduates to move on, to either the suburbs that grew in the wooded hills to the north of Paterson or the farmlands in Bergen County. During the 1950s, a new Christian elementary school opened in the then barely suburban, quasi-rural Wyckoff, and a new Midland Park Christian School was built. Building "B" in Riverside steadily declined as its supporters moved from the neighborhood. The new Wyckoff school spelled the end of Riverside, and North Fourth Street School closed in 1969.[26]

These eventual closings can be attributed to another success.

---

[23] "Program van de Ingebruikneming der Christelijke School."
[24] Carr, *The Savage Frontier*, 212.
[25] "Will Probably Be the Barnert Site," *The Morning Call* (9 Sept. 1910): 1. "Boys Break School Windows," *The Morning Call* (9 Oct. 1908): 2. Mrs. Smit's candy store, located across Halpine Street, functioned as a common space where students from both schools would routinely line up to buy their candy, pretzels, and ice cream during recesses, with the elderly "Smitty" serving as both peacekeeper and dispenser.
[26] Ostling, "In thy Light," 16-20.

Dutch Immigrants and Education 319

Eastern Academy, North Eighth Street

During the 1910s, Dutch American parents no longer routinely expected their children would be mill workers and manual laborers. Mills required office clerks, as did the banks and other businesses that supported the mills. The demand for commercial education grew, both in Paterson and throughout the country. Paterson's public school system had a commercial department, and there were a few business schools in the city, as well. But they cost money to attend—more than the Dutch immigrants were willing to pay. Their answer was to urge the Christian school to expand beyond the eighth grade and organize an American high school that would include commercial education at a cheaper price. In 1919 the newly organized Eastern Academy opened on the third floor of the North Fourth Street School, with a commercial component in the curriculum. Since the state of New Jersey required all high schools to include physical education among the courses, and North Fourth Street had no facilities for that and no room to fit a gymnasium on the property, the academy's board looked "up the hill" once again to purchase a big house to renovate into a school, to which a major addition (including a gym) would be added in 1924. Eastern Academy would reside on North Eighth Street for thirty years before it morphed into Eastern Christian High School and headed for the Borough of North Haledon in 1954.[27]

The opening of the high school, with its commercial component, created yet another crack in the solid wall which Christian school

---

[27] Cornelius Bontekoe, *An Historical Review of Eastern Academy, 1919-1944*, n.d., 11-34.

supporters believed would ensure the endurance of the bit of Holland in northern New Jersey. By the 1920s, commercial/secretarial work tended to be viewed as work suitable for women. When the Amity Street School opened in 1893 and the first pictures of the student body were taken, the placement of the students betrayed where the emphasis was in providing education for children. The boys were lined up in the front, consistently. When Eastern Academy graduated its first class in 1923, that distinction disappeared. In fact, for a number of years, women would outnumber the young men in the graduating classes. As for the male graduates, a distressing trend soon set in. A successful high school would send its best and brightest to college. For Paterson's Dutch Calvinists, that meant going west to Grand Rapids. Many of those who followed that path never returned. Hence the high school produced a brain drain. Beginning in the 1920s, Paterson would lose the likes of William Spoelhof and John Timmerman, both of whom graduated from Eastern Academy in the same year and returned to the city only for occasional visits during their long tenures of service on the Calvin College faculty. Their presence there, along with other expatriates from Paterson and Passaic, lured even more high school graduates to sojourn in West Michigan.[28]

Two competing missions propelled Dutch immigration of the Calvinist variety: redeeming the world and keeping the faith. The definition of both parts of the equation changed with time and circumstances. Notions of what a godly social order entailed changed. Ideas of how to equip young people with the tools for a godly life changed. The means by which one discussed the faith and prayed changed. For people who believed in Christian education, every change demanded soul searching, because if the school was Christian in the first place, and now change was required, then had they been unfaithful? Many of the Dutch Calvinists emigrated in order to remain Dutch Calvinists. But as James Bratt describes in *Dutch Calvinism in America*, being a Dutch Calvinist in the Netherlands was not the same thing as being a Dutch Calvinist in North America.[29] Change inevitably involved loss, as well as gain. With time, the ratio between Dutch and American (or Canadian) changed, with one of the terms, usually the latter, looming larger in

---

[28] Dr. John Timmerman was the featured speaker at the 1967 Eastern Christian High School graduation ceremony, the author of this paper being among the graduates.

[29] For an analysis of this process, see James D. Bratt, *Dutch Calvinism in Modern America* (Grand Rapids, MI: Eerdmans, 1984), 113-19.

the minds of those who lived within the communities that considered themselves Dutch American.

Postscript

It is very unlikely that any Dutch immigrants inhabit Paterson's North Ward today. Other immigrants live there now. The Amity Street building survives as a machine shop; the North Fourth Street School site is a parking lot for School No. 12, and Eastern Academy's building now houses a Muslim grade school, all symptoms of inevitable change. But the legacy those Dutch immigrant schools created while they thrived will live on as long as there are those who remember, or rediscover, their connections to those Dutch immigrants. For a moment in history, they *were* the North Ward and went to school there and, ironically, were equipped to leave by the institutions they aspired to establish there more one hundred years ago. Among them was my great-grandfather, John Minnema. The "Eastern Academy" sign is still there on the building, on the side that looks out over the city of Paterson and the wider Passaic Valley—a place where Dutch immigrants, like John's family, once called home.

CHAPTER 18

Farming across the Line: An Historical Reflection on the Hollander Fires

Keith Fynaardt

In an eighteen-month period from the spring of 1918 to the fall of 1919, American arsonists in southern Iowa near the Dutch enclave of Pella set fire to Dutch schools and churches. Under cover of night, they sloshed kerosene onto straw bales in the haylofts of the barns of Dutch farmers and struck a match or took a last drag on a cigarette and dropped it and then retreated to watch the flames rise fifty feet high, perhaps more, sending an unmistakable signal to their immigrant neighbors: "You Dutch, you don't belong here."

The place was Prairie Township, Mahaska County, Iowa, bordered by the small towns of Peoria on the west and New Sharon on the east, as the crow flies, about twelve miles from Pella or sixty miles southeast of Des Moines. Like all townships measured off in rods and chains in the Public Land Survey System, Prairie is six miles square, containing thirty-six sections of 640 acres each. During the golden age of American agriculture, in the first two decades of the twentieth century, at least four farmers lived on every square-mile section of land. By contrast, today, four sections of land are often managed by one farmer. Aptly named, Prairie Township lies on a borderland, where the rough hills of southern Iowa give way to gentle swells of tall grass rising above deep topsoil; where coal hills near Oskaloosa reach, to the north, toward New Sharon, and to the west, toward Pella; where softer swales of rolling countryside are more suitable to row crops than cattle pastures, the kind of prairie land which H. P. Scholte and his Dutch flock had claimed in 1848 as their home, their "safe haven," their Pella.

By 1918 jingoist nativist elements of the American population were growing more visible, stoked by President Wilson's declaration of war on Germany, with the warning, in reference to the vast numbers of German-born immigrants in the United States, that "If there should be disloyalty, it will be dealt with, with a firm hand of stern repression." More incendiary for immigrants in Iowa was the rhetoric and indeed the legal decree handed down by Governor William L. Harding in his infamous Babel Proclamation that declared the use of all languages other than English to be outlawed in public, in schools, on the train, in churches, and even on the telephone. The excessively patriotic mood in the nation, stirred up by inflammatory politicians with their propaganda that caricatured Germans as a blood-thirsty enemy, and the resulting anxiety was enough to turn neighbors into enemies. It caused those who imagined themselves to be more American than any of their immigrant neighbors (whether they spoke Deutsch or Danish or Dutch) to feel justified in their prejudice and paranoia, and in some cases, to take violent action.

Understandably, immigrant vs. American tensions and violence flared up across the country during the war, especially where recent German settlements and pacifist Mennonite sects neighbored older American towns. It is worth remembering, in reference to our Iowa example, that a convincing argument has been made that the Middle West, as it was settled in the century preceding World War I, was seen paradoxically as both a place to restart in a new world and a place to replicate life in the Old World. On the one hand, American migrants with long-established histories in older states, such as Pennsylvania and Ohio, saw the Midwest as a place for a new start, a distinctly American restart, without the baggage of the Old World. They left behind the Old World ethnic, social, linguistic, and religious tribalism, which had permeated New England and the American colonial world. On the other hand, immigrant groups, predominantly from northern and western European nations, were seeking exactly the opposite—to recreate in the newer states of Wisconsin, Minnesota, Nebraska, and Iowa, the very places they had left behind across the Atlantic.[1] There is no more powerful metaphor to describe this latter impulse than Scholte's own "safe haven." World War I turned hands to fists as the two competing visions fought over nothing less than the national identity.

The Hollander Fires, as they have come to be known, included the burning of two barns of Dutch farmers, who lived within two miles west of New Sharon; two churches, the Christian Reformed Church in Peoria and the Dutch Reformed Church in New Sharon; the Peoria Christian School, next door to the church; a commercial grain elevator in New Sharon (by far the largest economic loss); and a farmhouse recently purchased by a Dutch farmer a half-mile south of New Sharon. In addition to these cases, two further attempts to destroy Dutch property and institutions occurred: one to burn the Sully Christian School (in a small town ten miles north of Peoria), which failed to ignite, and another to use dynamite (found unexploded, with a partially burned fuse) to destroy the parsonage of the Dutch Reformed Church in New Sharon.

The barn of Martin De Jong, who lived a mile west and a mile north of New Sharon, was burned to the ground on the night of April 10, 1918. It was a total loss, including ten horses, five hundred bushels of corn, cords of split firewood, farm equipment, feed grain, harnesses, and rope. For livestock farmers and horse-powered, row crop farmers, the traditional post-and-beam barn of the era, with its stanchions for milk cows, stalls for horses, feed bins, and haymow, was the economic centerpiece of the farm. To strike at it was both to strike at the heart of one's livelihood and to send up a dramatically visible public threat. The local paper, the *New Sharon Star*, detailed the losses and reported the origin of the fire to be "a mystery."[2] Eighteen months later, as the plot was uncovered to burn out the Dutch and send them back west toward Pella, from whence they had migrated, all evidence pointed to the De Jong barn as the first incident that fit the evolving pattern. Those who had conceived and funded the plan were arrested, and their trials were pending.

After the shock of the fire, and with the adrenaline spent, the clean-up became a meditative process, where the implications of what had happened would take time to settle in. As the ashes smoldered and

---

[1] Jon Gjerde, *The Minds of the West: Ethnocultural Evolution in the Rural Middle West 1830-1917* (Chapel Hill: University of North Carolina Press, 1997).

[2] James P. Dahm and Dorothy J. Van Kooten, *Peoria, Iowa: A Story of Two Cultures, With an In-Depth Look at the "Hollander Fires," 1853-1993* (Pella, IA: Pella Printing Co., 1993), 85.

the screams of the horses diminished in the memory, the smell of smoke lessened. And after days of raking down glowing embers, there was still the matter of disposal of the charred carcasses, coils of wire, and the giant metal cupola that stove inward as it fell. The foundation stone would have cracked in the heat. Deep pits would need to be dug to bury what did not burn. De Jong must have faced these daunting tasks. Yet, in the historical record, I have not found any evidence that De Jong testified in the trials in the county courthouse in Oskaloosa, nor was his barn mentioned in the evidence against the perpetrators. I do know that he did not move out. He rebuilt his barn, and by the 1940s, he played an important role in the local threshing ring. A considerable number of Dutch farmers that were moving closer to New Sharon, pooled their resources for a machine of their own and shared the work of harvest as was typical of the era. De Jong's daughter and son lived on the farm until the 1980s.

The last of the fires, on September 27, 1919, destroyed the barn of Gysbert Vos, a prosperous Dutch farmer who owned a quarter section a mile-and-a-half west and a mile-and-a-half south of New Sharon. His barn was burned in a fashion similar to De Jong's. But by this time, the local authorities were on high alert for suspected cases of arson. The newly acquired farmhouse of Anthony Leyden, straight south of New Sharon, had been torched in February, and in July, the McVeigh grain elevator and feed mill in New Sharon had been burned. The burning of the McVeigh elevator and mill is a unique case, because up to this point, only Dutch property and Dutch institutions had been targeted. This time, however, the target was a prominent business owned by an American who was guilty by association, guilty of doing business with Dutch farmers. The loss was catastrophic—$40,000 for the structure and the grain it held. McVeigh hired a team of private investigators who worked parallel to the investigation conducted by the state fire marshals, the state Secret Service and the Iowa attorney general, who used the high-profile arson case and attendant press coverage to advance his own run for governor. By November 1919, the case was made, and the trials commenced, with the Vos barn used as key evidence.

The destruction of the barns, the farmhouse, and the grain elevator struck at the economic heart of the Dutch, but the church fires struck at their souls. Both Peoria and New Sharon had enjoyed decades of church history before the Dutch arrived. Christianity was not some new threat to the towns, but the Dutch language was, especially after the Babel Proclamation. Dutch prosperity, combined with the dramatically increased number of Dutch buying up farmland that spread farther east of Pella; the suspicions that arose about Peoria minister J. J. Weersing's loyalty to the war effort; and these Dutch-speaking church communities were, in the eyes of their neighbors, all guilty convictions of the Dutch setting themselves too far apart. As is well documented, within the Dutch community itself, there was hot debate about expressions of loyalty to the American cause at the time—flying the flag, buying war bonds, and the war effort with the Christian mission. Accusations flew from the pulpit and in the papers. Important for Peoria's case was the founding of the Peoria Christian School Society in 1907. This was the oldest of Iowa Dutch Christian School Societies, except for those founded in Orange City in 1904 and Sioux Center in 1905. Earlier attempts in the 1860s in Pella to provide distinctly Christian education for young people in the Dutch language had come to naught. Pella's own Christian school dates from 1912. The Peoria Christian School was located within yards of the church, and on the night of June 13, 1918, some citizens reported seeing the school burn first and then the wind igniting the church.

Is it important to know whether the arsonists doused with kerosene the school or the church or both? Perhaps not. Perhaps the arsonists knew the wind would carry the flames and were merely making the task of burning both structures simpler. But if the target was the school, it says something important about the limits of expressing one's immigrant identity in the eyes of American neighbors—at least in that time and place.

In the course of the trials, two young men from New Sharon, who had grown up with less fortunate backgrounds, confessed to being paid cash by prominent area farmers to burn out the Dutch. All the farmers were acquitted for lack of evidence; one perpetrator was found mentally incompetent, and the ten-year sentence of the other was reduced to eighteen months. He served a little over a year. It appears the attorney general, who wanted the notoriety of the case and the credit for solving it, was reluctant to indict wealthy American farmers for crimes against "suspicious" immigrants, especially in an election year.

Years later, in a letter reflecting on the fires, the trials, and the local sensation they caused, Rev. Edward Huibregtse, the former minister of the New Sharon Dutch Reformed Church (whose church was burned and who discovered the unexploded dynamite under his house), penned an important and enduring metaphor for what had occurred in Prairie Township during World War I. Huibregtse said that prominent American farmers "drew a line" through Prairie Township north to south, across which, no Dutch immigrant would farm. They had made a pact and initiated a system of cash payments to burn the Dutch out from those places that were seen to be already too far east—across the line.[3]

Two miles west of New Sharon, Iowa, on a gentle curve of the county blacktop, stands a two-and-a-half story Dutch colonial farmhouse, with high dormers cut into the gambrel roof, east and west. Anyone versed in the vernacular architecture of Midwestern farmsteads can see in an instant that this place was once the embodiment of the American agrarian dream. The house had once belonged to one of the prominent New Sharon farmers who had hatched the plan to burn out the Dutch immigrants, and in a story that is perhaps apocryphal, it is rumored that on the night of June 13, 1918, he and the other farmers who had colluded against the Dutch gathered in the upper story of this house to watch, five miles distant, on a hill in Peoria, the church and the schoolhouse burn.

I was born across the line. My grandfather had purchased our homestead a mile-and-a-half west of New Sharon in 1947, so many years after the Hollander Fires that he had claimed to have never heard anything about. He went to church in Peoria and sent his children to the Peoria Christian School; he did not belong to the farmer's co-op in New Sharon nor did he do any business there. The same was true for my father. My brother now farms the homestead, and several cousins, nephews, and dozens of others with Dutch roots also farm in the area. Some even farm *east* of New Sharon. They now serve on the co-op board of directors, together with their American neighbors. On the roster of the volunteer fire department, one will find Dutch last names, as well as some of the surnames of those farmers accused in 1918. But now we are all inclined to joke about "the line," if we talk about it at all.

Farming is as competitive ever, especially the demand for land, but economic tensions do not flare up along ethnic lines as they did during the political climate of World War I. The Peoria Christian School is hanging in there, struggling for enrollment like much of private education, and has taken steps in recent years to embrace the homeschool movement and become a facility where those families can gather. And unlike the Dutch Reformed Church in New Sharon, which had disbanded by 1934, the Peoria Christian Reformed Church celebrated its 125th anniversary in the spring of 2019.

---

[3] Dahm and Van Kooten, *Peoria, Iowa*, 94.

Postscript

The spring of 2019 was exceedingly wet across much of the Midwest; the corn and soybeans should have been in the ground by mid-May, and by mid-June, the planting was way behind schedule. In early June, I received a call from a farmer friend who, like most every farmer in Sioux County, has deep Dutch roots. He also "covers a lot of ground," as his envious neighbors say. He apparently was either desperate enough or had enough misplaced confidence, to ask an English professor if he would be willing to drive one of the tractors on the planting crew. "Sure," I said, "I'm on summer break."

I soon found myself behind the wheel of a five-hundred-horsepower, Case-IH quad track. The seat was seven feet off the ground; the fuel tank held three hundred gallons, and the digital controls, gauges, and monitors glowed like something designed by NASA. Behind the tractor was a forty-eight-foot-wide soil finisher, ready for action. I was one of two soil finishers in the fields, along with three twenty-four-row planters, sprayers, attendant fuel trucks, seed tenders, and more. The barns that house twenty-first-century farm equipment are so large they look like airport hangers.

In the morning, we drove west and crossed the Big Sioux River on a narrow bridge, as approaching cars, seeing the size of our machines that filled both lanes, ducked for cover. We left Dutch Sioux County and entered South Dakota, where my friend had recently acquired new fields and was expanding his operation. I soon settled into the controls—the throttle and the power-shift transmission—and got used to the width of the tillage tool, and my familiarity with tractors all came back, like riding a bike, only bigger—much bigger. Cresting the next hill and making a turn along the fence row, I suddenly found myself aligned, just across the county road, with a neighbor's tractor, and he, too, was pulling a tillage tool, but it was quite a bit smaller than mine. He took one look at my unfamiliar face, a foreigner in his backyard, and throttled up for a little drag race in the field. I simply pushed the power-shift button from sixth to eighth to tenth gear and left him in my dust.

CHAPTER 19

Publication as Pedagogy: How Dutch Reformed Churches Used Reading to Inspire Congregants

Justin R. Vos

Education has always played a large role in the development of the Dutch American community—schools, colleges, and universities affiliated with the Dutch Reformed tradition are scattered across the Midwest and Canada. For most of the Christian Reformed Church's history, Christian day schooling has been a key marker of its identity, creating a distinction from its older sister, the Reformed Church in America, which has traditionally been a strong supporter of public schooling.

Education, however, does not begin or end with formal schooling. For the faithful within the Dutch Reformed tradition, Sundays provide further educational opportunities through sermons, catechism, and Sunday school. Besides corporate worship, in the nineteenth and early twentieth centuries, Dutch Americans sought out Dutch books to read and published their own Dutch-language newspapers.[1] Reading and literature in the Dutch American community provided a depth of knowledge beyond the formal educational structure. Church-based

---

[1] Hans Krabbendam, *Freedom on the Horizon: Dutch Immigration to America, 1840-1940* (Grand Rapids, MI: Eerdmans, 2009), 266-79.

publications provide one example of how education and Christian formation permeated the daily lives of members of the Dutch Reformed community.

Daniel Vaca, an historian of American religion, devoted two chapters of his dissertation to the growth of Dutch Reformed publishing. Concentrating on the 1930s, Vaca describes the development of the Wm. B. Eerdmans and Zondervan publishing companies and highlights the importance of publishing and reading within the Dutch Reformed community. In linking the growth of these publishing efforts to the language shift from Dutch to English, he argues that Dutch Reformed leaders saw the need to create resources for their community in their new language. Both Eerdmans and Zondervan filled this gap.[2]

It is commonly recognized that the *Banner*, the official publication of the Christian Reformed Church (CRC), along with other church-related periodicals, played an important role within the theological realm of the church. This is evident in various histories of the denomination. James Bratt's study of ecclesiastical developments centers around debates in church periodicals. Similarly, Robert Swierenga's discussion of theological issues in the CRC in the second half of the twentieth century draws from articles in the *Banner* as markers of theological change. Within the CRC, the *Banner* served as a forum for discussing issues within denominational life.[3]

What if, however, one looked at the *Banner* in terms of its other functions? Could studying the publication from the perspective of education provide new insight about the values of and developments within the denomination? In the 1950s and 1960s, the *Banner* covered a wide variety of issues and topics for its readers. Exploring these various topics reveals that the *Banner* served as an educational tool that reached beyond theology and denominational life.

---

[2] Daniel Vaca, "Book People: Evangelical Books and the Making of Contemporary Evangelicalism" (PhD dissertation, Columbia University, 2012). See also, Vaca, *Evangelicals Incorporated: Books and the Business of Religion in America* (Cambridge, MA: Harvard University Press, 2019). For an additional discussion of Dutch Reformed publishers, see Janet Sjaarda Sheeres, "Of Making Many Books... Dutch Immigrant Book Publishers in Grand Rapids: The Early Years," *Origins* 35, no. 2 (2017): 4-13.

[3] James Bratt, *Dutch Calvinism in Modern America: A History of a Conservative Subculture* (Grand Rapids, MI: Eerdmans, 1984), and Robert P. Swierenga, "Burn the Wooden Shoes: Modernity and Division in the Christian Reformed Church in North America," in *Reformed Encounters with Modernity: Perspectives from Three Continents* (Stellenbosch: International Society for the Study of Reformed Communities, 2001), 94-102.

I hope to expand Vaca's focus on Dutch Reformed publishing by examining the *Banner* from 1950 to 1968.[4] Both Eerdmans and Zondervan allowed for the Dutch Reformed community to continue both publication and consumption during the transition to English— reading and writing held the community together. Likewise, the *Banner* served to shape individuals within the Christian Reformed denomination, but how exactly did the publication serve as an educational tool?

During the eighteen years from 1950 to 1968, the *Banner* evolved and grew under the editorships of H. J. Kuiper and John Vander Ploeg and gained importance within CRC denominational life. Reports given to synod show a consistent increase in readership. In 1949 the *Banner* sent out 32,500 publications.[5] Five years later, circulation had increased to over 38,000.[6] By 1960 the *Banner* had over 40,000 subscribers, and by 1968, that number had risen to 42,800.[7] The *Banner*'s growth coincided with that of the denomination. From 1963 to 1968, denominational membership rose from 256,000 to 278,000, and in 1968, around 65 percent of CRC households received the *Banner* weekly.[8] For many within the denomination, the *Banner* held a consistent place in their everyday life.[9] The prevalence of the *Banner* within the lives of CRC

---

[4] I begin with 1950 and end with 1968 for practical reasons. Much of my research material came from the library of the Reformed Theological Seminary in Orlando, whose collection of the *Banner* begins with 1950. I end with 1968 because I originally explored the material for a separate project regarding the civil rights movement. For this other project, I ended with the coverage concerning the assassination of Martin Luther King Jr. in 1968. Ideally, I would have continued through the end of Rev. John Vander Ploeg's editorship in 1970.

[5] *Acts of Synod*, 1950 (Grand Rapids, MI: Christian Reformed Publishing House), 320.

[6] Ibid. (1955), 309.

[7] Ibid. (1961), 168; (1969), 302.

[8] Historical membership statistics can be found on the CRCNA website. See https://www.crcna.org/sites/default/files/membership_stats_2019.pdf. I calculated the readership ratio by dividing the reported number of subscribers by the number of families reported in the membership statistics. Due to the untraceable factor of nondenominational subscribers, I subtracted several percentage points to arrive at an estimate of 65 percent.

[9] The *Banner* was not the only official magazine during this time frame. *De Wachter*, the denomination's Dutch-language periodical, played a similar role for Dutch speakers within the denomination. Readership of *De Wachter*, however, had fallen during the first half of the twentieth century. In 1968 *De Wachter* served 3,250 subscribers (1,800 of the 3,250 were in Canada, which may point to the newer migrants' fast adoption of English). Despite serving a different population within the denomination, the larger readership of the *Banner* gave it greater weight in denominational life. Thanks to Albert van der Heide for bringing the *De Wachter* to my attention.

members allows for viewing the publication as an educational tool; it shaped the thoughts, attitudes, and actions of its readers during a period of denominational growth.

Providing a diet of Scripture

The *Banner* included a weekly biblical devotional, one reading for each day of the week. For instance, in June of 1952, Henry Verduin led readers through the book of 1 Kings. The devotions served to guide the reader through Scripture, including three questions that parents could ask children about the passage. The *Banner* intended these devotions for evening use, paired with the separate denominational devotional, *Daily Manna*, which the *Banner* listed for morning use. In addition to the morning *Daily Manna* and the evening meditation, the *Banner* also provided a noon scripture passage. Morning, noon, and evening, the *Banner* sought to guide the scripture reading of its subscribers and to structure their daily life around Bible reading, creating a common liturgy of scripture.[10]

This daily diet of Scripture, structured around mealtimes, provided an avenue for Reformed teaching to be continually provided to the faithful. An advertisement for the *Daily Manna* devotional emphasized that the "daily meditations [were] prepared by ministers of the Christian Reformed, Reformed, and Presbyterian denominations."[11] Emphasizing the theological and denominational credentials of the writers effectively promoted the devotional to *Banner* readers. The *Banner* and the *Daily Manna* structured Bible reading, supplied members with daily religious formation, and expanded Reformed teaching beyond the Sunday sermon by reaching families around their dinner tables.

Creating Reformed readers

Beyond Bible reading, the *Banner* also sought to influence the broader reading material of its subscribers. Book reviews provided recommendations for readers, serving to guide theological consumption. *Banner*-endorsed books centered on Dutch Reformed authors.

---

[10] Henry Verduin, "For Your Daily Devotions: A Guide to Family Worship," *The Banner* (27 June 1952): 818. Unless noted otherwise, all further citations are taken from the *Banner*. When possible, I have provided the author and title of articles. For most advertisements, however, the author and title are not as clear. Therefore, for advertisements, I provide the main headline as the title, along with the date and page number.

[11] "Daily Manna Calendars" (27 June 1952), 823.

For example, a review of a book by Herman Bavinck concluded that he "presents Jesus as the central, the determining, figure. This is reason sufficient to buy and read this book."[12] Besides academically oriented works, the *Banner* also endorsed Marian M. Schoolland's book for children, *Forest Folk Tales*, for "constantly direct[ing]" children's attention from "the creature to the Creator."[13] The endorsement of Schoolland, a contributor to the *Banner* and a CRC member, came naturally.

In contrast to Bavinck and Schoolland, works by non-Dutch Reformed authors earned a more reserved recommendation. For example, a book published by the evangelical InterVarsity Press gained praise for "strik[ing] a lance against the liberals." The reviewer, however, also criticized the book for not including John Calvin in its argument.[14] The *Banner* printed reviews as recommendations for church members, guiding them to Reformed resources. In 1952 the editors listed books received for possible review. Yet, they cautioned that the list "should not be construed as a recommendation. A review of those found in this list which we regard as having value for our circles will be given later."[15] Placed together, the list and the warning demonstrate how the magazine served as an intellectual monitor, guiding Reformed readers toward useful books, while weeding out those either with theological issues or seen as insufficiently Reformed.

Besides broader works of theology, the *Banner* also promoted books connected directly to the Christian Reformed denomination. On October 5, 1956, the *Banner* advertised Rev. Peter Y. De Jong's *The Christian Reformed Church: A Study Manual*, a short history and discussion of the distinctives and character of the denomination. The *Banner* emphasized how the manual could be utilized for a variety of different church groups, such as "young couples' clubs, study groups, young people's societies, catechism classes, etc."[16] From the perspective of the denominational publication, De Jong's manual provided a way to educate members about CRC history.

As well as guiding the content of denominational reading, the *Banner* also strove to increase the amount of its subscribers' reading.

---

[12] Alexander C. De Jong, "Review of *Mensen rondom Jezus*, by Dr. J. H. Bavinck" (27 June 1952), 819.

[13] Mrs. Alexander De Jong, "Review of *Forest Folk Tales*, by Marian M. Schoolland" (25 July 1952), 957.

[14] John H. Bratt, "Review of *The Meaning of Inspiration*, by F. E. Gaebelein, and *Christian Students in a Communist Society*, by D. H. Adeney" (27 June 1952), 819.

[15] "Books Received" (25 July 1952), 957.

[16] "The Christian Reformed Church, by Peter Y. De Jong" (5 Oct. 1956), 1,239.

In 1964 editor John Vander Ploeg wrote an article emphasizing the importance of reading not only for healthy church life but also for strengthening the individual Christian life. He warned that "Religious illiteracy is sure to take its toll in the life of the church." Furthermore, he claimed that "familiarity with wholesome reading matter pays off in rich spiritual dividends for the individual member as well as for the church in and through which he is called to serve." Vander Ploeg averred that reading religious material served to strengthen the spiritual health of the church and its members.[17] While stressing the spiritual benefits of reading, Vander Ploeg used the prospect of material gain to prick his readers' consciences, in particular, in a discussion of the Tax Reduction Act of 1964, which lowered the tax rate for all income levels.[18] Vander Ploeg asked his American readers what the most beneficial use for their extra income would be. Highlighting the importance of church and Christian education, he concluded: "The question is, *Are we really putting first things first?*"[19] Vander Ploeg hoped that readers would think more carefully about how they spent their money, giving more to church-related causes. Reading and giving went hand-in-hand as part of one's commitment to the religious community. Therefore, the *Banner* promoted a vision of Christian living that gave new importance to the contents of people's bookshelves and the activities of their checkbooks.

Exploring science

During the 1950s and 1960s, the coverage of the *Banner* expanded beyond biblical knowledge and doctrinal education to include articles devoted to science. In the early 1950s, these articles explained elements of natural science or engineering, such as botany, chemistry, or the technology of radar.[20] These discussions had the dual purpose of explaining the scientific aspects of the topic and connecting the various concepts to a theological framework of God as creator. The *Banner* tied scientific knowledge to spiritual growth and understanding.

Some of the articles provided simple experiments to explain scientific principles. Designed as family exercises, these activities were

---

[17] John Vander Ploeg, "The Church Library—Defunct or Dynamic?" (17 April 1964), 8-9.
[18] For a discussion and listing of the rate cuts, see Joseph A. Pechman, "Individual Income Tax Provisions of the Revenue Act of 1964," *The Journal of Finance* 20, no. 2 (1965): 247-72.
[19] Vander Ploeg, "The Church Library," 8-9. Emphasis in the original.
[20] See "Plants After Their Kind" (11 July 1952), 874; Thedford P. Dirkse, "What is Radar?" (12 Sept. 1952), 1,098; Anne De Boer Deckard, "Like Fuller's Soap" (12 Oct. 1956), 1,259.

intended to be fun and interactive, and just as the *Banner* provided devotional resources to shape the spiritual life of families, so also the science experiments enhanced learning. In outlining an experiment concerning acid-base reactions, Anne De Boer Deckard described how the experiment could help make an "appreciation of God's handiwork an important part of... family life."[21] The *Banner* not only made biblical devotions a part of daily family life but also promoted "the viewpoint that God's glory is revealed in every part of his creation."[22]

Highlighting elements of the natural sciences within the context of creation provided a biblical framework for science education, but other science-focused articles developed more directly out of theological controversy. Edwin Y. Monsma, who regularly wrote science articles for the *Banner*, provided the two-part series: "A Brief History of Evolutionary Thought." Monsma explained how Charles Darwin inherited the concept of evolution from Greek philosophy and the earlier work of Comte de Buffon and Jean-Baptiste Lamarck, who had emphasized that "an age of materialism and religious modernism helped the rapid spread of [Darwin's] ideas." For Monsma, philosophical presuppositions sat at the root of the scientific community's acceptance of evolution. "Why is it that [scientists] adhere so tenaciously to their evolutionary views?" asked Monsma. He concluded that they lacked faith in the authoritative nature of the Bible, but he ended on a hopeful note, concluding that "nothing will be able to detract from the first sentence of the Bible."[23] Monsma's discussion of evolution highlights a connection between theology and science, giving readers a way to think about scientific concepts from a Christian perspective. The *Banner* expanded beyond teaching science by also working to shape how its readers thought about science.

Most science articles related to the natural world, but in 1964, a series of articles by CRC minister Ralph Heynen discussed the issue of mental health. Topics ranged from "healthy family relationships" to communication to how to relate to people diagnosed with mental illness. Heynen served as the chaplain at Pine Rest Christian Hospital for almost thirty years.[24] His articles provided a shift away from linking

---

[21] Anne De Boer Deckard, "A Family Activity—An Acid-base Reaction" (28 Sept. 1956), 1,195.
[22] Ibid.
[23] Edwin Y. Monsma, "A Brief History of Evolutionary Thought" (14 March 1952), 330.
[24] See the biographical note for the Ralph Heynen Collection, 1943-72, kept in Heritage Hall, Hekman Library, Calvin University.

knowledge of the natural world with a better understanding of God and discussed the issue of mental illness from a perspective of compassion, striving to help families and individuals with the daily struggles of life.[25] The *Banner* employed Heynen's experience in ministering to those struggling with mental health as a way to educate readers about a variety of mental health and relationship issues.

In addition to instruction in doctrinal issues, the *Banner* also provided readers with a biblical perspective on the natural sciences, presented in a way similar to family devotions, and with a close connection to theology, but which, at times, also became intertwined with broader discussions of worldview. Furthermore, Heynen's study of mental health issues shows how the *Banner* sought to educate by giving practical advice in relation to family life.

Discussing politics

The Cold War era fostered new challenges and worries for those within the Dutch Reformed community, as well as for most North Americans. Despite being shaped by their particular social geography, Dutch Reformed people also shared the common concerns of Americans in general, but the *Banner* provided readers with a specific perspective for understanding events occurring in the nation and around the globe.

In the mid-1950s, Rev. Edward J. Tanis wrote the World Today section of the *Banner*. Tanis, on the verge of retiring from ministry, discussed a variety of world events, ranging from the issue of apartheid in South Africa to alcohol on commercial airlines.[26] A decade later, Paul G. Schrotenboer wrote the World Today section. Highlighting the importance of the Cold War, Schrotenboer discussed the issue of religious persecution in the Soviet Union, emphasizing the need for "Christians in the free world [to] pray for God's mercy on his people in tribulation."[27] In the same issue, in a special article concerning the issue of disarmament, CRC minister Richard J. Frens provided a lengthy excerpt of the US State Department's "program for General and Complete Disarmament in a Peaceful World," followed by his own discussion of the issue. Frens provided no easy answers, emphasizing the problem of the "unreliability of the Communists." Concerning

---

[25] See, for example, Ralph Heynen, "Healthy Family Relationships" (14 Feb. 1964), 14; Heynen, "Talking Things Over" (21 Feb. 1964), 10; Heynen, "Overcoming Carelessness" (28 Feb. 1964), 14.
[26] Edward J. Tanis, "The World Today" (5 Oct. 1956), 1,226.
[27] Paul G. Schrotenboer, "Soviet Drive Against Religion" (1 May 1964), 6.

disarmament, he took the middle ground, stating: "We do not trust them [the Communists] very far when they are unarmed. We trust them still less when they are armed to the teeth." After giving his readers this conundrum, Frens concluded by emphasizing that war could be completely avoided only with the "gospel of the Prince of Peace." Furthermore, he directed his readers to the 1963 synodical committee report on warfare.[28] The *Banner* guided subscribers concerning the issues of the Cold War, provided opinions itself, and pointed readers to denominational guidance regarding the issue.

Readers also expressed their opinions on current events within the Voices section of the publication based on letters to the editor. In the 1960s, readers weighed in concerning the civil rights movement. In 1964 one contributor suggested a connection between the civil rights movement and communism, criticizing the CRC minister and congregation of Manhattan for participating in civil rights marches.[29] Gordon Negen, minister of Manhattan CRC, responded to the criticism, arguing for the "Christian's duty to make his voice heard in matters of civil rights."[30]

Although the *Banner* may have projected a unified stance regarding the Cold War and communism, seeds of division became apparent in issues of race and civil rights. Readers' opinions highlighted the ideological division that existed within the community. Subscribers may have been united around issues of Reformed theology, but the authority of the *Banner* faltered regarding controversial political issues, where it served more as a forum for discussion than an authoritative voice.

Promoting church-related events

Just as it emphasized the importance of reading, the *Banner* also provided opportunities for church members to participate in religious events outside of their local congregations with announcements and advertisements for church-related events.

In the early 1950s, the *Banner* announced many events occurring at the Christian Reformed Conference Grounds. Founded by five CRC families in 1951, the conference grounds is a retreat in Holland,

---

[28] Richard J. Frens, "Arms Control and Disarmament" (1 May 1964), 4-5. In addition to the Frens article, the 8 Nov. 1963 issue included Synod's "Statement on War."
[29] Bertha J. Bierma, "Strange Company for Calvinists" (21 Feb. 1964), 23.
[30] Gordon Negen, "Reply to Strange Company for Calvinists" (21 Feb. 1964), 23.

Michigan, on the shore of Lake Michigan,[31] a place where the CRC community weave together leisure and church life. The conference grounds hosted a full week of events for the July 4, 1952, holiday, including "inspirational speakers," hymns sings, a Reformed Bible Institute Course, and "sports for the children."[32] Additionally, every Wednesday during the summer of 1952, the conference grounds hosted a midweek Bible study, led by CRC minister Leonard Greenway.[33] The conference grounds also hosted a mission rally in 1952, featuring the choir from the CRC mission school in Rehoboth, New Mexico.[34] And in August, the conference grounds featured a "Neighborhood Evangelism Rally," which promised "inspiration, recreation, and Christian fellowship."[35]

Beyond the conference grounds, West Michigan served as a key location for other CRC-focused events. A "Double Header," including a lecture by Peter Eldersveld, host of the denominational radio program, the *Back to God Hour*, and a choir performance that took place at Eastern Avenue CRC in Grand Rapids, was publicized by the *Banner*.[36] The West Michigan Youth Bible Conference near Saugatuck included CRC minister Richard R. De Ridder.[37] The Forty-First Annual Mission Fest also invited youth to attend its event at John Ball Park in Grand Rapids, featuring the minister from the Rehoboth Mission.[38] For the conference grounds, and West Michigan more generally, the *Banner* served as a community bulletin board.

Other events intended for the Dutch Reformed community also took place around the Midwest. In February of 1952, the *Banner* advertised a "*Back to God Hour* Rally" in Des Moines, Iowa. Similar to the West Michigan double header, the rally featured an address by Eldersveld and a choir performance. Sponsored by the CRC Pella League of Men's Societies, organizers intended for the event to appeal to the Dutch Reformed faithful, with the advertisement including a map with arrows pointing to the prominent Dutch American settlements of Pella

---

[31] From the author's personal correspondence with the current Christian Reformed Conference Ground director, in the author's possession.
[32] "Bible Conference Program for the Week" (27 June 1952), 821, 823.
[33] "A Rare Treat" (27 June 1952), 826.
[34] "Mission Rally" (11 July 1952), 891.
[35] "Neighborhood Evangelism Rally" (1 Aug. 1952), 987.
[36] "Young People, Get Your Tickets" (20 Jan. 1950), 95.
[37] "Young People!" (11 July 1952), 891.
[38] "41st Annual Mission Fest" (11 July 1952), 891.

and Newton.[39] The Green Lake Youth Bible Conference in Wisconsin featured the teaching of three CRC ministers and also carved out time for swimming, golfing, and boating.[40] Whereas the Green Lake conference attracted youth, the Christian School Convention targeted their parents. Held at the Conrad Hilton Hotel in Chicago, the convention of 1952 explored "Christian Education in a World of Chaos." Conference organizers intended the convention to be useful for both educators and parents. Several Christian Reformed ministers served as speakers, along with Calvin College president William Spoelhof and Grand Rapids publisher Herman Baker.[41]

Similar to other areas of life, the *Banner* provided CRC readers with a source of information for connecting with others within the denomination. Families could relax at the conference grounds while learning from CRC ministers; parents could be assured that their children interacted with other CRC youth under the guidance of CRC leaders, and they themselves could learn more about Christian schooling, alongside others with the same convictions. Life in the postwar CRC focused on connecting those with like-minded convictions through learning and fellowship. For the most part, these events brought together regional CRC communities, with the majority centered around West Michigan. Some, however, such as the Christian School Convention, had a broader national appeal. The *Banner* sought to inform readers of these various opportunities, bringing members together both locally and nationally.

Encouraging giving through investment

The *Banner* put the needs of a variety of CRC communities at the forefront of readers' minds. Alongside John Vander Ploeg's question concerning readers' financial priorities, advertisements provided subscribers with specific opportunities to give to various causes within the CRC community. Based on frequency of appeals, Christian Reformed Churches and Christian day schools connected with the National Union of Christian Schools (the precursor to the current Christian Schools International) were the most visible institutions soliciting support. First CRC of Salt Lake City, Utah, posted a plea for financial help, stressing urgency by declaring their "New Sanctuary Delayed!" They followed up this bad news by stating that the congregation "Desperately need[s] 700

---

[39] "Midwest Back to God Hour Rally" (15 Feb. 1952), 215.
[40] "Have You Registered?" (1 Aug. 1952), 961.
[41] "Christian School Convention" (25 July 1952), 951.

investors."[42] From a more positive perspective, the Community CRC of Tacoma, Washington, announced "Growth in the Northwest," before asking for investments to aid sanctuary construction. The Tacoma advertisement informed readers that the congregation was "under the supervision of the Denominational Home Missions Board," implying that financial support would bolster the denomination's evangelistic outreach.[43] Holland Christian Schools advertised 5.5 percent interest on investments required for the construction of a high school building.[44] These advertisements highlight a denomination-wide focus on giving. Giving to congregations or schools across the denomination connected CRC members around the country, so that a CRC member from New Jersey could potentially aid the development of the congregation in Tacoma, Washington. Denominational unity could be found not only in theological distinctives and shared events but also in common recipients of financial support.

Personal investments made to individual churches and schools supplemented the Church Help Fund, which the denomination incorporated in 1902.[45] By 1962 the fund provided loans to 278 congregations.[46] Organizationally, the fund served as a practical way to support denominational growth. Yet, advertisements in the *Banner* seem to signify a further development—linking benevolence to investment and financial return. Advertisements for support did not simply ask for donations but also displayed percentages of return on investment.[47] One could be assured not only of supporting a denominational cause but also earning interest. Advertisements provided clear guidelines for how often interest would be paid, and some assured potential donors: "Requests for premature redemption will be given full consideration."[48]

---

[42] "Help" (13 March 1964), 23.
[43] "Growth in the Northwest" (20 March 1964), 21.
[44] "Holland Christian Schools" (3 June 1966), 25.
[45] *Acts of Synod* (1902), 79.
[46] *Acts of Synod* (1962), 359-64. Around this same time, in 1958, the RCA began to offer personal debt securities through RCA Extension Foundation. See https://www.rca.org/church-growth-fund/cgf-history.
[47] The linking of investment and giving within the CRC coincides with the general development of church techniques surrounding giving in the years prior to WWII. See James Hudnut-Buemler, *In Pursuit of the Almighty's Dollar: A History of Money and American Protestantism* (Chapel Hill: The University of North Carolina Press, 2007), ch. 5.
[48] See "Growth in the Northwest" (20 March 1964), 21, and "Valley Christian Reformed Church" (3 June 1966), 23.

The *Banner* helped create a new form of financial involvement in church life. Giving extended beyond local tithing in both geographic range and method. A financial supporter could potentially become an investor in other communities within the denomination. This system placed Vander Ploeg's editorial question into a new perspective. For those who chose to invest, what did "putting first things first" mean? Did the cause come first, or did one's opportunity for financial gain? The technique of giving through investment not only blurred the lines between generosity and financial gain but also provided connections within a growing denomination. The *Banner* advertisements facilitated the growth of this new strategy of religious charity.

Guiding vacationers

Besides advertising theological books, publicizing church-related events, and broadcasting investment opportunities, the *Banner* also ran other promotions highlighting the economic and demographic changes in the Dutch Reformed community. In the United States, post-World War II prosperity prompted changes in the habits of Dutch Americans.[49] With extra income and more free time, Dutch Americans traveled farther and vacationed more frequently. Advertisements for CRC churches in Florida, Arizona, Southern California, and Hawaii demonstrated this expanding Dutch Reformed geography.

Peter Y. De Jong recognized this growing trend in an article in 1952. He wrote, "In these days of lush prosperity, the practice of going on vacations for at least a week or two during the summer months has become very prevalent among us." De Jong admitted that a change of pace could have many benefits, but he also warned the Reformed community of the "perils connected with our vacations." He worried about spiritual issues created by vacations, particularly with regard to Sabbath observance. De Jong admitted that the Bible never explicitly commands the observance of specific Dutch Reformed Sabbath traditions, such as attending two worship services. Nevertheless, he concluded: "Those who are spiritually mature and sensitive will be persuaded in their hearts that all these matters [Dutch Reformed traditions] are proper and indisputable inferences from the plain teachings of the Bible." De Jong worried that the changing material

---

[49] Hans Krabbendam emphasized the general prosperity of the Dutch migrant community and their success in entrepreneurship and agriculture. The postwar period continued this trend. See Krabbendam, *Freedom on the Horizon*, 191-222.

habits of the community would lead to a negative impact upon their spiritual practices.[50]

Congregations located in vacation areas, likewise, realized that they needed to attract Reformed vacationers who might venture outside of Reformed preaching during their time away from home. The Orthodox Presbyterian Church (OPC) of Fort Lauderdale, Florida, urged *Banner* readers to not "lay aside Calvinism with [their] overcoat" and emphasized that the "Reformed faith is truth." With the presence of Reformed churches in Florida, a vacation was no excuse to take a break from worship. Notably, the OPC took advantage of such CRC anxiety and targeted CRC members by advertising their use of the CRC psalter hymnal and Sunday school materials.[51] But Florida did not serve as the only destination for vacationing Dutch Reformed folk. The CRC congregations in Arizona advertised the benefits of their climate for physical health, reminding readers that a "dry climate [is] helpful for respiratory diseases, arthritis, rheumatic fever, etc."[52] The CRC of Hawaii assured readers that a "warm aloha awaits you."[53] Even more modest locations, such as Cadillac, Michigan, and St. Louis, Missouri, sought to attract CRC vacationers to their churches.[54]

The growth of CRC churches in vacation centers, such as Florida and Arizona, seemed to follow a reactive pattern. An increase in short-term vacations and season-long escapes from northern winters (by 1959 over 600 people attended Dutch Reformed chapels in Florida) prompted the creation of churches in these new areas. This pattern of church growth in the wake of the "re-settlement" of (mainly) Dutch retirees, compares to the chain migration process of the initial Dutch migration, when congregations followed Dutch settlement westward.

De Jong's concerns, however, demonstrate how this newer movement differed from the community's earlier westward migration. Most Dutch Americans intended their time in Florida or Arizona to be temporary—several months at most. This led to new practices, such as the founding of winter chapels in Florida. In January of 1950, a chapel in St. Petersburg held afternoon services, led by both RCA and CRC ministers. Many viewed this chapel, along with the one established south of Tampa Bay in Bradenton, as a temporary measure, due to the

---

[50] Peter Y. De Jong, "Worship and Vacations" (6 June 1952), 716.
[51] "When in Florida" (13 Jan. 1950), 61.
[52] "Arizona" (13 Jan. 1950), 56.
[53] "Hawaii Calls!" (21 Jan. 1966), 30.
[54] "Cadillac Christian Reformed Church" (27 June 1952), 815; "St. Louis Invites You!" (21 Jan. 1966), 30.

Publication as Pedagogy   345

lack of a full-fledged CRC congregation in the area. Indeed, by 1959, one *Banner* contributor suggested that the chapels should be closed due to the establishment of the Bradenton, Florida, CRC congregation.[55] The Bradenton chapel continued, however, due to the Bradenton church's lack of space for all of the tourists during the height of the season. *Banner* editor Henry J. Kuiper, informed readers: "We believe [the chapel's] services will be discontinued as soon as it is apparent that they are no longer needed."[56] Several months later, the Committee of the Bradenton Chapel wrote to the *Banner* that they still saw a need for their services within the community of Reformed vacationers and tourists, emphasizing how the starting of the chapel developed the Reformed presence within the area and drew an even-greater number of vacationers to the region. Yet, the committee also concluded: "When there is no longer any need for the chapel, it will be discontinued."[57]

The worries and disagreements surrounding the vacation practices of the various Dutch Reformed communities highlight a bigger story, one of Reformed members' understanding of their place within North America. The CRC presence in Florida and Arizona developed, not from evangelism, but from the movement of those already within the fold. Through advertisements and articles, the *Banner* played a role in expanding the social geography of the Dutch Reformed community. Religious and cultural ties created safe places for the faithful to vacation. Bradenton, just one of many tourist towns in Florida, became associated with the chapel and later the CRC congregation. With an expanded geography of social connections, the Dutch Reformed could escape the northern winter but still hold on to their community and culture. The *Banner* informed readers of this expanded geography and orchestrated these communal connections.

Conclusion

In the 1950s and 1960s, the CRC community experienced growth and change, following broader national trends. The *Banner* provided a common link and source of information that allowed for connection across the expanding geographic reach of the denomination. CRC

---

[55] Joseph Vande Kieft, "Suggests That It Would Be Better to Discontinue Florida Chapels as Churches Are Organized There" (16 Jan. 1959), 29.
[56] Henry J. Kuiper, "Rev. H. J. Kuiper Replies to Explain Why Services Are Still Being Held in Two Florida Chapels" (16 Jan. 1959), 29.
[57] The Bradenton Chapel Committee, "Replies to William Heynen Regarding Bradenton Chapel" (6 March 1959). The Bradenton Chapel continues up to the present.

members could use a common devotional, read the same books and political opinion pieces, express their views on a variety of issues, attend the same events, and invest in each other's future. The *Banner*'s role in developing and informing readers of these various connections gave it a formative role in shaping the daily lives of its readers. Whereas formal education molded children and provided the Dutch American ethnic community with a distinct marker of identity, the *Banner* worked toward denominational solidarity within an expanding CRC community, developing and maintaining a common culture and worldview amidst growth and evolving lifestyles.

CHAPTER 20

Fifty Years of Dutch Studies at the University of Michigan

Ton Broos

Let me take you back to the Netherlands in 1708 and read parts of the story of a Dutch boy stranded on an island called Krinke Kesmes, somewhere in the unknown Southland near Australia. He meets inquisitive inhabitants and is soon teaching them Dutch. I quote:

> I am very properly provided for here; my School never consists of more than six young People, whom I instruct in the Dutch language, which I make them understand, speak, read, and write. These Southlanders believe that the happiness of their country, and of its good and very magnificent government, depends entirely on the good education of youth, therefore, no slatternly crones are allowed to be Schoolmistresses, nor drunken topers, or ill-mannered men to be Schoolmasters; such people are despised, as are those who lack common sense, as well as laggards and whiners, who are not well-spoken. They believe here that all, or most, failings that seem to be inborn in many people, have been received in their Youth from those who educate and instruct them, and which then stay with them through habit. Therefore,

Schoolmasters here have to be sensible, observant, prudent, and courteous. I adapted myself to their laws, and ever since have lived as decently as I can.[1]

This description struck me powerfully when I read it for the first time; it was as if I had looked into a mirror. I came to Michigan in 1982 and started Dutch instruction in Ann Arbor, trying to be just as sensible, observant, prudent, courteous, and decent as my nameless Dutch boy, whose story is part of an imaginary voyage published in Amsterdam in 1708. I found it in the Hubbard Imaginary Voyages Collection[2]—stories often referred to as Robinsonades, after Daniel Defoe's *Robinson Crusoe*—collected and donated to the University of Michigan by Lucius L. Hubbard in 1923.[3] This is just one example of the many thousands of Dutch holdings in our library.[4]

My own story is as truthful as memory allows, and it leans on the archives and libraries of the University of Michigan (U of M). A recent publication contains the most comprehensive account of the teaching of Dutch throughout the years, as well as observations for future educational approaches, anecdotes, related topics, and lists of visitors and their subjects of interest.[5]

How Dutch studies started at U of M is the first relevant question, and that is more easily asked than answered, since it depends on memories, viewpoints, documents, and so forth. In spite of considerable interest in Ann Arbor in all things Dutch from early in the twentieth century, the first documentation of the language being taught at U of M is a 1968 letter from Willard C. Wichers to U of M dean Robert L. Williams.[6] Wichers refers to the interest of his friends

---

[1] Hendrik Smeeks, *The Mighty Kingdom of Krinke Kesmes (1708)*, presented by David Fausset, trans. Robert-H. Leek (Amsterdam: Editions Rodopi, 1995), 86-87. Krinke Kesmes is an anagram of author Henrik Smeeks.
[2] https://www.lib.umich.edu/online-exhibits/exhibits/show/storied-acquisitions/hubbard-imaginary-voyages-coll.
[3] Hubbard was a Michigan state geologist from 1893 to 1899 and regent of the university from 1911 until his death in 1933. Ibid.
[4] Ton J. Broos, "The imaginary voyages of Lucius L. Hubbard: examining a collector and his illustrious collection, with a closer look at the Dutch holdings," in *Robinson Crusoe in the Old and New Worlds* (Ann Arbor, Groningen: Stichting Bibliographica Neerlandica, 1992), 13-35.
[5] Ton J. Broos, Annamarie Toebosch, and Karla Vandersypen, *Dutch is Beautiful: Fifty Years of Dutch and Flemish Studies at the University of Michigan* (Ann Arbor: University of Michigan, 2020).
[6] Willard C. Wichers, Netherlands Information Service, Holland, MI, to Robert L. Williams, Office of the Vice President for Academic Affairs, Ann Arbor, MI,

at the Dutch Embassy in the "course being offered in the study of the Dutch language by your graduate student, Mr. van Rosevelt." There had been discussions between the university and the Dutch government since 1945 about establishing a professorship devoted to Dutch history and culture. That initiative started a longstanding visiting professorship program, which brought in a series of professors from the Netherlands. The program began in 1950 and ran until 2010, when the Dutch Academy of Sciences ended its support. This termination of support was unfortunate because, over the years, we had had at least fifty-five visiting scholars who had covered a wide array of disciplines from history to economics to engineering, architecture, and chemistry. Of course, there are still visiting professors from the Low Countries but not on the official, state-sponsored level.

The formation and teaching of a Dutch language course took longer to establish. The first listing of a beginning Dutch course was in the 1970-71 academic year. In 1972 Dean Frank Rhodes corresponded with Van Rosevelt about plans to offer a second-year course in Dutch, and he also referred to the possibility of a gift from the Netherlands government toward the cost of a chair (of Dutch) within the department. The gift did not materialize, and in fact, Van Rosevelt's appointment was terminated at the end of the 1973-74 academic year.

But the U of M Dutch program had other advocates. In June 1973, Dean Charles Witke argued for the maintenance of the "present vigorous program in Dutch literature," which was "most essential for not only the Program in Comparative Literature, the Center for South and Southeast Asian Studies but [also] for other components of our University, such as political science, history, philosophy, and others." Dean Carruth responded: "I believe the German Department to be committed to Dutch not only for the excellent intellectual reasons which you cite but also because of the strong cultural ties which exist between Michigan and Holland." U of M's *Language, Science, and Arts Bulletin* for 1973-74 lists four Dutch courses, plus an independent study and "Modern Dutch Poetry and Prose in English Translation."[7]

The Dutch studies program did continue, thanks to the diligent work of the various visiting professors appointed for short terms. For 1974-75, Dr. Bep Bos, from the University of Amsterdam,

---

University of Michigan, Vice President for Academic Affairs staff files, box 29, Netherlands Visiting Professor, 1968, Bentley Library, Ann Arbor, MI.

[7] History and quotes about Dutch studies in: Ton Broos, Annemarie Toebosch, and Karla Vandersypen, eds., *Dutch Is Beautiful: Fifty Years of Dutch and Flemish Studies at the University of Michigan* (Ann Arbor: University of Michigan Press, 2019).

was named visiting associate professor. In addition to the beginning Dutch sequence, she offered an advanced seminar in Dutch linguistic theory. And by September of 1975, an agreement had been worked out between the Netherlands Ministry of Education and the U of M Department of Germanic Languages, whereby the Dutch government funded half the salary of a triennially appointed instructor, recruited in the Netherlands. This person was to hold the rank of visiting lecturer. The first incumbent of this position was Henk F. Meulenbeld, from the University of Leiden, who taught Dutch from 1975 to 1977. In addition to the first-year language course, he added a two-semester, second-year sequence, plus an advanced seminar on his specialty, middle Dutch literature, especially the Dutch play, *Elckerlyc* (1495), authored by Peter van Diest, a medieval writer from the Low Countries.

Meulenbeld's successor was Dr. Kees Snoek, who taught Dutch at U of M from 1977 to 1982, and under whom, the course offerings were expanded to include courses and colloquia on modern Dutch literature. He was also involved in the inauguration, in 1981-82, of the Dutch writer-in-residence program, as well as the U of M arrangements for the celebration of the two hundredth anniversary of the Treaty of Amity and Commerce between the Netherlands and the United States (1782). Queen Beatrix visited Michigan and U of M in July of that year.

I just missed that visit when I became the visiting lecturer in Dutch in the 1982-83 academic year. The original agreement appointing a different incumbent every three years was revised, and I continued until my retirement in 2012. In addition to the four-semester, beginning-language sequences, I supervised many independent studies, including Indonesian history and seventeenth-century documents, and taught numerous seminars in Dutch literature. In 1993 I inaugurated the course entitled Anne Frank in Past and Present, which, to my great delight, turned out to be immensely popular among students. In the course, students examine, in translation, not only the famous diary but also other accounts of the Dutch Holocaust, as well as other more general material related to World War II. In the fall semester of 1998-99, I offered for the first time a course entitled the Dutch Colonial Experience. This freshman seminar continued for several years and was taken over by my successor, Annemarie Toebosch, who refocused the course, now entitled Amsterdam. Under her leadership, the Anne Frank course has increased in popularity and remains in high esteem among students and faculty alike, also through linkage with Judaic studies. The various visiting and long-term professors have clearly shaped the program according to their own personal and scholarly interests. Their persistent hard work and ability to make connections with other fields and disciplines has made the program increasingly stronger.

What benefit is there to learning the Dutch language? This is not an easy question. For contrast, I love to give two examples from the history of English-speaking students. In 1780 John Adams put his two sons, John Quincy and Charles, age thirteen and eleven, respectively, in the hands of a Dutch teacher in the so-called Latin or middle school in Amsterdam. It was a failure, because they did not speak Dutch properly, and the schoolmaster thought they were unruly. Father Adams sent them to Leyden to get one-on-one tutorials and attend the occasional lecture at the university. Although we do not know how the young Adams boys fared, the country also known as the United Provinces looked favorably on the United States. When John Adams as the first ambassador in Holland successfully negotiated loans, it was the province of Friesland that recognized the United States in February 1782, even before France did. No Dutch influence is found in the later lives of the Adamses.[8]

Also, at about that same time in the eighteenth century, we find a most diligent student in Utrecht, James Boswell, the biographer of the famous Dr. Johnson, and we have some examples of his attempts at written Dutch. His father had instructed him to work on his Dutch, because "we must own that the English is a good deal borrowed from [the Dutch language]."[9]

There was considerable unrest in the New World colonies at that time, and the Dutch had already put their footprint clearly in the development of America as an independent nation. Alexander Hamilton's wife was Elisabeth Schuyler, and his in-laws were the famous Van Rensselaers. Many Americans identified with the Dutch and reflected their anti-British sentiments, as shown in the arts, fashion, and antiques of the nineteenth century. There is, of course, also a president who, in 1838, kept the many Dutch traditions alive. That was our eighth president, Martin Van Buren, born in Old Kinderhook, which, as legend would have it, is the source of the term "OK."

Readers of this volume know well the large immigration of Dutch to Michigan and the Midwest during the nineteenth century. The stories

---

[8] L. H. Butterfield, Marc Friedlaender, and Mary-Jo Kline, eds., *The Book of Abigail and John: Selected Letters of the Adams Family 1762-1784* (Cambridge, MA: Harvard University Press, 1975), 281-82.
[9] Frederick A. Pottle, *Boswell in Holland 1763-1764* (NY: McGraw-Hill, 1952), 110.

of Van Raalte and Scholte in promoting Christian education are well known, and their Calvinist predecessor was Dominie Jonas Michaelius, who already in 1628 had established instruction in New Amsterdam. "At the outset, preaching and cathechizing [sic] were the forms of education most widely practiced in each of the North American colonies planted during the first half of the seventeenth century."[10] At least 115 Dutch Reformed ministers served in the American colonies. Their stories are the subject of many studies. The struggles that we have had at U of M to establish or maintain Dutch instruction are somewhat similar to the ministerial work of convincing and winning souls. It must have been somewhat easier at Calvin College in Grand Rapids.

The relationship between Dutch studies at U of M and Dutch studies at Calvin College has always been of a cordial nature, albeit somewhat distant, not only in direct miles but also in opinions. When I inquired about teaching opportunities at Calvin College from my previous position in England, my good friend Walter Lagerwey advised me:

> We have an opening in our Dutch Department, but for it, we can consider only persons who are of the Reformed (Gereformeerd) conviction and persuasion, and who stand within that tradition, and are committed to articulate the Christian vision and life and world view in their teaching: we are a Calvinist institution.[11]

This was somewhat problematic in my case since my Roman Catholic parents had baptized me Antonius Jozef Maria. After my appointment in Ann Arbor, Walter and I became respected colleagues, and we worked together on the board of the American Association for Netherlandic Studies. Walter was a formidable treasurer, and I was a hanger-on, who did some newsletters. He once wrote: "For me, the sound of the wind, which more than anything else stands for home, symbolizes the Dutch identity. It is in the littleness itself that the greatness of Holland is comprised, the wind of freedom, the wind of the spirit."[12]

I recently came across another more direct characterization in a wonderful WWII memoir: "The Reformed Church played its part in

---

[10] Lawrence A. Cremin, *American Education: The Colonial Experience 1607-1783* (NY: Harper & Row, 1970), 176.
[11] Walter Lagewey to the author, 12 Feb. 1980.
[12] Ton Broos, Walter Lagerwey, "Pionier van de Neerlandistiek in de Verenigde Staten," *Neerlandia/Nederlands van Nu* 3 (2012), 38-39.

giving the Dutch their national character: direct, house proud, and determined to offer a respectable exterior to the outside world."[13]

The 1992 Interdisciplinary Conference on Netherlandic Studies in Grand Rapids inspired me to consider new teaching methods. I followed up with an invitation to a colleague, and as a team, we started the Anne Frank course. This course has brought in the number of students that impress the bean counters. It is currently the most popular course in the Department of Germanic Languages, with some one hundred students and a waiting list. In part because of it, U of M boasts the largest Dutch program in the United States.

To highlight the success of the Dutch program, we established an annual lecture series,[14] now in its twenty-sixth year. Our speakers have ranged from a member of the Dutch Supreme Court to a member of parliament, Holocaust survivors, and writers on topics such as Dutch Indies literature, New Amsterdam, Flemish art, and Spinoza. I vividly remember Robert P. Swierenga and his presentation about the Dutch garbage collectors in Chicago. His granddaughter was one of my students.

You might remember that I mentioned Henk F. Meulenbeld, one of my predecessors and one of the first instigators of Dutch Studies in the 1970s, who taught a course on *Elckerlyc*, a Medieval Dutch drama, now regarded as the original to the famous English *Everyman*. My colleagues Martin Walsh and Clifford Davidson of Western Michigan University and I, made a new and updated translation in 2007, which was well received. It is a sign of the changing times, however, that over the years not even a hundred copies have been sold, even at a student-friendly price. In other words: student interests are moving away from literature, in favor of communication studies or other topics, like colonialism, racism, political activism, and other isms. The young have many aspirations, and I have reminiscences.

---

[13] Bart van Es, *The Cut Out Girl* [*vergeet mij niet*, in Dutch]: *A Story of War and Family, Lost and Found* (NY: Penguin Press, 2018), 135.

[14] "In 1996 the Dutch Studies Program was further enriched by the addition of the De Vries-Van der Kooy Memorial Lecture. Jan de Vries, a Dutch physician with the World Health Organization, who taught at the University of Michigan, and Meindert van der Kooy, Director of Plant Operations at U of M, were instrumental in the formation of the Netherlands America University League in Ann Arbor. In honor of their extraordinary efforts to promote the study of the language and culture of the Low Countries, the annual De Vries-Van der Kooy Memorial Lecture has been held annually since 1996." https://lsa.umich.edu/german/undergraduate-students/dutch-flemish-studies/devries-vanderkooy-lectures.html.

What can Dutch teachers in the United States learn from this? I believe that the Dutch (and Flemish) slice of the American pie can add significantly to the international—or global, multicultural—contribution to a worldwide understanding of the human condition. Improved technological developments help us face our brothers and sisters across the ocean in one-on-one encounters, look at their newspapers and television programs, exchange music in real time, look into all the libraries of the world, and have Dutch historical literature on our desks in seconds. What is sometimes called *Neerlandica extra muros* is a growing field with flexible borders.

The teaching of Dutch at U of M began as language courses, with the usual vocabulary and grammar tests, but soon branched out to include literature, occasional art historical subjects, the colonial experience in southeast Asia and the West Indies, and the history and actuality of Amsterdam, as well as excursions into other disciplines. Dutch and Flemish studies under my successor put more emphasis on diversity, equality, and inclusion, which means more attention to colonialism, social activism, and culture awareness. There is no limit to the possibilities. Passion and enthusiasm were the requirements that drove the first teaching ministers in the seventeenth century, and I believe we have that in abundance in our modern-day teachers.

The links between Grand Rapids and U of M are stronger than just the Dutch language and literature studies that I have referred to. Grand Rapids native Jack Lousma, with Frisian ancestry, attended Pioneer High School in Ann Arbor and U of M and became an astronaut. As a member of the support crew in Texas, he received the message from Apollo 13, "Okay, Houston, we've had a problem here." The most famous link, of course, is President Gerald R. Ford, a Wolverine quarterback. Whereas the beautiful Gerald R. Ford Presidential Museum is in Grand Rapids, the Gerald R. Ford Presidential Library is in Ann Arbor. As the story goes: "The day after Ford left office, nine trucks moved fifteen million papers to a storage facility in Ann Arbor." The privately funded library was completed in 1979.[15]

Many prominent professors with Dutch Michigan ancestry have come through the doors of our university, and many Dutch professors have joined us from across the ocean. They all kept the Dutch and Flemish connections alive. The Dutch and Flemish studies programs demonstrate that U of M is more than a "Big House" football stadium with a college attached to it.

---

[15] Susan L. Nenadic and M. Joanne Nesbit, *Legendary Locals of Ann Arbor* (Charleston, SC: Arcadia Publishing, 2016), 67, 92.

CHAPTER 21

Betsy DeVos's Dutch Heritage, Media Reporting, and the Misuse of Dutch American History

Michael J. Douma

The current (2019) US secretary of education, Betsy DeVos (1958-) was born and raised in Holland, Michigan. She is of Dutch descent, but in all branches of her family tree, she is at least three generations removed from late nineteenth-century immigrants from the Netherlands to the United States. Her father, Edgar Prince (1931-1995), also born in Holland, Michigan, founded the Prince Corporation, which became a very profitable manufacturer of die cast machines and interior components for the automobile industry. DeVos attended Holland Christian High School and then Calvin College in nearby Grand Rapids. In 1979 she married Dick DeVos, Amway executive and son of company cofounder Richard DeVos. The Prince and DeVos families are known for their philanthropy and support for conservative policies. Betsy DeVos previously served as the chair of the Michigan Republican Party and was the Republican National Committeewoman for Michigan. Through private giving and political lobbying, she has advocated for charter schools.

When Betsy DeVos was nominated to become the US secretary of education in 2016, journalists desperately sought to explain how she could believe what she believed. Perhaps there was something about DeVos' background that would explain why she supported the free market in education, charter schools, Christian schools, and vouchers. The investigative reporting that followed seemed to be motivated not so much by an inquisitive, "*Why* does she support these things?" but by an accusatory, "*How could she* believe these things?" Seeking answers about DeVos, journalists—primarily East Coast progressives—flocked to West Michigan like anthropologists studying a primitive tribe to observe the scenery and take notes on the local inhabitants.

In January 2017, articles in *Politico* and *Mother Jones* established a narrative that DeVos' ethnic heritage was the dominant underlying factor that explained her views. These articles begot more articles, which begot WordPress comments, which in turn begot tweets and retweets, such that, for a short time in 2017, and again with an article in the *Economist* in 2018, the history of Dutch American education was a major news story. Following the establishment of this ethnic heritage thesis, the discourse turned more toward DeVos' supposed inheritance from Abraham Kuyper, her billionaire status, her lack of experience, and other topics. In the process, quite a bit of damage was done to the public's perception of the Dutch American legacy. Through poor research, absent fact checking, a combination of outsider mistakes and intentional, apparently politically motivated misrepresentations, journalists butchered Dutch American history.

The history of Dutch Americans and the history of education in the Netherlands, many observers surmised, explains how DeVos came to her beliefs. This argument—poorly defended and without any evidence—sometimes borders on a kind of historical determinism in which one's beliefs are thought to be determined either by one's identity or some environmental factor.

I contend that media accounts of DeVos in *Politico*, *Mother Jones*, the *Atlantic*, the *Economist*, and the *New York Times*, among other sources, oversimplified and misrepresented Dutch American history, sometimes in order to score political points and often with reckless disregard for nuances on the ground and the established research on Dutch Americans. I do not have a political argument in this paper. What I think of DeVos' political views is immaterial to my purpose as an historian, which is to rectify errors in the interpretation of the history of Dutch American education that appeared in the media in the wake of DeVos' nomination and eventual swearing in as secretary of education. I will trace the story of how the media handled DeVos' ethnic background, expose their factual errors, and explain what we know unequivocally about her Dutch and Dutch American influences. Finally, I will argue that historians are responsible to correct such public misconceptions of history and that we members of AADAS, myself included, missed an opportunity to do so when the media began its critique. I trust this paper begins the corrective process.

"If you ain't Dutch"

"To understand the DeVos family, it helps to understand West Michigan," wrote Zack Stanton at *Politico* in early 2017. He continued:

Broadly speaking, it's a region where people are deeply religious, politically conservative, and unfailingly polite—think Utah, if it were settled not by Mormons but by Dutch Calvinists. "There's an old expression here," chuckles Gleaves Whitney, director of the Hauenstein Center for Presidential Studies at Grand Valley State University in Grand Rapids, "If you ain't Dutch, you ain't much."[1]

The idea that the Dutch of West Michigan are like the Mormons would be repeated in later news coverage of DeVos. It is an inferred notion of Dutch insularity, isolation, whiteness, and conservatism that drives the narrative. More on this isolation narrative later. First, let us deal with the phrase, "If you ain't Dutch, you ain't much." My experience suggests that not one out of a hundred people in West Michigan has uttered this phrase in any kind of seriousness. If used, it serves as a joke, or perhaps as a commentary on an individual's behavior. Yet, this phrase is repeated numerous times in media accounts as evidence of Dutch chauvinism in West Michigan.

We even get it in an article from a journalist in the Netherlands who covered the DeVos story:

The West of the state of Michigan, where there are cities and villages with names like Holland, Zeeland, and Borculo, is very Republican, conservative, and fundamentalist Christian. Many of the inhabitants are descendants of the Dutch Reformed (*gereformeerden*) who in the 19th century emigrated to the U.S.

---

[1] Zach Stanton, "How Betsy DeVos Used God and Amway to Take Over Michigan Politics," *Politico*, 15 Jan. 2017. https://www.politico.com/magazine/story/2017/01/betsy-dick-devos-family-amway-michigan-politics-religion-214631).

"If you ain't Dutch, you ain't much" they still always say in West Michigan.[2]

The emphasis on this phrase is a perfect example of the failure of outsiders to understand the history and culture of a place. Research on the origin and background of the phrase, "If you ain't Dutch, you ain't much," yields little. During my investigation of this phrase, I searched for it in delpher.nl., the *New York Times* historical database, ProQuest, newspaperarchive.com, advantage-preservation.com, and other newspaper databases. There was nothing there. In addition, there are extensive newspaper archives for West Michigan and for other places of Dutch settlement, like northwest Iowa. Although many Dutch American newspapers have been digitized, a search of *De Grondwet*, the *Sioux Center Nieuwsblad*, the *Holland City News*, and the older *Sheboygan Nieuwsbode* yielded no results for this phrase. Given the controversy over the history of the term "No Irish Need Apply," one must always hold out ultimate judgment, since other results may someday come to light.[3] These searches do, however, suggest that the phrase, "If you ain't Dutch, you ain't much," is not of long standing.

From all the available sources, I discovered that the earliest printed use of the term comes from Iowa in the year 1980. "If yer not Dutch, yer not much," and "If you ain't Dutch you ain't much" were mentioned by students in Hawarden, Iowa, in 1980, as favorite t-shirt sayings.[4] The two separate versions may indicate the linguistic immaturity of the phrase, that it had not been fixed in usage. The "ain't Dutch" variety appeared in the *Sioux Center News* a few months later.[5] It seems this phrase originated in northwest Iowa, then spread to Pella,

---

[2] "Het Westen van de Staat Michigan, waar stadjes en dorpen liggen met namen als Holland, Zeeland, en Borculo, is zeer republikeins, conservatief en fundementaal-christelijk. Veel van de inwoners stamen af van gereformeerden die in de 19de eeuw naar de VS emigreeden. 'If you ain't Dutch, you ain't much,' zeggen ze nog altijd in west Michigan." Bert Wagendorp, "Betsy DeVos's missie: christelijke privescholen in een godelijke samenleving," *De Volkskrant*, 10 Feb. 2017. https://www.volkskrant.nl/nieuws-achtergrond/betsy-devos-missie-christelijke-privescholen-in-een-godgerichte-samenleving~b35bcfb4/.

[3] In this case, what was once thought of as fact came under attack as a "myth"; in the long run, however, the initial understanding—that NINA was, indeed, an historical reality—proved to be true. Richard Jensen, "'No Irish Need Apply': A Myth of Victimization," *Journal of Social History* 36, no. 2 (Winter 2002): 405-29. Rebecca Friend, "No Irish Need Deny: Evidence for the Historicity of NINA Restrictions in Advertisements and Signs," *Journal of Social History* 49, no. 4 (Summer 2016): 829-52.

[4] *The Independent*, Hawarden, IA (3 April 1980): 6.

[5] *Sioux Center News*, IA (2 July 1980): 8.

from whence it was carried to Canada, where, in 1982, the *Globe and Mail* used it in a review of a book by Berton Roueché, in referring to his visit to Pella, Iowa.[6]

Historically, it seems that this phrase did not originate in West Michigan, nor was it limited to use there. It was used not only to exclude non-Dutch, rather—and this is crucially important for the current analysis—the term was used to insult and ridicule the Dutch, as well as the non-Dutch. It appeared in Canada, the United States, and the Netherlands in a few forms. It may have been used in earlier decades but was captured in print only in the 1980s and popularized in the 1990s. Mostly, however, the phrase has been used in humorous ways to refer to the Dutch in the Midwest, as well as those in New York and even the Pennsylvania Dutch.

So, in the *Politico* article, when Gleaves Whitney calls the phrase "an old expression," we need to clarify that, in fact, it is a recently established expression, not an old one. It does not appear to be "old" in the sense that it has been around since the days when Dutch was the dominant street language of Holland, Michigan, for instance. Bert Wagendorp implies in his above-mentioned article that in West Michigan, people "still" use this phrase, which certainly insinuates that this was a common phrase and attitude from an earlier age that persists today. It appears that it was not and is not.[7]

Understanding DeVos

Back to the main theme of this chapter. In 2017 numerous articles purporting to explain DeVos' views appeared from the hands of journalists working for major media. There are many people who believe in a free market for education and many more who support charter schools. But with DeVos coming into a position of power, more explanation was needed for "why" people held these views. Why

---

[6] *The Globe and Mail*, Toronto, CA (9 Oct. 1982): 17.
[7] The Dutch media, although interested in DeVos' Dutch background, is much more likely to point out that she is rich (many sources use the term *steenrijk*) and Christian. See, for another example, Louis Hoeks, "Trump kiest minister met Hollandse wortels," *Financieel Dagblad*, 24 Nov. 2016. Ironically, there is more evidence for an earlier date of the anti-Dutch rhyme: "Dutchman, Dutchman, belly full of straw, can't say nothing but ja, ja, ja" (or yaw, yaw, yaw), which older Dutch Americans in the 1970s recalled as a phrase from their childhood. For one example, see Clarence DeGraaf, Oral History Interview, 22 Jan. 1977, Digital Commons of Hope College, Joint Archives of Holland, and the reminiscences of Nellie Ruite Baas in 1970 at (http://www.ruitersporen.nl/verhalen/verhalen.php?story=78), accessed 4 Jan. 2019.

did she believe this? For many, the answer came from the unique history which DeVos brought to her worldview. The history of Dutch Americans, combined with the history of education in the Netherlands, they surmised, would explain how DeVos came to her beliefs. Common were statements of the type: "DeVos's educational convictions aren't necessarily surprising, considering her hometown's ethnic, religious, and cultural ties to the Netherlands."[8]

In their zeal to explain DeVos' ideas by way of historical background and context, many a journalist made simple mistakes about Dutch Americans and their history. Most of these mistakes, however, seem to have been born of ignorance, not malice. For example, we can excuse the ever-dumbed-down *USA Today* for writing something that is more awkward than inaccurate: "The Christian Reformed Church, formed by Dutch immigrants settling the Midwest in the 1800s, grew out of Dutch Calvinism."[9] And the *Huffington Post* recently (but not, however, in any reference to DeVos) made the error of thinking that Holland, Michigan, was once full of Dutch-looking buildings: "Much of the original architecture [in Holland, Michigan] was destroyed in an 1871 fire, but the city still has many tributes to its Dutch heritage."[10]

A number of high-profile sources seem to have gone out of their way to make unfair characterizations of Dutch Americans as the Mormons of Michigan or some long-lost and long-left-behind tribe. For the *New York Magazine*, Lisa Miller wrote, "Holland is the kind of religious and ethnic American enclave, like Salt Lake City or Monsey, New York, where a dramatic homogeneity is preserved by geographic isolation."[11] What kind of homogeneity is that? Is it racial/ethnic homogeneity? Then she has not looked very closely at the census; more than a third of the residents of Holland, Michigan, are Latinos. Is she referring to political homogeneity? Ottawa County is Republican, but Democratic voters within the city of Holland now have a slight majority. And the argument that Hollanders are conservative because they have voted for Republican presidential candidates since the 1860s,

[8] Emily Deruy, "A Tale of Two Betsy DeVoses: The generous Grand Rapids resident and the tone-deaf Trump official," *The Atlantic*, 8 March 2017.
[9] https://www.usatoday.com/story/news/nation/2017/02/07/5-faith-facts-betsy-devos/97601374/.
[10] Caroline Bologna, "14 U.S. Cities with a European Vibe," *Huffington Post*, 15 Nov. 2018, https://www.huffpost.com/entry/us-cities-european-vibe_n_5beb2eaee4b07 83e0a1d139c.
[11] http://nymag.com/intelligencer/2017/07/betsy-devos-secretary-of-education.html.

fails American History 101. Historians regularly teach that political parties change platforms over time and evolve. Has Holland, Michigan, been more conservative over the long run than, say, Central Alabama, just because Central Alabama used to vote for conservative Democratic candidates and now votes for conservative Republicans? Perhaps Lisa Miller's comment about "dramatic homogeneity" refers to religious homogeneity. In that case, her story falls apart with a quick glance at the phonebook to see all the churches from traditions outside the Dutch Reformed.[12]

Rizga as the source of errors

These mistakes pale in comparison to the worst DeVos article of them all, a piece by Kristina Rizga in the March/April 2017 issue of *Mother Jones*. This article first appeared online in January 2017. Like other journalists, Rizga consistently misrepresents the West Michigan Dutch so she can "explain" the background of Betsy DeVos.[13] There are so many historical inaccuracies about Dutch Americans in her article that it is hard to know where to begin. Rizga opens with these lines:

> More than 150 years ago, Dutch immigrants from a conservative Protestant sect chose western Michigan as the setting for this idealized replica of Holland, in part because of its isolation. They wanted to keep American influences away from their orthodox community.

The Dutch Americans who settled in West Michigan 150 years ago did not come from one "sect" but from a variety of Protestant and Catholic backgrounds. One could assume that Rizga chose the word "sect" instead of denomination because "sect" has the connotation of a marginalized cult.

More importantly, the Dutch immigrants in West Michigan did not want isolation, nor did they choose Michigan because they wanted to be left alone. Indeed, it was very much to the contrary. Albertus C. Van Raalte, the founder of Holland, chose Michigan partly because it was more developed and settled than Wisconsin. The earliest Dutch to settle in West Michigan went there because land was inexpensive,

---

[12] Lisa Miller, "Who is Betsy DeVos, and how did she get to be head of our schools?" http://nymag.com/intelligencer/2017/07/betsy-devos-secretary-of-education.html.

[13] https://www.motherjones.com/politics/2017/01/betsy-devos-christian-schools-vouchers-charter-education-secretary/.

and there was enough land available to settle together so they could replant their churches and re-establish the social networks they had in the Netherlands. But from the very first years, the Dutch of Holland, Michigan, welcomed non-Dutch into their community. Dutch Americans in West Michigan did not want to "keep American influences away"; they wanted to keep sinful influences away. Although some of those sinful influences were American, the settlers generally welcomed Americans. Indeed, they tackled the English language; they studied American politics and history; they applied for citizenship as soon as they could; they struggled with questions about slavery, and they sent soldiers to fight for the Union in the Civil War.

Free market oriented from the start, the Dutch in Holland, Michigan, particularly wanted to attract businessmen who could furnish the city with capital. They also wanted American bankers, merchants, and schoolteachers. The Dutch cut roads out of the wilderness and petitioned the state of Michigan to build roads and railroads to their city so that they could talk and trade with other Americans. They dug a harbor channel again and again to reach the markets of Chicago. They sought connections with the Reformed Church in New York and New Jersey. The Dutch settled in ethnic enclaves in Grand Rapids, Michigan, and in Chicago, but so did the Germans, the Lithuanians, the Polish, and every other ethnic group in the Midwest in the nineteenth century. The Dutch were no more isolationist than the Norwegians or Swedes. Indeed, they were not isolationist at all. Settling together did not make them isolationists.

Despite Rizga's stereotype, Holland was never intended to be an idealized replica of the Netherlands. Certain elements were replicated in the Tulip Time parade, an event that was initiated and promoted by the non-Dutch American citizens of Holland to beautify the city and bring in tourist dollars during the bare-boned 1930s. Some of the Dutch Americans played along, and some of them detested the event, but most of them did not resist the annual extravaganza and came to embrace it for its commercial impact on the community.

Rizga then lists several strict laws that either are or were until recently on the books in Holland, Michigan. This, she maintains, is a sure sign of the city's backward conservatism. It is, of course, quite easy to find silly laws of the "no spitting on the sidewalks" variety on the books in any American municipality. There are also many places that restrict alcohol sales or maintain regulations for mowing the grass or otherwise disturbing the peace, and so forth. On this theme of conservative law and order, Rizga writes that, in present-day Holland: "Most locals say rules like these help keep Holland prosperous, with low unemployment, little crime, good city services, and Republicans at almost every government post." I am quite certain that she did not interview "most locals," and I am also quite certain that most locals would say nothing of the sort. Most locals would probably say that there are local ordinances because the people want to live in a clean, orderly town. Cities that elect Democrats have similar objectives and similar laws.

Rizga continues to make erroneous claims. She claims that the Dutch Seceders who made up a large portion of the Dutch American immigrants "rebelled against the Dutch government when it tried to modernize the state Calvinist church, including by changing the songbooks used during worship and ending discriminatory laws against Catholics and Jews." The implication is that the Seceders were rebelling because they wanted the government to discriminate more against the Catholics and Jews. The majority of Protestants in the Netherlands, not just the Seceders, were against full Catholic rights, but it was not a major theme in the Seceders' justification for secession. The Seceders' main complaint was about restrictions on their own freedom to worship, not on the state's limitations on other faiths. This, of course, is a trick with ambiguity in the English language. One can read Rizga's line about the Seceders and the Catholics and Jews in at least two ways: that the Dutch Seceders were rebelling either *while* this other stuff was going on or *because* of it. Frankly, it is a dishonest style of writing. Last, one could dispute that there was a state church in that period. The Dutch state privileged the Hervormde Kerk, but it was not officially a state church.

Rizga's inaccuracies get worse: "In the city of Holland, they recreated their Dutch villages. And just like back home, their church was essentially their government, influencing every part of farmers' lives." Physically, Holland, Michigan, was not built on the model of a Dutch village. The grid design of its streets was American, and its early buildings were mostly in the American fashion, since the Dutch immigrants did not bring a lot of architects and city planners along with them. The churches in Holland were a powerful presence in the community, but they were certainly no stand-in for government. Holland, Michigan, was never a theocracy. In the first year of the city, the Dutch formed a *volksvergadering* (people's assembly), an explicitly secular democratic governing body. The churches upheld a code of conduct in the city before secular government could be formed, but from the beginning, civil punishment for major crimes was doled out at the county level in Grand Haven.

Writing for the website of the John C. Danforth Center on Religion and Politics, Abram Van Engen, an associate professor of English at Washington University in St. Louis, points out some of Rizga's mistakes. Van Engen, who prefaces his remarks with a statement of his personal disagreement with DeVos, is a graduate of Calvin College, with a background in the Christian Reformed Church. He points out that historical backgrounds do not determine one's ideas. "That's the thing about religious traditions," he writes. "They can be highly formative without yielding predictable results. "Membership in the CRC does not lead inexorably to free market conservative policies, Amway, or wealth."[14] For evidence of this, there has been a long tradition of liberal-progressive politics at Calvin College and among the intellectuals in the CRC. Lester DeKoster, writing for the *Reformed Journal* in 1958, spoke for this group when he declared that Calvinism and the Democratic Party, and Calvinism and state regulation, were more intertwined historically than either Calvinism and capitalism or Calvinism and free markets.[15]

Instead of pushing back on Rizga for her historical errors, we see a bit of the opposite—some Dutch Americans wrote responses in support of Rizga's interpretation. On March 6, 2017, religiondispatches.org, which styles itself as "your independent, non-profit, award-winning source for the best writing on the critical and timely issues at the intersection of religion, politics, and culture," posted an article by Peter Laarman, in which he repeats the line from Rizga about the Seceder discrimination toward Catholics and Jews. These "'Seceders' [quotes used by Laarman] were unhappy that the Dutch government at the time (1840s) was doing away with some relics of the old Calvinist theocracy in the Netherlands, e.g., ending discrimination across Catholics and Jews." Laarman ends that sentence with the snarky, "We can't have that, can we?" Piling on, Laarman ascribes racist motives to the vouchers movement, connecting modern Dutch American Calvinism with Dutch Calvinist racial discrimination elsewhere in history. "Let's just say that

[14] Abram Van Engen, "Advancing God's Kingdom: Calvinism, Calvin College, and Betsy DeVos," 30 Jan. 2017, https://religionandpolitics.org/2017/01/30/advancing-gods-kingdom-calvinism-calvin-college-and-betsy-devos/.

[15] Lester DeKoster, "Calvinists and Democrats," *Reformed Journal*, Oct. 1958. Reprinted in James D. Bratt and Ronald A. Wells, *The Best of the Reformed Journal* (Grand Rapids, MI: Eerdmans, 2003), 47-53.

Dutch Calvinism has never been especially kind to people of African descent." Think slave trade and apartheid, he implies.¹⁶

To Rizga's article, Dutch American author James Calvin Schaap, responded with praise: "I don't know Kristina Rizga, but she's been following the Betsy DeVos story for some time already; and it's clear she's done her homework on [the CRC]." Schaap, apparently, does not recognize any of Rizga's historical errors.¹⁷

In her attempted coverage of Dutch American history, Rizga never mentions Abraham Kuyper. But later writers would link DeVos more to Kuyperian educational ideas than to the views of the early Seceders. This was the point of a May 27, 2017, article by Willemien Otten, professor of theology and the history of Christianity at the University of Chicago Divinity School, writing for that school's Martin Marty Center for the Public Understanding of Religion. The title of her article, "The Hidden Roots of Betsy DeVos' Education Policy," suggests a conspiracy or some intentional attempt to "hide" DeVos' true influences. Otten produces a reasonable account of the rise of the Dutch Kuyperian educational system, but she provides no evidence of Kuyper's influence on DeVos. Otten links DeVos with Kuyper with this one line: "Growing up in the Christian Reformed Church in Western Michigan and attending Calvin College, Betsy DeVos was heavily influenced by Abraham Kuyper (1837-1920), an early Dutch advocate of 'Schools with the Bible.'" Otten is critical of the Kuyperian educational system in the Netherlands for its "lack of credible representation," while one of her primary worries about such a system in the United States is that schools would be free to discriminate on various grounds. Otten's overriding concern, however, seems to be this: "By sidetracking funds from public education, a shadow system of privately run schools is created that undermines the flourishing of a once viable national public school system." That seems like an overly limited picture of the history of American public education, one in which the role of private Christian education is not part of the landscape.¹⁸ Note the implicit pejorative implications in terms like the "shadow system" of schools, DeVos' "hidden" ideas, and the looming threat to national public education by Christian schools.

---

[16] Peter Laarman, "Dutch Treat: Betsy DeVos and the Christian Schools Movement," http://religiondispatches.org/dutch-treat-betsy-devos-and-the-christian-schools-movement/.

[17] James Calvin Schaap, "Betsy DeVos and the Kingdom," 19 Jan. 2017, https://www.christiancentury.org/blog-post/betsy-devos-and-kingdom.

[18] https://divinity.uchicago.edu/sightings/hidden-roots-betsy-devoss-educational-policies, 25 May 2017.

After a year of trying to understand DeVos, the *Economist* jumped into the fray with an article that received perhaps the most attention of all in this genre. Inspired by both DeVos' ascendency and the nomination of the conservative former congressman Peter Hoekstra as ambassador to the Netherlands, this article was titled, "Why are Dutch-Americans so different from the Dutch?" And it lumps together all Dutch Americans—meaning a few Michigan politicians and the residents of the city of Holland, Michigan—to explain why they are such backward conservatives. The article's subtitle betrays the game the author wants to play: "The most conservative Americans, the most liberal Europeans."[19]

By what measure are Dutch Americans the most conservative Americans? Perhaps the author is unaware of Orthodox Jews, the Amish, or the average southern or midwestern evangelical, who, culturally, is likely to be more conservative than the average Dutch American.

To learn more about the topic, the *Economist* interviewed Jay Peters, local Democratic politician and failed mayoral candidate in Holland, Michigan. Peters' response is full of hyperbole. "The people who left the Netherlands were some of the most conservative Dutch-speaking people on the planet." Well, since most of the Dutch-speaking people on the planet were in the Netherlands, this is hardly a surprise. Then again, it is not even entirely true. The Dutch-speaking Boers of South Africa, the colonial administrators of the Netherlands East Indies, the slave-holding plantation owners in Dutch Suriname were, in a variety of ways, more conservative than the backwater Dutch peasants who immigrated to the United States.

The *Economist* wants to know what accounts for the cultural gulf between conservative Dutch Americans and the liberal Dutch nationals. Any short article is necessarily limited in scope, but this article finds its explanation on only one side of the ocean. What it neglects is that the Netherlands was a relatively conservative country until the 1960s. What it also neglects is that both sides have changed. Dutch Americans are conservative, but not overwhelmingly so, and their political and social views today have changed to some degree since Van Raalte first arrived in Michigan in the winter of 1846-47. Historians looking at the Dutch Americans of the nineteenth century have found communitarian and egalitarian elements that contrast with the image of modern-day conservatism.

---

[19] This article at the *Economist* got widespread attention. It was reposted at History News Network, https://historynewsnetwork.org/article/169145.

What we know about DeVos's Dutch connection

What does Betsy DeVos have to say about her own background, about the history of Dutch Americans, and about Abraham Kuyper that would indicate the source of her ideas? Very little, it turns out. Why are journalists and pundits digging and turning out (somewhat inaccurate) narratives? This is partly because of the relative silence of DeVos herself. During her confirmation process, she was not allowed to give interviews. About this, DeVos says, "I wasn't able to talk with the media at all. I wasn't able to express anything from my perspective. So it gave weeks and weeks of open shots for my opponents to take."[20] When she could talk to the media, things did not go much better. A tense interview on CBS's *60 Minutes* in March 2018 brought her widespread criticism for being unprepared. Perhaps to avoid the critical spotlight, she has given few further interviews.[21] Although she actively defends certain elements of her educational platform, she seems reluctant to outline her foundational philosophical beliefs, which may interfere in her attempts to act more pragmatically in the Department of Education. She has not spoken publicly about either her Dutch heritage or her intellectual debts.

DeVos' Kuyperian influence is only tangentially evidenced, and the media's focus on this theme can to be traced to a comment from Richard Mouw in an interview with the *Washington Post* for an article about DeVos in 2016.[22] Mouw once served on a committee with DeVos at Mars Hill Church. When this shared committee work happened and what the extent of their relationship was is unclear. Mouw is reported to have said that DeVos was "heavily influenced" by Kuyper. This article in the *Washington Post* also quotes Mouw as saying that he would not consider DeVos to be either right-wing or in the religious-right camp. These latter comments, less useful for the narrative that many reporters tried to tell, did not appear to have been taken up by later

---

[20] https://www.politico.com/magazine/story/2017/11/01/betsy-devos-secretary-education-profile-2017-215768.

[21] Some examples include: https://www.the74million.org/article/74-interview-education-secretary-betsy-devos-on-freedom-scholarships-why-parents-deserve-more-school-options-the-noisy-status-quo-protecting-cabal-fighting-her-agenda/; https://omny.fm/shows/business-for-breakfast/betsy-devos-june-26.

[22] Sarah Pulliam Bailey, "Betsy DeVos, Trump's education pick, is a billionaire with deep ties to the Christian Reformed community," *Washington Post*, 23 Nov. 2016. https://www.washingtonpost.com/news/acts-of-faith/wp/2016/11/23/betsy-devos-trumps-education-pick-is-a-billionaire-philanthropist-with-deep-ties-to-the-reformed-christian-community/?utm_term=.ab8b540ea6cd.

writers. Instead, the "heavily influenced" by Kuyper line became part of her standard bio online. The article by Willemien Otten, which linked DeVos to Kuyper, while providing a short history of Dutch educational policy, also helped to promote this perception.

Word of DeVos' Kuyperian lineage spread from there. The World Socialist website informs us that, "Billionaire heiress Betsy DeVos is a devotee of neo-Calvinist Dutch theologian and Prime Minister Abraham Kuyper, an ultra-right-wing opponent of the French Revolution."[23] This is how quickly we go from learning the hidden history of DeVos' Kuyperian heritage to her status as a devotee. A professor of African American history at the University of Illinois repeated the view that DeVos was a "devotee of the neo-Calvinist theologian" Kuyper to link her to support for pillarization, segregation, South African apartheid, and Dutch slavery.[24] It quickly spirals out of control in the comments on other websites: "Oh, and Betsy DeVos' intellectual hero is Abraham Kuyper, who was also a hero of Hendrik Verwoerd."[25] *De Volkskrant's* Bert Wagendorp reports that "Her thinking is, in her own words, above all influenced by one man: Abraham Kuyper."[26] Unless Wagendorp has access to something we do not, there seems to be no public record of DeVos saying that she is above all influenced by one man—Abraham Kuyper. This is like a bad, trans-Atlantic version of the telephone game. At the end of Wagendorp's article is a correction: "In an earlier version of this column, Grand Rapids was called the capitol of Michigan. That is not correct. Lansing is the capitol of Michigan."[27]

In sum, what the public knows or can know about DeVos is extremely limited. The entirety of the Kuyperian angle has been triangulated from the fact that she attended Calvin College and from the short mention of Kuyper in the press made by Richard Mouw.

---

[23] Nancy Hanover, "US education secretary attacks separation of church and state, 21 May 2018, https://www.wsws.org/en/articles/2018/05/21/devo-m21.html.

[24] Sundiata Cha-Jua, "Real Talk: The Destruction of Public Education," 21 Jan. 2018, *The News-Gazette* (east-central Illinois), http://www.news-gazette.com/opinion/columns/2018-01-21/sundiata-cha-juareal-talk-the-destruction-public-education.html.

[25] https://www.scoopnest.com/user/AfricasaCountry/827191231893602304-oh-and-betsy-devos-s-intellectual-hero-is-abraham-kuyper-who-was-also-a-hero-of-hendrik-verwoerd.

[26] "Haar denken is naar eigen zeggen bovenal beinvloed door een man: Abraham Kuyper." Bert Wagendorp, "Betsy DeVos's missie: christelijke privescholen in een godelijke samenleving," *De Volkskrant*, 10 Feb. 2017.

[27] "In een eerdere verise van deze column werd Grand Rapids de hoofstad van Michigan genoemd. Dat klopt niet, Lansing is de hoodstad van Michigan."

Perhaps DeVos really is a devotee of Kuyper; maybe she has a picture of him on her wall at the Department of Education. But, at present, there is very little to indicate that she has more than a passing familiarity with Kuyper and that the influences on her thinking about education and school choice have more to do with her experience as a philanthropist and little to do with her Dutch heritage.

In a 2013 interview with the magazine *Philanthropy*, DeVos was asked how she had become interested in the school choice movement in the first place. Her answer was that it was a gradual process, but one important event was a visit to the Potter's House Christian School, which garnered her sympathy for those who could not send their kids to whatever school they believed was best for them.[28]

Perhaps the journalists are correct, and DeVos has secret motivations for her views, but the general narrative of the press is not in line with the reasons DeVos has given. In the *New York Times*, DeVos gives only one reason for her support for private education, charter schools, and voucher programs. Namely, she wants to empower "parents with a right that she was afforded by privilege: choice."[29]

Conclusion

To some observers in the media, it is obvious that DeVos' Dutch American heritage and background are responsible for her views. To Willemien Otten, it is equally obvious that DeVos is an heir of Kuyper. To others, DeVos' views are explained by her Calvinism or maybe her conservatism, evangelicalism, social status, and business aims. Instead of imagining that a person may entertain any number of ideas, the conversation has turned to background causes that have supposedly determined her views.

It is natural that we look for a narrative to connect the dots of evidence that we do have. Does Betsy DeVos' Dutch American heritage, her upbringing, or her reading of Abraham Kuyper determine her views? Perhaps to an extent they do. But anyone's ideas are more than a response to their conditions. DeVos has certain ideas that she justifies with reasons, with arguments. Her reasons for holding her views may be

---

[28] https://www.philanthropyroundtable.org/philanthropy-magazine/article/spring-2013-interview-with-betsy-devos-the-reformer.

[29] Erica L. Green, "To Understand Betsy DeVos's Educational Views, View Her Education," https://www.nytimes.com/2017/06/10/us/politics/betsy-devos-private-schools-choice.html, *New York Times*, 10 June 2017.

right or wrong, but they are more than the inevitable outgrowth of her Dutch American heritage.

To their credit, a few voices have been trying to correct historical and contemporary factual errors that have risen about the Dutch in West Michigan since Betsy DeVos' entrance into the national spotlight. Calvin College's James K. A. Smith, for example, took to Twitter in November 2016 to educate the *New Yorker*'s Jane Mayer about some basic errors in her article on DeVos. He objected to Mayer's sentence, "The DeVos family belongs to the deeply conservative Dutch Reformed Church and has pushed for years to breach the wall between church and state on education, among other issues." Mayer was unable to see what was wrong with that and asked for clarification. Smith doubled down with a flood of capitalized words:[30] "There Is No Denomination Called The Dutch Reformed Church. She is Not A Member of Any Reformed Church. Christian Reformed Church Usually Dismissed As 'Liberal' By Evangelicals. And BDV Doesn't Q Church/state Dist." Mayer refused to admit her error and called it a matter of opinion.

In the *Chicago Tribune*, Heather Wilhelm ridiculed this trend of news articles about the conservative, religious Dutch Americans. With not a little tongue in cheek, she wrote:

> My childhood in western Michigan was rather ordinary, I suppose. Together with my Dutch-imported family, I'd gather on weekends at the local Christian Reformed Church, eating piles of imported Voortman wafer cookies, while plotting how to best install a theocracy in our unsuspecting Midwestern state. During the week . . . we'd . . . cook up a menu of ideas to destroy the American education system. In our free time, we'd do our best to enforce repressive and arbitrary laws in our small, idyllic, largely Dutch town, marching in lockstep as we aimlessly purchased windmill-shaped tchotchkes and engaged in the occasional public shaming.[31]

Betsy DeVos-induced reporting about the history of Dutch Americans has been factually incorrect and borders on unethical. Journalists have an obligation to get their facts right, and they need to understand the principle of charitable interpretation. We like to look

[30] https://twitter.com/james_ka_smith/status/801636417306820608/photo/1.
[31] Heather Wilhelm, *Chicago Tribune*, 20 Jan. 2017. https://www.chicagotribune.com/news/opinion/commentary/ct-betsy-devos-charter-schools-perspec-0120-md-20170119-story.html.

for simple dichotomies, like liberal and conservative, and it is easy to draw historical lines connecting Van Raalte with Peter Hoekstra, Betsy DeVos, and Eric Prince (DeVos' brother), but these long lines are a stretch. There are reverberating threads of history, the kind of history that does not repeat, and does not rhyme, but echoes.

When I finished my dissertation on Dutch American history, I treated the story of Dutch American history as more-or-less a closed book. I knew Dutch American history would go on, but I figured it would become marginalized as a source of personal and collective identity. I assumed that the debates about the Dutch American past were over. Boy, was I wrong.

CHAPTER 22

All but the Saloon: Nineteenth Century Dutch Immigrants, the Wilderness, and the Idea of Progress

Jan J. Boersema and Anthonia Boersema-Bremmer

In 1976, on the occasion of the two hundredth anniversary of the United States, painter and professor Chris Stoffel Overvoorde (1934-2019) made four paintings, each with an episode of the history of Dutch emigration to the United States. The paintings had been commissioned by the Dutch Immigrant Society and were intended to be offered to then-president Gerald R. Ford. They characterize four stages in the relationship of the Netherlands to this continent since Henry Hudson's journey in 1609.

The second painting in the series, *The Mid-West Migration*, depicts immigration in the nineteenth century. We can see the transformation of the landscape as the immigrants found it: the majestic forests of West Michigan and the rolling prairie of the Midwest. By the beginning of the twentieth century, these forests had largely disappeared, and on the prairie, there were no longer huge herds of grazing bison, but corn was growing. The log cabin (or is it a log church?) in the painting symbolizes the simplicity of the beginning, and the new era arrives in the form of a four-lane highway with cars ("modern highway" in the caption). This transformation was generally seen as progress, and

373

The Mid-West Migration, by Chris Stoffel Overvoorde, 1976

people were proud that the Dutch immigrants had contributed to it. Except for some moral issues (lost piety, the arrival of a saloon in town), signs of progress were welcomed across the board.

In the foreground are the leaders of the emigration, which had gained momentum in 1847. On the far right, we can recognize Albertus C. Van Raalte, the founder of Holland, Michigan, and next to him, his colleague, Rev. Hendrik Pieter Scholte, the leader of the Pella, Iowa, settlement. Just behind these two is Rev. Cornelius van der Meulen, the pioneer of Zeeland, Michigan. Martin Van Buren, president of the United States from 1837 to 1841 and of Dutch descent, is depicted at the top right corner, slightly apart from the rest of the company.

This chapter is about the Dutch emigrants who were part of the Midwest migration. A considerable number of them belonged to the so-called Seceders (Afgescheidenen, in Dutch) in the Netherlands. Once in America, these immigrants often stayed together and founded settlements, churches, schools, and colleges. As a result, a relatively large amount of this group's culture has been preserved.

To investigate how Dutch immigrants and their offspring thought about progress, we have researched their ideas of progress in letters, memoirs, pageants, newspapers, periodicals, and other publications from 1847 to about 1920. We wanted to find out if people wrote about progress and, if so, then how, and what they saw as signs of progress (which apparently was a popular topic). We recorded all sentences that referred to progress and advancement, and in this way, we have collected a solid corpus of quotations. The work reported here is part of a long-term research project previously published.[1] Two questions are central to this chapter. First, the question of how to put in context and explain the nineteenth-century enthusiasm for progress, and second, the question of why the decline of the wilderness was seen as progress.[2]

The idea of progress[3]

According to influential British historian John B. Bury, progress can be defined as the idea that civilization has moved, is moving, and will move in a desirable direction.[4] Alternatively, to quote Charles van Doren, it is about "irreversible meliorative change."[5]

Following Herbert Spencer, Bury considers the idea of progress to be a modern invention, most notably of the Enlightenment. Marquis de Condorcet's *L'Esquisse d'un tableau historique des progrès de l'esprit humain*, published in 1795, just after his death, is considered by many to be the zenith of the idea of progress.[6] In this booklet, De Condorcet presents the history of civilization as one of progress in the sciences. He claims that there is an almost causal connection between scientific progress and the development of human rights and justice and outlines a future rational society entirely shaped by scientific knowledge. According to De Condorcet, the progression of the human race was to continue throughout the course of our existence, as humanity continually progressed toward a perfectly utopian society. His phrasing of the idea of progress has moral undertones and features of a (secular) belief system.

---

[1]   Jan J. Boersema and Anthonia Boersema-Bremmer, "'The Wilderness has been made to Blossom': Nineteenth-Century Dutch Immigrants and the Natural World," in *Sharing Pasts: Dutch Americans through Four Centuries* (Holland, MI: Van Raalte Press, 2017), 25-50. Jan J. Boersema and Nella Kennedy, "A Hunter's Experience. Henry Takken's Memoir and the Demise of the Passenger Pigeon (*Ectopistes migratorius*)," in *Dutch Muck—and Much More: Dutch Americans in Farming, Religion, Art, and Astronomy* (Holland, MI: Van Raalte Press, 2019), 207-20.
[2]   We would like to thank Ite Wierenga for his help with the English language.
[3]   For this paragraph, we have made use of Jan J. Boersema, "Progress," in *Vocabulary for the Study of Religion*, 3 vols. (Leiden: E. J. Brill, 2015), 3:136-39.
[4]   John Bagnell Bury, *Idea of Progress. An Inquiry into its Growth and Origin* (London: Macmillan, 1932), 2.
[5]   Charles van Doren, *The Idea of Progress* (NY: Praeger, 1967), 7.
[6]   Marie-Jean-Antoine-Nicolas Caritat, Marquis de Condorcet, "Outlines of an historical view of the progress of the human mind," being a posthumous work of the late M. de Condorcet. Translated from the French (Philadelphia: M. Carey, 1796). https://oll.libertyfund.org/titles/1669.

This belief system, with its rational and optimistic view of humanity, was at odds with political conservatism and the (French) traditional institutionalized religion of the Ancien Régime. It also constituted a break with the notions of some classical Greek and Roman thinkers that there had once been a Golden Age in the history of mankind and that since then, there has only been decay.

The aforementioned particular idea of progress—science based, secular, ongoing improvement in every direction, and an Enlightenment invention—has been contested and adapted ever since its inception.[7] Scholars, such as Ludwig Edelstein and Robert Nisbet, for example, have traced the idea of progress—in a certain form—to antiquity.[8] They point out that the philosophers of classical antiquity (starting with Xenophanes in the late sixth century BC) mooted the idea of human progress, as well as the idea of a lost golden age. According to Aristotle, progression in a society is by gradual improvements, later defined by Lucretius as step-by-step progress (*pedetemtim progredientis*). Lucretius is therefore considered to be the first to apply the word "progress" to societal developments.[9]

More importantly, the relationship between belief in progress and religion, especially Christianity, does not seem to be one of contrast, but rather, one of interconnectedness. Lynn White points out that the Christian conception of time (and, therefore, of history) as a linear process has formed a fertile soil for the belief in progress.[10] In essence, this view of history as an ongoing process with a past, present, and future, refers back to the Old Testament. Aurelius Augustine, himself one of the most influential fathers of the church, supported this linear image of time. It was he who stated: "The wicked walk in a circle."[11]

[7] Gabriel A. Almond, Marvin Chodorow, and Roy Harvey Pearce, eds., *Progress and Its Discontents* (Berkeley: University of California Press, 1982); Arnold Burgen, Peter McLaughlin, and Jürgen Mittelstraβ, eds., *The Idea of Progress* (Berlin: De Gruyter, 1997).

[8] Ludwig Edelstein, *The Idea of Progress in Classical Antiquity* (Baltimore, MD: Johns Hopkins University Press, 1967); Robert Nisbet, *History of the Idea of Progress* (NY: Basic Books, 1980).

[9] *Usus et impigrae simul experientia mentis, paulatim docuit pedetemtim progredientis* (All were taught gradually by usage and the active mind's experience as men groped their way forward step by step, trans. by Penguin Classics), Lucretius, *De Rerum Natura* (Cambridge, MA: Harvard University Press, 1959), 5:1448ff.; see also, Abraham C Keller, "Lucretius and the Idea of Progress," *The Classical Journal* 46, no. 4 (1951): 185-88.

[10] Lynn White Jr., "The Historical Roots of our Ecologic Crisis," *Science* 155 (1967), 1203-7.

[11] Aurelius Augustinus, *De Civitate Dei* (Cambridge, MA: Harvard University Press, 1966), 12:14, 15.

According to Augustine, the God of the Bible is the God of history. He was at the beginning and goes with his people until the end of time in a continuous movement. We are all living in between Genesis and eschatology. This is reflected in his ideas about time as set out in his main writings *The City of God* and *Confessions*. In this linear view of time moving like an arrow, the present is, by definition, different from the past, and the future will be different from the present. Of course, recurrence happens, even with Augustine—think of the seasons—but there is no return of "the same"; time always has a direction. By combining recurrence and moving in a direction, the arrow takes the form of a spiral. Linearity implies change. If nothing changes, time, as it were, stands still. Change, on the other hand, opens the possibility of improvement. The scientist of religion, Walter Burkhart, identified offering hope as a core characteristic of religion.[12] That certainly applies to Christianity, which is rightly called the religion of hope.

Thanks to recent scholarly work, we now know that Bury also undervalued the role of religion in the rise of science. David Lindberg and others showed that the so-called "scientific revolution" of the seventeenth century had a long run-up.[13] The contributions of ancient philosophers, medieval scholars, and institutions, such as monasteries and universities, are hard to ignore, although there are still views that overlook or downplay their role.[14] During the Reformation, Protestant denominations adopted a more historical reading of the Bible, and in one of their creeds (the Belgic Confession, Confessio Belgica) professed that studying the "book of nature" could lead to true knowledge of God and His creation. There emerged a climate in which natural theology, with its rational investigative approach to reality, also paved the way for modern science.[15]

When we look at material developments, the Enlightenment marks the beginning of what is called "the great acceleration."[16] Its most

[12] Walter Burkhart, *Creation of the Sacred. Tracks of Biology in Early Religions* (Cambridge, MA: Harvard University Press, 1998).
[13] David C. Lindberg, *The Beginnings of Western Science. The European Scientific Tradition in Philosophical, Religious, and Institutional Context, 600 B.C. to A.D. 1450* (Chicago: University of Chicago Press, 1992); Edward Grant, *The Foundations of Modern Science in the Middle Ages* (Cambridge: Cambridge University Press, 1997).
[14] See David Wootton, *The Invention of Science: A New History of the Scientific Revolution* (London: Allan Lane, 2015).
[15] Peter Harrison, *The Bible, Protestantism, and the Rise of Natural Science* (Cambridge: Cambridge University Press, 1998).
[16] Will Steffen, Wendy Broadgate, Lisa Deutsch, Owen Gaffney, and Cornelia Ludwig, "The Trajectory of the Anthropocene: The Great Acceleration," *The Anthropocene Review* 2, no. 1 (2015), 81-98.

spectacular element is the exponential growth of world population, beginning around 1750. As part of a broader project, economist Angus Maddison and historian Jan Luiten van Zanden documented the statistics of these developments over a period of two centuries after the Enlightenment.[17] Their results reveal the impressive changes that started in Western Europe and soon spread to the New World. During this period, life expectancy doubled to around eighty years, of which, on average, about sixty years could be expected to be in reasonable health. People grew taller, and vaccinations against diseases became available. The infant mortality rate declined sharply, and child labor was replaced by education. The work week was reduced to an acceptable level, and hunger was virtually eliminated. Stinking cities and grinding poverty in the slums largely disappeared, and garbage was collected. In many aspects of life, there was progress. It was shaped by science and technology, resource based, and kept going by extracting and burning fossil fuels. The human appropriation of planet earth had increased dramatically.[18]

Century of progress

North America occupies a special place in this modernization process, particularly the United States in the second half of the nineteenth century, continuing to the First World War. This young nation expanded strongly westward, and progress began to accelerate. Nowhere was the landscape so thoroughly transformed; nowhere had innovation changed life so greatly; nowhere did so many new residents enter the country, and nowhere did so many of the original inhabitants, both human and nonhuman, have to leave the field. One technological or industrial development followed another, and the country grew into an economic world power. The mood was unprecedentedly optimistic, and progress was sung about, described, and depicted in many ways.

Two works of art stand out in both popularity and expression in the late nineteenth century. In 1862 Christian Schussele (1824-1879) painted *Men of Progress*, a group of men who, in his opinion, shaped this progress with their inventions and businesses. Shortly afterward,

---

[17] Angus Maddison, *Monitoring the World Economy 1820-1992* (Paris: OECD Development Centre Studies, 1995); Angus Maddison, *Contours of the World Economy 1-2030 AD* (Oxford: Oxford University Press, 2007); Jan Luiten van Zanden, ed., *How Was Life? Global Well-Being Since 1820* (Paris: OECD Publishing, 2014).

[18] Helmut Haberl et al., "Quantifying and Mapping the Human Appropriation of Net Primary Production in Earth's Terrestrial Ecosystems," *PNAS* 104, no. 31 (2009): 12,942-47.

Century of Progress stamp issued at the Chicago World's Fair in 1933

in 1872, John Gast (1842-1896), on an even grander scale, painted his famous canvas *American Progress*. In it, the trek to the west is represented as a triumphal procession of the goddess of progress, who, going from the east to the west and guided by science and technology, drives away the wilderness and darkness. The plow, the mail coach, and the train accompany and symbolize this victory over the uncivilized world. It is, therefore, no wonder that a stamp was issued at the world exhibition in Chicago in 1933 with the text: "Century of Progress 1833-1933." Overvoorde's work described above also illustrates that image and shows that this view of progress and the nineteenth century had lost little force for the Dutch community half a century later.

The Dutch immigrants were very aware of this special place called North America, and they embraced progress in every possible way; a large proportion of these immigrants had left the Netherlands in search of a better future, not only for themselves but also for their children. For example, in 1869, shortly after his arrival in Wisconsin, the Roman Catholic Jan Smits, born in the poor regions of East Brabant, wrote to the Dutch weekly *Venloosch Weekblad*: "Everything is progress here, with you, there is standstill, if not decline."[19]

Historian Van Stekelenburg believed that this quote was so typical that he made it the title of his book about the emigrants from the southern part of the Netherlands. The predominantly Protestant immigrants we investigated found themselves on the same page. In the words of Rev. Henry Utterwick: "Calvinism, freedom, progress—these

[19] H. A. V. M. van Stekelenburg, *"Hier is alles vooruitgang": Landverhuizing van Noord-Brabant naar Noord-Amerika 1880-1940* (Tilburg: Stichting Zuidelijk Historisch Contact, 1996).

three words were read on many a page of modern history."²⁰ When in 1927 the settlers in Iowa looked back on their early years in Pella in an historical staging, they titled their play the *Pageant of Progress*. In this play, Miss Pella addresses her audience soon after she meets a character called Progress: "Onward Pella, wherever Progress goes, we will follow."²¹

The journalist Theodore de Veer, visiting "our Hollanders in (Zeeland) Michigan," draws the same conclusion as Jan Smits: "Everything there points to prosperity and constant forward motion."²² But D. Broek is more specific when he lists the various areas in which progress has occurred: "We have since grown in numbers and in material prosperity, in knowledge, science, and development; we have progressed in almost every area."²³ One of the leading periodicals, *De Grondwet*, connected progress with civilization and the Enlightenment when it typified the ruling era with this opening phrase: "Now, in the enlightened nineteenth century and in this land of progress and civilization."²⁴ And another periodical, *De Hollander*, writing about the new constitution of 1851, noted: "It should correspond to the forward-looking spirit of the time."²⁵ In his article about the importance of agriculture and the need to use science for the furtherance of agriculture, the editor of *De Hollander* ended with the catchy phrase: "Progress should be the password."²⁶

For the Dutch immigrants, science was important and not at odds with their religious beliefs. The importance of and relationship between science and faith found expression in *De Grondwet*, in which the editor-in-chief wrote in December 1879:

> They go hand in hand. As soon as faith rejects science, it becomes zealotry, and people return to the days when the sea captain

[20] Rev. Henry Utterwick, no. 6, box 4, Van Schelven Papers, Holland Historical Trust (HHT), Holland, MI.
[21] *Pageant of Progress*, staged July 4, 1927, Pella, IA, prologue.
[22] In the original language of Dutch, the repetition makes it more powerful: "En alles, alles wijst er op voorspoed, op 'n maar immer gestadig 'vooruit,'" in Henry S. Lucas, *Dutch Immigrant Memoirs and Related Writings* (Grand Rapids, MI: Eerdmans, 1997), 2:498 (English), and 2:14 (Dutch).
[23] "Wij zijn sedert dien gegroeid in getallen en stoffelijke welvaart, in kennis, wetenschap en ontwikkeling; bijna op elk gebied zijn wij vooruitgegaan," D. Broek, *De leiders der landverhuizers*, box 5, Van Schelven Papers, HHT (trans. JJB).
[24] *De Grondwet*, 12 Aug. 1873.
[25] "Dat zij overeenkomt met den voorwaarts strevenden geest des tijds," *De Hollander*, 13 March 1851 (trans. JJB).
[26] "Vooruitgang moet het wachtwoord zijn," *De Hollander*, 10 Jan. 1872 (trans. JJB).

would employ diviners to bring favorable winds, and the churches resounded with prayers against the effects of comets. However, if science rejects religious belief, it becomes Atheism.[27]

In line with this, great emphasis was placed on education. Laying a cornerstone for a new school building was "a mark of progress."[28]

Signs of progress galore

Looking at the tangible signs and carriers of progress, almost everything in modern life is mentioned, from central heating to the lawn mower. But two things really stand out: the railroad and agricultural machinery. In a letter dated December 26, 1855, sent to his family in the Netherlands, Peter Lankester from Milwaukee, Wisconsin, shows not the slightest doubt: "Railroads are the key to progress in this country."[29]

He expressed the general feeling. As soon as houses and farms were built, and a settlement grew, the residents tried to get a railroad to that place. Not getting a railroad and/or a station was a major setback. Prosperity was attributed to the presence of a railroad. Gerrit van Oostenbrugge from South Holland described the construction of tracks through Lage Prairie as "a sure index of rising land values and of general prosperity."[30]

According to William van Eyk: "The progress in the means of transportation is one of the brightest chapters in the world's history."[31]

Even the bike was hailed as a promising invention. The number of horses displaced by the bicycle was enormous wrote Van Eyk in 1897, and he continued: "The bicycle, it may be said, has abrogated some of the laws of political economy."[32]

Given the importance of agriculture for the settlers—many of whom came from rural areas and either had been or would become farmers—it is not surprising that the spectacular developments in this

[27] "Het is het hand aan hand gaande Godsdienstig geloof en de wetenschap. Zoodra het geloof de wetenschap verwerpt wordt het dweeperij en keert men terug naar de dagen toen de zeekapitein van de Laplandsche Wichelaars gunstige winden kocht en de kerken weer klonken van de gebeden tegen de gevolgen van staartsterren. Zoo echter de wetenschap het godsdienstig geloof verwerpt, wordt het Atheisme," *De Grondwet*, 30 Dec. 1879 (trans. JJB).
[28] "Die hoeksteen is een merkteeken van vooruitgang," *De Grondwet*, 12 Sept. 1879.
[29] Brinks, *Dutch American Voices* (Ithaca, NY: Cornell University Press, 1995), 347.
[30] Lucas, *Dutch Immigrant Memoirs*, 2:64.
[31] William van Eyck, "Transportation in Colonial Days," in Lucas, *Dutch Immigrant Memoirs*, 1:440.
[32] Ibid.

area are discussed at great length in our sources. "The prospects of agriculture are full of hope and promise. The heart of the people rejoices amidst all their privations, in the mercy of God, which has given them such a goodly land and such great progress."[33]

Isaac Wyckoff wrote this optimistic assessment in his report on the colony in 1849. At that time, the real agricultural inventions were yet to come. And they did come, the one even more spectacular than the other. We find them everywhere in the sources: the hay bailer; the threshing machine run by four, six, or ten horsepower; the Kirkby Self Rake Reaper; a sowing machine; the potato digger; the corn husker; and the harvesting self-binder. Many letters resound with surprise at and admiration for these wonders. Ulbe Eringa wrote in 1892 to his sister: "Mr. Hunt has cut one hundred and fifty acres with the self-binder. This large machine, drawn by four horses, cuts the grain, which it also ties into sheaves and then drops them on the ground. You should see this—it is an invention that is almost unbelievable."[34] In Charles Dyke's words: "A machine that did the whole job without any human assistance, except the driver, was to us a novel and even astounding piece of mechanism."[35] Mechanization progressed so quickly that Harry Eenigenburg from Roseland, Illinois, got used to the pace of change. "We see something new every day and without any surprise."[36]

Finding black swans

Philosopher Karl Popper tells us that science advances if we search for "black swans," challenging our default hypothesis of all swans being white. Black swans are views that either are not very positive about progress or highlight the shadowy side. We found only three black swan quotations. All were related to moral progress. The first comes from Evert Zagers, one of the pioneers of 1847. He thought, looking back, that in addition to progress, there had also been loss. "Alas! How things have changed; but they have not become better. Our fields indeed have cleared, and we have gone forward in material matters, but we have lost much of our earnestness and piety."[37]

[33] Isaac N. Wyckoff, "An Official Report on the Dutch *kolonie* in Michigan, 1849," in Lucas, *Dutch Immigrant Memoirs*, 1:452.
[34] Ulbe Eringa, letter, 22 Aug. 1892, in Brian W. Beltman, *Dutch Farmer in the Missouri Valley: The Life and Letters of Ulbe Eringa, 1866-1950* (Urbana: University of Illinois Press, 1996), 52.
[35] Charles L. Dyke, *The Story of Sioux County* (Sioux City, IA: Verstegen Printing Co., 1942), 174.
[36] Lucas, *Dutch Immigrant Memoirs*, 2:60.
[37] Ibid., 1:89.

Rieks Bouws expressed the same feeling in his memoir, *How I spent my early years*, published in 1882:

> I recall those days with pleasure and thankfulness, especially when I consider what progress we have made in the temporal aspects of our social life and what welfare we are now enjoying. But alas! We have lost much of our former seriousness in spiritual life and have become lax. When I think about this, I become ashamed.[38]

Another settler saw his settlement of South Holland as thriving, and he appreciated "all progress but the saloon."[39] There were undoubtedly more immigrants, in particular the people of the first hour, who felt that material prosperity was threatening initial piety and simplicity. But we could find little of that in the written sources. On the contrary, there are even a few texts that are very positive about moral and social development. Henry J. Brown, a former student of the Holland Academy, returned to Holland and was amazed by the change. "Patient industry and . . . have transformed crude nature into a region abreast of any in the State for material wealth, intellectual activity, and moral grandeur."[40]

In the archives of Northwestern College in Orange City, Iowa, we found a document titled "The Essentials of Progress." It appears to be a lecture delivered by R. B. Le Cocq in 1923 and is an almost modern, liberal document. Le Cocq, a second-generation immigrant, wrote in this lecture:

> From a social standpoint we have also made wonderful progress. . . . Slavery was forever abolished from free America. . . . We have granted to woman her long delayed right of equal suffrage. We have opened our great public schools to young and old, to rich and poor alike.[41]

In this relatively late document, we seem to be close to Enlightenment ideals, which may indeed look very similar, but reading

---

[38] Ibid., 1:110.
[39] "The saloon is a means of destruction of body and soul and cannot be regarded as a positive asset of the community," Gerrit van Oostenbrugge, Lucas, *Dutch Immigrant Memoirs*, 2:67.
[40] Henry J. Brown, "Recollections of an Early Student at the Holland Academy," box 6, Van Schelven Papers, HHT.
[41] R. B. Le Cocq, "The Essentials of Progress," Archive of Northwestern College, Orange City, IA.

through all the letters, memoirs, periodicals, and other sources, we found one major difference. Progress and prosperity may be the result of their hard work, technological innovations, the railroad, or education and science, but in the end, it is all perceived by the immigrants as being a blessing from their heavenly father, which they received in great gratitude. In the words of Cornelius van der Meulen: "This is not mere human praise or empty boast, it is a matter for which we must be thankful."[42]

Wilderness

In the spring of 2019, one of the hymns sung in the service of the Third Reformed Church in Holland, Michigan, was no. 243, *One People, Here, We Gather*. It is a beautiful song, and it was sung with enthusiasm, including the third verse:

> One world invites our nurture, a stewardship of care
> for oceans, fields and forests, one habitat we share.

When I, Jan, realized what we were singing, I wondered about "stewardship . . . for oceans." Could Van Raalte and his band of 1847 pioneers ever have sung this hymn in their log church? I doubted it. Over lunch we talked about it, and my coauthor doubted it too. Through all our reading, another hymn came to mind, by far the most beloved one by the immigrants: Psalm 66, especially verse 3: *God baande door de woeste baren, en brede stromen ons een pad*.[43]

The psalm, always sung in the Dutch language, could be translated: "God cleared for us a path through stormy seas and broad rivers."[44] Stewardship for oceans was definitely not on the immigrants' minds. These words reminded them of their dangerous crossing of the Atlantic Ocean.

And what to make of "stewardship for fields and forests"? Kaspar Lahuis, to name just one early immigrant, would have understood little of this expression. In 1887 he commemorated the struggle of the pioneers with fields and forests to not be one of stewardship when

---

[42] The original Dutch is more powerful: "Het is geen menschelijke roem of grootspraak. Het is dankzaak." Address at Zeeland, 18 Sept. 1872, Lucas, *Dutch Immigrant Memoirs*, 1:183.
[43] Psalmberijming 1773 (Versed Psalms 1773).
[44] The translation we found in Lucas: "God prepared through barren wastes. Through spacious streams for us a path" (memoir, Adriaan Pleune, Lucas, *Dutch Immigrant Memoirs*, 1:345) does not match the "threat" in the Dutch original.

he wrote: "The pioneer's clearing is the foundation of our material progress."[45]

A line in a poem written by Henry Dosker on the fortieth anniversary of Zeeland in 1887, tells us what happened to the forests: "Triumph, triumph at long last. The fight has been fought. The giant of the forest lies exanimate."[46]

Apparently, the immigrants saw their relationship with the wilderness as a struggle and a fight. How is this to be explained? The first possible explanation is of course the unruly nature of nature itself. To start farming, fields had to be cultivated, that is, the forest giants had to be cleared, and the heavy prairie sod had to be dug away. And to continue farming, the locusts, the raccoons, and the squirrels had to be kept at bay. But that is not the whole story. The language in which the natural world is described also points to something else. Nature is not seen as a single category. Careful reading of all the "nature quotations" reveals a clear difference, a dichotomy, between the domesticated, civilized, human-made or human-friendly kind of nature and the majestic, undomesticated, threatening, and at times, chaotic, wild nature or wilderness. Livestock, flowers, and the garden belong to the first category. ferocious wolves and shrieking owls, to the latter.

The Hon. G. J. Diekema, a lawyer in Holland, Michigan, at the turn of the twentieth century, has provided us with a colorful and almost complete description of these "two faces of nature":

> We owe to our fathers the transformation of impenetrable forests, damp dismal swamps, dark jungles, and tangled thickets infested with poisonous reptiles and beasts of prey and loaded with the germs of pestilence, disease, and death, into fertile fields waving with golden grain, rich gardens, vine-clad hill, shaded groves, and grassy meadows covered with horses and cattle. To them we owe this transfiguration, this redemption of nature.[47]

"Transfiguration... redemption"—that is religious language. Here Diekema expresses a view of nature that has its roots in the Bible, in particular, the development of the story of paradise in Genesis. Central

---

[45] "De pioneer's clearing is de grondslag van onzen welvaart," in Lucas, *Dutch Immigrant Memoirs*, 1:437 (translation JJB). ["*Welvaart*," here translated "material progress," may also be rendered "prosperity." Van Raalte's use of "pioneer's clearing" in his sermon notes appears to be a mingling of English words with Dutch.—Eds.]

[46] "Triomf, triomf in 't eind! De strijd is afgestreden. De woudreus ligt ontzield," poem by Henry E. Dosker, box 7, Van Schelven Papers, HHT.

[47] Historical souvenir of the celebration of the sixtieth anniversary of the Hollanders in Western Michigan; held in Zeeland, MI (21 Aug. 1907), 52.

to this is the idea that harmony in creation has been disturbed by the Fall. Because of this, man has lost his natural knowledge of creation and his original dominance. The Fall has also changed nature's character; it has, in part, become hostile to humanity. Nature has two faces. In the Old Testament, there is, on the one hand, a world that can make a home for man, where he can live in peace and harmony under his own fig tree and with his own vineyard and his own grain field. On the other hand, there is a world with chaos, blood and wildness, deep waters, inhospitable deserts, and drought. That wild side of nature demands respect and admiration, but mostly fear. Man has to resist it. The task that was given to man in the Garden of Eden, that is, "to cultivate it and keep it,"[48] outside the garden, became to fight the wilderness and cultivate the earth. That became humanity's mission in life, our cultural mandate (in Dutch, our *cultuuropdracht*). The earth had to be cultivated. Wherever possible, it had to become a garden again. The dark forests were not only a source of wood to build houses and churches, or money in the bank (in Van Raalte's view), they were also a kind of no-go area for civilized people. According to Dingeman Versteeg: "Only the half-civilized, wandering Indian and wild beasts of the forests could live there and dispute the supremacy in this unbroken wilderness."[49]

The idea that nature has two faces and that our actions against the wilderness are, therefore, legitimized ethically is not an exclusively Biblical notion. We also find it among Greek and Roman philosophers. For example, Lucretius, known as one of the most "animal-friendly" writers of antiquity, wrote the following in his *Moralia*:

> There is no injustice, surely, in punishing and slaying animals that are antisocial and merely injurious, while taming those that are gentle and friendly to man and making them our helpers in the tasks for which they are severally fitted by nature.[50]

This thinking about the consequences of the Fall for man and nature has subsequently found its way into the Christian-humanist tradition of the West. The extent to which it is anchored is evident from

---

[48] Gen. 2:15 (NASB).

[49] "Slechts de half beschaafde, zwervende indiaan en het wild gedierte der wouden konden er leven en betwisten elkaar de opperheerschappij in deze ongebroken wildernis," Dingeman Versteeg, *De Pelgrim—Vaders van het Westen* (Grand Rapids, MI, 1886), 89.

[50] Plutarch's *Moralia*, book 12, *Whether Land or Sea Animals are Cleverer* (Cambridge, MA: Harvard University Press, 1968), 353:964F.

the following quote, among others. It is from the English philosopher Francis Bacon (1561-1627), one of the fathers of modern science:

> For man by the fall fell at the same time from his state of innocency and from his dominion over creation. Both of these losses, however, can even in this life be in some part repaired; the former by religion and faith, the latter by arts and sciences. For creation was not by the curse made altogether and forever a rebel, but in virtue of that charter, "In the sweat of thy face shall thou eat bread," it is now by various labours (not certainly by disputations or idle magical ceremonies, but by various labours) at length and in some measure subdued to the supplying of man with bread, that is, to the uses of human life.[51]

The positive quotations about civilized nature and the many negative about the wilderness in the writings of immigrants fit seamlessly into this tradition.[52] The language used to speak about the wilderness is peppered with Old Testament expressions. Genesis is one of the sources referred to, as evidenced by the following quotations:

> Our people were strongly moved. Everywhere they spoke about America. They read the Bible, they learned that emigration not only was permitted, that indeed it was the Lord's purpose, plan, and command [to] "be fruitful and multiply the earth."[53]

P. J. Risseeuw, who truthfully describes the immigrants in his historical novels, has his character Arjaan say: "But the earth is given to man to control and to labor for her in the sweat of his face for sin's sake. The first people to be driven out of Paradise have also faced the unbridled nature."[54] Wilderness is not a neutral category from a religious point of view, as the following quotation from a sermon by Van Raalte shows:

> God will pluck up what he has planted, break down what he built, and withhold what is good. Israel heard the good news, but

---

[51] Francis Bacon, *Novum Organum* (1620), 2:lii.
[52] See Boersema and Boersema-Bremmer, *Sharing Pasts*, 2017.
[53] Cornelius van der Meulen, on the twenty-fifth anniversary of Zeeland, 1872, in *1847 Ebenezer 1947*, 32. Memorial souvenir of the centennial commemoration of Dutch immigration to the United States held in Holland, MI, 13-16 Aug. 1947, prepared for the Centennial Commission of Holland, MI, by Henry S. Lucas.
[54] P. J. Risseeuw, *De Huilende Wildernis* (Baarn: Bosch & Keuning N.V., 1946), 17.

their unbelief and sin cast them back into the wilderness. Sin is the source of trouble. . . . We had to say these things, occasioned by Jeremiah's message, not only concerning Israel but with equal emphasis to every person and nation to the end of time. For therein are proclaimed God's immutable principles for his governance of the world.[55]

In our 2017 paper, my coauthor and I concluded: "Rolling back the wilderness was not only an inevitable condition for carving out an existence; the process itself was a symptom of progress and civilization *per se*."[56] We can now conclude that it was also seen as a religious mission to make the wilderness bloom like a rose. The fact that the wilderness and its inhabitants were almost completely "transformed" was considered progress.

---

[55] Sermon on Jer. 18: 5-10. Gordon J. Spykman, *Pioneer Preacher: Albertus Christiaan Van Raalte, A Study of His Sermon Notes* (Grand Rapids, MI: Calvin College and Seminary Library, 1976), 102.

[56] Boersema and Boersema-Bremmer, *Sharing Pasts*, 48.

CHAPTER 23

Teaching the Past: History Education among Dutch Americans

David Zwart

What should Dutch American children learn about their own religio-ethnic legacy in history class? Educator John Van Asselt—under the alias of Derek Knikkerbakker—sought to answer this question in a professional journal for teachers in Christian schools, started by and serving mainly Dutch Americans and Canadians. Vanasselt asserted that the teaching of history had been highjacked by "presentism"—the assessment of the past on the basis of current values and mores with the intention to make history more relevant. He maintained that "such an approach to the study of history is less than the discipline deserves." History requires one to study the past on its own terms to avoid naïve opinions about the present.[1] Vanasselt's assertion was part of a larger conversation about the direction and purpose of history education in the twentieth century in North America, specifically for Dutch American and Canadian children.

---

[1] Derek Knikkerbaker, a.k.a John Vanasselt, "History in the Christian School," *Christian Educators Journal* 26 (Feb./March 1987): 23-24. Vanasselt was the principal of Woodland Christian High School of Breslau, Ontario.

Like Van Asselt, twentieth-century history educators and school leaders answered this question within a matrix of competing interests. Since at least the nineteenth century, common schools in the United States and around the world have introduced children to the collective memory of their nations.[2] This collective memory was meant to inspire a patriotic, if not a nationalistic, identity. Educators and policy makers hoped students would become patriotic citizens through common school education, while they learned reading and writing. History education lay at the heart of citizenship, and there were always competing ideas about citizenship education. Some argued that students needed to learn a patriotic narrative, and others argued the merits of other approaches to history education. These debates in both private and parochial schools were layered with other competing interests about citizenship and collective memory.[3]

Private schools in the twentieth century, founded and supported within Dutch American communities, were one place where goals and interests often varied from mainstream American education. These private schools answered to their own constituency, not just to local, state, and national educational initiatives. Yet, they found themselves within the broader context of education in America. The history of education in the United States includes various streams, but all with the goal of citizenship. Deviation from this central goal, including attacks on private and public schools in the 1920s, often brought suspicion and distrust. This struggle was the setting for the development of the National Union of Christian Schools (NUCS) in the 1920s.[4]

Teachers and policy makers of NUCS, which served predominately Dutch American pupils, experienced the tension between the needs of the local community and those of the American educational culture. They needed to decide what to teach the children and what rationale to provide for their decisions. The ideas surrounding the history curriculum reflected this tension throughout the twentieth century. As educators decided what students should learn in history class, the mix

---

[2] Joel H. Spring, *The American School: From the Puritans to No Child Left Behind*, 7th ed. (Boston: McGraw-Hill, 2008), and Ron Evans, *Social Studies Wars: What Should We Teach the Children?* (NY: Teacher's College Press, 2004).

[3] For instance, see William J. Galush, "What Should Jankek Learn? Staffing and Curriculum in Polish-American Parochial Schools, 1870-1940," *History of Education Quarterly* 40, no. 4 (Winter 2000): 395-417.

[4] Harro W. Van Brummelen, *Telling the Next Generation: Educational Development of North American Calvinist Christian Schools* (Lanham, MD: University Press of America, 1986), 135-58.

of immigration and theology that had produced NUCS schools had an impact on the articulated purpose of history education. A justification for the chosen purpose was needed, even if the actual history education encountered in the classroom did not differ much from the general tendencies of history education in the United States and Canada.

In 1978 NUCS changed its name to Christian Schools International (CSI).[5] These schools were primarily located in areas with high concentrations of Dutch Americans, particularly those associated with the Christian Reformed Church (CRC).[6] Studying history education in these schools provides a glimpse into the way historical context shaped the choices Dutch Americans made in how they taught their children about history. It clarifies the collective identity they wanted to emphasize for their children as they were raised to be God-fearing citizens. NUCS schools wanted to be isolated and distinct on the one hand, but on the other hand, they often mirrored and even sanctioned the general tendencies of American classrooms in the twentieth century.

Although a longer history of NUCS schools can be found elsewhere, a brief overview here provides the background for understanding history education among these Dutch Americans. As Harro Van Brummelen has argued, the Dutch immigrants who started Christian schools had decided that they could not get the kind of Christian education they sought for their children in the common schools. The Christian schools were supported mainly by people in the CRC, so the church could retain its Dutch and "conservative, isolationistic outlook on life."[7] The Christian schools opened in Kalamazoo, Grand Rapids, and Muskegon, Michigan, were sure that the communities could maintain this outlook, even when they did not control the schools in rural, homogeneous villages. The yearbooks of the CRC in the 1880s printed the number of students enrolled in these early parochial schools.[8]

The close connection between the CRC and the private schools of NUCS continued through at least the first three-quarters of the

---

[5] Although colleges and academies would also be rightly labeled as Dutch American schools, they are outside the scope of this paper.
[6] On this connection, see Van Brummelen, *Telling the Next Generation*, and James D. Bratt, *Dutch Calvinism in Modern America: A History of a Conservative Subculture* (Grand Rapids, MI: Eerdmans, 1984).
[7] Van Brummelen, *Telling the Next Generation*, 49.
[8] Ibid., 55. Van Brummelen lists only six schools in the 1886 yearbook; by 1894 there were fifteen schools with over 2,350 students. *Jaarboekje ten dienste de Holl. Chr. Geref. Kerk in Noord America voor het Jaar 1894* (Grand Rapids, MI: J. B. Hulst, 1894).

twentieth century. By 1920 about one-half of the children in the CRC attended NUCS schools.[9] Every ten years thereafter, NUCS produced a report showing the percentage of CRC children enrolled in Christian schools, and that number continued to grow. These reports also included a map where "Christian school centers are printed in red." By 1970 about 80 percent of children in CRC congregations were enrolled in NUCS schools.[10]

This close connection to the CRC shaped the overall rationale and purpose of curriculum in NUCS schools. Bible instruction was paramount, but the particulars of the rest of the curriculum were up for grabs. The tension within what others have called the "mentalities" of the Dutch American community often bubbled to the surface.[11] For instance, both defensive and introverted church members (Confessionalists and Antithetical Calvinists)[12] advocated a history curriculum that focused on telling the story of *ons volk* (our people) and church history. This church history placed Calvinism at the apex of developments in the church. They saw themselves as God's chosen people who needed to stick together to defend Calvinistic orthodoxy.

The more outgoing, optimistic folks (Reformed Church "West" and Positive Calvinists[13]) saw the possibilities of the world and the impact they could have. For them, an emphasis on national and world history should be the focus. A 1915 curriculum guide with this approach by B. J. Bennink called for using "any leading history textbook" with a positive American story but that the teacher should shape the instruction to show a Christian perspective.[14]

Both postures toward history education, a defensive Calvinistic history and a positive national story, were really two sides of the same coin of history education. For both sides, history education equaled cultural literacy—students should learn the right information to be part of a collective identity, either an inward-looking identity or an

---

[9] Van Brummelen, *Telling the Next Generation*, 74.
[10] NUCS *Christian School Directory, 1970-1971* (Grand Rapids, MI: NUCS, 1971).
[11] Bratt, *Dutch Calvinism in Modern America*, 37-54.
[12] Confessionalists emphasize loyalty to the historic Reformed standards as articulated in the Reformed creeds. Antithetical Calvinists distrust the prevailing culture and seek guidance from within Reformed organizations.
[13] The Reformed Church "West" perspective emphasizes the importance of moral living as the way to influence the broader Protestant society. Positive Calvinists build institutions to prepare their members to transform the larger society.
[14] B. J. Bennink, *The Elementary School for Christian Instruction* (Grand Rapids, MI: The Alliance of Christian Schools of Michigan, 1915). Available in Christian Schools Papers Collection, Heritage Hall, Hekman Library, Calvin University.

outward-focused identity. The pedagogy emphasized that the teacher should just teach, and the students would then learn the names, dates, and events of the past to gain a shared collective memory.

This matches what was largely happening in history classrooms across America in the early twentieth century. Most history classrooms in the United States focused on memorization of important names, dates, and events, so that students would be conversant in the story of America.[15] Curriculum and pedagogy focused on heroes and important dates from both American history and the broader Western tradition. This default curriculum matched the context of the era, with a high number of immigrants who required a concerted effort to unite Americans around a shared story.

Although classrooms defaulted to this kind of cultural literacy, some national leaders and reformers proposed alternative ways to teach history to the cultural literacy model. Starting in the late 1800s, these efforts sought to revise history education to be more than just transmitting culture and myth, patriotism and good citizenship, and cultural literacy. As the culture itself became more "scientific" in the late 1800s, the American Historical Association (AHA) took the lead in proposing revisions to the teaching of history. Its 1892 Committee on History, Civil Government, and Political Economy was part of a larger effort of the National Education Association to reform the secondary curriculum. This committee, made up of historians, such as Woodrow Wilson, called for teaching history to train students to think critically and avoid mere lists of lifeless dates. The AHA also stressed the importance of writing proficiency and critical examination of primary documents using the skills of analysis comparable to those needed for a laboratory science. The AHA produced another report in 1896 that emphasized the idea of "thinking historically."[16] Supported by a growing number of professionally trained history faculty, the AHA reports advocated teaching students to understand the nature of history as a field of study crucial for individual intellectual development.

Progressive reformers and educators, inspired by John Dewey, were not satisfied with this "scientifically based" approach to history education that focused on intellectual development. They wanted a

---

[15] Evans, *Social Studies Wars*, 5-20; D. Antionio Cantu and Wilson J. Warren, *Teaching History in the Digital Classroom* (Armon, NY: M. E. Sharp), 3-18; Anne-Lise Halvorsen, *A History of Elementary Social Studies: Romance and Reality* (NY: Peter Lang, 2013), 183.

[16] Cantu and Warren, *Teaching History*, 3-6.

curriculum that addressed current social problems and needs.[17] A 1916 report by a committee of secondary school educators advocated an instrumentalist approach to teaching history, that is, using historical examples to study specific societal problems. This social studies approach coalesced in the formation of the National Council for the Social Studies (NCSS). This organization would continue to advocate for an activist approach to social studies education throughout the twentieth century.

These two approaches then, the individual intellectual growth model versus the social-problems model, have largely set the ends of the spectrum of the curriculum and pedagogical debates about history education in the United States for the last century. The pendulum seems to swing between these two poles depending on the historical context. But these alternating approaches to teaching history have often had a hard time penetrating classroom practices, which continue to focus on transmitting cultural literacy. The continuing debate reflects not only the context of the time but also the desire by leaders and reformers to change what they see as deficiencies in the stubborn cultural literacy paradigm of classroom history instruction.

NUCS writers and leaders made their history curriculum suggestions within the context of these general developments within that field. They recrafted the broader history education program to fit the unique requirements of their own schools. They needed to do this for their Dutch American Calvinist constituency, who had varying views on the goals of history education. Most often, during the first decades of the twentieth century, NUCS dismissed both the more disciplinary-based approaches of the AHA and the more socially progressive approaches of NCSS. A basic cultural literacy approach to history education guided NUCS until the 1930s. A 1926 collection of NUCS convention papers, although emphasizing the citizenship aspect of Christian schools, mostly focuses on how students needed to study history in order to be good citizens, to know the heroic past of the nation.[18] In 1933 Mark Fakkema, the full-time general secretary of NUCS, wrote about the importance of facts in history education. Christian history education was about transmitting the important aim that God is behind all these facts. History was about helping students

---

[17] Cantu and Warren, *Teaching History*, 5; Evans, *Social Studies Wars*, 21-45.
[18] *Educational Convention Papers, 1926* (Grand Rapids, MI: NUCS, 1926), Christian Schools Papers Collection, HH.

catch "a vision of the majesty of our God."[19] Fakkema never explained how this rather lofty idea would shape instruction, but it was clear that, whatever religious guise it took, history education was about learning the facts of history.

By the time World War II had engulfed the world and the Cold War had heated up, history education reformers were again arguing about the best approach to history education. Many called for a method that highlighted a defense of the West's democracy and capitalism. This move meant that the policy makers' push for either intellectual development or a social studies curriculum took a back seat to full-on advocacy for (patriotic) cultural literacy. This consensus de-emphasized any critical-thinking approaches that some, such as Harold Rugg, had advocated in the 1930s.[20] The reformers of this era regularly found confirmation of the need for more cultural literacy. There was consistent lament about the lack of knowledge about the past. For instance, the *New York Times Magazine* published the results of a survey in May 1942 that had historian Alvin Nevins lamenting that young people did not know American history. He believed that a lack of core knowledge of the facts of history left young men "without a very deep faith in the democratic way of life."[21] Belief in the power of historical, cultural literacy to make a patriotic people was pervasive during these years.

As the number of NUCS students and schools increased rapidly in the years after World War II, leaders emphasized the distinctive nature of learning history in a Christian school.[22] The leaders started to advocate for more curricular materials and textbooks that would bring a uniquely Christian approach to fields of study, including history. This distinctiveness, however, did not preclude students from learning to be patriotic Americans but inferred that they might be better Americans because they were strong Christians. The 1947 *Course of Study*, published by NUCS, laid out history objectives, including "the increased knowledge of God as revealed in history," "the acquisition of significant historical information," and "the development of patriotism and desirable citizenship."[23]

The *Course of Study* suggested various textbooks that could be useful but cautioned that educators should take "extreme care in

---

[19] Mark Fakkema, "The Starting Point in Teaching History," *Christian Home and School Magazine* (June 1933), 7.
[20] Evans, *Social Studies Wars*, 46-69.
[21] As cited in Evans, *Social Studies Wars*, 86-87.
[22] For numbers, see Van Brummelen, *Telling the Next Generation* and also NUCS reports.
[23] NUCS, *Course of Study for Christian Schools* (Grand Rapids, MI: Eerdmans, 1947), 216.

the selection of a textbook," because the texts lead to predetermined goals that might not match those of the Christian school. The teacher must "constantly exert an influence which is both corrective and constructive" to the textbook. In the "Graded Course Suggestions," the authors propose in detail what the history curriculum should look like. American history in the middle grades (4-6) should emphasize that "God prepared a haven for His persecuted children," and that "The Pilgrims were willing to suffer extreme hardships for God's sake." In the end, "These grades can contribute significantly to the development of patriotism." By the "Higher Grades" of 7-8, the curriculum should be a "carefully prepared outline [that] furnishes the pupil with a basic pattern for a unified picture of history."[24] This kind of cultural literacy, complete with lists of names, dates, and events, shows the extent to which the NUCS history curriculum fell in with the general parameters of history education at that time. It also made room to see history as God-ordained. This provided the theological framework for history education in the private schools.

The context of the Cold War particularly shaped how NUCS schools conceived of their overall purpose. Convention addresses published in the 1950s had a foreboding view of the world, with titles like "Christian Education in a World of Chaos."[25] In the early 1960s, NUCS published *Under God*, a textbook to promote patriotism, as well as provide a resource unit on communism.[26] The implications were that the United States was a Christian country and that pupils learning its history and politics in the NUCS schools could be counted on to be good citizens. Articles appeared in the *Christian Educator's Journal* (*CEJ*) and *Christian Home and School* that supported and reinforced the commonalities of both Christian and American cultural literacies. Frederick Nohl, for instance, authored two articles for *CEJ* in 1966 about communism.[27]

One notable exception to merely defending a cultural literacy approach is an article by Robert Swierenga, in which he notes that three-quarters of the thirty-two Christian high schools associated with NUCS were using textbooks that had been criticized by E. Merrill Root, who believed that these texts were too progressive for the Christian

---

[24] Ibid., 222.
[25] NUCS, *Christian School Annual* (Grand Rapids, MI: NUCS, various years). "Christian Education in a World of Chaos" was published in 1951.
[26] NUCS, *Christian School Directory, 1961-1962*, and *1962-1963*.
[27] Frederick Nohl, "Communism: Three Convictions and Four Concerns," *Christian Educators Journal* 5 (Feb. 1966): 11-14; Frederick Nohl, "Communism in the Classroom," *Christian Educators Journal* 5 (April 1966): 27-29.

schools.²⁸ Instead of simply agreeing with this diagnosis, Swierenga calls for teaching history to rely on the latest history scholarship and current debates in the field about American history. This approach, harkening back to the original AHA position from the 1890s for how history should be taught, seemed a unique call in the 1960s, a period when NUCS schools were using history to strengthen American patriotism.

By the late 1960s and 1970s, the context of American history education shifted again, as progressive ideas started to break through at the policy and theoretical levels. According to Jerome Bruner, students should learn the deep structures of the disciplines in order to be good citizens.²⁹ Innovations in this era included *Man, A Course of Study* and other progressive curricula that were meant to get students engaged in doing history and social studies. The NCSS stressed the importance of problem- and issues-based social studies education as related to the struggles of the culture. The curriculum this group emphasized questioned the power structures of the era. Despite these policy and theoretical trends, most classrooms stayed set in a cultural literacy paradigm of fighting over who was and who was not in the story of the past and how the past should be taught.³⁰

For Dutch Americans in private NUCS schools, the broader cultural changes of the 1960s encouraged many to re-emphasize a curriculum and approach centered on a Christian view of history. NUCS particularly worked in the later 1960s and throughout the 1970s to establish a "philosophy" of curriculum development. The hope was that this philosophy would help in the production of distinctive history textbooks.³¹ This perspective often meant christening America as a Christian nation. Curriculum and articles emphasized this approach. To manage the growing social studies catalog and related vital work, NUCS hired historian Gordon Oosterman in 1966.³² This hire showed teachers that history education had the attention of NUCS and its schools. Curriculum production started to grow as NUCS churned out materials for classroom use and tried to implement a broader vision of history education from "a Christian perspective." For instance, a textbook on European history by John DeBie had a large reach. Other

---

28   Robert Swierenga, "Book Burning is Not the Answer," *Christian Educators Journal* 6 (Dec. 1966): 27-28; E. Merrill Root, *Brainwashing in the High Schools: An Examination of Eleven American History Textbooks* (NY: Devin-Adair, Co., 1958).
29   Cantu and Warren, *Teaching History*, 10-11; Evans, *Social Studies Wars*, 123-32.
30   Cantu and Warren, *Teaching History*, 9-12; Halvorsen, *A History of Elementary Social Studies*, 123-54.
31   NUCS, *Christian School Directory, 1967-1968*.
32   Ibid., 182.

textbooks and resources were produced and promoted by Oosterman and NUCS.[33]

NUCS also grew with many new schools opening in Canada. More-recent immigrants from the Netherlands and the schools they started would bring a significant change to just how "distinct" NUCS schools would view themselves. The influence of a stronger, positive Kuyperian Calvinism would fundamentally push for curriculum innovations that more fully captured the Kuyperian vision.[34] Furthermore, discussions about how to be more positively engaged in the world—rather than just isolationists—would cause noticeable tension in the curriculum process. The 1976-77 directory, for instance, expressed concern about a curriculum development center starting in Ontario.[35] NUCS started to produce social studies curricular material specifically for Canada. The challenge of the Canadian arm of the Christian schools was more than just perspectival. It forced Dutch Americans in Christian schools to think about patriotic citizenship more broadly than just US-centered. With members in Canada, leadership needed to think outside of the US perspective.

By the 1980s, the history education landscape in America had shifted again. With the release of *A Nation at Risk*[36] in 1983, schools were blamed for the nation's decline in international economic competition. A Bradley Foundation-funded commission outlined the way history curriculum should respond to that book. It called for a return to using history to instill American democratic values, to build a sense of national identity and common culture.[37]

The result of these reports was the beginning of the standards movement. Standards were intended to "raise the bar" and dictate what basic information students needed in order to thrive in the modern world. The debate over what was "basic information" in history would lead to much political friction. One attempt at establishing

---

[33] John DeBie, *Story of the Old World* (Grand Rapids, MI: Eerdmans, 1954). There were subsequent editions in 1984 and 1992 showing the textbook's continued popularity. For information on curriculum projects, see the NUCS directory, 1968-77.

[34] According to Van Brummelen, the Kuyperian vision entails "preparing children to become Christian critics and reformers of society," 191. Van Brummelen, *Telling the Next Generation*, 188-92, 215-19.

[35] NUCS, *Christian School Directory*, 218.

[36] *A Nation at Risk: The Imperative for Educational Reform* (Washington, DC: United States Department of Education, 1983).

[37] Gary B. Nash, Charlotte A. Crabtree, and Ross E. Dunn, *History on Trial: Culture Wars and the Teaching of the Past* (NY: Vintage Books, 2000).

national standards in United States history was developed by the National Center for History in the Schools at UCLA. With support from the National Endowment for the Humanities, then headed by Lynne Cheney, the standards seemed to be without controversy, until conservative pundits called them "ideology masquerading as history." The Senate voted against them 99 to 1.[38] With this failure to establish national standards, states started to write "frameworks" and standards documents. Whatever the particular standards were in any given situation, this was largely a fight about students not knowing enough basic cultural literacy. It was not about the goals of history education; it was not a replay of the debate about intellectual development via inquiry and discipline-based practices or about the problem- and issues-based social studies education. It was about who was to be included in the list of historical actors and how to articulate the story of the past, not about how to teach students about the past.

These debates about standards in history would eventually spill into the CSI schools. How these schools reacted depended more on their state and the personnel in the school than on any official position at the national level. Most standards rarely challenged basic assumptions about American progress. Many schools were comfortable with standards as long as they enshrined the kind of history the schools wanted. Few leaders in CSI curriculum advocated for history education that emphasized conceptual or discipline-specific skills. Dealing with the challenges of the late twentieth century in the CSI schools meant to maintain what had worked for the previous century.

Debate about history standards continues today. The Michigan State Board of Education voted to approve revised (but contested) K-12 Standards for Social Studies in June of 2019. The debate about this over the past five years has shown that people care about what is taught about the past.[39] But the debate is not limited to Michigan or even to the United States. In the Netherlands, as James Kennedy attests, discussion continues over the appropriate "historical canon" for that nation.[40] Today's debate about what is in and what is not in the story of

---

[38] Evans, *Social Studies War*, 167; Nash, Crabtree, Dunn, *History on Trial*, 221-58.
[39] John Wisely, "Conservatives, liberals fight over Michigan social studies standards," *Detroit Free Press*, 15 April 2019, https://www.freep.com/story/news/education/2019/04/15/social-studies-standards-michigan/3434048002, accessed 16 April 2019.
[40] "Another Shot at the Dutch Canon: What the Historians Say," DutchNews.nl, 11 June 2019; https://www.dutchnews.nl/news/2019/06/another-shot-at-the-dutch-canon-what-the-historians-say, accessed 11 June 2019.

the past continues a long tradition. The intensity of the debate shows that people believe that the stories we tell about the past matter. People believe that knowing the "right" things about the past will make us act "better" in the present. The debate has little to do with pedagogical methods of history education; rather, the focus is on the patriotic or religious utility of learning an approved legacy.

Examining the way schools with a Dutch American constituency conceptualized history education provides a deeper look at one main point of contention among Dutch Americans. The rhetoric has called for being distinctive, Christian, and maintaining a certain worldview. NUCS private schools worked hard to justify their existence to both their constituency and their outside critics by stressing their uniqueness. The reality, though, is that the thought leaders in history education in NUCS schools largely followed a cultural literacy approach well within the mainstream of most classrooms in America. NUCS schools focused on filling students with information about specific names, events, and dates. Students needed to hear about patriotic heroes and great deeds of the past to be inspired to be better citizens. The list of what they should study might have differed slightly from the public school curriculum, but the methods were "drill and kill" (learning by rote). Progressive education reforms in history education that focused on social problems have never gathered much support in Dutch American circles.

This brief examination of history education in NUCS schools contributes to our understanding of the memory culture of Dutch Americans. It provides another clue as to how Dutch Americans understand themselves within the North American, twentieth-century context. It shows that being distinctively Dutch American has had little to do with what is taught in the history classroom. The memory culture, at least in these schools, has put Dutch Americans squarely in the middle of mainstream American education. Maybe more "American" than they would like to admit.

Contributors

Henk Aay, PhD, Clark University. Aay is a senior research fellow of the Van Raalte Institute, Hope College. He is professor emeritus of geography and environmental studies and holds emeritus status for the Frederik Meijer Chair in Dutch Language and Culture, Calvin University. He regularly publishes research on Dutch American topics and is currently taking the lead on an atlas project mapping Dutch Americans. A past president of AADAS, Aay is an editor of the 2015 AADAS conference proceedings, *Sharing Pasts: Dutch Americans through Four Centuries* (2017).

Douglas Firth Anderson, PhD, Graduate Theological Union. Anderson is a retired professor of history at Northwestern College. In retirement, he is the part-time archivist for Northwestern College. He won the Woodrow Wilson Award of the Presbyterian Historical Society (1994) and the Arrington-Prucha Prize of the Western History Association (2003). Besides many published articles and reviews, he is coauthor with Eldon G. Ernst of *Pilgrim Progression: The Protestant Experience in California* (1993) and lead coauthor with Tim Schlak, Greta Grond, and Sarah Kaltenbach of *Orange City* (2014).

Anthonia Boersema-Bremmer, MA, Utrecht Univerity. In addition to her studies in language and literature at Utrecht University, Boersema-Bremmer has undertaken cultural studies from Open University, the Netherlands.

Jan J. Boersema, PhD, University of Groningen, the Netherlands. Boersema is a professor of the principles of environmental sciences at the Institute of Environmental Sciences of Leiden University. He is an honorary research fellow of the Van Raalte Institute, where he is a past visiting fellow. His most recent books are *The Survival of Easter Island* (2015) and *Beelden van Paaseiland* (2020).

Ton Broos, PhD, Radboud University, Nijmegen. Broos studied Dutch language and literature at the University of Amsterdam. Broos worked at the Royal Library in The Hague, taught Dutch at Sheffield University in the United Kingdom, and was director of Dutch Studies at the University of Michigan from 1982 until 2012. He has published widely on 18th-century Dutch literature, Dutch medieval translations (Elckerlyc, Mariken van Nimwegen), Anne Frank, and most recently on the history of Dutch studies at the University of Michigan (*Dutch is Beautiful*, 2019). He is retired and lives in Ann Arbor, Michigan.

Donald J. Bruggink, PhD, University of Edinburgh. Bruggink is a senior research fellow at the Van Raalte Institute. For thirty-seven years, he taught at Western Theological Seminary and is the James A. H. Cornell Professor of Historical Theology Emeritus. As general editor of the Historical Series of the Reformed Church in America for fifty years, he oversaw the publication of ninety-four titles and ninety-eight volumes. As general editor emeritus, he was responsible for the 2020 publication, *A Constant State of Emergency: Paul de Kruif, Microbe Hunter and Health Activist*, by Jan Peter Verhave.

Ken Bult, MFA, Governors State University. Bult grew up in the Calumet region of Illinois and still lives in that area. He currently teaches computer graphics, photography, and art history in northwest Indiana. He is the author of *The Dutch in the Calumet Region* (2015), and, as a visiting research fellow at the Van Raalte Institute, he is using photography to trace the westward migration of Dutch settlements.

Herman J. De Vries Jr., PhD, University of Cincinnati. De Vries is a professor of Germanic languages at Calvin University, where he also holds the Frederik Meijer Chair in Dutch Language and Culture. He has served as president of AADAS. He has also held leadership roles in the American Association for Netherlandic Studies and is the North American board member of the Internationale Vereniging voor Neerlandistiek. His recent scholarship has been on the issue of English versus Dutch as the operative language in higher education in the Netherlands. He also served as guest editor of *Dutch Crossing: Journal of Low Country Studies* 38, no. 3 (2014).

Michael J. Douma, PhD, Florida State University. Douma is an assistant research professor and director of the Georgetown Institute for the Study of Markets and Ethics at the Georgetown University McDonough School of Business. His most recent publications include a book on the philosophy and methods of teaching history, *Creative Historical Thinking* (2018), and an introduced and edited book of Dutch-to-English translations, *The Colonization of Freed African Americans in Suriname: Archival Sources Relating to the U.S.-Dutch Negotiations, 1860-1866* (2019).

Keith Fynaardt, PhD, Northern Illinois University. Fynaardt is a professor of English, department chair, Humanities director, and coordinator of the first-year seminar at Northwestern College in Orange City, Iowa. He has published articles on the poetry of such disparate lyricists as Wendell Berry ("'What I stand for is what I stand on': Prepositions in Wendell Berry's Poetry of Cultivation," *The Journal of Kentucky Studies* 12 [1995]) and William Cullen Bryant ("The Spirit of Place as a Usable Past in William Cullen Bryant's 'The Prairies,'" *Midamerica: The Yearbook of the Society for the Study of Midwestern Literature* 21 [1994]). He has also published creative nonfiction about the life and work of Frederick Manfred and the paintings of Pieter Bruegel the Elder.

Adrian Guldemond, DEd, University of Toronto. Guldemond began his high school teaching career in 1969 in Toronto as an historian and finished there as an administrator. In 1979 he became the executive director of the Ontario Alliance of Christian Schools, mandated to develop a Reformed and Canadian identity for the schools. Over the course of thirty years, he taught courses in history, administration, and legal ethics at Calvin, Redeemer, and Kingswood Universities. Although he has written many articles and editorials, he is happiest with having edited *Religion in the Public Schools of Ontario: Progress in the*

Courts (1990) and his retirement project, *Inspired by Vision... Constrained by Tradition* (2013). More articles about the politics of education in Canada are on the drawing board, but golf and grandchildren beckon mightily.

George Harinck, PhD, Vrije Universiteit, Amsterdam. Harinck is a professor of the history of Neo-Calvinism at the Vrije Universiteit Amsterdam and of the history of Protestantism and director of the Neo-Calvinism Research Institute at the Theological University Kampen. Recent publications include *'Men wil toch niet gaarne een masker dragen,' Brieven van Henry Dosker aan Herman Bavinck, 1873-1921*, edited and annotated with Wouter Kroese (2018), and *Domineesfabriek. Geschiedenis van de Theologische Universiteit Kampen*, with Wim Berkelaar (2018).

Pieter Hovens, PhD, Radboud University, Nijmegen. Hovens is a cultural anthropologist who specializes in Native North American Studies at the University of British Columbia (Vancouver, Canada). As a senior policy assistant with the Dutch government, he worked in the fields of ethnic minorities, volunteerism, and the remembrance of World War II in contemporary society. He was also curator of the North American Department at the National Museum of World Cultures in Leiden. He has published widely on gypsies, Native North American art, material culture, and history. Recent retirement enables him to continue publishing on Indian-Dutch relations between 1800 and 1940.

Earl Wm. Kennedy, ThD, Princeton Theological Seminary. Kennedy is a senior research fellow at the Van Raalte Institute, where his three-volume opus, *A Commentary on the Minutes of the Classis of Holland 1848-1876. A Detailed Record of Persons and Issues, Civil and Religious, in the Dutch Colony of Holland, Michigan*, was published by the Van Raalte Press (2018). He served as senior editor of the 2017 AADAS proceedings, *Dutch Muck—and Much More: Dutch Americans in Farming, Religion, Art, and Astronomy* (2019). Kennedy is professor emeritus of religion at Northwestern College.

Andrew Klumpp, MDiv, Duke University. Klumpp is currently completing his PhD at Southern Methodist University and has been appointed editor of the *Annals of Iowa* with the State Historical Society of Iowa. He serves as the treasurer for the Society for US Intellectual History and previously served on the national Graduate Student

Committee for the American Academy of Religion. His research has recently appeared in the *Annals of Iowa,* the *Middle West Review,* and the *Society for US Intellectual History Blog.*

Donald A. Luidens, PhD, Rutgers University. Luidens is a senior research fellow and director of the Van Raalte Institute. Among his publications is *Divided by a Common Heritage: The Christian Reformed Church and the Reformed Church in America at the beginning of the New Millennium* (with Corwin Smidt, James Penning, and Roger Nemeth) (2006). Recently, he co-edited *Jack: A Compassionate Compendium. A Tribute to Dr. Jacob E. Nyenhuis: Scholar, Servant, Leader* (with JoHannah M. Smith) (2018), and *Dutch Muck—and Much More: Dutch Americans in Farming, Religion, Art, and Astronomy* (with Earl Wm. Kennedy and David Zwart) (2019).

Rhonda Pennings, MBA, Northcentral University; EdD, University of South Dakota. Pennings is the dean of Arts and Sciences/Business and Health at Northwest Iowa Community College in Sheldon, Iowa. She is currently the president of the Iowa Women in Higher Education (Iowa chapter of American Council on Education Women's Network group), where she writes a quarterly newsletter. She is working on an article to be published in a forthcoming issue of *Origins* magazine.

Mary Risseeuw, MA and MFA, Northern Illinois University. Risseeuw is a professional genealogist, historian, writer, lecturer, teacher, and artist. She has researched nineteenth- and twentieth-century Dutch immigration to Wisconsin for thirty years and has lectured throughout the Midwest and the Netherlands on the subject. She is a past president of AADAS. Her most recent articles have appeared in *Origins* (2019), *Dutch Muck—and Much More: Dutch Americans in Farming, Religion, Art, and Astronomy* (2019), and *Repast: Quarterly Publication of the Culinary Historians of Ann Arbor* (2014).

Robert Schoone-Jongen, PhD, University of Delaware. Schoone-Jongen is a professor emeritus of history at Calvin University. His research, writing, and teaching have focused on immigration to the United States, especially Dutch immigration since 1850. He has contributed chapters to a wide variety of books, including *Immigrants in American History*, edited by Elliott Robert Barkan (2013), and *Four Centuries of Dutch American Relations*, edited by Hans Krabbendam et al.

(2009). Currently, he is assembling the story of Dutch immigration to northern New Jersey, where he grew up.

Suzanne M. Sinke, PhD, University of Minnesota. Sinke is director of graduate studies and associate professor in the Department of History at Florida State University. Since the fall of 2018, she has served as editor for the *Journal of American Ethnic History*. A specialist in migration and gender studies in the US context, she is the author of *Dutch Immigrant Women in the United States, 1880-1920* (2002) and co-editor of *Across Borders—Dutch Migration to North America and Australia* (2010). She has received several teaching accolades, including two Fulbright teaching awards. Sinke's extensive list of journal articles includes venues such as *International Migration Review*, *OAH Magazine*, *Gender Issues*, *Journal of American Ethnic History*, and *History of the Family*.

Stephen Staggs, PhD, Western Michigan University. Beyond his duties as a Calvin University professor, Staggs is currently revising a manuscript for publication that analyzes Indian-Dutch relations in New Netherland/New York between 1609 and 1750. A chapter from that manuscript will appear in *Dutch and Indigenous Communities in 17th-Century Northeastern North America: What Archaeology, History, and Indigenous Oral Traditions Teach Us about their Intercultural Relationships* (forthcoming 2020). He is also working on a new research project that examines race and religion in the Dutch Reformed Church in New York and New Jersey between 1772 and 1827. This new, long-term project has received funding from the Louisville Institute, a Calvin Research Fellowship, and the Frederik Meijer Chair in Dutch Language and Culture.

Robert P. Swierenga, PhD, University of Iowa. Swierenga is a Timothy Christian Schools alumnus, having graduated from the Cicero grade school over seventy years ago. He completed his secondary education at Chicago Christian High School in 1953. His teaching career began at Pella [Iowa] Christian High School (1958-61), continued at Calvin College (1961-62, 1965-68), and culminated at Ohio's Kent State University. Since 1996 he has been the Albertus C. Van Raalte Research Professor at the A. C. Van Raalte Institute. His latest book is *His Faithfulness Continues: A History of Timothy Christian Schools of Chicagoland* (2020).

Phil Teeuwsen, PhD, Brock University. Teeuwsen is an associate professor of education and director of teacher education at Redeemer University College in Ancaster, Ontario. His recent publications focus on experiences with diverse pedagogies and different approaches to teacher education. His other research interests revolve around the more social/cultural contexts in education. His recent publications have appeared in *Studies in Higher Education* and *South African Journal of Higher Education*.

Justin R. Vos, MA, Florida State University. Vos is currently a PhD candidate in history at FSU, with special focus on immigration studies, Dutch ethnicity, and religious history. He currently serves as president of the History Graduate Student Association and teaches various courses in American history.

Douglas J. Vrieland, DMin, Fuller Theological Seminary. Vrieland is a retired Christian Reformed minister and United States Navy chaplain. He was deployed to New York City following the September 11, 2001, attack on the World Trade Center; Iraq in support of the Global War on Terrorism; and Ishinomaki, Japan, following the March 11, 2011, earthquake, tsunami, and nuclear disaster. He also has a forthcoming publication, *The Fort: Growing up in Grosse Pointe during the Civil Rights Movement* (Trimble Hollow Press).

David Zwart, PhD, Western Michigan University. Zwart is an associate professor and assistant chair in the History Department at Grand Valley State University. Prior to his appointment at GVSU, he was on the history faculty at Dordt University. He has published numerous articles on Dutch Americans in the twentieth century, the rural Midwest, and history education. Among his recent articles are "Rural Identity among Dutch Americans," in *Dutch Muck—and Much More: Dutch Americans in Farming, Religion, Art, and Astromony* (2018), and "For the Next Generation: Commemorating the Immigration Experience in the United States and Canada," *Tijdschrift voor Sociale en Econonmische Geschiedenis* 7, no. 2 (2010).

AADAS Conferences 1977 to 2019

"Dutch Americans and Agriculture, Past and Present" (Fulton, IL, 2017). Proceedings published in *Dutch Muck—and Much More: Dutch Americans in Farming, Religion, Art, and Astronomy*. Edited by Earl Wm. Kennedy, Donald A. Luidens, and David Zwart. Holland, MI: Van Raalte Press, 2019.

"The Dutch in America Across the Centuries: Connections and Comparisons" (New Netherland Institute, Albany, NY, 2015). Proceedings published in *Sharing Pasts: Dutch Americans through Four Centuries*. Edited by Henk Aay, Janny Venema, and Dennis Voskuil. Holland, MI: Van Raalte Press, 2017.

"The Dutch American Involvement in War: U.S. and Abroad" (Central College, Pella, IA, 2013). Proceedings published in *Dutch Americans and War: United States and Abroad*. Edited by Robert P. Swierenga, Nella Kennedy, and Lisa Zylstra. Holland, MI: Van Raalte Press, 2014.

"Past and Present: The Importance of History for Dutch Americans" (Lakeland College, Sheboygan, WI, 2011). Proceedings published in *Diverse Destinies: Dutch Kolonies in Wisconsin and the East*. Edited by

Nella Kennedy, Mary Risseeuw, and Robert P. Swierenga. Holland, MI: Van Raalte Press, 2012.

"Across Borders" (Redeemer University College, Ancaster, Ontario, CA, 2009). Proceedings published in *Across Borders: Dutch Migration to North America and Australia*. Edited by Jacob E. Nyenhuis, Suzanne M. Sinke, and Robert P. Swierenga. Holland, MI: Van Raalte Press, 2010.

"Arts & Letters" (Hope College, Holland, MI, 2007). Proceedings published in *Dutch American Arts and Letters in Historical Perspective*. Edited by Robert P. Swierenga, Jacob E. Nyenhuis, and Nella Kennedy. Holland, MI: Van Raalte Press, 2008

"Dutch Immigrants on the Plains" (Dordt College, Sioux Center, IA, 2005). Proceedings published in *Dutch Immigrants on the Plains*. Edited by Paul Fessler, Hubert Krygsman, and Robert P. Swierenga. AADAS, 2005.

"The Dutch in Urban America" (Trinity Christian College, Palos Heights, IL, 2003). Proceedings published in *The Dutch in Urban America*. Edited by Robert P. Swierenga, Donald Sinnema, and Hans Krabbendam. AADAS, 2004.

"The Dutch Adapting in North America" (Calvin College, Grand Rapids, MI, 2001). Proceedings published in *The Dutch Adapting in North America*. Edited by Richard H. Harms. Mimeograph copy. AADAS, 2001.

"Dutch Enterprise" (Central College, Pella, IA, 1999). Proceedings published in *Dutch Enterprise: Alive and Well in North America*. Edited by Larry J. Wagenaar and Robert P. Swierenga. Mimeograph copy. Holland, MI: Joint Archives of Holland, 2000.

"The Sesquicentennial of Dutch Immigration: 150 Years of Ethnic Heritage" (Hope College, Holland, MI, 1997). Proceedings published in *The Sequicentennial of Dutch Immigration: 150 Years of Ethnic Heritage*. Edited by Larry J. Wagenaar and Robert P. Swierenga. Mimeograph copy. Holland, MI: Joint Archives of Holland, 1998.

"A Century of Midwestern Dutch American Manners and Mores—and More." Northwestern College, Orange City, IA, 1995 (in conjunction with the 1995 quasquicentennial of Orange City). Made possible by a grant of the Iowa Humanities Board and the National Endowment for the Humanities. Proceedings published in mimeograph form, 1995.

"The Dutch and their Neighbors in Transition" (Calvin College, Grand Rapids, MI, 1993). Proceedings published in *The Dutch and Their Neighbors in Transition: The Formation, Growth, and Dissolution of Ethnic Centers in Grand Rapids, Chicago, and other Places*. Mimeograph copy, 1993.

"The Dutch and Their Faith" (Hope College, Holland, MI, 1991). Proceedings published in *The Dutch and Their Faith: Immigrant Religious Experience in the 19th and 20th Centuries*. Coordinated by Larry J. Wagenaar. Mimeograph copy, 1991.

"Suffering and Survival: The Netherlands, 1940-1945" (Dordt College, Sioux Center, IA, 1990). No published proceedings. Some presentations were published in *Pro Rege*, a Dordt College publication. Eighteen audiocassettes are available at Calvin University's Heritage Hall.

"Dutch Chicago" (Trinity Christian College, Palos Heights, IL, 1987). Proceedings published in *The Dutch in America, Perspectives 1987*. Convened by Hendrik Sliekers. Mimeograph copy, 1987.

"Dutch Settlements West of the Mississippi" (Northwestern College, Orange City, IA, 1985). Proceedings published in *Proceedings of AADAS, September 1985*. Mimeograph copy, 1985.

"Dutch Settlements" (Hope College, Holland, MI, 1983). Proceedings published in *The Dutch in America: Papers presented at the Fourth Biennial Conference of AADAS*. Compiled by Elton J. Bruins. Mimeograph copy, 1984.

"Third Biannual conference on Dutch American Studies" (Pella, IA: Central College, 1981). No published proceedings. A paper by Philip E. Webber is available in the AADAS files at Calvin University's Heritage Hall.

"Status of Dutch American Research" (Grand Rapids, MI: Calvin College, 1979). No published proceedings.

"Initial Conference on Dutch American Studies" (Grand Rapids, MI: Calvin College, 1977). No published proceedings.

Index

A Nation at Risk, 398
Aardsma-Hoekstra, Alice, 247
Aay, Henk, xvii, 401, 409
Abbink, John, 77
Adams, Charles, 351
Adams, John Quincy, 351
Adams, John, 210, 351
African Americans, xvi, xxi, 106, 202n3, 211n22, 217n2, 220, 225, 233, 236, 292, 298, 309, 368, 403
Afscheiding (Secession), 41, 45n18, 46, 106, 192n36
Álvarez de Toledo y Pimentel, Fernando (3rd Duke of Alba), 109
Americanization, xvii, xxvii, 21, 24, 44, 95, 301, 313

Amity Street Christian School, xxiii, 307-8, 316
Anderson, Douglas Firth, xix, 283, 401
Aristotle (Greek philosopher), 376
arson, xxiv, 323, 326-27
Assink, Charlotte, 297
Augustine, Aurelius (Saint Augustine), 376-77
Avink, Harm, 266
Azariah, L. V., 297
baby boom (postwar), 25, 28
Bacon, Francis (English philosopher), 387
Bai, Mercy Rani, 299
Banner, The, xxiv, 31, 152, 231-32, 235, 239, 315, 332-46

Barkan, Elliott Robert, 405
Batts, John, 226
Bavinck, Herman, 55, 192, 195-97, 335
Bavinck, Jan, 188, 190
Beadie, Nancy, 105
Beardslee, John Walter, 291
Beardslee, John, Jr., 291-92
Beatrix, Queen (the Netherlands), 350
Beets, Henry, 238-39, 246, 250
Beijer, Dina, 265
Beijer, Herman, 269
Belgic Confession, 6, 133, 136-37, 377
Bennink, B. J., 30, 392
Berger, Peter L., 167-68, 173, 176-77
Berkhof, Louis, 137
Berrien, John Macpherson, 210, 212-13
Berrien, Judge John (grandfather), 213
Berrien, Major John (father), 213
Berrien, Margaret Macpherson, 213
Berry, Wendell (American poet), 403
Betten, Antonie Jacob, Jr., 46
Beuker, Henricus, 191-92, 196-97
Bewulda, Klaaske, 269
Bhabha, Homi, 168-69
Bible study, 32, 244, 248-49, 340
Blekkink, Clarence, 72
Blocker, Simon, 293
Bloemers, Harms, 71
Bloemers, Vera Holle, 71
Boer, G. Egberts, 187-88, 191-94, 196
Boer, Harry, 232

Boer War, 52-53
Boersema-Bremmer, Anthonia, xxv, 402
Boersema, Jan J., xxv, 402
Bolks, Seine, 41, 46, 108-9, *109*, 110
Boogaart, Thomas, 298
Bos, George, 264
Bos, Gerda, 285
Bos, Gerhardus, 264
Bosman, Willem, 203-5
Bosscher, Jacob H., 240, 243, 250
Boswell, James (Scottish biographer), 351
Botts, Harold, 223-25, 227
Boughton, Willis, 212
Bouma, Mark, 240, *241*
Bouma, Mrs., *241*
Bouws, Rieks, 383
Brandt, Cora, 247-48
Bratt, James, 320, 332
Breiner, Leon, 220
Brink, J. W., 241
Brink, L. P., 239-40, 243-44
Brink-Vander Wagen, Dena, 247
Brink, Wilhelmina, 247
Broek, D., 380
Broekstra, Marinus, 57
Broekstra, Martin, 54
Broos, Ton, xxv, 402
Brouwer, Willem, 265
Brown, George, Jr., 299, 301
Brown, Henry J., 383
Brownson, James V., 299
Brown, Timothy, 300
Bruegel, Pieter, 403
Bruggink, Donald J., xxiii, 402
Bruins, Elton J., 411
Brummelkamp, Anthony, Jr., 189-90

Brummelkamp, Anthony, Sr., 191
Bruner, Jerome, 397
Buechner, Frederick, 122-23
Buis, Harry, 297
Bult, Ken, xviii, 402
Bultmann, Rudolph, 293
Burggraff, Winfield, 292
Burkhart, Walter, 377
Burr, Aaron, 206
Bury, John B., 375, 377
Buursma, Ale, 95-98
Calhoun, John C., 212
Calvin University (formerly College), xx, 134, 149-50, 152, 154, 170, 183-98, 263, 281-82, 320, 352, 355, 364, 368
Calvinism, xix, xxii, 344, 364, 369, 392, 398
Calvin, John, 166, 335
Calvin Theological Seminary, xx, 183-98
Canons of Dort, 6, 133
Carpenter, Ginny, 285
Central College, 263
charter schools, 36, 355-56, 359, 369
Cheeko, George, 248
Chino, Wendell, 292
Christelijke Gereformerde Kerk, 187, 189, 191, 196-97
Christian Educators' Journal, 31, 396
Christian Home and School, 31, 153, 396
Christian Indian, The, 239
Christian School Herald, 149, 153
Christian Schools International, 22, 127, 141, 156, 341, 391. *See also* National Union of Christian Schools
Chun, Young Chang, 292

Church Herald, The, 76
Cicero race riots (1951), 233
citizenship, xx, 362, 398; education for, 13, 240, 275, 390, 393-95
Civil War, 219-20, 273, 362
Clinton, George, 206
Cobo, Albert, 220-21
Cold War, 338-39, 395-97
Collier, John, 249
Colonial New Netherland, 5-12, 21, 202, 313
communism, 339, 396
control of schools: parental, 22, 30, 152, 159, 196, 225; Native American, 252
Cooke, Dave, 224
Cook, James I., 298
counterculture, 62
creationism, 240
Cruz, Virgil, 298
curriculum (Christian), 32, 157
Daily Manna, 334
Darrow, Clarence, 220
Darwin, Charles, 337
Davidson, Clifford, 353
Davidson, Matt, 140, 142
De Boer Deckard, Anne, 337
de Brés, Guido, 137
de Buffon, Comte (French naturalist), 337
de Cock, Helenius, 188, 191
de Cock, Hendrik, 184, 188
de Haan, Tamme Foppes, 184-85
De Jong, Conrad Keith, 75
de Jong, Garrett, 74
De Jong, Geertje, 83
De Jong, Hendrik, 83-84
De Jong, Martin, 325-26
De Jong, Nellie, 246, 261-62

De Jong, Peter Y., 335, 343-44
DeKoster, Lester, 364
de Lange, Willem, 259
de Lespinasse, Adolph Frederik Henri, 42-43, 46, 63
De Master, Augusta, 71
De Master, Hazel, 71
De Ridder, Richard R., 340
De Spelder, John A., 110, 125
De Velder, Joyce Borgmann, 297
De Vries, Herman J., Jr., 402-3
dean of women, 274, 277, 280-84, 286-87
DeBie, John, 397
DeBraal, Daniel, 72
Defoe, Daniel (English writer), 348
DeJong, Selina Peake, 84
Dekker, Frederick G., 305, 307, 310, 313
demographic changes, xv, xix, xxi, xxvi, 343
Depression (the Great), xv, xix, xxi, xxvi, 343
Derks, Anna, 240, *241*
Deus est Lux (God is Light), 113, 115, 124
DeVos, Betsy, 355-57, 359-61, 364-71
DeVos, Richard, 355
Dewey, John, 393
Diamond, Neil, 201
Diekema, G. J., 385
Dieleman, Suzanna, *241*
Diez, Paul, 293
diversity: cultural/ethnic, 61, 139, 214, 285, 289-301, 354; religious/ecclesiastical, 15, 137, 143, 228
Dolfin, Frederic, 73

Dooyeweerd, Herman, 151
Dordt University, xiv, 284-86
Dorsey, Chris, 300
Dosker, Henry, 385
Douma, Michael J., xxv, 403
Droppers, Dorothy, 71
Droppers, Oliver, 72
Drukker, Roelof, 308
Duenk, Arnie, 71
Duer, William, 211
Duer, William Alexander (son), 210-12
Dutch language: in church xv, 21, 188, 310-11, 326-27, 384; in school, xv, xxv, 19, 21, 49, 184, 188, 193, 257, 267, 269, 310-11, 332, 347-54
Dyke, Charles, 382
Dykhuizen, Cornelius, 72
Dykhuizen, Dorothy, 244
Dykstra, Broer Doekeles, 103, *104*, 111-12, 118-21, 123
Dykstra, John D., 125
Ebbers, Alva, 72
Edelstein, Ludwig, 376
Eenigenburg, Elton M., 293
Eenigenburg, Harry, 382
Eerdmans, Wm. B., 51n38; publishing co., xxiv, 332-33
Eldersveld, Peter, 340
Elhart, Cora, 247
Elzinga, Mel, 155
Englund, Harold, 294-95
Erasmus Hall Academy, xxi, 201-15
Eringa, Alys, 262
Eringa, Dora, 262
Eringa, Jessie, 260, 262
Eringa, Thryze, 262
Eringa, Ulbe, 382

Ernst, Eldon G., 401
Eves, Ernie, 159
evolution, 58-59, 152, 161, 337
Fakkema, Mark, 394-95
Fennema, Jack, 154
Ferber, Edna (American novelist), 84
Feringa, Phil, 225
Fessler, Paul, 410
Flaherty, Jim, 159
Flipse, Eugene, 72
Flipse, Martin Eugene (son), 66, 76
Flores, Daniel, 301
Ford, Gerald R. (US president), 354, 373
Ford, Henry, 220
Fortuin, H. J. L., 51
Francken, Aegidius, 185, 191
Frank, Anne, 350, 353, 402
free market, 356, 359, 362, 364
Free University (Vrije Universiteit), Amsterdam, 151, 195-96, 292, 298-99
Frens, Richard J., 338-39
frontier, xviii, xx, 12, 18, 93, 95, 98, 290
Fryling, Herman, 238, 245-46
Fryling, Sophia, 247
Furens, Elizabeth, 262
Fynaardt, Keith, xiv, 403
Ganzevoort, Herman, 165
Gardner, John, 228
Gast, John, 379
gender issues, xxi-xxiii, xv-xvi, 161, 255-71, 273-87, 289-301
George, Thotathill Mathai, 297
Gereformeerde Kerk, 166, 309
Germany, Lamar, 223
Germany, Louise, 223

Geronimo (Apache warrior), 120
Giago, Tim, 251
Gibson, Stanley, 70
Gilmore, Christina Van Raalte, 280, 286
Gilmore, William Brokaw, 280, 290
global perspective, 97, 163, 286, 354
Gloucester, John, 210
Goldsmith, Oliver (Irish novelist), 208-9
Gorter-Brouwer, Ante, 267
Gorter-Brouwer, Betje, 267
Goudberg, Anna, 247
Goudberg, William, 249
Goulooze, William, 292-93
Graham, Billy (evangelist), 76
Greenway, Leonard, 340
Greydanus, Frances, 307
Groendyk-Houtman, Anna, 281
Groenewold, John, 222
Grond, Greta, 401
Grondwet, De, 380
Grosse Pointe Christian Day School, 217-36; board, 218, 223, 227, 234
Grotenhuis, Louis, 72
Grotenhuis, Willard, 71, 81
Guldemond, Adrian, xix, 130-31, 142, 403-4
Haan, Sheri, 156
Hamilton, Alexander (American stateman), 206, 210, 351
Hamilton, Elisabeth Schuyler, 351
Hamming, Nellie, 247
Harding, William L., 324
Harinck, George, xx, 404
Harms, Richard H., 281-82, 410

Harris, Mike, 157
Hartog, Cocia, 240, *241*, 243
Hartt, Rollin Lynde, 103
Hausch, Adrienne Flipse, 76
Haverkamp, Anthony, 72, 79
Hayashi, Paul, 293
Hayzlett, George, 238
Havenga, Calvin, 246, 248
Heemstra, Jacob, 123-24, 283
Heemstra, James, *124*
Heemstra, John F., 115, 125
Heidelberg Catechism, 6, 111, 133, 224
Heidenwereld, De (later, *Missionary Monthly*) 53, 239
Heinen, Charlotte, 296
Hemkes, Gerrit K., 189, 191
Henderlite, Rachel, 294
Hengstman, Albert, 151
Herbert, Victor, 283
Hesselink, Clarence, 72
Hesselink, Harold, 72
Hesselink, I. John, 75, 297-98
Heynen, Ralph, 337-38
Heyns, William W., 191
Hiemenga, John J., 314
Hillyer, Karl, 283
Hinkamp, Paul, 68
Hoekema, Houkje, 259, 271
Hoekema, Klaas, 259, 271
Hoekstra, J., 188
Hoekstra, Peter (congressman), 366, 371
Hoff, Marvin D., 298-300
Hofman, Effie, 263
Hofstra, Peter, 312
Hollander, De, 380
Hooglandt, Adrian, 202
hooks, bell, 174

Hope College (Holland, MI), 65, 74, 263, 274, 278-81, 290, 298
Hospers, Hendrina, 75, 118-23
Hospers, Henry, 41, 93-99, 106-10, 120
Hovens, Pieter, xxii, 404
Hoving, Arnold, 135, *136*, 138
Hsieh, Peter, 292
Hubbard, Lucius L., 348
Hubbard, Orville, 225
Hudson, Henry, 373
Huenink, DeLloyd, 72
Huenink, Gerald, 73
Huibregtse, Edward, 72, 327
Huizenga, Lee S., 240
Huizenga, Peter H., 135
Hull, Marion, 283
Hultink, Henk, 155
Hunsberger, George R., 299
indiginization, 252
integration, 217-36
Itoh, Katsuhiro, 297
Jacobsma, H., 21
Janssen, Ralph, 191
Jasper, Mr. (Jacobus Jans Jasper), 48n30
Jay, John (first chief justice of the US), 206
Jefferson, Thomas (US president), 204-5, 212
Jentink, Bernice, 71
Jeremiah (biblical prophet), 122, 388
Jim (interviewee), 174-75
Johnson, Lyndon B. (US president), 235
Johnson, Samuel (English author), 208
Jones, William Atkinson, 238
Kaiser, Christopher, 298

Kaltenbach, Sarah, 401
Kampen Theologische School, xx, 55, 183-97, 292, 309, 313
Karsten, John H., 91-93, 99
Kay, Elaine, 297
Keng, Moses, 295
Kennedy, Earl Wm., xvii, 290, 404-5, 409
Kennedy, Gerard, 160
Kennedy, James, 399
Kennedy, Nella, 409-10
Kerber, Linda, 274
Key, Francis Scott, 213
Kilpatrick, W. H., 9
Kimura, Kumaji, 290
King, Martin Luther, Jr., 221
Kleinheksel, Ruth, 296
Klumpp, Andrew, xviii, 404-5
Knikkerbakker, Derek, 389
Koeppe, Edwin, 72-73
Koeppe, Elizabeth Renskers, 73
Koester, Reinhard, 293
Kollen, Gerrit, 65
Kolyn, Matthew, 125
Konig, John, 72
Koning, A. A., 251
Koning, John W., 76
Koning, Mildred Te Ronde, 76
Koops, Enne, 166
Koops, Hugh, 296, 298
Koskamp, Dorothy, 71
Krabbendam, Hans, 406, 410
Kroese, Wouter, 404
Krygsman, Hubert, 410
Kuiper, Henry J., 333, 345
Kuiper, Klaas, 54
Kuipers, Cornelius, 244, 247-49
Kuitert, Harry, 152
Kuyper, Abraham, 44, 55, 62, 147-48, 153, 166, 172, 192, 268-69, 309, 356, 365, 367-69

Kuyper, Cornelius, 74
Kuyper, Everdene, 74-75
Kuyper, Lester J., 292-93
Kuyperian paradigm, 57, 59, 147-48, 152, 162, 170, 195, 197, 306, 365, 367-69, 393
Laarman, Peter, 364
Lagerwey, Walter, 352
Lahuis, Kaspar, 384
Laman, David, 73
Lamarck, Jean-Baptiste, 337
Lammers, Barend W., 66
Lammers, William, 66
Lam, Nellie, 249
Lankester, Peter, 381
Law, Elsie Wen-Hua Shih, 294-95
Law, Jeremy Chung Hian, 295
Le Cocq, R. B., 383
Lefferts, Peter, 206
Lensink, John, 72
Lewis, Viola, 71
Leyden, Anthony, 326
Leys, Fanny, 240
Lindberg, David, 377
Linn, John Blair, 210-12
Linn, William, 210
Lin, Stanley H. K., 295, 297
Lisa (interviewee), 179-80
Livingston, Edward, 211
Livingston, John, 205-6, 208
Locke, John, 208
Lothers, Charlotte, 284
Lott, Johannes, 206
Lousma, Jack (astronaut), 354
Lowe, Peter, 204-5
Lubbers, Anthony, 79
Lubbers, Arend (Anthony's father), 66, 79n24
Lubbers, Arend Donselaar (Don), 80, 294-95

Lubbers, Arthur, 80
Lubbers, Clarence W., 80
Lubbers, Elaine E., 80-81, 294, 296, 298
Lubbers, Elmer H., 79-80
Lubbers, Harold, 80
Lubbers, Irwin J., 80
Lubbers, Jennie, 79
Lubbers, Kathryn Huenink, 80
Lubbers, Melvin B., 80
Lubbers, Raymond J., 72, 79
Lubbers, Wilhelmina, 79
Lubbers, William, 80
Lucas, Henry, 90
Luckmann, Tomas, 173
Luckman, Sid, 201
Lucretius (Roman philosopher), 376, 386
Luidens, Donald A., 405, 409
Lupton, Brandt Schuyler, 208
Lupton, William, 208
Macpherson, Margaret, 213
Maddison, Angus, 378
Madison, Brian, 300
Madison, James (US president), 212
Maluleke, Samuel Tiniyiko, 299
Manfred, Frederick, 403
Maodush-Pitzer, Diane, 299
Maria, Antonius Jozef, 352
Marsden, George, 143
Masselink, Benjamin Henry, 40-41
Mattison, Robin, 299
Mayer, Jane, 370
McGuinty, Dalton, 159
McIntosh, Lachlan, 213
Mead, Sidney, 63
media, 389-400
Meengs, Raymond, 72

Melling, Robert, 225-26, 236
Memmelaar, Jean, 248
Mennenga, George H., 292-93
Meulenbeld, Henk F., 350, 353
Michaelius, Jonas, 99, 352
migration: 1840s, 3, 16, 368, 373; 1880s, 16, 43, 93, 368, 373; colonial, 16; from the Netherlands, xiii, xv, xvii, xxiii-xxi, 16, 23, 320; twentieth century, 25, 28, 146, 165-66, 170, 177-78, 391
Miller, Lisa, 360-61
ministers/pastors, 21, 53, 72-76, 153, 170, 222, 234, 286, 334, 341, 352, 354; and training, 67, 98-99, 183-96, 232, 234, 290-91, 299
ministers' wives, 72, 81
Minnema, Frances, 307
Minnema, John, 305, 307, 313, 316, 321
missions/missionaries, xvi, xviii, xxii, 72-76, 92, 96, 98-100, 120, 262-63, 271, 290, 297. *See also* Rehoboth
Mol, Joseph, 257-58
Moncada, Antonio, 292
Monsma, Edwin Y., 337
Morgan, Jacob Casimero, 240, 249
Mouw, Richard, 367-68
Muilenburg, Hubert, 121
Muilenburg, James, 118, 121-23
Mulder, John R., 293-94
Mulder, Yge Yges [Jr.], 41, 45-51, 62
multiculturalism, 354
National Union of Christian Schools, 17, 127, 149, 341,

Index 421

390. *See also* Christian Schools International
Native Americans, xvi, xxii, 72, 75, 106, 212, 237-53, 292
nativism/jingoism, xxiv, 324
Navajos, xxii, 238-46, 249-53, 263
Negen, Gordon, 339
Nemeth, Roger, 405
Neo-Calvinism/Calvinists 21, 32, 190, 192, 196-97, 268, 368
Nevins, Alvin, 395
New Brunswick Theological Seminary, 292, 313
New Deal, 120, 249
Nies, Helenius, 306
Nisbet, Robert, 376
Nohl, Frederick, 396
Noordhoff, Nellie, 240, 263
Northwestern Classical Academy (Junior College/College), xvii-xix, 46-47, 54-55, 91-101, 103-26
nurses, xxiii, 71, 74, 81
Nyenhuis, Jacob E. (Jack), 235, 280, 410
O'Brock, E., 75
Oggel, Henry Peter, 47, 50-54, 56, 62-63
Oghimi, Motoichiro, 290
Okazaki, Sayuri, 299
Ongna, Reuben, 73
Ontario Alliance of Christian Schools (OACS), xx, 145-63
Oosterman, Gordon, 397-98
Orsi, Robert, 314
Osterhaven, M. Eugene, 293
Otte, Frances Few Christie Phelps, 279
Otten, Willemien, 365, 368-69

Oudersluys, Richard C., 293
Overvoorde, Chris Stoffel, 373
Paarlberg, Widow, 84
Padilla, Alvin, 301
Park, Soo Am, 297
parochial schools, xx; Catholic 44, 59; Reformed/Dutch 5-6, 10, 12-15, 19, 22, 30, 56-62, 390-91
Pass, George, 112
Patmos, Louis A., 317
patriotism, xviii, 51, 56, 58, 315, 393, 395-97
Penning, James, 405
Pennings, Rhonda, xxii, 405
Peterkin, Janelle, 215
Peters, Jay, 366
Phelps, Eliza, 279
Phelps, Philip, 279-80
physicians, 42, 69-71
Piet, John H., 297-98
Plekenpol, Lester, 71
Plekenpol, Mabel Weavers, 71
Plumbe, Edward O., 43, 63
Poel, Mary, 284
Polinder, Ron, 252
politics, xxiv-xxv, 97, 160-61, 338-9
Pope Paul VI, 295
Popper, Karl, 382
Postma, Dirk, 184-85, 191
Potts, Willis J., 69-70
primary schools, xiii, xvi, xxii, 25, 43, 46-47, 73, 95, 186-87, 308
Prince, Edgar, 355
Prince, Eric, 371
professionalization/professionalism, 30, 35, 105,

260, 291-2, 294
professors, 154, 187, 191, 193, 269, 291-92, 349, 354; female, 273-87
progress/progressive, 108, 154-57, 249, 276, 356, 364, 373-88, 393, 396-97, 400; provincialism, 107
Proper, Herman, 158
Protestant Reformed Christian School, 89-90
Protestant Reformed Church, 34-35
race relations, 201-15, 217-36, 237-53
Rae, Bob, 157
Ramaker, Harvey, 78
Reed, Bessie, 248
Reformed Creeds, 6, 12, 16, 19, 133, 148
Reformed Protestant Dutch Church (later Reformed Church in America), 9, 202, 204-5, 207, 313
Rehoboth, 238-45, 250-53, 340; boarding school, 239-41, 246, 249, 252-53
Rhem, Richard A., 299
Rhodes, Frank, 349
Rich (interviewee), 171
Richardson, Wilson Duke, 292
Ridder, Herman J., 295
Risseeuw, Mary, xviii, 405, 410
Risseeuw, P. J., 387
Rizga, Kristina, 361-65
Robinson, Arthur, 77
Romeyn, Dirck, 210
Romney, George (Michigan governor), 221
Rooks, Albertus J., 194-95

Roosevelt, Franklin D. (US president), 249, 314
Root, E. Merrill, 396
Rosbach, Katherine, *241*
Roueché, Berton, 359
Rudenga, Liz, 285
Rufus, Mahamimai, 297
Rugg, Harold, 395
Runner, H. Evan, 170
rural schools, 13, 65-66, 262, 265, 269
sacred canopy, 167-69, 177, 180
Sadler, George, 283
Said, Edward, 169
Salinger, J. D. (American author), 152
Santer, A. G., 78
Schaap, James Calvin, 365
Schieffelin, Samuel, 15
Schlak, Tim, 401
Schmidt, John, 298
Schnell, Diane, 70
Scholte, Hendrik Pieter, 108, 324-25, 352, 374
school boards, xvi, 18, 142, 147, 152, 155, 158, 162, 175, 258, 271, 316
Schoolland, K., 195
Schoolland, Marian M., 335
Schoone-Jongen, Robert, xxiii, 405-6
Schram, Henry, 240
Schrotenboer, Paul G., 338
Schussele, Christian, 378
Schutter, William L., 298
Schuttinga, Bethany, 284
Scudder, Ida, 74
Seceders, xx-xxi, 18, 184-86, 188, 195-97, 268, 363-65, 374

secondary schools, xiii, xvi, xviii, xxii, 25, 35, 105, 186-87, 201, 207
secularization/secularism, 62, 107, 143
segregation, 105, 219-20, 225, 234, 368
Shao, Wesley, 293
Shih, Paul, 293
Shu, Stephen, 299
Sietsema, John, 65
Sinke, Suzanne M., xxii, 406, 410
Sinnema, Donald, 410
slavery, 202, 212, 214, 262, 368
Sliekers, Hendrik, 411
Smidt, Corwin, 405
Smies, Geraldine, 73
Smies, Gerry, 73
Smies, Lillian, 73-74
Smith, Amanda McAdams, 283
Smith, Clarence K., 283
Smith, Clarice, 283
Smith, Fern, 283-84, 286
Smith, James K. A., 370
Smith, Leona, 283
Smith, Paul, 298
Smith, Ronald T., 297
Smith, Sidney, 70
Smits, Jan, 379-80
Smitter, Jan, 54
Snoek, Kees, 350
socialism, 58, 314
Society for Christian Instruction, 30, 40, 84
Soulen, Philip, 103, 125
Spencer, Herbert, 375
Spoelhof, William, 320, 341
Spyker, John, 240
Staggs, Stephen, xxi, 406

standards: educational, 135, 149-50, 160, 225, 227, 248, 259-60, 273, 262, 398-99
Stanton, Zack, 357
Steen, Franklin, 218, 235
Steen, Stacy, 235
Steffens, Nicholas (Nicolaus) M., 190, 291-92
stereotypes: Dutch, xxv, 362
Stewart, Sonja (Mrs. John), 296, 298, 300
Stob, Leonard, 142
Stob, Renzina, 240, 250
Stoffel, John, 234
Streisand, Barbara, 201
Stronks, John, 155-56
Stuart, William, 51
Sue (interviewee), 172, 175, 179-80
Sutherland, Jane Graham, 291
Suzuki, Makomoto, 297
Sweet, Ossian, 220
Sweet Trials (1926), 220
Swierenga, Robert P., xix, 190, 268, 332, 353, 396, 406, 409-10
Tanis, Edward J., 338
Te Paske, Anthony, 108, 121, 124
teacher training, 22, 46, 259, 263
Teeuwsen, Phil, xx, 406-7
Ten Haken, Reuben, 73
ten Hoor, Foppe M., 191-92
Ten Houten, Carrie, 240
Ten Pas, Alwin, 72
ten Zythof, Gerrit, 297
Teologiese Skool (Cape Province, South Africa), 185, 187
Theonugraha, Felix, 301
third space, 168-69, 180
Third Way (philosophy of schooling), xx, 145-63

Three Forms of Unity, 6, 36, 61, 133
Tietema, Kasper, 45-46
Timmer, Gerrit, 125
Timmer, Johanna, 281-82, 286
Timmerman, John J., 194, 320
Timothy Christian Schools, 127-43, 232-34, 236
Tod, James, 208
Toebosch, Annemarie, 350
Tolley, Kim, 105
Trinity Christian College, xiv, 285-87
Troup, George McIntosh, 210, 212-14
Umberto I, King, 314
"Un-American" (schools), xviii, 62
urban schools, 31, 62, 129, 258
Utterwick, Henry, 379
Vaca, Daniel, 332-33
Van Asselt, John, 159, 389-90
Van Beek, Cornelius, 88
van Beek, Meindert, 246
Van Brummelen, Harro, 391
Van Buren, Martin (US president), 351, 374
van Dellen, Idzerd, 55, 57-63
van den Berg, J. F., 51
van den Hoek, Arie, 267, 270
van den Hoek, Teunis, 264
van den Hoek, Willempje, 264
Vanderbilt, John, 206
Vander Brug, Duane, 232
Vander Brug, Mel, 223-24, 232
Van de Riet, Gerrit, 217, 219, 223, 225
Vande Riet, Gertrude, 261
van der Meulen, Cornelius, 374, 384
VanderMey, Albert, 166

Vander Ploeg, John, 231-32, 235, 333, 336, 341, 343
Van der Riet, Anna, 247
Vander Wagen, Andrew, 238, 245-46, 248
Vander Wagen, Dick, 240
Vander Werp, Douwe J., 183-85, 187, 191-92
Van der Zee, John, *86*
Van De Vrede, Edna, 75
van Diest, Peter, 350
Van Dijk, Johanna, 166-67
van Doren, Charles, 375
Van Dyke, Martin, *86*
Van Dyken, Joanna, 247
van Dyken, Mattie, 240
Van Engen, Abram, 364
Van Engen, Charles, 298
van Eyk, William, 381
Van Goor, Klaas, 312
van Hetloo, Elbert, 313
van Hinte, Jacob, 268
Van Leeuwen, W. H., 183
van Nimwegen, Mariken, 402
Van Nostrand, Margaret, 291
van Oostenbrugge, Gerrit, 381
Van Prooyen, Dan, 140
Van Raalte, Albertus C., 41, 46, 108, 280, 290-91, 301, 352, 361, 366, 371, 374, 384, 386-87
Van Raalte, Christina de Moen, 280
Van Roekel, Gertrude, 75
Van Stekelenburg, H. A. V. M., 379
Van Til, Clara, 283
van Velzen, Simon, 188
Van Vlaanderen, John C., 316
Van Vlaanderen, Peter, 308-10
Van Vuren, Marie, 75
Van Wyk, Nancy, 297

van Zanden, Jan Luiten, 378
Van Zanten, Jacob, 65, 110
Van Zanten, Nellie, *132*
van Zanten, Wesley, 70
van Zanten, William, 70
Venema, Catherine, 240
Venema, Janny, 409
Venloosch Weekblad, 379
Verduin, Henry, 334
Verhage, William, 78-79
Verplanck, J. D., 249
Verspoor, Shirley, 223, 226
Versteeg, Dingeman, 386
Verwoerd, Hendrik, 368
vocational training, 241-43, 245, 319-20
Volksvriend, De, 42-63, 92-94, 97, 120
Voogd, J., 51
Vos, Geerhardus, 190-92
Vos, Gysbert, 326
Vos, Jan H., 191
Vos, Justin R., xxiv, 407
Vos, Marie, 249
Voskuil, Dennis, 296, 300, 409
Voskuil, Homer, 71
Voskuil, Robert, 77
Voskuyl, Anthony, 76
Voskuyl, Roger, 76-77
Voss, Carol, 285
Vreugdenhil, Jim, 158
Vrieland, Curtis, 223
Vrieland, Douglas J., xxi, 407
Vrije Hollander, De, 52
Wachter, De, 31, 57, 239
Wagenaar, Larry J., 410-11
Wagendorp, Bert, 359, 368
Walchenbach, John, 312
Waldron, Representative [Robert E.], 224

Walsh, Martin, 353
Walvoord, Anthony, 75
Walvoord, Cornelia, 65
Walvoord, Florence, 75
Walvoord, William, 72
Washington, George (US president), 213
Wassink, Marian, 71
Webber, Philip E., 411
Weelink, Bernard Rensink, 263
Weener, Jay R., 299
Weersing, J. J., 327
Welmers, Thomas, 115-17, 121-22, 125
West, Mae, 201
Western Theological Seminary, xxiii, 289-301
Westervelt, John, 317
White, Lynn, 376
Whitney, Gleaves, 357, 359
Wichers, Willard C., 348
Wielenga, Douwe K., 190
wilderness, xxv, 362, 373-88
Wilhelm, Heather, 370
Williams, Eric, 300
Williams, G. Mennen, 219
Williams, Robert L., 348
Williams, Samuel, 292
Wilson, Woodrow (US president), 393
Wilt, Paul, 77
Winter, Egbert, 65
Winter, Jerry P., 56-63
Wisconsin Memorial Academy, xviii, 65-81
Witke, Charles, 349
World War I, 69, 266, 325
World War II, 28, 70, 148, 173, 250, 292, 294, 343, 352, 395
Wyckoff, Isaac, 382

Wynveen, Benjamin, 72
Yates (Kremers), Amy, 280
Yff, George, 249
Zagers, Evert, 382
Zondervan (publishing), xxiv, 332-33
Zunis (Zuni Pueblo), xxii, 245-49, 251-53
Zwaanstra, Henry, 194
Zwart, David, xxvi, 177, 405, 407, 409
Zwemer, James F., 111-12, 115, 125
Zylstra, Lisa, 409

www.ingramcontent.com/pod-product-compliance
Lightning Source LLC
Chambersburg PA
CBHW030101170426
43198CB00009B/441